THE SEARCH
FOR DIGITAL
EXCELLENCE

Other Books From CommerceNet Press

Opening Digital Markets: Battle Plans and Business Strategies for Internet Commerce **by Walid Mougayar**

Understanding Digital Signatures: Establishing Trust over the Internet and Other Networks **by Gail L. Grant**

THE SEARCH FOR DIGITAL EXCELLENCE

James P. Ware
Judith Gebauer
Amir Hartman
Malu Roldan

McGraw-Hill

New York San Francisco Washington, D.C. Auckland Bogotá
Caracas Lisbon London Madrid Mexico City Milan
Montreal New Delhi San Juan Singapore
Sydney Tokyo Toronto

Library of Congress Cataloging-in-Publication Data

The search for digital excellence / James P. Ware ... [et al.].
    p.   cm.
    Includes index.
    ISBN 0-07-027057-0
    1. Electronic commerce—United States—Case studies. I. James P.
Ware
    HF5548.325.U6S4 1997
    658.8'00285—dc21   97-38056
                                            CIP

McGraw-Hill

A Division of The McGraw·Hill Companies

1 2 3 4 5 6 7 8 9 0   DOC/DOC   9 0 3 2 1 0 9 8

ISBN 0-07-027057-0

The sponsoring editor for this book was Scott Grillo, and the production supervisor was Sherri Souffrance. It was set in Fairfield by Lisa M. Mellott through the services of Barry E. Brown (Broker—Editing, Design and Production).

Printed and bound by R. R. Donnelley & Sons Company.

McGraw-Hill books are available at special quantity discounts to use as premiums and sales promotions, or for use in corporate training programs. For more information, please write to the Director of Special Sales, McGraw-Hill, 11 West 19th Street, New York, NY 10011. Or contact your local bookstore.

CONTENTS

ACKNOWLEDGMENTS

This book represents the culmination of our year-long journey into the exciting world where digital excellence is in the earliest stages of its formation. It was an exhilarating journey, often tinged with the realization that the frenzied activities and products of the San Francisco Bay Area companies we studied are imprinting the character of future businesses, institutions, and ways of life. At the same time, the journey was challenging, as the frenzy and the pace of change necessitated much ambiguity and not enough time for introspection. In our efforts to build useful insights out of this constantly shifting phenomenon, we have benefited from the generosity of the many, many individuals who helped us. They made time for us in the midst of their own frenzied lives, and then took the time to engage us in conversations about their own experiences, to challenge our own understandings, and to teach us what digital excellence is all about. We will inevitably but unintentionally omit some of them, and for that we apologize in advance.

We are especially grateful to the sponsors of the Fisher Center for Management and Information Technology at the Haas School: Jack Hancock, Chair of the Fisher Center Advisory Board; Cindy Andreotti, Senior Vice President of MCI Telecommunications Corp.; Dr. Paul Blumberg, Director of Product Development Systems, Ford Motor Company; Dennis "Mick" Connors, Senior Vice President of The Gap, Inc.; Deems Davis, Senior Vice President of Fireman's Fund Insurance; Kathleen Earley, Vice President of EasyCommerce Services, AT&T; Donald Fisher, Chairman of The Gap, Inc.; Tim Graumann, Vice President of Corporate Information Systems, SBC Services; Robert Guidrey, Vice President of MCI Telecommunications Corp.; William A. Hasler, Dean of the Haas School of Business; Dr. Gerald D. Held, Senior Vice President of Oracle Corporation; Patricia Higgins, Vice President and CIO of Aluminum Company of America; Dawn Lepore, Chief Information Officer at Charles Schwab; Denise Miller, Vice President and Director of the California IT Division of Kaiser Foundation Health Plan, Inc.; Mike Polosky, Executive Vice President of AirTouch Cellular;

Michaele Rittenberg, Vice President of Sun Microsystems Corporation; Phil Schaadt, Senior Vice President for Strategy, Architecture, and Standards at Bank of America; Yuji Shibuya, Manager of Systems Consulting at Nomura Research Institute; Ed Solomon, Vice President of the Western Region of Interim Technology; Carmine Villani, Corporate Vice President and CIO of McKesson Corporation; and Diana Whitehead, Vice President and CIO of SBC Services. Their financial support made our research possible. Just as importantly, their vigilance in pushing for relevance in the research propelled us beyond the comforts of our preconceived models of business practice. We also thank them and their staffs for their generosity in sharing their experiences in applying Web technologies to their business. Their war stories are captured in many of the cases in this book. We also want to thank the Fisher Center's Faculty Director, Professor Arie Segev, for building the network of colleagues and resources that made our research both practical and meaningful.

We are grateful to our faculty colleagues and students: the Haas School faculty, undergraduates, MBAs, and executive MBAs, an international array of visitors and practitioners who engaged and challenged us in various courses and events sponsored by The Fisher Center, Berkeley's Haas School of Business, the Department of Electrical Engineering and Computer Science, and the School for Information Management and Systems and CommerceNet, whose early recognition of the importance of digital commerce inspired much of our interest and many of our ideas. Often times, as it turned out, we were more students than teachers. We are especially grateful to the second generation of the "Berkeley Internet Mafia": N. Aronson, M. Bhuptani, K. Billings, V. Bobba, J. Bracken, M. Breitbard, D. Cain, N. Cutajar, E. Defty, M. Fernandez, A. Ferrier, M. Gankema, C. Gill, R. Glithebo, A. Goel, L. Han, A. Hayward, T. Hicks, P. Hoff, L. Horvath, B. Howell, R. Hutcherson, A. Ip, F. Jeanneau, M. Kan, M. Keudel, A. Laszlo, C. Lee, T. Leung, S. Li Peha, C. Liu, P. Piccirilli, S. Potter, E. Raber, J. Redo, S. Rundfelt, T. Ryglinski, R. San Andres, S. Schiller, K. Schulz, D. Schwanenflugel, E. Sigler, T. Sparkman, M. Suppiger, M. Typrin, H. Uhrig, C. Vichare, B. Wahl, P. Watridge, S. Westlake, and

M. Zambianchi. Their energy, creativity, and enthusiasm generated much of the field research that produced the case studies in this book.

We would also like to thank the many individuals who gave generously of their time to help us document the stories of their own early efforts at implementing Web technologies: Dan Joaquin, Michael McCadden, Tom Stromberg, Suzanne Luger, and Debbie Gardner at The Gap, Inc.; Kevin Brown at Inktomi; Alan Fisher at ONSALE; Al Allegre, Mike Gottlieb, Dan Gray, Bob Kyle, Rob Jensen, and Debra Ohlsen at McKesson, Corp.; Ed Callan at Pacific Bell Internet Services; Peter Granoff and Cyndy Ainsworth at Virtual Vineyards; Linda Glick and David Samson at Levi Strauss & Co.; and Pete Solvik at Cisco Systems. We also thank them for continuing to help us hone our understanding of their experiences by patiently reading and re-reading the case write-ups that we prepared for this book.

We want to thank our editors, Scott Grillo at McGraw-Hill and Loel Mcphee at CommerceNet Press, for their commitment to this book and to us. They have both patiently and diplomatically supported us through the many trials and stresses of collaborating on a book that covers a rapidly evolving phenomenon. We are also greatly indebted to their marketing and production partners, most notably Judy Kessler, Barry Brown, and Kellie Hagan. They were all essential to helping us hone our message into a coherent, compelling whole.

Our journey, as it turns out, has only begun. We look forward to continuing this conversation with our old friends, acknowledged here, as well as with new ones, perhaps including you, our readers. We owe our best insights to such a discourse, although of course we claim any inaccuracies as our own.

This is a very special time in human history. Never before has a technology swept across the world as quickly or with as much an impact as the Internet has over the past several years. Never before have so many organizations embraced a radically new way of doing business so readily. Never before have literally millions of individuals been able to communicate directly with each other easily and cheaply, or with the richness that text, graphics, sound, and video can bring to millions of desktops all over the world.

But also—and this is a very important "but"—never before has a technology been so full of hype and so burdened with unrealistic expectations. Thousands of start-up companies and millions of existing organizations are experimenting simultaneously with this new way of creating, storing, accessing, and transmitting information. New business models are being invented daily, and some of them even appear to be working. Yet in 1997 there are still only a handful of companies that can honestly claim to be making money on the Internet. Internet-based IPOs have already created hundreds of new millionaires, and an almost equal number of bankruptcies. At the same time, there are hundreds of firms, both new and old, that are saving millions of dollars through creative deployments of the Internet, World Wide Web sites, and intranets. The "killer apps" that transformed the 20-year-old Internet into an "overnight" success and created the World Wide Web were, without question, HTML (hypertext mark-up language) and the graphical browser interface. Together these software programs enable Web surfers to click from one site to another almost as if they were flipping the pages in a book of all the world's knowledge. Today each of us can act as if all the computers in the world are on our own desk, because in a very real sense they are. Yet all too often the Web is more promise than reality.

What is the poor, confused business or technology manager to do? Is the Web the greatest invention of all time or is it a passing fad? Is the digital economy really all that different? What are the principles for defining digital business strategies?

Does it make sense for every company to have a Web site in order to offer products and services for sale over the Internet? What is a Web site really good for, anyway? And how in the heck can a Web site or an intranet be integrated into your existing technology platforms? What kind of business and technology skills do you need to do it right? What does it cost to build and maintain an effective Web site, and what kind of return can you realistically expect from a Web site investment? Most importantly, what are companies *really* doing today? What works and what doesn't? What mistakes can you avoid because someone else has already made them? What does it take to be successful?

These are the questions that motivated us to put this book together. We are fascinated by the Internet, intrigued by the possibilities it offers, and just as frustrated as you are at the blooming, buzzing confusion that surrounds it. We have read the news stories and professional publications, watched the TV shows, attended the industry conferences, and listened to the speeches from vendors, consultants, pundits, and other so-called gurus (Michael Hammer once commented that he prefers being called a *guru* because it's easier to spell than *charlatan*). But we have also talked to real, live managers in dozens of organizations about what they have done, are doing, and plan to do with these new technologies. We have listened to their experiences and learned from them what really does work and what doesn't. We have compiled their stories, and we have developed our own ideas about what it takes to be successful in the emerging digital economy. But our focus is clearly on what is happening "out there" in the real world: this is a book about practice, and about what practitioners are doing.

We wrote this book to help us make sense of what we are seeing, hearing, and experiencing. In our teaching and research activities at the Fisher Center for Management and Information Technology and at the Haas School of Business at the University of California at Berkeley, we are surrounded by bright, energetic, and creative students who have their eyes on what is happening in Silicon Valley and around the world. Many of them have their own Web sites, and several have built and sold Web-based businesses while we were compiling the stories in this book. They have taught us much.

We are very fortunate to be located so close to Silicon Valley, the engine of the digital economy. Because of that proximity we have been able to visit with many of the digital revolutionaries—the entrepreneurs, engineers, venture capitalists, and business executives who are creating the new technologies and business models that are driving the new digital economy and making these capabilities available on a global basis. Most importantly, we have been working with the senior business and technology executives in many leading-edge organizations all over the country—the practitioners who are learning how to transform established business strategies and existing business processes to exploit the unique characteristics of the Web and the Internet. They, too, have taught us much.

What have we learned? The single most important *aha!* (and the basis of this entire book) is that the digital economy is *not* really about new technology. Of course, technology is at the heart of it, but digital excellence is all about building new kinds of relationships: relationships with suppliers, customers, employees, business partners, investors, regulators, the press, consultants, and every other constituency in your business and social environment. We are convinced that software-mediated and software-supported relationships really *are* different, and you can't succeed in this new world without understanding those differences.

We are also convinced that if there is a secret to succeeding in the digital world, it is that deploying these new technologies effectively means changing almost *everything* about the way you do business. Digital excellence involves rethinking marketing strategies and value propositions, reconnecting with customers and suppliers, restructuring organizations, redesigning jobs, reconstructing technology platforms, and reskilling both your business and your technology professionals. Sadly, it's a big job and it isn't easy.

Obviously, this new global communications infrastructure called the Internet offers you direct, individualized, low-cost, multimedia access to millions of individuals and billions of bits of data. But having access isn't what matters. How you exploit that access and how you position your business is what will determine your success. Doing it well definitely isn't easy, but the pioneers we have learned from and whose stories we have compiled here can indeed show you the way to digital excellence. And the good news is that it's unquestionably worth the effort.

THE ORGANIZATION OF THIS BOOK

We begin our search for digital excellence with a broad look at the shape and characteristics of electronic commerce, focusing in particular on how we got to where we are today. We then zoom in on the building blocks of the digital economy: the hardware, software, communication channels, and business entities that together comprise the global electronic infrastructure that we call the Internet (and its multimedia subset, the World Wide Web).

In Chapters 4 through 9 we describe how you can use these building blocks to create completely new organizational forms, and to transform an established business into something altogether different. In the course of looking at these transformed businesses, you will also discover—surprise!—that these new entities compete (and collaborate) in radically new ways, creating a very new, electronically mediated marketplace. Value chains become value webs; many businesses are disintermediated, while new intermediaries are springing up every day.

There is an intriguing dance between the new technologies themselves and the organizational forms they enable, a continual interplay between technology architectures and business architectures. Our discussion of this dance alternates between close- in analysis of the technology foundations, on the one hand, and the organizational and business practices those foundations enable and occasionally mandate, on the other.

In Chapter 10 we come up for air and take a broad, sweeping look at how our neighborhoods, our communities, and society as a whole are all being affected by this digital revolution. We consider how even governments are being transformed, and raise questions about the ability of national governments to "control" the Internet in any meaningful way.

In Chapter 11 we pull these threads together and offer some guidelines for business and organizational success. We base our recommendations on our observations and interpretations of what the winners have done, as well as on our own understanding of what it takes to achieve digital excellence.

We conclude our search in Chapter 12, where we toss our focus on actual experiences aside and simply speculate a bit about where the digital revolution might be going. We don't claim any fortune-telling capabilities, but we do try to look ahead, to extrapolate the most important trends, and to explore some basic discontinuities that might make today's most obvious trends completely irrelevant.

As part of our emphasis on practical experiences, we have included over a dozen specific case studies and many more shorter examples from a variety of businesses and industries. We believe very strongly that cyberspace is one place where practice is currently way, way ahead of theory, and that the only way to understand what the digital economy is really all about is to go where the action is: to the board rooms, conference rooms, team rooms, desktops, and Web sites of the corporations that are building and using the new digital tools.

We are strong believers in the power of real-world experience, but we would never presume to pass judgment on the successes and failures of the managers and companies described in our case studies. Rather, we offer these real-world stories as "postcards from the edge," a sort of collage of current experiments and experiences. While some of our examples are clearly success stories, in most cases the stories aren't finished; we simply tell them to provide you with a much broader perspective on what is happening "out there" than you could get otherwise.

CAN A BOOK BE WEBIFIED?

Finally, we want to emphasize that we view this entire book as just the opening chapter in a much longer story about the birth of a fundamentally new economy (and a fundamentally new society). That story will be written in full by all of us together, including each and every one of you who reads this book.

In a digital world, a printed book like this is in many ways an anachronism. Yes, we wrote these words on our desktop and laptop computers, and we transmitted them to our editors over the Net. We also used the Net extensively in our research. But you are reading our words in a book whose form is not all that different from the Gutenberg Bible that was printed over five hundred years ago. Even the monks who predated Gutenberg as the scribes of knowledge would feel comfortable with the form and format of this book. A book is still a collection of atoms, drops of ink on paper. A book is a physical thing that must be produced, shipped, displayed on shelves, purchased, and taken home the old-fashioned way.

Regrettably, a book is very much a one-way flow of information. We wish it could be more individualized and interactive, more like the new digital world whose stories fill these pages. We want to continue listening, learning, pursuing digital excellence, and telling *your* stories in the future. We can't engage each and every one of you the way we could if this were a Web page, but we do want to do the next best thing. Send us e-mail and tell us your story, disagree with us, or ask us provocative questions. We will do our best to respond; at the very least we'll learn from you, and will include your lessons in our future teachings and writing.

Now *click here* (turn the page) to begin Chapter 1.

—*Jim Ware (jware@haas.berkeley.edu)*
Judith Gebauer (gebauer@haas.berkeley.edu)
Amir Hartman (hartman@haas.berkeley.edu)
Malu Roldan (roldan@haas.berkeley.edu)
Berkeley, California
February, 1998

INTRODUCTION

Now, as the power and reach of these technologies sky-
rocket, the Information Revolution promises to touch—
and in some cases radically transform—every aspect of
life: our work and leisure, all manner of scientific techniques, and virtually every method for recording and
transmitting knowledge . . .

—*Business Week, 1994, p. 12*

A PARADIGM SHIFT

If you haven't heard yet, we're having a revolution. Or is it a paradigm shift? Whichever it is, it's happening now. How do we
know? Well, for one thing, *Business Week* says so. Apparently,
the revolution is being led by information and communication
technology, and the poster-child for this revolution is the
Internet. In the past few years, much has been said and written
about this paradigm shift/revolution and the changes it will
bring about—so much so, in fact, that, with respect to air time
and column space, most news items pale in comparison. These
apparently are great times in the making. We're being promised
a transformation in almost every fiber of our lives, and if we
look around us, we can see clear signs of the changes. A "new
world order" is being created that is being driven by the Internet

and emerging information technologies. Yes, we are certainly hearing the tolls of the coming era. Our gurus de jour are promoting a "new and improved" society. Far be it from us to make light of a revolution; it's a serious matter.

The "information age," as it is so often called, is ushering in an era where economic and social order is dictated not by physical resources but by knowledge and the ability to manage it and create value from it. Today the Internet and its related technologies are fostering a new realization that knowledge can indeed be created, stored, transmitted, and sold for economic value. However, although magazines such as *Business Week* can be given part of the credit (or blame depending on how you look at it) for disseminating these ideas, the notion of a "postindustrial" or "information" society is certainly not new. People like Daniel Bell, Peter Drucker, and Alvin Toffler made this view popular several decades ago.

The most important and most vivid aspect of the so-called postindustrial society is that we are entering a radically different stage in history, separating from the past, and breaking with previous values, social relations, and modes of production. According to Daniel Bell, "knowledge and information are becoming the strategic resource and transforming agent of the postindustrial society." What this message promises to organizations is a fundamental shift in social relationships and modes of production: empowerment of workers, democratization of knowledge and decision making, and a reduction in hierarchies.

At the heart of this transformation lies the assumption that knowledge and technology, specifically information technology, are the driving forces of the revolution. Through the use of metaphors such as the "information revolution" and the plethora of "post" terms (postindustrial, postcapitalist, postbureaucratic, and post-Fordist), we are being told over and over again that present and future circumstances and management practices will differ radically from past ones.

Business has always looked to technology for help, be it to improve productivity, lower labor costs, make the workplace safer, create new products and markets, or understand customers more completely. However, there seem to be some fundamental differences embedded in the newer breeds of information technology that have recently helped place information at the center stage of the economy. Why have information and knowledge suddenly become so important? Simply put, they have characteristics, shaped by the emerging digital technologies, that are fundamentally different from traditional sources of production. Emerging digital technologies enable us to create, transmit, replicate, and customize information faster, cheaper, and more broadly than ever before.

There are four primary characteristics of the new digital world that make it fundamentally different from the world we all grew up in:

INFORMATION CREATION. Historically, information creation has been the domain of the elite, from monks and monasteries before the printing press, to the intellectuals in universities, to the wealthy of modern times who owned (and often still do) the means of information production and distribution: network television and radio stations, newspapers, magazines, and other publication outlets. Now, with the creation of digital technology such as PCs and other devices that are more affordable and are rapidly being adopted by the mainstream population, individuals in all walks of life have an unprecedented ability to create and disseminate their own information, or become "authors"—a very radical concept if you stop to think about it. When else have so many people, in organizations and countries around the globe, been able not only to access information instantaneously, but to create it themselves? Millions of individuals can now tell stories about their families and the great experiences they've had; their companies, products, and services; and injustices in their own countries that might otherwise go unnoticed. Authorship is empowerment, and digital technology in the hands of ordinary people is a very novel and empowering reality.

INFORMATION TRANSMISSION. A few months ago, a couple of us were talking with an organization about creating and teaching an electronic commerce seminar to business managers. We were in Palo Alto, one of the meccas of the information age, putting together the content and structure of the seminar as well as the promotional material. At day's end, we drove home to Berkeley and continued with our daily routines. However, when we got to our office late that evening, we had a voice-mail message from one of our colleagues back in Pittsburgh. The message was from someone who we stay in touch with regularly but speak to directly only about once a month. What was so special about this message was that our colleague finished it off with "Oh yeah, I hear you guys are going to be doing an electronic commerce seminar in Atlanta." We were completely taken aback. How in the world did he know about the seminar? The Web, of course. As we left Palo Alto, a brief promotional piece on the seminar was placed on the Web, and our colleague happened upon it while we were driving back to Berkeley. He had literally seen the information before we had. That was truly fast, and it was that experience that drove home to us the recognition that this technology is really different from previous ones. It is instantaneous, ubiquitous, and global.

INFORMATION REPLICABILITY. Quite different from most physical products, information can be sold or distributed without transferring ownership, and it can be used without being exhausted. In other words, you can create information and then sell it or give it to someone else without losing possession of it yourself. This is a very simple concept, but it is radically different from a physical product, where once you sell it or give it to someone you have to create another one in order to sell it to another party or have it for yourself.

INFORMATION CUSTOMIZATION. Information is "soft." That is, it is malleable, unlike most physical products. You can present information in many different forms, be it text, graphics, video, or audio. For example, consider the ability to send e-mail messages to colleagues—messages that can be customized for a particular individual and include information from widely different sources, which can be combined and integrated to include text, an audio message, or even a personal video. In the same way a company can send highly customized messages to thousands of employees or customers, and can tailor Web pages and banner ads to the individual characteristics or interests of each Web surfer.

OLD WINE?

Many pundits have theorized about the changes in work organization and management due to computerization. Much of the most influential work has come in the form of best-seller books such as Toffler's "The Third Wave", and Naisbitt's "Megatrends". Thought leaders have flirted with this topic for many years, and have popularized such descriptive terms for the "organization of the future" as postindustrial, postcapitalist, postbureaucratic, and post-Fordist.

An interesting feature of these predictions of changes in work organization and control is their optimism, particularly concerning the impact of computerization on the workplace. This optimism is even more apparent within the popular media, where you get the sense that information technology will be able to solve practically every social ill—a sort of "liberation technology" if you will. Most of us tend to see technology as isolated from the world around us. "Technology is just a tool; it can be used for good or bad" is the most common view.

What is our fixation with technology? We like it, no, we love it. We enjoy creating and building technology, but even more we enjoy consuming it, much like a drug. As a society we seem to be addicted to technology. We like the power and the speed it gives us. And the more speed and power we get, the more we need. We can't stop. And the best news is that it's affordable! We have come to count on technology as a key sustenance and source of wealth generation.

The dominant view when it comes to understanding and implementing technology is one of "technological determinism." This is the notion that technological development is autonomous with respect to society: it shapes society, but is not influenced by it. We maintain that such a perspective is wholly unsatisfactory because technologies do not, in practice, follow any predetermined course of development or acceptance. Also, although technologies clearly have consequences, the nature of those consequences is not intrinsic to the technology, but depends on a broad range of social, political, and economic factors.

To make this point further, we can look more closely at the effects of computerization in the workplace. For example, there are many instances where e-mail has helped to reduce the communication barriers between people at different levels of hierarchy in an organization. However, in other situations participation in e-mail has actually led to less open communication. In one company, certain employees formed a private conference and used it to air their gripes and support each other, and senior managers were so upset they took a number of actions that eventually generated a culture of fear and intimidation.

It is precisely these contrasting images that serve as intuitive evidence that the growth and acceptance of computerization and technology in general is much more a social process than it is a technological one.

What does this mean for the latest new generation of information technology and its place in business? It means that technology does not develop in a vacuum, but rather is very much created, driven, and used in a complex social, political, and economic "web." What seems to be missing in many approaches to technology-enabled change, however, is the realization that two antithetical conditions—one favoring technology and the other actively resisting it—often reside within the same organization, and that such conditions are a product of social forces both inside and outside the organization.

Our goal is to broaden your perspective and place internetworked technologies and their effects within the proper context: a web of historical, political, and economic forces that must be examined and understood in concert with technology. In other words, we will describe opportunities for achieving digital excellence.

This book is an attempt to identify and articulate strategies for digital excellence. We want to make salient the need for thinking strategically and holistically about Internet-based technologies. We want to move beyond addressing IT solutions as "quick fixes" and away from "cut-and-paste" solutions. We want to develop a roadmap that will help you think about how to compete in this emerging economy and how to exploit these powerful technologies for real value creation.

So, what exactly is different about the new breed of Internet-/ Web-enabled technologies? What is it about this technology that will change the world? The answer lies in its very makeup. The characteristics inherent in Web-based technologies enable radically new types of processes and interactions, as shown in the following table:

CHARACTERISTICS	OPPORTUNITIES
Interactivity	Entertain and engage; capture customer knowledge
Immediacy	Collect, integrate, and distribute information; quickly respond to customer needs
Connectivity	Create space for communication and collaboration
Interoperability	Direct and seamless communication with customer
Media richness	Customize products and services
Ease of use	Empowerment

INTERACTIVITY. The interactive nature of Web-based technologies enables a very different type of activity with computers, whether human/machine interaction, new business processes, or person-to-person activities supported by technology (by *interactivity* we mean the way these new communication technologies allow for reflection, response, and engaging in real-time dialog). Words like *playfulness* are not usually associated with traditional communication media, but the Internet clearly enables and encourages a level of creative "play" that goes far beyond what older generations of technology made possible. Technologies of the past put people in a very passive role. They pushed information to us regardless of whether we wanted it or found it useful. The new technologies allow us to engage with each other and with information, and to become actively involved in far more interesting dialog. It is no wonder that "browsing" or "surfing" the Web has become so addicting and time-consuming for so many people.

IMMEDIACY. All communication is sensitive to time, but the Internet allows us to reshape time and give new meaning to distance and time zones. Our ability to "informate" many products and all forms of information into a digital format allows us to transmit those bits of information instantaneously to any other location around the globe or even in space. Whether it is information about a product—such as a price change that can be updated on the fly—or news about happenings around the world that otherwise would have gone unnoticed, we now truly live in the "global village" that Marshall McLuhan wrote about over 30 years ago. When we need information, we just turn to our desktop computers and get what we need. Consider, for example, your ability to get immediate information about the status of an order you placed or a package you sent or are waiting to receive from Federal Express or UPS. What about needing financial information about a company you are considering investing in, then just signing onto the SEC's EDGAR site and downloading the latest 10-K. Want to check your bank account or transfer some funds? Just do it—from home, office, hotel room, or airplane. No matter where you are or what time of day it is, you can access the information you need, communicate with colleagues, or act on your decisions.

CONNECTIVITY. With the growth and proliferation of digital communication technology not only within an organization but around the globe, people and organizations alike are able to acquire information that previously was either completely inaccessible or very time-consuming and costly to access. Moreover, the ability to access information irrespective of geographical proximity creates not only more informed and more satisfied customers (both individual consumers and business customers), but also enables new forms of organization and community. No longer are people constrained by their location in terms of who they work for, who they interact with, and what type of work they do, and no longer are organizations limited to the human resources available nearby. Companies can now attract and employ the best talent from around the country and even around the world. This global connectivity makes distributed teams not only feasible but imperative.

INTEROPERABILITY. Networks and the ability to communicate with anyone anyplace are not new. Organizations have been able to link electronically to business partners such as suppliers and contractors for decades. However, the networks behind those linkages were almost always expensive, proprietary, and closed systems that required large financial investments and extensive coordination of technology platforms. Today's Web-based internetworked communication technologies allow individuals and institutions with different types of technology platforms and different performance capabilities to communicate in a common language and to create information that can be accessed and used by others.

RICHNESS. Richness is the ability of a communication channel or medium to convey the full complexity of information. Communicated information can be very diverse in terms of complexity. Face-to-face conversations, for example, are quite rich. The parties involved not only exchange content, but can see each others' nonverbal expressions and hear intonations, enabling them to express themselves in a fuller and more expansive manner. In comparison, text-based communications such as letters and e-mail are less rich because they convey just the message's content with almost none of its emotional undertones. For example, it would not make sense to plan a complicated new product design using memos alone because of the uncertainties and different perspectives that all the involved participants would have. The new technologies, however, are enabling much richer forms of communication within traditional text-based channels. The ability to digitize and send information such as an audio clip of a speech or a video clip of a product creates a much richer and more complete communication environment.

EASE OF USE. Computer and communication technologies have been getting easier to use for some time, but being able to point, click, and type familiar words and then have those simple actions perform highly complex functions is quite empowering. Average individuals and organizations with little specialized expertise are now able to create knowledge and disseminate it to anyone they want. And certainly these technologies and the ones to come will become even easier to use, thereby creating an even greater opportunity for empowerment. Granted, we often find ourselves wasting hours just surfing the Web and struggling to find the information we want, but that's not the point. The point is that never before have so many people, whether inside or outside organizations, been able to express themselves and inform themselves so easily. That is a powerful concept. And for all our talk in academia, governments, and companies about empowering individuals, here is a set of tools that finally makes that talk real.

We argue here that the emergence of Webbed technologies, with their core characteristics, has created an opportunity to create a "rupture" or "leap" in the equilibrium, which can foster new types of relationships, generate new forms of knowledge, and create new economic value. Dell Computer Corporation has successfully been able to create and exploit such a rupture, reshaping the competitive landscape of the PC industry. Through the use of Internet technologies, Dell has redefined and extended the direct distribution model to reach operational excellence in its logistics, creating a built-to-order paradigm that is a significant competitive advantage. Only time will tell whether or not the company can sustain such an advantage.

An interesting observation regarding Dell's Internet success and its sustainability is how other companies, especially those within the PC industry, are responding. Overwhelmingly, companies are trying to emulate Dell's success by copying their business model. This, however, might cause more damage than good, as companies disregard their own business strategies, structures, and core competencies to chase someone else's success. This is a response that many, even those in other industries, will unfortunately find inadequate. How are companies to react, then? Such a quandary gives us insight into the complexities of the emerging business ecosystem, and has led us to identify five key principles that companies should keep in mind when navigating these competitive waters:

PRINCIPLE 1. Competitive advantage will be more difficult to attain and even more difficult to sustain in this emerging economy. Companies will find that the competitive landscape in most industries will be one of fast environmental changes. Competitiveness will be based more on one's ability to identify and capitalize on emerging opportunities, shore up the intellectual capital and resources required to exploit the opportunity, and ruthlessly implement a strategy, rather than building long-lasting sustainable solutions that competitors cannot overcome.

PRINCIPLE 2. Solutions that are driven by emerging Internet technologies are perhaps necessary but for the most part easily replicable by competitors who have the resources and capabilities to react. The ease of use and development of Internet-related technologies has enabled many business opportunities, but it has also made it easier for others to do the same.

PRINCIPLE 3. The emerging economy requires companies to shift from static planning to holistic and dynamic planning, in other words, moving toward a strategy development process that is constantly questioning itself and trying to discover new opportunities. Gone are the days of long-range planning. Companies today have to be in a constant discovery and change mode because of the ever-changing competitive landscape.

PRINCIPLE 4. In order to be competitive, companies cannot be completely isolated, but must form constellations of relationships (even with competitors). The formation of these constellations helps companies bring together the core competencies and capabilities for capitalizing on opportunities. Moreover, it reduces the risk normally involved in going after opportunities. A company's ability to bring together the players to form these relationships is a distinct advantage in this emerging economy.

PRINCIPLE 5. Companies must focus their Internet technology initiative along their core competencies and key value delivery drivers, but not be too fast to give away all noncore capabilities, because of the dangers of a quickly changing environment. In these days of outsourcing, companies should be careful to not give away Internet development projects that are crucial to their business or can serve to differentiate them and their competition. Those companies that do not have the capability to execute technology solutions should develop ways of bringing those capabilities and taking control as quickly as possible. A case in point is Charles Schwab, who originally outsourced the development of their online trading application (eSchwab), but immediately brought the capability in-house to make sure they could stay ahead of up-and-coming competition like eTrade.

We view this emerging economy along four dimensions: political, economic, cultural, and technological. Throughout the book we will be reporting on how these four crucial dimensions must be coordinated and managed to take full advantage of the opportunities that the new digital, Webbed world offers.

POLITICS

Governance, be it in organizations or in nations, has historically been defined and maintained by those with significant power. Within organizations, power normally flowed to those who controlled the means of production and/or financial capital. Within nations, the controlling power was often held by the same people, although in some cases those who controlled the military controlled the government as well.

Democracy was very much influenced by economics. In other words, those who controlled the wealth were also able to dictate policy, and were certainly more involved in the political process. Information, a crucial element of democratic involvement, was top-down, tightly controlled, and slow-moving. Even in commercial organizations, involvement in the strategic decisions was the role of top management, not the front-line worker. Workers were forced to be doers, not thinkers. The workers' primary concern was building products as efficiently as they could, not creating information or having a say in how things were done. These values were carry-overs from Taylorism and an engineering way of doing things.

Today, however, through emerging information and communication technologies, knowledge and constant learning is much more widely shared. Technologies like the Internet are making the access, creation, and dissemination of information far easier. People anywhere in a country can now access information about proposed legislation, for example, as it is being deliberated. Moreover, they can voice their opinions on the matter and communicate their wishes directly to their elected representatives. Theoretically, the public has always been able to voice its opinion, but in the past it was much more difficult to do so and consequently did not often happen. In this new environment, "ordinary" people such as citizens and front-line workers can easily and effectively express their ideas and desires, and thus influence crucial decisions. The implications of this revolution in decision-making processes are only just beginning to be understood.

ECONOMY

Organizations in the past were large, slow, functional pyramids focused on "command and control" management practices. Success was based on things you could touch, buildings and plants that could house the workers and production processes, machines to create the product, workers who were physically present to work the machines, and vehicles to deliver the products. Products were made of "atoms," to use the term originated by Nicholas Negroponte of MIT's Media Lab. That is, products were tangible hard goods, like tables, cars, houses, and industrial equipment.

Today's products are less atomic and less tangible. By far the largest portion of the economy produces information-based products and services that require "brain force" instead of "brute force."[1] Because these products and services are comprised primarily of information, they are easier to transport, require less packaging, take up less space, and are easy to duplicate. Take, for example, the music industry, where not only traditional companies like Capitol Records but emerging upstarts like N2K allow consumers to find music, sample it, and purchase it in digital form instead of physical form such as CDs. Such changes reduce the transaction cost on behalf of the consumer, and also make the development of music products more efficient.

In today's emerging digital economy, it is the creation and dissemination of information, not the ownership of land or machines, that is the means to control. Successful organizations in the new economy are flexible, dynamic, and dramatically smaller. The quality and productivity of information workers, rather than the volume of production, defines the new economy. The information age will require nations and organizations to be more open to and driven by:

· Empowered and demanding customers
· Time, value, and services

· Escalating global competition
· Rapid change and flexibility

CULTURE

Leisure and quality of work life has been put on the back burner for many people due to a tightening economy and overly burdensome workloads. Over the last several decades, families have had to work longer hours and, in the majority of cases recently, have needed two people working in order to maintain a decent lifestyle. Education, recreation, the arts, and other leisure-time activities were for the high-income minority, often born into wealth, who could afford to pay for them.

This condition created a political/economic/cultural gap in the industrialized nations, where the working class had to work harder and harder just to maintain a basic standard of living. Today, emerging information technologies enable the work force to be more productive, and theoretically allow them more time to enjoy the pleasures of life like education, recreation, and family. Cultures from around the globe are more accessible because of this emerging medium, and learning processes are facilitated. Widespread and inexpensive access to news, entertainment, and other kinds of information has contributed to a great leveling, even a homogenization, of cultures around the world. Just consider how good news—like the fall of the Berlin Wall or the Olympic Games—and bad news—like Tianenman Square or the deaths of Princess Diana and Mother Theresa—were shared by millions of people in every major country. As communication bandwidth continues to increase and costs fall, the global sharing of news, information, and personal experiences will become even more common.

TECHNOLOGY

In the past, technology was a tool that often replaced manual labor, usually devaluing the contributions of the work force and taking many crucial skills away from workers. Technology was often a means for management to reduce labor costs, because machines could do many tasks faster and cheaper than humans and could certainly be controlled more easily. It should be no surprise that many workers and their unions were alienated by these developments and often actively fought the introduction of new technologies.

Today's information technology, with its ability to be interactive, ubiquitous, playful, and easy to use, allows people in an organization to be creative, to collaborate, to share, and most importantly to feel a part of the organizational process. Continued developments in the core technologies—microprocessors, storage devices, communication bandwidth, switches, routers, and other networking components—will continue to drive new business models, new management practices, and new lifestyles for more and more people.

One thing is certain: the Internet and related technologies have become extremely visible in highly industrialized societies, especially within the workplace. In the last several years, we have witnessed the internationalization of labor, the growth of worldwide competition, and instant and constant communication from anywhere to anywhere. Moreover, the last three years have engendered an onslaught of new technology practices revolving around networks. Beyond creating an unprecedented amount of new business (e.g., consulting, information directory services, network hardware and software), these networked technologies have brought with them the promise of change: change in the way we work, change in the way we shop and learn, change in the way we relate to each other, change in power structures and decision-making processes, and change in the structure of our society. The challenge lies in addressing the following questions:

- What are the fundamental difference between and similarities of "Webbed" organizations?
- What does it take to become "digitally excellent," and how do I get there?
- Which strategies and business models work and which don't?

In our research and consulting efforts, we have been lucky enough to gain insight and understanding into how dozens of companies are capitalizing on these new technologies. We have observed and consulted with companies ranging from Fortune 1000 firms with over 100,000 employees to Internet startups with fewer than 50 employees. Our work has taken us into all sectors of the economy, including banking, finance, automotive, consumer products, high technology, entertainment, insurance, and healthcare.

These experiences have made it clear to us that there are some fundamental similarities among those companies where the Internet has played a significant role in changing the way business is done. Organizations that are successfully moving into this new marketplace carry with them new-generation values that drive their thinking and the approaches they use to achieve Internet-enabled change.

We see the following seven values as being the cornerstones to success in the networked economy:

BE VISION-DRIVEN, NOT APPLICATION-DRIVEN. Most organizations building Internet applications are doing so within a very narrow framework, simply applying cut-and-paste solutions to existing practices. In order to be successful in the long run, companies must stop asking themselves "Should we build an Intranet application that will help us reduce paper?" and start asking the more difficult questions like "Where do we want to move?" or "What role can we play in changing our industry?" or "How can this new technology be exploited to radically shift our competitive position?"

RELISH EXPERIMENTATION AND FAILURE. Many organizations, especially North American ones, are understandably very cautious, and are fundamentally driven by short-term results. This behavior often creates a paralysis in companies that can be very unhealthy and usually leads them to be highly reactionary. Digitally excellent companies embrace experimentation and welcome the risks of failure. They know that many projects might not succeed, but they mitigate those risks by allowing and encouraging people to be creative and take intelligent chances. Sun's Java is a perfect example of this. A few years ago, Java was a failed experiment. Today it is not only alive, but at the cornerstone of Sun's strategy; it has become a catalyst for new jobs, new companies, and new industries.

THINK STRATEGICALLY AND HOLISTICALLY. To see long-term benefits, companies must start now to build strategies for this new environment. Senior managers must understand the environmental forces at play within their organization and industry, and place Internet opportunities within a broader strategic context. Companies must address issues of customer requirements, core competencies, organizational culture, industry competitiveness, buyer and supplier power, and political factors, or their Internet initiatives will develop in a complete vacuum that will reap little value.

IF IT AIN'T BROKE, BREAK IT. Organizations that have found digital excellence go well beyond automating existing processes. They seek to break rules and radically transform organizational processes and existing industry dynamics, creating new opportunities even if they do not appear at first to work. Leaders don't just transform their processes; they transform their industries by inventing wholly new ways of creating value for customers.

BE CUSTOMER-CENTRIC. Successful organizations build value propositions from the customer's point of view. Moreover, they have a larger view of what constitutes a "customer." Your marketplace includes not only end consumers, but all other parties involved in a particular process, be it internal or external to the organization. This definition includes end consumers, business partners, suppliers, investors, internal departments, employees, government entities, local communities, and even the public at large.

DISPLAY A FUNCTIONAL/HEALTHY PARANOIA. Digital excellence is often a function of paranoia, or discontent with the status quo. Winning organizations are constantly on the lookout for new ideas, for what will give them an edge in their industry, and for what the competition, both existing and potential, is doing. Winners never rest easy. As Satchel Paige once put it, "Don't look back; they may be gaining on you."

EMPOWER EVERYBODY.   There has been a lot of talk of empowerment in recent years. Most of it has been just that—talk.
However, this new technology carries with it the potential to
provide employees and customers with genuine power. It is trite
but true that "information is power," and the Internet is all
about information access and dialog.

Thus, the Internet is not just a new tool. It is not even just a
new platform. It is a new platform that has the potential to revolutionize just about every aspect of our lives. But it won't do that
alone. In the course of this book we will take you on a journey
through several dozen companies, new and old, that are actively
experimenting with these new technologies and the surrounding
management systems needed to make them effective. The chapters to come will address issues from strategy formulation; to specific applications along business-business, business-consumer,
and intrabusiness relationships; to the management of technology; to future developments within the Internet space.

We will share with you our ideas about what these experiments mean, and suggest how you can—no, must—conduct
your own experiments. Come with us, then, on our search for
digital excellence.

NOTE

[1] This terminology comes from Alvin and Heidi Toffler, who differentiate the third wave
(information era) from the second wave (industrial era) largely on the basis of the increased importance of knowledge and brain power as sources of wealth creation.

THINKING STRATEGICALLY ABOUT ELECTRONIC COMMERCE

As your company embarks on its quest for digital excellence, it will face a great many decisions that will determine the different paths it will take and the success or failure it will encounter along the way. In making these decisions, business leaders are faced with some of the most difficult circumstances ever. Not only are they being bombarded by Internet "success stories" and proclamations about how this new environment will revolutionize business, but the rapid evolution of these technologies makes forecasting and investing in them an almost impossible task. What is clear, however, is that for the past three years of the corporate Internet craze, many companies have not reaped the benefits expected from their Internet-related investments.[1] It is this fact, in part, that drives us to articulate a strategy development process and framework for organizational decisions and the building of Internet initiatives.

This chapter starts by reviewing the concept of electronic commerce, including its history and current incarnation. This review will underscore the fact that electronic commerce has much in common with past networked information systems. As such, it is imperative that it be treated with the same level of strategic oversight—even though it might be tempting to let the latest, trendiest technologies drive a firm's electronic commerce activities. Ultimately, taking a strategic approach is not only prudent but essential. To assist you with this approach, we recommend a seven-step strategy and implementation plan development process. This process is summarized at the end of this chapter and discussed in further detail in the rest of the book.

WHAT IS ELECTRONIC COMMERCE?

Before we start, we want to build a common lexicon with which to communicate. This is not as trivial as it might seem, because in the corporate world you'll find a diversity of perspectives.[2] Ask ten different people what their definition of *electronic commerce* is, and you'll get at least as many answers. We will start out with a simple definition, and subsequently broaden it in order to capture a fuller picture. (p.29)!

Electronic commerce is not a new phenomenon that was invented with the commercialization of the Internet or the development of the World Wide Web; as a general concept it has been in use for decades. According to the Electronic Commerce Association, a simple definition for *electronic commerce* is "doing business electronically."[3] This phrase implies the exchange of information using a combination of structured (EDI) and unstructured messages (e-mail), data, databases, and database access across the entire range of networking technologies. At the core, electronic commerce clearly implies electronic links between dispersed sources of information.

Basic technologies such as e-mail and electronic data interchange (EDI) have long been combined into sophisticated systems to facilitate the exchange and distribution of information within and across organizational boundaries, to enable transactions and automated data processing, and to facilitate electronic marketplaces—all categories of applications that are still valid today, as we will highlight in numerous ways throughout the book. Here are a few prominent examples of early electronic commerce applications:

EARLY INTRANETS.   IBM's Professional Office System (PROFS) and early versions of Lotus Notes are examples of the 1980's forerunners to what are called *intranets* today (discussed in greater detail in Chapter 5). These systems basically provided links between end-user PCs and mainframe computers. They were deployed with the objective of enhancing office productivity by allowing employees to communicate over a network of terminals, to create and share documents, to retrieve, review, and print stored reference materials, and to update and exchange calendars.

AUTOMATED INVENTORY AND ORDERING. During the 1970s and early 1980s, pharmaceutical wholesaler McKesson and hospital supply manufacturer and distributor American Hospital Supply (now Baxter Healthcare) both installed terminals in customer facilities to automate inventory management and ordering processes. These two systems are examples of an earlier generation of today's internet and Web-based business-to-business applications (discussed in more detail in Chapter 6).

AIRLINE RESERVATIONS. Reservation systems such as American Airlines' well-known SABRE and United Airlines' Apollo were early examples of the concept that today we call *business-to-consumer electronic commerce* (discussed in detail in Chapter 7). They provided end consumers (through their travel agencies) with access to flight and ticket information, and online ticketing.

ELECTRONIC MARKETS. Information systems bringing together dispersed buyers and sellers and supporting business transactions were in use long before the current Internet frenzy. Although applications in the financial sector receive the most attention (e.g., The London or New York stock exchange), electronic markets were also established many years ago for less obvious industries like agricultural products (e.g., Telcot). Electronic brokering systems have long been in use and have influenced the transformation of established market structures and business practices.

Most of the systems that represent early examples of electronic commerce were initiated by large companies and reflect their attempt to gain sustained competitive advantage by establishing tight linkages with their business partners and by providing business value to them—effectively raising the cost of switching to competitors. The systems were usually based on proprietary technology; in fact, there were often not very many other choices, since only a few open and widely accepted standards existed at the time.

Electronic connections were often based on leased lines, offered by value added network (VAN) providers, and were usually very expensive. Most of the systems were purely text-based and otherwise had very limited functionality. Additionally, they were inflexible, making it difficult to add new partners or features or to integrate them with other applications and databases. As a result, most early electronic commerce applications remained islands of automation, consistent with the basic idea of electronic commerce but not realizing the benefits of synergy among various systems. Although they were often touted as being on the verge of a major breakthrough, technologies like EDI never reached truly widespread diffusion, especially among small- and medium-sized companies.[4]

COMPANIES IN THE FOREFRONT

The Internet, the "network of networks" (which is based on open standards), and especially its hypertext-based, multimedia-supporting spin-off, the World Wide Web, have opened a wealth of new opportunities that easily explain the hype and rebirth of the "old" idea of electronic commerce (see Chapter 3). Not only are applications such as e-mail, EDI, and online ordering systems now greatly facilitated and achievable at a much lower cost, but some organizations have shown impressively how these technologies can in fact change businesses and eventually spill over to transform whole industries.

DELL AND CISCO

For example, both Dell Computer Corporation and networking technology giant Cisco Systems are not only enabling transactions for their customers via the Web, but also creating one-to-one customized silos of interactivity and transactions that are, in essence, transforming business practices. Dell allows all customers to configure, buy, and receive support for products online, and it also establishes individualized Web sites for key customers—sites that incorporate special pricing, reporting tools, and direct access to an account team (for more details, see Chapter 6).

The impact of Dell's online ordering system has been phenomenal (see Figure 2-1). Not only has the company extended its "built-to-order" and direct distribution methods to the Web, but it has also succeeded in changing the nature of product distribution in the entire PC industry. Leading PC manufacturers like Apple and distributors like Gateway have now established online ordering systems patterned after the Dell model.

Such industry changes, however, point out an underlying burden when competing in the new digital economy: the never-ending pursuit of digital excellence and the difficulty of sustaining any kind of competitive advantage. Sustaining moves such as Dell's is by no means easy, as fellow industry players and emerg-

	Features	Benefits
Marketing Merchandising	Rich product info Segment merchandise Company info	Quick access to company info Customized information
Purchasing	Configurator for PCs 2 stores for PCs and complementary products Electronic orders	Convenience and control Product customization One stop shopping
Service & Support	Real time order status Rich reference info Troubleshooting tools	Improved service levels Reduced service costs Convenience
1:1 Customer Sites	Approved configuration and special prices Reporting tools (history, balance)	Improved customer relationships Management control Better prices

FIGURE 2-1. Dell's offering.

ing competitors follow suit. A close look at Dell reveals two strengths that place it in a sustainable strategic position. First, Dell's extended Web business model is just that, an extension of a business model that has been in operation for years. Dell has traditionally sold directly to customers, which is a luxury that companies like Compaq and Hewlett-Packard don't have. These other companies have existing channels of distribution to consider, thus the Web operation might lead to the cannibalization of existing channels. Second, Dell's real strength lies in two key areas: its supply-chain management and cost structure, which is superior in the industry; and most importantly its ruthless commitment to this extended digital business model. Although any other PC manufacturer could emulate Dell's model, there is no guarantee it will have the competencies in place to succeed.

ONSALE

ONSALE provides an example of the effort to bring together both buyers and sellers in a virtual arena to do business. The company has successfully established a forum where computer hardware and electronics OEMs, resellers, and consumers trade in an online auction format. It has, in essence, become an Internet-based "market maker" (see the case study in Chapter 7).

One of the major reasons for ONSALE's great success is the very clear value proposition that exists for both buyers and sellers. Buyers have the opportunity to "win" and not just buy products at an extremely competitive price. Such an environment has created a new type of economic output, "an experience," far more valuable than commodity-oriented products. For resellers and OEMs, the value proposition is even stronger. In essence, ONSALE takes from them the burden of moving "dead" inventory. This is an enormous benefit for companies like Compaq, whose relationship with resellers requires it to write off the costs incurred for products that are not sold or become obsolete.

FEDERAL EXPRESS

Consider the development efforts of a company like Federal Express. Clearly, a company does not have to be "born on the Web" to be successful or to take the Internet seriously. Also, success does not happen overnight; it comes through constantly being driven to change and do things better than others. Although Federal Express is often highlighted as a success story in the Internet arena, its success was achieved through long years of building competencies in key areas, and having a strong and visionary management team that led the way. Figure 2-2 illustrates Federal Express' Internet commerce evolution. Sixty percent of all Federal Express shipping orders are now placed electronically, and most users of the Web service are repeat Web customers. In addition, to further leverage its competencies, the company has established FedEx Logistics, an organizational unit that can take over all aspects of a company's logistics operations—from ordering to distribution to customer service.[5]

Thus, when we compare the current "wave" of Internet-based electronic commerce to the decades-old examples of networked information systems, it is evident that, although today's technologies differ significantly from the ones available in the "old days," the basic principles required in planning, designing,

1973–1976	Proprietary COSMOS system to track status of every package in the Federal Express Distribution network.
1984	Free dedicated PCs for PowerShip to high volume customers for direct connect to COSMOS.
1987	Free dial-up FedEx Ship software for any PC to connect to COSMOS to: Process shipping orders Arrange for courier pickup Track packages Create laser printed air bills
1994	World Wide Web site to track packages in real time
1996	Shipment ordering via the Web
1996–1997	Creation of Web-based end-to-end storefront and logistics services for small to medium sized organizations.

FIGURE 2-2. Federal Express's electronic commerce development.

and managing them remain unchanged. As before, and despite the apparent acceleration in the pace of change, organizations would do well to avoid a technology-driven vision of electronic commerce. Rather, it is prudent—even wise—to seek alignment between a firm's Internet and World Wide Web initiatives and its strategic goals.

DIFFERENT APPROACHES

One thing that is common to most organizations that have failed to capitalize on Internet initiatives is that they tend to be driven by either applications or opportunity, rather than strategy or vision. Why is an opportunistic approach dangerous? For starters, given the rapidly evolving technological environment, a fervent commitment to a specific technology or application can put a company in a very risky position. For example, organizations who hold fast to the belief that UNIX is the operating system of the future will naturally hire system administrators and programmers well versed in that operating system. Because UNIX personnel are scarce and in great demand in current IT workforce markets, such organizations will have to compensate these technicians quite handsomely in order to attract them. The organizations might then become locked into a position of over-paying their personnel should the current trend towards Windows NT continue and UNIX fall into disuse.[6]

A technology-driven, opportunistic approach to Internet strategy development ignores the real issues that companies must face: a more complex and fast-paced competitive environment; increasingly sophisticated, never-satisfied consumers[7], and the need for flexibility. It is these latter issues, as well as a company's overall corporate strategy, that should be the driving forces of Internet technology adoption, innovation, and use. To illustrate our point, we present a comparison of four approaches to electronic commerce: technology-driven vs. customer-driven strategies, "me too" vs. vision and core competency strategies, legacy vs. digital business models, and islands of Webification vs. portfolio of continuous applications.

TECHNOLOGY- VS. CUSTOMER-DRIVEN STRATEGIES

The hype of the technology and "success stories" of a few high-achieving companies have all too often led other companies down the path towards Internet commerce. This is not surprising given the elegance and simplicity of many Internet applications, the exciting hype surrounding them, their potential to bring hoards of new consumers to a company's doorstep, and the promise of radically reducing costs. We recommend, however, that the needs and wants of your customers and other constituents (consumers, business partners, vendors, employees) be the impetus for your Internet development. Understand which business opportunities create real value, or you might find that much of your effort will fall far short of your goals. Chapters 4, 6, and 7 provide techniques and ideas for building a deeper understanding of how a firm can use electronic commerce to support and strengthen its customer relationships.

LEGACY BUSINESS VS. DIGITAL BUSINESS MODELS

The initial impulse in many companies is to "Webify" existing processes, rather than to create new ways of doing business or to restructure key practices. The bottom line is that putting makeup on a monster only makes a pretty monster (if it does anything at all). Such an approach will lead to building the legacies of tomorrow. We recommend instead that you rethink your business models and processes and, in most cases, recreate them from the ground up to fit this new digital environment. Chapter 3 provides background material and concepts for assisting you with this rethinking.

"ME TOO" STRATEGY VS. VISION AND CORE COMPETENCY FOCUS

Too many companies have tried to "keep up with the Joneses" with respect to Internet solutions. A prime example is the intranet/extranet domain. The belief seems to have been that you can plop down an intranet within any organization and it will have the same impact regardless of corporate culture, strategy, structure, and business needs. Ultimately, the way a specific electronic commerce effort addresses these requirements will determine the project's success—or failure. We believe that your Internet initiatives must be focused on supporting a vision and building on the organization's core competencies. The processes we present at the end of this chapter and in Chapter 8 will provide you with a basis for achieving this alignment.

ISLANDS OF WEBIFICATION VS. A PORTFOLIO OF CONTINUOUS APPLICATIONS

Unintegrated "islands" of Internet activity can be found in most organizations. On the one hand, this is good because it indicates that people are being empowered to create and are accountable for their efforts. On the other hand, this situation can become quite problematic in terms of coordination, maintaining service levels, and building solutions that drive organizational success. Thus, islands of Webification are Internet/Web initiatives that are created in isolation from each other and are not tied to an overall architecture. Ideally, companies should strive to build a portfolio of complementary, integrated applications and to view these applications as needing continuous growth, development, and updating. Realistically, the desired level of integration must be balanced with the overhead expenses required to achieve and maintain this integration.

Given the fast pace with which technologies change, a technology- and application-driven focus can be disastrous. Technology becomes outdated quickly, and competitors can enter the market rapidly and easily as development tools and technology become more mature and more manageable. Furthermore, the new business models developed from the application of electronic commerce technologies can be copied very easily. Thus, established brand names like Barnes & Noble can enter the market and take market share away from the innovative new competitors like Amazon.com, the Internet startup that claims to be "earth's biggest bookstore."

"Davids" such as Amazon.com must be careful to avoid ending up as a historical footnote—being remembered as just the company that paved the way for the "Goliaths" such as Barnes & Noble. A comparison of the Web applications of those two companies reveals surprising similarities, and some observers claim that the much better-funded Barnes & Noble has made significant improvements to Amazon.com's original model. Barnes & Noble is reportedly prepared to lose $7 million dollars a year to build market share online.[8] In reaction, Amazon.com slashed its prices in the fall of 1997 and has attempted to build brand awareness in traditional media channels, e.g., radio commercials touting the benefits of doing holiday shopping at Amazon.com.

This scenario of well-funded dominant players coopting the ideas of creative and promising (albeit still unprofitable) upstarts is being played out in a wide range of online arenas—most prominently (and tragically) in the browser battle between Microsoft and Netscape, but also in other industries like auto distribution (GM vs. Auto-by-Tel[9]). It will be interesting to watch how market shares shift as new and cheaper Internet technologies make electronic commerce accessible to mass consumers—a population that is significantly less computer-savvy than the majority of current online consumers.

A company that wants to maintain or even increase its online market share despite these shifts would do well to pay attention to the relationships it maintains with its customers. Our extended definition of electronic commerce, therefore, revolves around relationships:

> Fundamentally, we see *electronic commerce* as the electronic support and transformation of social and economic intercourse through internetworked technologies. As such, it inherently involves the creation, transformation, and redefinition of *relationships* for value creation within organizations, between organizations (business-to-business), and between organizations and individuals (business-to-consumer).

In Chapter 4 we will discuss this relationship-focused view of electronic commerce in some detail. That chapter will also introduce concepts and techniques for describing and then building a strategy for using electronic commerce technologies to support and transform your company's web of relationships. Chapters 5 through 7 will present extended discussions of how such support and transformation can be achieved for relationships internal to the company, for relationships among business partners, and for relationships between the company and its consumers.

As a guide to starting to think strategically about electronic commerce, we will end this chapter with an overview of a strategy development process that we have found to be effective for thinking through the business, organizational, and technological choices you must make to build a successful online business. This overview will focus on the steps in the process you can use to describe your company's current position with regard to electronic commerce applications. We've filled Chapters 3–7 with ideas and concepts that will assist you in developing a map of where you might want to take that strategy. Chapter 8 provides practical steps for implementing the strategy that you have built.

ELECTRONIC COMMERCE STRATEGY DEVELOPMENT

In essence, this seven-step strategy development process focuses on the following basic questions:

- Where are you along the continuum of possible electronic commerce applications?
- Where do you want to go?
- How are you going to get there?

These are crucial questions to address if you want to take a strategic approach to the application of electronic commerce technologies. How do companies increase their ability to exploit digital economy opportunities for a sustainable value? Having the proper framework is the key to building capabilities of identifying and capitalizing on the opportunities. We have developed an assessment and planning methodology, and an approach to clarifying goals and expectations. The questions listed at the end of each of the steps illustrate the types of questions any enterprise should pursue in understanding and evaluating their Net-readiness, as well as the Net-readiness of potential business partners, affiliates, or anyone with whom they are engaged in market-based opportunity relationships.

STEP 1: MAP THE FUTURE

To align business strategy and Internet initiatives, you must create scenarios for the future that are not constrained by existing ways of thinking about business. When companies do not analyze the future marketplace, they often risk missing out on opportunities. In the Internet environment, planning scenarios around how the Internet and its key sources of innovation could affect the business are absolutely crucial. Chapters 9 through 12 provide useful perspectives for thinking about these scenarios. The questions to answer are:

- What is the current and future value chain of your business?
- How could the Internet impact the future value chain?
- What possible value propositions will the Internet bring about?
- What business could you be in due to the Internet (service vs. product)?
- How can the Internet be used to break "unbreakable" industry rules or challenge common assumptions?

STEP 2: VISION STATEMENT

In order for any initiative to be effective, a vision from senior management must be in place to drive Internet initiatives and make certain they are understood to be a serious and integral part of the business. Moreover, such a vision goes a long way towards getting the appropriate resources and funding for Internet initiatives. For example, Cisco Systems has total support from senior management for its Customer Connection Online Web site. This has resulted in the well-recognized success of Cisco's Internet commerce strategy and continues to drive future efforts and direction. The questions to answer are:

- Does your company or division have a well articulated vision for its Internet initiatives?
- Is the vision defined in business terms? Does it address how the new initiatives will provide new value to customers?
- Is that vision widely communicated and understood?

- Is senior management heavily involved in the development and support of Internet initiatives?
- Is senior management attuned to the opportunities/threats enabled by the Internet?

STEP 3: IDENTIFY AND TRANSFORM KEY VALUE CONSTELLATIONS

A company's strategy and vision should give rise to identifying the core practices and processes that Internet technologies could most affect. This analysis should not be limited to internal processes nor to a linear value chain. Increasingly, companies are learning to pay attention to the webs of relationships in which they are invested, as well as the value propositions for each relationship in that web. These webs of relationships and matching value propositions are called *value constellations*.[10] Companies should choose the processes that are most directly linked to customer value creation, and therefore provide the best opportunities for breakthrough performance. Charting out a business's value constellations and listing the expectations of each customer served by the key elements of the value constellation usually opens up many new opportunities to apply Internet technologies. The questions to answer are:

- What is the value proposition?
- What business processes are involved in delivering the value proposition?
- What are the key drivers of the value proposition and their associated information?
- How can the Internet enhance or transform the value constellation?
- How can we use the Internet to change the methods (and cost) of distribution of value?

STEP 4: DEVELOP A PORTFOLIO OF INITIATIVES

Having identified possible opportunities from the previous steps, the team in charge should articulate conceptually what key Internet initiatives it wants to pursue. Also, it is here you should check for the alignment or synergy among the various proposed initiatives. The questions to answer are:

- What key business-to-business initiatives will you undertake?
- What key business-to-consumer initiatives will you undertake?
- What key intrabusiness initiatives will you undertake?
- Is there synergy among these initiatives?
- Is it clearly understood and defined who will drive the strategy, development, and implementation of these initiatives?
- Are the roles, responsibilities, and accountability for these initiatives clearly defined?
- Where and how will you obtain the requisite skills and competencies (internal or external, local or global, recruit or train)?

STEP 5: DEVELOP YEAR-BY-YEAR OBJECTIVES

Explicitly outlining plans for Internet initiatives not only helps to crystallize the importance of the initiatives, but also provides the basis for developing measures of the effect these initiatives will have on the organization. Aside from assessing progress and performance, the outcomes suggested by these measures are crucial to determining future refinements to your electronic commerce strategy. The questions to answer are:

- Does your organization have an explicit and flexible system for measuring the success of Internet initiatives?
- What factors will dictate success: improved internal communication, enhanced knowledge sharing, enhanced cultural unity, cycle time reduction, increased customer share, process improvement, increased sales, etc?
- Will the Internet solution be flexible enough to accommodate change over the plan period?
- Do you have the technological infrastructure and competencies to engage in these initiatives?

- How much money is specifically allocated to fund these initiatives?
- Do you understand both the direct and indirect costs of these initiatives?
- Have you clearly identified and targeted manageable projects (3 to 6 months in duration)?

STEP 6: IMPLEMENTING THE CHANGE

This is the step where the rubber meets the road. The project participants not only have to deliver a system, they must also undergo the changes in attitudes and behavior that such a system requires. This is the point when the greatest resistance to change often emerges. The resistance is usually related to the degree of change required and the degree of mobilization and buy-in generated from the start. It is helpful to keep a project's scope within manageable limits— taking into account that any information system implementation engenders a wide variety of organizational and individual upheavals, requiring resources, time, and attention to be managed to successful conclusion. The questions to answer are:

- Which potential manageable project areas have the greatest probability of success?
- Do you have measures in place to monitor the success of the projects?
- Are the interdependencies that exist between those impacted understood?
- Who is responsible for managing these relationships?

STEP 7: METRICS

Although it is the final step, monitoring the overall plan is perhaps the most crucial activity. One of the biggest mistakes organizations make with Internet initiatives is thinking that the work is done when the new systems are up and running. This couldn't be farther from the truth. Successful companies take a "we are never done" approach to Internet applications. We cannot overstate the need to continuously revisit your strategy and the ongoing evolution of Internet initiatives. The questions to answer are:

- How are you going to measure the impact of Internet initiatives over time?
- Are there mechanisms in place to regularly review and revisit the strategy?
- Is there a plan to continuously evaluate the metrics that are currently being used?
- Can the metrics be modified if needed?
- How do emerging Internet technologies and business models affect our plan?
- What will the likely response of our competition be to these initiatives? What could it be?

This seven-step strategy development and implementation process summarizes the general technique we recommend for bringing electronic commerce into your organization. We also suggest taking an evolutionary approach to applying this seven-step process. In other words, at this point you might want to go through the seven steps quickly, building a preliminary strategy and implementation plan. Then, as you read through the rest of the book, you can revisit your preliminary strategy and plan, enriching it based on ideas and insights that emerge. Chapter 3 kicks off this enrichment process by providing you with a high-level overview of the technologies that enable electronic commerce.

NOTES

[1] Lou Bertin. "Look at the Long Term." *Information Week*, Oct 13, 1997: 45–50.

[2] Allison Lucas. "What in the World is Electronic Commerce?" *Sales & Marketing Management*, SMT Supplement, June 1996: 24–29.

[3] http://www.eca.org.uk/index.html.

[4] David Baum. "Transcending EDI." *InfoWorld*, March 24, 1997: 67–68.

[5] Todd Lappin. "The Airline of the Internet." *Wired*, 4.12, December, 1996.

[6] "Unix vs. Windows NT." *Byte*, May 1996.

[7] Regis Mckenna. *Real Time*. Boston: Harvard Business School Press, 1997: 36.

[8] Anthony Bianco. "Virtual Bookstores Start to Get Real." *Business Week*, October 27, 1997.

[9] Jeanne C. Lee. "Can GM Sell Cars on the Web?" *Fortune*, September 29, 1997: 243–244.

[10] Noel P. Greis and John D. Kasarda. "Enterprise Logistics in the Information Era." *California Management Review*, Summer 1997: 55–78.

THE BUILDING BLOCKS OF ELECTRONIC COMMERCE

In this chapter we will provide an overview of the essential hardware and software components that form the infrastructure for electronic commerce. Since electronic commerce technologies are still in their early stages of development and are rapidly evolving, it is impossible to describe them completely in a single chapter. Our goal here is to provide you with a basic, high-level view of the technologies essential for conducting business over the Web and point out some trends to watch. We aim to equip you with a framework for tracking the evolution of these technologies and for discussing their application with individuals in your organization who are technically oriented. The chapter ends with a discussion of capabilities that are enabled by the application of these technologies. This discussion will serve as a springboard for the more detailed discussions, later in the book, of the impact of electronic commerce technologies on the conduct and structure of business operations.

One of the simplest ways of characterizing the infrastructure that supports electronic commerce is as a network of clients and servers (see Figure 3-1). Viewed in this manner, the computing paradigm of the Web is usually characterized as a client-server system. As such it continues the trend towards such modular computing infrastructures where processing and

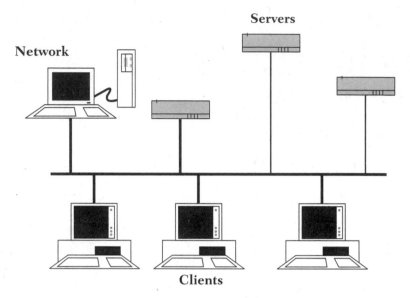

FIGURE 3-1. A framework for understanding and tracking electronic commerce technologies.

storage are parcelled out among various computers connected by a network allowing the sharing of resources (e.g., printers) and gaining efficiencies. Generally:

· Clients receive, display, and/or execute files. They constitute the component of the client-server system with which the user interacts. Clients range from $200 Web TVs to desktop PCs and high-end workstations.

· Servers handle the storage, processing, and delivery of files to clients. These components of the infrastructure constitute the workhorse of the entire infrastructure. In general, most of the heavy-duty storage and processing involved in the computing system occur in these components. Servers range from high-end PCs and workstations to special-purpose processors to the largest mainframes and supercomputers.

· Networks link clients and servers so they can exchange files and instructions. Networks include the web of public networks linked together to form the Internet, internal corporate local area networks, far-ranging wide area networks, and the rapidly growing wireless communications infrastructure.

Although the majority of information and program process-ing occurs at the servers, clients and networks are capable of processing as well, albeit generally on a smaller scale. We will use this simple client-server-network structure to organize our overview of electronic commerce technologies. We will then re-view some overlays to this structure in order to cover other technologies that are essential to conducting electronic com-merce. These overlays include a security infrastructure and a payment system infrastructure.

CLIENTS

HARDWARE

Clients are generally composed of the systems that sit on users' desks (see Figure 3-2). Users can be the entire range of em-ployees, customers, and other individuals who access your sys-tems. It is especially important to be aware of what client systems you are going to reach with your electronic commerce applications. The capabilities of clients generally influence the features of your electronic commerce applications. To get the

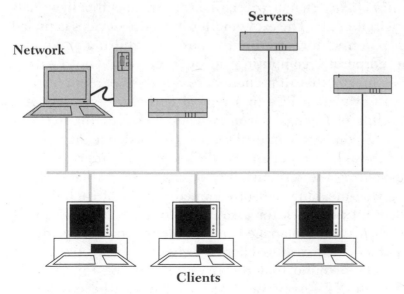

FIGURE 3-2.   Client/server network, emphasis on *client*.

most value from your investment, it is best to offer features that your users' clients can access easily, or you run the risk of losing a possible contact or sale because the user gave up on accessing the site. For example, most clients need special add-on programs (called plug-ins) to run sophisticated animation. If your target users have only an average amount of computer knowledge, they are likely to be uncomfortable with adding these programs to their systems. Thus, you would have to either simplify your Web application to reach average users or provide such users with alternative, less feature-filled Web pages. This latter option is usually the preferred design because currently there is a wide range of client hardware and software configurations that any company has to reach—from those based on pure text to fully loaded, state-of-the-art browsers linked to unlimited bandwidth. More sophisticated sites will offer users a choice of either a simpler low-bandwidth version or a high-bandwidth one. Others generate pages "on the fly" based on the type of browser a user is viewing the site with.

At this point, client hardware can range from $200 Web TVs to basic PCs and laptops, all the way to high-end workstations. An important trend to watch is the emergence of client devices with scaled-down processing and storage capabilities, called *thin clients*, that are designed to work specifically in network environments. The excitement over these devices is fueled by their potential for lowering the cost of acquiring and maintaining corporate computing infrastructures. The Gartner Group estimates that thin clients are 30 to 40 percent less expensive to own than PCs in a typical corporate environment. The amount of savings is somewhat dependent on the efficiency of a company's information systems department since some of those savings accrue from keeping maintenance and troubleshooting the responsibility of expert IS staff instead of allowing well-meaning, self-proclaimed experts at each department to hunt and peck for a solution to a system problem. A company with a well-managed environment can expect only a 5 to 15 percent decrease in client hardware costs.[1] A study by Zona Research found that the five-year cost of 15 Windows PCs with an NT server was $217,663, while the cost of 15

Wyse Winterm clients with an NT/WinFrame server came to only $94,368. The savings accrue not only because thin clients (and the infrastructure to support them) are cheaper than PCs, but also because thin clients are easier to support. Thin clients break down less often than PCs, are simpler, and thus require less user training. Furthermore, thin clients enhance the standardization that makes support easier, by preventing users from installing their own software and/or conducting their own inefficient troubleshooting when the PC goes down. While thin clients will likely require a larger MIS department to provide support, a company saves in the long run because technical support will be performed by expert MIS staff.

There are generally two categories of thin clients. The first includes radically new devices designed primarily to run software developed in Java, a multiplatform object-oriented programming language developed at Sun Microsystems. To ease transition to this new platform, the devices also provide gateways to existing programs and data. Examples of these devices are Oracle Corporation's Network Computer and Sun's own Java Station. The second category includes devices that don't execute programs locally. These thin clients act like terminals with graphics capabilities. The clients enable users to run popular software programs like those based on the Windows platform. The difference is that these programs are executed on another machine to which the client is connected via a network.

SOFTWARE

An essential component of a client system is software to facilitate the access of files of data or applications. The software includes proprietary corporate software, off-the-shelf client applications, and Web browsers. A key factor in improving the user-friendliness among current systems are Web browsers. Web browsers are software packages that allow you to access and display data, and execute programs. They can display many different media, e.g., text, audio, and video, in a wide variety of formats. These browsers, incorporating well-established protocols, allow a wide variety of clients to access, view, and/or execute files stored on a server. Browsers have been key to allowing clients to do this because their early development was rooted in a philosophy that embraced cross-platform, user-friendly, multimedia systems.

One of the biggest proponents of this philosophy and the embattled leader in the Web browser market is Netscape Communications. It provides a browser, Navigator, that functions in essentially the same way across a wide range of client platforms: Windows, Macintosh, UNIX, etc. One of the biggest benefits of the cross-platform nature of browsers such as Navigator is that it allows companies to provide a unified interface to the disparate systems within their companies and across the various companies with whom they want to communicate. Most browsers also incorporate the type of graphical user interface that many users have become comfortable with in the over 20 years since Apple brought it to popular usage with the Macintosh. This simple, familiar interface, coupled with the ability to handle all forms of media—audio, video, and hypertext—provide companies with the potential for making their standardized interfaces much more accessible and engaging than ever before possible.

An important trend among browser packages is the movement to build integrated desktop suites that augment browser capability with additional productivity tools for functions like e-mail, discussions, and coordination of schedules among workgroup members. The ultimate goal is to make the browser the single desktop package that any user needs to do his or her work—supporting major activities as well as providing easy access to files and programs no matter where they sit on the global network. In early 1997, Netscape introduced Communicator, which significantly augments the capabilities of desktop programs. The full, production version of the package is expected to allow clients to share calendars and conduct discussions and controlled chats across networks like the Internet.

A trend to watch is Netscape's promotion of HTML as the standard for e-mail communications. This means that e-mail can go beyond plain text and contain essentially the same elements that make Web pages so engaging: graphics, audio, hyperlinks, animation, even Java applets. Intellipost (www.intellipost.com), a start-up providing targeted direct marketing via e-mail, uses HTML mail to send multimedia enhanced advertising e-mail to its subscribers. As information providers start to use this new form of e-mail to "push" and/or broadcast information customized to meet user interests, browsers are likely to have diminished prominence as a primary form of information access. This trend enhances the importance of other productivity tools included with the browser suites in current use.[2]

SERVERS

Servers are powerhouse computers that store files and perform the major processing that occurs in the electronic-commerce client-server network (see Figure 3-3). Servers range in size from Sun workstations to the digital supercomputer that sits behind the Alta Vista search engine. One of the most difficult tasks of any IS manager is planning for the future capacity of these servers. Many have addressed this issue by leasing machines from outsourcing vendors. A new paradigm emerging from work at UC

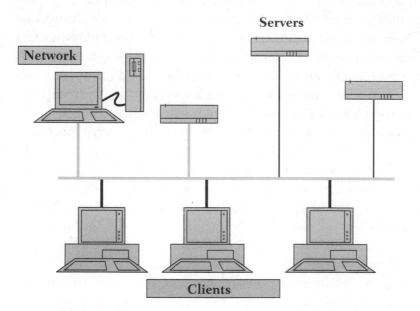

FIGURE 3-3. Client/server network, emphasis on *server*.

Berkeley's Computer Science department is to use networks of workstations (NOW). This is built on the premise that flexibility and incremental scalability is key to matching the rapid and unpredictable shifts in processing requirements. To this end, the NOW paradigm uses a high-speed network to cluster commodity workstations—e.g., Pentium Pros and Sun workstations—to make them function as a single machine. What this modular architecture allows a company to do is increase capacity by adding one workstation at a time to the network, thereby avoiding the complications involved with a "forklift upgrade"—replacing a huge mainframe with another, larger-capacity mainframe.[3] One of the first applications of the NOW architecture is the search engine HotBot (www.hotbot.com) Provider Inktomi was able to build HotBot's capacity to index 54 million documents using NOW technology. The company estimates that is provides 3–5 times price/performance advantage when compared with other leading search engine providers. While it is unlikely that the modular architecture of the NOW paradigm will replace the large computers that currently hold company's legacy databases, they will most probably play an increasingly important role in the storage and processing of new applications and databases. Already companies such as Bank of America and Wal-Mart are using clustered computing platforms to store and process their massive data warehouses of customer information. In late 1997, clustering is getting increasing attention with Microsoft's addition of Wolfpack, a clustering capability, to its highly successful Microsoft NT operating system (also known as Microsoft cluster server).[4]

All browser packages have corresponding server packages that manage the delivery of information and files to client browsers. At the same time, these server packages can collect information from clients, either by asking the user to enter information on a form or by tracking the status of the client and the online activities of the user. Some of the more sophisticated server applications use this collected data to customize the pages provided to a target client. These servers usually run intelligent agent and/or database systems to conduct the analyses and on-the-fly decisions required to achieve customization. Servers also run packages that use established protocols to perform common tasks like delivering e-mail messages to client machines, managing newsgroups, and matching descriptive names to the numerical IDs assigned to machines on a network. A growing trend is to place servers between companies' legacy systems and newer Web technologies. These servers run software that accesses or extracts pertinent data from legacy systems, then processes and formats the data for delivery to browser clients.

A useful by-product of the tracking capabilities of server software is that it can be used to collect information on users of corresponding clients. The most common way of doing this are through surveys, server logs, and cookies. *Surveys* are basically online versions of traditional hardcopy surveys. Companies usually motivate users to fill out these surveys by making them a requirement for accessing useful files like free software, samples, and customized information. Most server packages automatically generate listings (*server logs*) identifying which client machines access specific files on the server. These logs can then be analyzed to generate information on the most popular files. Identification information on most client machines also includes information on the domain where they come from, e.g., .edu for education, .gov for government, and .com for commercial. You can then use this information to further refine analyses of server logs by segmenting information on client accesses by domain. Lastly, *cookies* allow companies to send a small file to be stored on the client machine. This file can contain information on past activities of the client machine, e.g., login ID and password, browser version, page settings, and user preferences. The next time the client returns to the Web site, its browser software sends the cookie back to the server. The server can then act on the information on the cookie, as well as update it. The information in the cookie can also be used to track the same client's activities regarding a company's site, over time.

The tracking capabilities provided by server software are a potential windfall of data for determining the preferences of consumers and other users who visit a company's Web site. However, realizing this potential is hampered by two main difficulties. First, as with other measures of advertising and marketing impact, it is very difficult to make inferences and build useful information from the data collected by server software. Not only are there few established methods for making these inferences, but there are also many measurement problems involved. For example, numerous users might use the same client address, one person might use different client addresses, or a single Web page might require several file accesses to be displayed (one for each element in the page, e.g., one each for the text, Java applet, or graphic). Second, users are not entirely comfortable with the idea that companies can monitor their activities much more closely than ever before. For many users, giving up such a large part of their privacy is not worth the benefit of any customized information, products, and convenience that companies could provide to them based on the information collected.

THE BATTLE FOR ELECTRONIC-COMMERCE SOFTWARE DOMINANCE: MICROSOFT VS. NETSCAPE

One of the most interesting stories in the electronic commerce era is the battle between Microsoft and Netscape. Netscape started off the whole new paradigm for computing when it launched Navigator in 1994. Microsoft took a year or so to realize the potential of the Web platform for weakening its dominance over user desktops. Recognizing this in late 1995, Microsoft launched a major development and promotion effort fueled by a staggering reserve of resources. Within a year, Microsoft's own browser, Internet Explorer, and a whole slew of Internet development tools and applications established Microsoft as a legitimate player in the electronic commerce arena.[5] Internet Explorer's rapid dissemination was facilitated by Microsoft's control of the desktop system market and the company's financial, marketing, and legal clout; Explorer is bundled with the Windows operating system, it is free for anyone to download from the Microsoft Web site, it provided free subscriptions to popular Web service like the Wall Street Journal Interactive Edition, and it successfully fought or delayed action on Netscape's accusations of predatory trade practices.

In early 1997, Netscape introduced a new suite of browser applications called Communicator, which pushed the envelope of browser capabilities. At the same time, Microsoft was scrambling to fix security problems with its own Internet Explorer package. Both companies are building new desktop applications that blend these browsers, Web technologies, and operating systems to best support the network-centric computing that is gaining in importance as workers become increasingly mobile. Although both companies aim to provide users with seamless access to local and remote resources, their approaches to achieving this aim reflect contrasting corporate visions for the future of computing. Microsoft continues to push for a world where the Windows platform remains dominant. Its active desktop will always work better with the Windows operating system. Netscape, on the other hand, is pushing for complete location- and platform-independent computing. As envisioned, its Constellation desktop product will run on 18 different operating systems and provide users with a uniform interface no matter what machine they use to hook up with their home server—be it their own laptop or desktop, or a machine borrowed from a hotel or office they're visiting.

Microsoft, with its resources and market dominance, might well continue to provide superior, easily attainable products. Arguably, some will be built through co-opting innovations generated by companies such as Netscape. This period, however, will be recognized as a period of high creativity fueled by competition between two companies with strongly held yet opposing philosophies. No matter what the outcome, this creativity will likely benefit all users by fostering more user-friendly, interoperable, and useful software systems.

NETWORKS

Two concepts underlie most discussions of electronic commerce networks (see Figure 3-4): bandwidth and security. *Bandwidth* refers to the speed and capacity of a network, resulting from advances in network materials, modems, and compression technologies. *Security* addresses the processes and technologies used to ensure a level of propriety over the information passing through these networks. The level of security can range from private dial-up lines established between two companies to semiprivate networks established by industry consortiums (e.g., the insurance industry's IVAN) to public networks of the Internet.

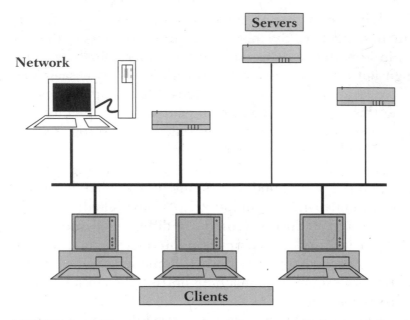

FIGURE 3-4. Client/server network, emphasis on *network*.

BANDWIDTH

A fundamental law of electronic commerce is that human beings have an insatiable appetite for bandwidth. Any advances in network speed and capacity are quickly "maxed out" by users eager for more functionality and multimedia capabilities from their Web applications. Thus, network providers and modem manufacturers alike are constantly in search of greater bandwidth. When you consider that network providers are composed of some of the largest companies, such as phone companies and cable operators, you realize the extent of resources that are being invested in this search. Furthermore, as phone companies struggle to operate within the new electronic commerce paradigm and cable companies struggle with resource constraints, major network vendors are slowly eating away at their advantage as installed network providers. These vendors are providing new and better network options much more quickly and at more affordable prices.

A useful way of classifying the four major types of networks linking clients and servers is by the conduits that achieve this linking: copper twisted-pair, fiberoptic, wireless, and coaxial cable. A major driver for the optimistic assessment of Internet commerce growth is that all these channels, save for fiberoptic, are currently available in the homes and businesses of a large part of the global consumer marketplace. Generally, the first two are laid and managed by phone companies, their subsidiaries, or spin-offs of subsidiaries. Wireless involves a wide range of providers from cellular phone vendors to UHF and cable companies.[6] The last, coaxial cable, is generally laid and managed by cable companies. All of these networks required special modems to translate any information running through the wires into a form that is readable by the computers linked to them. Thus, modem companies like U.S. Robotics and Hewlett-Packard also play major roles in the development of these networks.

Experts forecast huge increases in bandwidth in the coming years. Figure 3-5 compares a sampling of the most prominent network services currently available or in discussion. It portrays the dramatic increases in speed and capacity we can expect by the turn of the century. Compare the current standard for internal corporate LANs and the bottom bar, which is the prevalent U.S. standard for home access to the Internet. Modem and network technologies are developing at such a rapid pace and in the midst of much competition that projected prices suggest that much of this capacity will be affordable for the average telecommuter and even perhaps consumers. As these technologies become more affordable and accessible, we are likely to see an increase in the percentage of telecommuters within organization's personnel. It is important to note that these telecommuters are also consumers who will have the benefits of high-speed connections not only to their home organization servers but also to any organization servers connected to the Internet. These telecommuters will become a significant target group for any organization seeking to build a sophisticated Web service that capitalizes on such high-bandwidth capability.

Network performance can also be enhanced by the actions of additional components like switches and routers. *Switches* build virtual circuits within networks that allow a group of users greater access to a subset of network capacity,

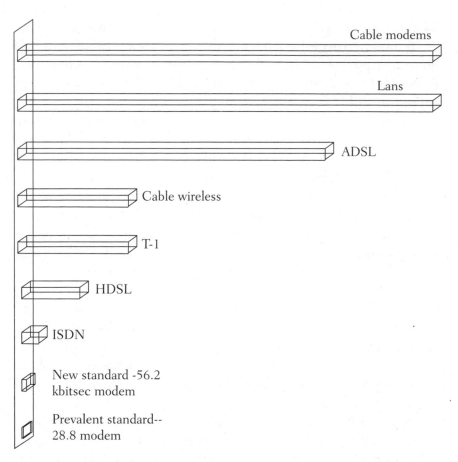

FIGURE 3-5. Comparing the maximum speeds of some of the most prominent network services currently or soon to be available.

and *routers* make automatic decisions on the most efficient routing for messages traversing a given network. There are also many debates raging about the appropriate and most efficient network configurations, both in the public arena and within private corporate networks. The lack of consensus on configurations has resulted in a highly complex telecommunications design and maintenance task. Individuals who have the expertise to make intelligent decisions about corporate networks are among the rarest and highly paid members of any IT organization.

The complexity of the problem has also resulted in the proliferation of consulting and outsourcing practices in this area.

Some of the major providers of such expertise are the leading systems integrators (e.g., Computer Sciences Corp., Andersen Consulting, and EDS), telephone companies (e.g., AT&T, Lucent Technologies, Inc., Northern Telecom, Inc., and DSC Communications, Inc.), and network equipment vendors (Cisco Systems, Inc., Cascade Communications Corp., Ascend Communications, Inc., and 3Com Corp.). In the future, as telecommunication practices mature, companies are likely to see basic telecommunications as a component of their infrastructure that is ripe for partnering or outsourcing arrangements.

SECURITY

One of the major advantages of the Internet as a network is its ubiquity, a legacy of almost 30 years of government and education funding in the United States and Europe. Originally envisioned as a fail-safe network, it allowed the government many alternate routes for its messages should any enemies of the nation disable part of the network. The protocols that allow such flexibility and redundancy also allow any transactions coursing the Internet today to take a myriad of routes through the public networks that comprise the Internet. With the rapid growth of business and consumer usage of the Internet, the transmission of corporate data over public networks (e.g., as part of Internet EDI applications), coupled with consumers' hesitancy about sending personal information over the same networks, has increased managers' awareness of the security risks of any form of network computing. Such awareness has helped develop stronger, more user-friendly technologies for securing the data moving through any networks that might be at risk. The three essential components for achieving such security are *firewalls*, which moderate traffic flowing between public networks and a company's private network, *encryption technologies*, which make the data unreadable to most individuals who might happen to access the data illegally, and a *public key infrastructure*, which certifies the identity of network users and distributes "keys" that make the encryption systems work.

Firewalls are essentially computers that store a list of instructions and databases used for assessing the access privileges of any user seeking to obtain files stored in an organization's servers. They generally guard the dividing line between computers that store private company data and those that serve up files for public access. User access can be categorized in a variety of systems, including passwords, user domain addresses, machine IP addresses, or digital certificates. Firewall systems that facilitate changes to user access privileges will become increasingly important tools in the current business era, where corporate flexibility is so much dependent on organizations' ability to easily create and sever links with experts, business partners, and temporary workers.

Encryption technologies and procedures help ensure that files sent over public networks are unreadable by unauthorized individuals. These technologies are essential to systems currently in use and being developed to ensure privacy and security on the Web, identify entities connected to the Web, and build virtual private networks. Encryption scrambles messages so anyone illegally accessing them cannot read the data unless he or she has the correct key to unscramble the message. Because they are aware of the crucial role security plays in encouraging electronic commerce, software manufacturers have made great strides in making encryption technologies easy to use. The major browsers and several e-mail packages already incorporate the ability to encrypt messages and other forms of information that might be transmitted over public networks like the Internet. In general, the size of an encryption key determines the degree of difficulty unauthorized persons will experience in trying to decrypt an encrypted message they might intercept over the Internet. The following table lists the maximum time required to decode a message (encrypted using the cryptographic system embedded in Netscape), relative to the length of the key used. These time estimates assume that decryption is done using "brute force," where a code-cracker tries every possible combination of bits. Note that 56-bit symmetric keys (DES algorithm) are the typical size allowed for export under the U.S. Department of State's International Traffic in Arms Control regulations, in late 1997. Note that in June 1997 a worldwide network of computers, linked by the Internet, cracked a message encrypted with a 56-bit key. It took them approximately three months to find a key to decrypt a message that was encrypted with the strongest encryption level allowed by the U.S. government for export.

KEY LENGTH	MAXIMUM TIME REQUIRED TO CRACK A MESSAGE ENCRYPTED USING THE GIVEN KEY LENGTH (IF THE CODE CRACKER DID NOT HAVE THE KEY AND ALL POSSIBLE KEY COMBINATIONS WERE NEEDED TO DECRYPT THE MESSAGE)
40 bits	15 days
56 bits*	2,691.49 years
64 bits	689,021.57 years
128 bits	12,710,204,652,610,000,000,000,000 years

*Note: The 56-bit key was cracked in June 1997 in much less time because the key was found after only 25% of all possible combinations were tried, and because the code crackers used a huge number of machines working in parallel.

The seamless use of encryption technologies is somewhat hampered by two issues, still to be resolved at the policy level. First, the U.S. Government, fearing its use for illegal activities, restricts the export of encryption technology that allows for keys longer than 56 bits. There has been a continuing and heated battle between law-makers and much of the computing industry regarding appropriate measures for addressing the government's discomfort with making such strong encryption available outside the U.S. Additionally, the U.S. government is pushing for measures that provide it ready access to private keys. Unfortunately, the government restriction of encryption opens the way for non-U.S. software makers to provide their own security solutions and potentially own the de-facto standard for such applications. Second, there is no agreed-upon method of exchanging encryption keys and certifying the identity of key owners. The heart of this issue is in building a public key infrastructure.

ENCRYPTION TECHNOLOGIES IN DETAIL
SYMMETRIC KEY AND PUBLIC KEY ENCRYPTION

*While software products incorporating encryption proce-
dures are making a very tedious set of protocols work seamlessly and transparently to most users, there are benefits to
spending some time understanding the processes underlying
such applications. Such understanding is invaluable in
helping managers envision new uses for such procedures,
understand some of the debates raging around the widespread adoption of encryption, and intelligently apply the
technologies to the organizations they manage and to their
personal work.*

There are two commonly used encryption methods—
symmetric key and *public key* cryptography. The two methods
are often used in combination—to speed up encryption processing and gain from the benefits of both. Symmetric key
encryption involves using the same key to both encrypt and
decrypt a message traveling from sender to receiver. While
simple, it presents a quandary—how does one transmit the
key from sender to receiver? This quandary is addressed by
public key cryptography. Still, since symmetric key cryptography is faster than public key cryptography, it is often used
to encrypt large documents. Public key cryptography is then
used to encrypt the symmetric key for its journey from
sender to receiver.

Public key cryptography addresses the problem of sending keys over the Internet by assigning key pairs to every
party wanting to be involved in private communications.
Each party generates a unique key pair consisting of a private
key and a public key. Anything encrypted with a public key
can be decrypted only by the matching private key, *and* vice
versa. Public key cryptography is built on the long challenged
but still upheld premise that it is very difficult to calculate
the private key given only its matching public key—essentially requiring one to factor a very large number into two
very large prime numbers. So, it is possible to distribute the
public key freely without compromising the cryptographic

system, since only the private key can be used to decrypt anything encrypted with the public key.

The private key is kept in a secure location—e.g., the owner's hard disk or better yet a smart card. The public key is published in the public arena—e.g., a directory, a Web page, a signature file. Ideally the public key is published to include certification from a trusted party—or a network of trusted parties—that the key actually belongs to the person who claims to own it. This is not a trivial matter on the Internet, where the ability to communicate with individuals anywhere in the planet requires well-established means of certifying the identity of the person on the other end of the "line." As of late 1997, wide-ranging certification systems are rudimentary at best.

Once parties have generated their key pairs, they can use them both to encrypt messages sent between them and to generate digital signatures that identify the message sender and guarantee the integrity of the message. These are done in two separate procedures. A sender uses a receiver's public key (Rpub) to encrypt a message to be sent to the receiver. This message can then be sent over public networks to the receiver. Once the message has arrived, the receiver decrypts it using the private key that matches the one used by the sender to encrypt the message (Rpriv).

Digital signatures and integrity checks take advantage of the fact that anything encrypted with a private key can also be decrypted with the corresponding public key. A sender wishing to sign a message first generates a summary number that is unique to the message, using a well-established mathematical procedure. The sender then encrypts this number with his/her private key (Spriv). The sender then usually sends a bundle to the receiver that includes the following:

1. The message encrypted with the receiver's public key (Rpub).

2. The summary number encrypted with the receiver's public key (Rpub).

3. The summary number encrypted with the sender's private key (Spriv).

When the receiver gets the bundle. He/she does the following:

1. Decrypts the message encrypted with Rpub using his/her private key (Rpriv).
2. Decrypts the summary number encrypted with Rpub using his/her private key (Rpriv).
3. Decrypts the summary number encrypted with Spriv using the sender's public key (Spub). This authenticates the identity of the sender.
4. Checks the integrity of the message by making sure that the summary number decrypted in step 2 matches the one decrypted in step 3.

As mentioned earlier, symmetric keys are usually used in combination with public keys to speed up the process of encryption. In the latter scenario, a unique symmetric key is randomly generated for a given message. The message is encrypted using the symmetric key and the symmetric key is encrypted using the receiver's public key. The procedures for generating summary numbers and digital signatures then match those outlined above. The bundle then includes:

1. The message encrypted with the unique symmetric key.
2. The symmetric key encrypted with the receiver's public key (Rpub).
3. The summary number encrypted with the receiver's public key (Rpub).
4. The summary number encrypted with the sender's private key (Spriv).

With variations in the mathematical procedures used and some concessions to government requirements, the above procedures generally match those embedded in many software programs that offer encryption capability today—including Netscape's and Microsoft's browser products and Lotus Notes. One of the leading providers of encryption products embedded in top software products—and an advocate for the widespread use of these technologies—is RSA Data Security (www.rsa.com). The growth in demand for secure network commerce has increased the visibility and, fortuitously, hastened the development of user-friendly encryption components. In a few years, we might all be adept in the use of such components and be able to take greater responsibility for our own privacy and identity in the digital realm.

A *public key infrastructure* (PKI) includes all the services supporting applications that require cryptography. When it comes to electronic commerce, these are any applications that involve the transmission of data that needs to be secured. Examples are all forms of EDI, consumer purchase transactions, consumer checks on the status of their bank or merchant accounts, and business customer inventory checks and purchases. Essential services to support such applications are systems for generating encryption keys, for authenticating the owners of such keys, for signing documents, and for providing time-stamped receipts that serve as legally binding audit trails for electronic commerce transactions. Building a PKI requires cooperation among businesses, governments, and infrastructure vendors both within the U.S. and worldwide. One of the groups coordinating these efforts is CommerceNet, which provides a useful site for tracking trends in this area.[7]

PAYMENT SYSTEMS

For commerce to sustain itself in the electronic commerce arena, there needs to be a medium of exchange that allows organizations to collect money for the services and products they provide over the Web and other networks. As of late 1997, the most common method of achieving this is by having buyers send payment and other confidential information over a secure channel—such as that afforded by Netscape's secure sockets layer. Several standards that improve the security and privacy of such transactions are in development, the most prominent being the SET initiative, which involves many traditional players in the electronic payments arena—including Visa and Mastercard. The SET initiative aims to develop the processes that will be used to allow the secure and reliable transmission of payments using traditional instruments like credit cards. This model is considered quite viable because it can leverage the level of trust people have in institutions like Visa and Mastercard and hopefully transfer such confidence to new channels for purchase transactions—e.g., the Internet. This model, however, is viable only for purchases above $10 since smaller purchases do not present a profitable value proposition to merchants and the organizations involved with SET. This limitation has resulted in opportunities for building a standard for micropayments, or payments below the $10 threshold established by the SET initiative.

Micropayment systems use various methods for allowing users to establish an account from which they can debit small amounts to be applied to electronic purchases. Examples of such systems available or being tested in late 1997 are Cybercoin from Cybercash and Digital's Millicent. The most common method is to have users charge a small amount on their credit card, say $20, using a channel they are comfortable with—e.g., the phone. This puts the $20 into what is usually called a "wallet." The user can then use a pin number associated with this wallet to pay for purchases over the Web in increments of $\frac{1}{10}$ of a cent to $5. Using this system, users can avoid sending their sensitive personal information like credit card numbers over a channel they perceive as insecure. The small dollar amount involved in each transaction requires that the systems sacrifice some security—to enable the high volume of transactions per second (approximately 2500 according to Digital's estimates) that could generate profits from revenue built on a tenth of a cent per pop! Should electronic commerce get to a point where users pay each time they access files or information over the Web, micropayment systems will likely serve as an important process for collecting money in exchange for such access.

ENABLING ELECTRONIC COMMERCE

This last section provides an overview of how the building blocks described earlier in the chapter result in the unique characteristics of Web technologies and, consequently, the unique capabilities of Web technologies. Many of these capabilities will be discussed later in the book. The capabilities include developing engaging front ends for business applications, integrating existing disparate systems, standardizing user interfaces and system configurations, digitizing organizational knowledge, and developing settings for real time, as well as enhanced interaction and relationship marketing.

Many of the unique characteristics of Web technologies described in Chapter 2 result from the features of browser software run on clients, the corresponding software running on servers, and the fact that these clients and servers are connected via a worldwide network that links private corporate networks with the public networks of the Internet. The following table allocates these capabilities between software running on clients and servers, and networks.

WEB IT CHARACTERISTIC	BROWSER/SERVER SOFTWARE	WORLDWIDE NETWORK LINKING PUBLIC AND PRIVATE NETWORKS
Interactivity	Yes	Yes
Immediacy	Yes	Yes
Connectivity	No	Yes
Cross-platform	Yes	No
Richness	Yes	No
Easy	Yes	No

Engaging front ends are built on the capability of browsers to access and display multimedia files, and their constant interaction with a server that can collect and analyze data about the users at the other end of the client browser. By exploiting this interactivity and multimedia capabilities, companies have been able to provide consumers with entertaining configurations of video, audio, text, and graphics that change in response to user input. At the same time, companies are able to exploit the same capabilities to provide more accessible and useful windows to legacy decision support systems and databases. Users no longer have to be satisfied with text-based views of systems and data. With multimedia capabilities, these views can include graphs, hypertext links, and even real-time video of corporate activities being monitored by a given system. With Internet connections, these views are available even to mobile and/or telecommuting users at remote locations. Interactivity also facilitates the rapid display of the results of any changes suggested by user inputs, for instance during a "what if" analysis. Any user input can quickly be processed at the server end and then the results used to generate a multimedia Web page that portrays the impact of the input on key measures.

The cross-platform nature of Web browsers and related technologies can greatly facilitate the integration of the disparate systems currently found in most organizations. Because browsers like Netscape's Navigator run on many different operating systems, developers can provide very similar formats and functionality to users running entirely different systems. The Java programming language adds functionality through applets that can be executed in a wide range of platforms as well. Once this cross-functionality is fully realized, organizations can use a browser to unify the interface by which employees access the systems and information they require to do their work. A range of programs, collectively known as *middleware*, then mediate the exchange of files between legacy systems and browsers. Such middleware is now becoming available from vendors such as Oracle and Microsoft. With middleware, the company in effect achieves standardization at the browser level despite running disparate systems on user desktops and even maintaining stable, long-established systems on the back end.

The link between servers and browsers provides another opportunity for the standardization of user systems—a goal with much promise for reducing cost, yet always elusive. Companies can mirror the software distribution methods pioneered by software companies, using the Web for such activities. They can use the same system to allow users download the latest files onto their own desktops in order to configure their systems and keep them in sync with all the other machines in the organization. New browsers and desktop systems also allow for the automatic updating of user desktops. This "push" model of file distribution has much potential not only for standardizing information and system configurations within an organization, but also for improving the company's marketing efforts. The model enhances a company's ability to reach a select group of customers that would be most interested in hearing about the company's products.

Browsers are also useful front ends for collecting data pertinent to building organizational knowledge. The link between client and server is two-way. As mentioned previously, servers constantly keep logs of client activities. Such logs can be used as a basis for auditing the efficiency of company operations as well as employees' adherence to manager-prescribed actions. Users can also enter information into forms that are directly linked to a database. This can be a useful tool for capturing organizational knowledge that would otherwise remain unarticulated and highly inaccessible—kept as they are in the heads of key employees. Such employees could be encouraged to enter their knowledge of specific operations and/or customers into a browser form that links up to a database, where the information could be organized and made accessible through a Web browser. For example, salespeople could be encouraged to enter daily notes on the customer visits they have made. These notes could then be collected and organized in a database and made accessible to all employees who contact customers. This system would not only facilitate information-sharing among employees, but also ensure that the corporation would not lose a significant part of its knowledge should an employee choose to leave the company.

New browser applications take advantage of the interactivity afforded by Web technologies to enable the building of rich settings for interaction. Browser users can now share a whiteboard to collectively draw diagrams or they can engage in collaborative browsing and conduct moderated chats over the Internet. As bandwidth becomes more available, companies will start having the option of transmitting video over the Web. This high-bandwidth application will allow the transmission of the social cues generally absent in text-based transmissions. At that point, conferencing over the Web will present a viable alternative to face-to-face interaction. Additional benefits of conducting such meetings over the Web is, again, the almost automatic digitization of organizational knowledge, which can be collected, shared, and digested in the meeting. Web technologies can store the video of the session, notes, audit trails, and other useful information, which can then serve as reference for future meetings, a basis for next action steps, and a way for managers to track the activities of teams and determine whether further guidance or incentives might be needed.

Lastly, the building blocks of electronic commerce all come together to enable the next generation of Web applications. These are generally applications that support relationship marketing. Relationship marketing aims to build long-term, repeat business from given customers through various techniques that include customization of products to meet customer needs and the use of rituals to build a strong bond between customers and the company. Customers can be external (consumers, business partners, etc.) or internal (e.g., employees and other departments). Chapter 7 will discuss in more detail the topic of relationship marketing in a digital environment. Key to this complex activity is the shaping and collection of information on user preferences, and the rapid customization of a product to meet these preferences. Shaping preferences is perhaps best achieved with rituals. A company can build a strong bond with its customers by mining the wide range of shared experiences for those that might best match its products. The rituals can then become very interactive over the Web—allowing customers to have some semblance of interaction with the ritual itself. Customer preference profiles can be built out of these interactions and across repeated interactions with the customer. The company can then build a link with its own manufacturing and production systems to build a customized product that meets the customer's needs. The matching of consumer preferences and customer products in a ritualized setting is one of the key ways in which a company can build a long-lasting bond with a given customer.

THE CASE OF INTERNET EDI: THE EVOLUTION OF INTERNET TECHNOLOGIES

The following cases[8] contrast the implementation of Internet-based EDI in two organizations: McKesson and Bank of America. The cases are a contrast in approaches, fueled partly by contrasting organizational approaches, but also by the rapid evolution of Internet-based EDI technologies. The cases illustrate how approaches to implementation can quickly change in response to the rapid deployment of Internet-based versions of traditional applications.

One of the most often cited reasons for limiting the adoption of EDI is the prohibitive cost of its implementation. Traditionally, these EDI implementation costs have included the cost of purchasing or developing the EDI translator, the cost of integrating the EDI translator with the corporate information system, and the cost of establishing a communications network among trading partners. These costs, along with the major effort and expense involved in making disparate corporate systems communicate seamlessly within EDI standards, mean that the spread of EDI has largely been fueled by pressure and/or subsidies from large manufacturers to their suppliers.[9]

Value-added network providers play an essential role in providing expertise for translating, tracking, and conveying EDI transactions among trading partners.[10] Still, Forrester Research estimates that this situation excludes up to 60 percent of the vendor marketplace, or 1.9 million companies, from current EDI networks.[11] A large part of the interest in using the Internet as a channel for EDI transactions is the potential for facilitating the entry of more suppliers in such networks—both by lowering set-up costs and by being a readily available network providing ubiquitous access.[12] This case assesses the impact the Internet might have on the growth of EDI networks, based on the results of two efforts at the early application of the technology and a preview of upcoming applications.

The Internet seems to present a cost-effective transmission medium for EDI transactions, but the decision to move EDI to the Internet is not a forgone conclusion.[13] Contrary to initial notions, the Internet is not always the cheaper alternative, for three reasons. First, to maintain their customer base, current transport medium carriers, e.g., value-added networks (VANs), are lowering their rates to stay competitive as an increasing number of companies consider moving their EDI transactions to the Internet. Moreover, since many VANs are now offering Internet-based services, organizations need not switch to an Internet service provider (ISP) to obtain Internet access or capability.[14] Second, the cross-platform user-friendly nature of Web technologies is fueling the growth of computer-based interorganizational services at many corporations. As EDI-aware corporations are beginning to realize, the Web paradigm facilitates interorganizational transactions that need not be based on EDI standards. For example, companies specializing in the transportation of goods and information, e.g., Federal Express, offer full-service logistics support without using EDI forms and standards for communications and tracking among trading partners.[15] Third, concerns over the security and reliability of public networks like the Internet mean that porting EDI to the Internet requires additional procedures to ensure the security and reliability of EDI transactions.[16] Any savings on the transport medium could easily be canceled out by the investment in developing and implementing such procedures, and the risks and costs of a large security violation or reduced service quality due to delay or the loss of EDI forms sent over the Internet.

This case illustrates two approaches to building an Internet EDI capability, and the approaches reflect the contrasting conditions in which they were applied: BofA/LLNL started developing their pilot in mid-1994 during the early days of Internet EDI evolution, while McKesson started its implementation in early 1996.

When BofA started its pilot, the design of Internet EDI systems was still being worked out; indeed, Premenos' Templar was still being tested and, with the cosponsorship of CommerceNet, the BofA/LLNL pilot was seen as part of the effort of refining Internet EDI specifications. The BofA/LLNL teams benefited from extraordinary conditions that shielded them from constant oversight and allowed them to experiment with the new technology for almost two years. Paramount among these conditions were the uncertainty over the ultimate application of a newly and enthusiastically appropriated technology (the Internet), the presence of well-recognized EDI and security experts at both organizations, and the relatively low cost of the entire experiment ($80,000). In essence, the pilot was sustained in a pocket of ambiguity and slack resources—similar to many organization's initial forays into Internet applications. When McKesson attempted its own implementation, the technology had matured to a point where production-grade systems could be purchased, albeit at an imposing price that limited the size of the trading network that could be built. At this juncture, the state of Internet EDI technology suggests that McKesson's quandary is a temporary one and that soon the cost of ramping up to EDI capability might be low enough to promote its widespread adoption.

BANK OF AMERICA

Before the Financial EDI (FEDI) pilot, BofA used two primary channels—private networks and VANs—to transmit FEDI and other EDI transactions. In late 1994, individuals at BofA were searching for a client partner to start a FEDI pilot project. Because of general concerns over Internet security, particularly for transmissions involving financial transactions, BofA expected that it would have a difficult time finding a willing partner. At about the same time, individuals at LLNL became interested in building the capability for FEDI over the Internet, as part of a planned overhaul of its accounts payable system. At LLNL, this was seen as a next step in its continuing leadership with innovation in the practice of EDI. Quite fortuitously, representatives from both organizations made contact at several CommerceNet and special-interest group meetings in the San Francisco Bay area, and decided to pursue a possible pilot for conducting FEDI over the Internet.

The key objective of the pilot was to demonstrate that it was possible to achieve secure and reliable transmission of sensitive data like payment instructions over the Internet. The pilot was meant to dispel negative perceptions of the Internet that were held by the general public and the business community. The pilot would be especially valuable in addressing the concerns in the banking industry over sending crucial financial data over the distributed public networks of the Internet. As discussed previously, these perceptions centered primarily on two concerns: security (that transactions over the Internet were easily intercepted and tampered with) and reliability and speed (that transactions tended to get lost and/or delayed as they were passed from node to node over the Internet).

The FEDI pilot included two phases. The first phase limited the exposure of both LLNL and BofA to the risk of financial losses due to compromised payment instructions. Success with this limited test led to the relaxation of the limits during the second phase of the pilot. The second phase also included volume testing to simulate any problems that might result from a full-scale implementation. In general, the pilot system involved the exchange of EDI documents containing payment instructions and acknowledgments. To achieve security, the documents were processed through servers running software built around the PEM/MIME standards at entry into and exit from each organization's existing network of EDI systems. A system of e-mail and human monitoring tracked messages through the system—ensuring that payments were completed accurately—and collected data to assess system performance. All throughout the seven months of the pilot, BofA project participants were also involved in designing a full-production platform to support Internet security for FEDI and similar applications.

Data from BofA's daily tracking log showed that almost 50 percent of problems stemmed from internal systems going down or offline. This figure reflects the difficulty in coordinating the separately managed systems that were part of the FEDI pilot process. This condition was magnified because BofA's PEM server was part of the firewall operation that resides in an R&D location, as opposed to a financial production environment. Thus, BofA's PEM server was at times accessible to individuals who were unaware of the impact of any processes they might run on the PEM server on the FEDI pilot. Furthermore, both BofA and LLNL went through several software problems and upgrades over the course of the pilot, resulting in further problems with compatibilities between the systems in the network. Much of the early work done by the project team involved solving these incompatibilities and instituting procedures to coordinate all the different systems involved in the pilot process. Most of these problems were resolved by January of 1996. It should also be noted that, despite these problems, all payments were completed within the agreed-upon time frame: two days from the time that LLNL sent a payment instruction to BofA.

In the assessment of participants at both BofA and LLNL, the results of the pilot supported the viability of the secure and reliable transmission of sensitive information over the Internet. Most of this support comes from the finding that none of the problems with payment transmissions were due to any breach of the network or tampering with the messages being transmitted. Most of the problems encountered during the pilot were due to nonrecurring software and procedural issues that were eventually resolved. The most striking finding regarding the reliability of the Internet for FEDI transmission is that none of the messages were lost in transit between BofA and LLNL. Any reliability problems encountered occurred within the internal systems of the pilot partners. The reliability measures also showed that, despite delays and problems, information on payment instructions, acknowledgments, and payments remained consistent. This suggests to the participants that, given the security measures used and despite its decentralized nature, the Internet has the capability of accurately transmitting crucial data like payment instructions.

The results of volume testing showed that, as the number of payment instructions contained in a message increased, the processing time also increased. However, this increase can be attributed to the increased time required to processes the instructions and not to increases in the time required to transmit the e-mail message over the Internet. Analysis of BofA logs shows that most of the time increase resulted from the greater time required to process the transactions at the BofA ECS server. There were no systematic or large increases in the message transmission times.

McKESSON

With $17 billion in revenues, McKesson is one if not the leading U.S. wholesaler in the pharmaceutical industry. Maintaining this leadership in an industry where average net profits hover around two percent requires constant innovation. McKesson has achieved continued leadership by growing its generic drug inventories, providing value-added services, and improving the efficiency of its own operations.[17] Key acquisitions and its own internal development have made McKesson a leader in providing value-added services to many segments of the healthcare industry. Many of these services involve the application of information technology to rationalize and improve the efficiency of distributing pharmaceuticals and of managed-care compliance. Its proprietary Economost product-ordering system, originally developed in the 1970s, today supports 6600 trading partners.[18] It has recently developed a suite of financial and managed-care applications to complement the back-end services it provides to a group of individual retail pharmacies that are operated as a virtual pharmacy chain.

Recently, the Internet-EDI involvement of the company was hastened by efforts to win a major contract that included requirements for Internet-based access to McKesson's product inventory and ordering systems. The specific requirements of the contract were direct FTP access into McKesson's systems for price checks and product availability, two-hour quantity and pricing confirmation on orders, and emergency ordering capabilities. Additionally, McKesson needed to build this functionality within 90 days in order to win the contract. Because of the security risks associated with providing such access, McKesson negotiated to meet the contract requirements using two systems: a browser-based system for emergency inventory checking and ordering single items, and an Internet-EDI system for routine ordering, invoicing, and other transactions.[19]

In addition to meeting the requirements of the customer contract, any solution chosen by McKesson had to meet the high access and security standards of the company. Due to its long history with mainframe-based computing, McKesson's managers were accustomed to the operation of crucial systems on a 24-hour-a-day, seven-day-a-week basis. The mainframe-era security standards and crucial nature of the data stored and processed by McKesson's systems dictated rigorous security measures for the proposed system.

To build the two systems, McKesson built a multidisciplinary team, headed by the vice president of Information Delivery. The team was composed of two project managers, programmers from the EDI area, five architects from the applications area, a Web developer, network engineers, UNIX engineers, and customer integration staff. The new system had to be integrated with legacy systems in the order processing, distribution, receiving, and accounting areas. The team had to knock down many organizational obstacles to meet its aggressive deadline and its additional goal of enhancing existing applications in the process.[20] The magnitude of the development effort supported a strong case for obtaining resources and convincing various organization members to break from traditional organizational practices. The size of the contract was also instrumental in justifying the half a million dollars spent in building the infrastructure and developing the software necessary to meet the customer requirements and McKesson's own high standards of security and availability. To meet these standards, McKesson purchased redundant Web servers and built a double firewall.

The browser-based system for emergency ordering was built using HTML and PERL on the Netscape platform. The use of these tools greatly reduced the development time for the emergency ordering application. The system is, in effect, an extranet that allows password-enabled access into McKesson's inventory and ordering systems. Authorized customer representatives can access the extranet using a Web browser. The system allows authorized users to check on inventory levels and order individual products.

McKesson purchased Premenos' Templar software for both its own system and a hub at its customer facility that could support 18 ordering sites. At the time, Templar was the only product that provided complete, secure Internet EDI capability using the Simple Mail Transfer Protocol (SMTP) messaging standard.[21] Despite being limited to one package, McKesson was reassured by successful applications and testing of the Templar product.[22] This software package interfaced with the company's existing EDI software and added software-level security and authentication procedures, including the encryption and signing of any EDI documents that were sent over the Internet. The package included key management capabilities that will be especially useful as McKesson increases the number of trading partners it conducts EDI with over the Internet.

The two cases of Internet-EDI implementation presented in this section illustrate the increasing "commodification" of a new technology: Internet EDI. The quick development tools, multiplatform nature, and reuseability of code generated for EC applications hasten the movement of technologies from standard building to off-the-shelf products. In early 1997, barely three years from the initial interest in Internet EDI, a proliferation of products were announced or made available by traditional EDI and enterprise computing vendors:

COMPANY	PRODUCTS/SERVICES
Harbinger	Harbinger Net Services
	TrustedLink Guardian
	TrustedLink Enterprise
	Trusted Link Commerce
	Trusted Link Banker
Sterling Software	Sterling Commerce:
	Gentran
	Commerce
	Connect
	Vector
GEIS	GE TradeWeb
	Business Network EDI
	EDI Application Integrator
	EDI Application Integrator for SAP
	EDI*CONNECT for DOS

COMPANY	PRODUCTS/SERVICES
	EDI*EXPRESS(SM) Service
Premenos	Templar
	Announced Systems
Actra Business Systems	Business Document Gateway
FourGen Software Inc.,	EDI/Internet order-processing solution that will
Seattle, and	integrate FourGen's Enterprise supply-chain
Frontec AMT Inc.	management applications and Frontec's advanced
	messaging technology, AMTrix
	(http://www.frontec.com/fourgen.html)
AT&T	AT&T EDI services
	(http://www.att.com/easycommerce/easylink/edi.html)
SAP & Microsoft	Internet EDI applications based on the Microsoft
	browser, a server, and OLE controls
	(http://www.microsoft.com/industry/sap/
	News/news2.htm)

Because these products emphasize interoperability and facilitation of setup using browser-based applications, their deployment could result in a situation where even small companies and occasional EDI users could quickly and inexpensively acquire the capability to handle EDI transactions. At that point, being EDI-capable would cease to be a competitive advantage for suppliers. Buyers need not be locked into suppliers solely because they are EDI-capable, and suppliers who are not EDI-capable need not be locked out of a trading networks. Such a scenario portends a transformation of the competitive landscape within such networks. Buyers can place less emphasis on pressuring suppliers to build up EDI capabilities and more on other aspects of buyer-supplier relationships: cost, trust, product quality, and codevelopment. Ideally, this could result in improvements in product quality, as organizations are no longer limited to EDI-capable firms in their search for suppliers. Ultimately, the winners might be the EDI infrastructure providers, as widespread adoption translates into major increases in EDI transactions. Albeit, the potential windfall for EDI providers is somewhat mediated by the potential competition from non-EDI-based interorganizational system solutions, e.g., logistics services provided by Federal Express and extranets.

NOTES

[1] "Thin Clients: Behind the Numbers" *Byte*, April 1997. http://www.byte.com/art/9704/sec6/art3.htm.

[2] "Net Applications: Will Netscape Set the Standard?" *Byte*, March 1997. http://www.byte.com/art/9703/sec6/art1.htm.

[3] Eric Brewer, Clustering Multiply and Conquer Data Communications on the Web (July 1997) www.data.com/tutorials/clustering.html.

[4] "What Wolfpack Means for Parallel Computing" *Byte*, May 1997. www.byte.com/art/9705/sec7/art8.htm.

[5] Kathy Rebello, "Bill Gates' Quiet Shopping Spree" *Businessweek*, January 13, 1997. www.businessweek.com/1997/02/b3509221.htm.

[6] Jonatan Marshall, "Wireless Web Surfing" *San Francisco Chronicle*, Page C1, September 16, 1997.

[7] http://www.commerce.net/work/taskforces/pki/pki.html.

[8] These cases were prepared in collaboration with Arie Segev and Jaana Porra, Fisher Center for Management and Information Technology.

[9] C. Iacovou, I. Benbasat, and A. Dexter. "Electronic Data Interchange and Small Organizations: Adoption and Impact of Technology." Management Information Systems Quarterly, 19, No. 4, December 1995: p. 470; T. Mukhopadhyay, S. Kekre, and S. Kalathur. "Business Value of Information Technology: A Study of Electronic Data Interchange." Management Information Systems Quarterly, 19, No. 2, June 1995; G. Premkumar and K. Ramamurthy. "The Role of Interorganizational and Organizational Factors on the Decision Mode for Adoption of Interorganizational Systems." Decision Sciences, 26, No. 3, May/June 1995: p. 307; E. Wang and A. Seidmann. "Electronic Data Interchange: Competitive Externalities and Strategic Implementation Policies." Management Science, 41, No. 3, March 1995: p. 415.

[10] B. Fox. "Internet: Bane or Boom for EDI VANs?" Chain Store Age, 72, No. 6, June 1996; Hitchcock Publishing Co. "Is the Internet a better way?" Manufacturing Systems (Master the Supply-Chain Challenge Supplement), August 1995; J. Ross. "Retailers Explore EDI on the Internet." Stores, 78, No. 7, July 1996.

[11] Hitchcock Publishing Co. "Internet breaks price barriers for small and mid-size companies." Manufacturing Systems, 14, No. 8, August 1996.

[12] J. Gebauer. "Internet-Based EDI." Fisher Center For Information Technology and Management Briefings Paper, 96-BP-001, December 1996.

[13] C. Curtis. "EDI Over the Internet: Let the Games Begin." Communications Week, 627, No. 59, September 1996; C. Frye. "EDI Users Explore Internet as Tool of Trade." Software Magazine, 15, No. 13, December 1995; P. Gill. "Manufacturers Cautious on the Internet." Software Magazine, 16, No. 5, May 1996; C. Harler. "Logistics on the Internet: Freeway or dead end?." Transportation & Distribution, 37, No. 4, April 1996; E. Messmer. "The Internet Rocks EDI Boat." Network World, 13, No. 18, April 1996; E. Messmer. "Harbinger Gives EDI an Internet Twist." Network World, 13, No. 15, April 1996; K. Nash. "Internet EDI on Horizon." Computer World, 30, No. 5, January 1996; A. Segev, D. Wan, C. Beam, B. Toma, and D. Weinrot. "Internet-Based Financial EDI: A Case Study." The Fisher Center for Management and Information Technology Working Paper, CITM-95-WP-1006, August 1995; K. Weisul. "Heavy Hitters Open Doors to EDI over the Internet." Investment Dealers Digest, 62, No. 46, November 1996.

[14] C. Curtis. "EDI Over the Internet: Let the Games Begin." Communications Week, 627, No. 59, September 1996; J. Davis and M. Parsons. "EDI vendors adjust strategies in face of growing Internet." InfoWorld, 17/18, No. 52, December 1995/January 1996; B. Fox. "Internet: Bane or Boom for EDI VANs?" Chain Store Age, 72, No. 6, June 1996; C. Harler. "Logistics on the Internet: Freeway or dead end?." Transportation & Distribution, 37, No. 4, April 1996; D. Kilbane. "Services Enable EDI Exchanges by Internet." Automatic I.D. News, 12, No. 9, August 1996; E. Messmer. "Harbinger Gives EDI an Internet

Twist." Network World, 13, No. 15, April 1996; J. Minkoff. "Internet Appeal to Business." Discount Merchandiser, 36, No. 3, March 1996; J. Ross. "Retailers Explore EDI on the Internet." Stores, 78, No. 7, July 1996; G. Socka. "EDI Meets the Internet." CMA Magazine, 70, No. 5, June 1996.

[15] T. Lappin. "The Airline of the Internet." Wired, 4, No. 12, December 1996.

[16] C. Frye. "EDI Users Explore Internet as Tool of Trade." Software Magazine, 15, No. 13, December 1995; J. Gould. "EDI Over the Internet." ec.com, 3, No. 1, January 1997; P. Gill. "Manufacturers Cautious on the Internet." Software Magazine, 16, No. 5, May 1996; C. Harler. "Logistics on the Internet: Freeway or dead end?." Transportation & Distribution, 37, No. 4, April 1996; K. Nash. "Internet EDI on Horizon." Computer World, 30, No. 5, January 1996; A. Reinbach. "Internet Commerce: Slow, But Moving Forward." Bank Systems & Technology, 33, No. 10, October 1996, J. Smith Bers. "Diving into Internet EDI." Bank Systems and Technology, 33, No. 3, March 1996.

[17] S.L. Oswald and W.R. Boulton. "Obtaining Industry Control: The Case of the Pharmaceutical Distribution Industry." California Management Review, 38, No. 1, Fall 1995.

[18] V. Wheatman. "EDI Over the Internet: McKesson Case Study." The Gartner Group Electronic Commerce Strategies Research Note, June 1996.

[19] Ibid.

[20] Ibid.

[21] Ibid.

[22] S. Gore. Electronic Data Interchange (EDI) Over the Internet. National Information Infrastructure Testbed. http://www.infotest.com, 1996.

BUILDING A WEBBED ORGANIZATION

In this chapter we propose guidelines for developing your company's Internet commerce strategy. The approach taken in this chapter results from our premise that emerging Web technologies occasion a shift in the conceptualization of strategies—both in the IT arena and ultimately organization-wide. This shift takes into account the myriad of relationships that envelope an organization and drive its present and future operations. Understanding the many facets of these relationships is key to supporting and transforming them with Web technologies. In this chapter, we will introduce a tool to help you build a comprehensive view of your company's relationships: the relationship matrix. We will then discuss five principles for guiding your thinking about how these relationships might be transformed by Web technologies. The chapter ends with a summary of implementation issues that you need to consider in building your strategy. These implementation issues will be revisited in more detail in Chapter 8.

The chapter also illustrates how several companies—e.g., McKesson Corporation and Federal Express—have used the Web to support and enhance such relationships. McKesson Corporation has had a history of exploiting information technology to gain a competitive advantage in the wholesale drug distribution industry. As the "webbing" of American business threatens its intermediary position in the industry, the company is searching for ways to use the Web as a delivery tool for improving the value it provides to its customers. Similarly, Federal Express has built its industry position by successfully using information technology to enhance the courier services it provides. The Web affords it the opportunity to expand its range of services—aiming to provide complete order fulfillment services to any company who wants to do business on the Web.

FOCUSING ON RELATIONSHIPS

In this book we propose a major shift in the way managers construct strategies. A core premise of the book is that focusing on business relationships is essential to building a successful strategy for exploiting Web technologies. The networked nature of Web technologies forms a natural infrastructure for supporting and transforming relationships. This is especially pertinent—and opportune—in a business environment that emphasizes partnering and relationship building. A major feature of Web technologies is their ability to rapidly build links among entities that seek to exchange assets—e.g., information, technical skill, and raw materials. Yet companies cannot fully mine the capabilities of these new information technologies without thoroughly understanding the myriad of relationships in which they are involved. Only by recognizing the intricate and shifting constellations of relationships that involve their companies can managers go beyond just mirroring current relationships—problems and all—to fully achieve the potential these technologies have for supporting and transforming such constellations.

An important first step in building a Web commerce strategy is to locate the company in its network of relationships. As discussed in Chapter 2, the emphasis on networks necessitates a shift from the traditional tool for building strategy, the value chain. The value chain, while useful, tends to be limiting in three ways. First, its focus on activities undermines the importance of continuing and shifting relationships among the entities engaging in these activities. Identifying the activities that bring raw materials into the company's plants is not enough. A thorough and useful description would need to characterize the multiple facets of the company's relationship with the entities that provide such materials. This information is useful for guiding the development of systems that not only improve the efficiency of value chain activities but, more importantly, promote the maintenance and enhancement of the relationships a company has with the entities engaging in these activities. For example, in the realm of customer relationship, studies show that corporate profits rise significantly with customer retention. Just a 5 percent decrease in customer defection has been shown to boost profits by 25 percent to 85 percent.[1] Second, a thorough description of the current operations of most companies would need to go beyond the linear nature of the value chain. Nowadays, product manufacturing and service provision involves multiple, complex arrangements and information transfers among business partners, partners of business partners, and beyond. To complicate matters further, each entity in the value chain itself possesses its own constellation of relationships. Recognizing the nonlinear nature of such constellations creates opportunities for exploiting existing relationships in order to build new and profitable ones. Third, relationships are not built on the sum of the value chain activities that a company shares with a given entity. To understand how Web technologies might support and transform such relationships requires that a company pay attention to the aspects of relationships that are not built solely on such activities. These aspects include the personal contacts and rituals that surround traditional value chain activities. The Canon-Hewlett Packard relationship captures the rich characterization of relationships that we suggest should inform your applicaton of Web technologies.

INDUSTRY EXAMPLE: HEWLETT-PACKARD AND CANON

The Hewlett-Packard and Canon relationship is a perfect argument for focusing beyond the value chain and onto multiple and shifting relationships. HP and Canon are both collaborators and competitors; they collaborate on the design of laserjet engines, but compete in the production of inkjet printers. The dual nature of the

HP-Canon relationship has major implications for the design of the information systems that support it. A key goal for such an information system is separating information in the conduct of the companies' collaborative relationship from the information shared in the conduct of the companies' competitive relationship. Information technologies and systems of passwords and access restrictions go only part of the way toward making sure that the correct subsets of information are provided and accessed by the appropriate parties. Yet both companies recognize that this compartmentalization can be only partly achieved with technologies and legal contracts. Ultimately, it is the long-term relationship and desire to maintain that relationship that keeps each company from going beyond the bounds of access provided in support of their multiple relationships.

The networked computers enabled by Web technologies can mirror these multifaceted relationships and their shifts. The World Wide Web—through both its hard wires and the information they transmit—facilitates connections among businesses with complementary capabilities. Such connections enable companies to readily augment their core competencies. Furthermore, because of its ubiquity and relatively low cost, the Web also provides support for the fluidity of such relationships. It is much easier nowadays to modify the boundaries between the partners in such relationships in response to changing environmental requirements or the shifting nature of such relationships. The flexibility of such linkages can also potentially facilitate joint experimentation among partners. Since such linkages are readily set up, modified, monitored, and severed, companies might be more willing to engage in risky undertakings.

Opportunities also abound for transforming relationships. The ubiquity of networks across time and space, as well as the ease of building links among organizations, make possible opportunities for changing the links used to achieve company goals. As linkages become easier to form, companies might find efficiencies in disintermediating the agents and middlemen who used to provide the expertise necessary to form those linkages. At the same time, the rapid growth and evolution of Web technologies and the information they carry will create opportunities for the emergence of new intermediaries. Finding entities to fill these new intermediary positions could represent a huge sourcing issue for companies, as they try to determine what these new intermediaries are, how to find them, and how to value their services. On the more positive side, the new intermediary positions might also represent new lines of business for a given company.

The first step we recommend for building an Internet commerce strategy is to fully understand your core business strengths and how they are positioned in the constellation of relationships required to conduct your business. Carefully assessing your company's core strengths is important for differentiating essential relationships from less essential ones. It is also an important step in determining the key relationships you need to cultivate or transform in any endeavor your business might undertake. Also essential to this step is understanding the multiple facets of the relationships you have with the key players in this network.

As a guide to this understanding, we provide a relationship matrix. The matrix identifies several factors that can guide your thinking when crafting a strategy for supporting and enhancing your company's relationships. In this chapter we will define the key components of this matrix and how you might use it as a guide for crafting strategy. In Chapters 5 to 7, we will describe how you can use the matrix to guide strategy development for applications applied to the three main kinds of electronic commerce: business-to-business, business-to-consumer, and intrabusiness.

THE RELATIONSHIP MATRIX

The matrix in Table 4-1 augments traditional efforts for describing the various customer segments an organization tries to target. Traditionally, an organization lists the customer segments and then identifies the product or service configuration that best matches each target segment's preferences; e.g., cheap, white,

Table 4.1 The Relationship Matrix

CUSTOMER SEGMENT (VARIES BY COMPANY)	PRODUCT/SERVICE ATTRIBUTES (VARIES BY PRODUCT/SERVICE)			KINDS OF BONDS		
	Attribute 1	Attribute 2	Attribute 3...	No Bond	Structural	Emotional
Segment 1						
Segment 2						
Segment 3						
Segment 4...						

Note: Attribute and Segment items will vary depending on your company, customer segments, and products.

single-pocket T-shirts are preferred by the generation X customer segment. We propose to augment this matrix by recognizing the aspects of customer relationships not specifically linked to these product configurations. A relationship can also be based on the bond formed between the parties involved in it. The right part of the relationship matrix might be used to characterize these aspects of a given relationship. We define three types of bonds: no bond, structural, and emotional. These bonds can be found in any given relationship either alone or in combination. We define each type of bond as follows:

NO BOND.   The no-bond category refers to situations where a segment is composed of customers who are not seeking a relationship. A common strategy for attracting these customers is to make it convenient for them to access a company's services or products. A key characteristic of this bond is that customers do not incur a switching cost when choosing to go with another provider. An example of this type of approach would be magazine publishers who allow customers to sign up for trial subscriptions on the Web (e.g., *Wired*). A customer can sign up for the subscription by filling out a seven-item form, and no credit-card information is required. To exit the subscription, the customer merely writes "cancel" on the magazine bill and sends it back to the publisher. The price of entry is the little time spent filling out the online form. Exiting costs 32 cents (the stamp to mail back cancellation). Forming a year-long relationship costs about 15 bucks.

STRUCTURAL BOND. This category refers to situations where a segment is composed of customers who are locked into relationships with a company because it provides value-added services that make it difficult and/or expensive for customers to switch to another provider. The structural bond differs from the no-bond, purely convenience situation in that switching costs are high. It differs from the emotional bond in that the switching costs arise from offerings that directly affect the efficiency of access and/or operation of the company's product or service. Examples are the provision of information technology solutions like Federal Express's Powership or McKesson's Economost.

EMOTIONAL BOND. This category refers to situations where a segment is composed of customers who are locked into a relationship with a company because it has linked its products to a set of emotionally powerful symbols. It differs from the structural bond in that it builds customer loyalty using methods that do not directly affect the efficiency of access and/or the operation of the company's product or service. These methods usually involve some form of community-based ritual that links the company's offerings with icons and rituals that have a strong emotional impact within a pertinent cultural grouping. Examples are The Gap's use of attractive, sexy entertainment icons to imbue its clothing products with style and pedigree, or Nike's myth-building, myth-celebrating advertising campaigns.

Other key concepts in building a relationship matrix are customer segment and product attributes:

CUSTOMER SEGMENT. The groupings a company uses to differentiate the various types of target entities for its products or services. These customers include entities internal and external to the organization. Note that there need not be a one-to-one match between customer segments and products; one product might actually be appropriate for more than one customer segment.

PRODUCT ATTRIBUTES. The various components and characteristics of a product that a company manipulates to customize it
according to customer preferences. Components refer to parts
that make up a product, e.g., information, metal fittings, or
screws. Characteristics refer to key features of the product that
affect a customer's decision to purchase it, e.g., color, price,
and fit. Note that we do not assume that an exchange transaction has to occur upon delivery of a product.

This matrix is presented as an initial step for characterizing
the web of relationships that underlie company operations.
There are of course other aspects of these relationships that
will affect any strategies your company might choose to build.
These aspects include:

· Power differentials among partners in a relationship, whether
  partners have equal power or one partner dictates the terms
  of the relationship.

· The character of the relationship, whether the partners collaborate, compete, or both.

· The history that exists between partners. Partners with a long
  history and established relationship to draw on might benefit
  from the trust built through this history or suffer the consequences of past grievances.

Once you have a full map of the constellations of relationships
you both currently have and want to build, the next step is to
carve out a piece of that map that you want to involve in your
Internet commerce activities and applications. The key task is
to identify the value proposition that your organization currently offers as part of your relationship with these entities.
Useful questions to answer at this point are:

· What are your target relationships (internal or external)?

· What are the product, services, and/or activities that bring the
  most value to these relationships?

· What are the quantitative and qualitative benefits of building,
  augmenting, or discontinuing these relationships?

Having identified these relationships and your current value proposition, you are now ready to assess how Web technologies might transform them.

FRAMEWORKS FOR VALUE CREATION

A multitude of opportunities have been identified for mining the value from the application of Web technologies. As of early 1997, most of these opportunities cannot rely on the assumption that consumers will pay for content over the Web. Although likely, such a condition will have to wait for infrastructure improvements and much consumer education before it becomes a reality. This section highlights five basic high-level principles that managers can use to think about how they might profitably apply Web technologies to their business relationships. These principles include:

· Off-loading tasks to users
· Moving to cheaper platforms
· Informating products and processes
· Moving information, not mass
· Creating markets for information

   To illustrate how Web technologies can transform the relationships you have identified with the relationship matrix, we end each principle's discussion with a description of how the Web might be used to build a structural bond between a business and a customer.

OFF-LOADING TASKS TO USERS

Companies gain value by applying Internet commerce technologies to off-load tasks to users. Users include individual and business customers, employees, and business partners. Value is gained when savings accrue from reductions in the personnel used for the off-loaded tasks. These savings are likely to be large since the most common tasks are those that are most easily off-loaded to users. Businesses probably have the greatest experience with the task and thus have the knowledge of its complexities. Most surprisingly, businesses off-loading such activities often gain value in the form of improved user satisfaction. Despite taking on a greater burden for these tasks, users feel that they have greater control and knowledge of the results of the task. They also do not have to wait for an available customer service representative and explain what they need. They can just go ahead and find the information they want on their own time. There is also the benefit of anonymity, since users do not have to interact with a human being who could look into their confidential records (bank balances, benefits packages, etc.).

The most well-known cases of off-loading involve consumers. The most common tasks off-loaded are tracking customer orders, product development and deployment, and customer service. For example, the Federal Express Web site lets customers track the location of their package throughout the FedEx network. At the same time, customers can get useful information directly from the Web site, often removing the need to call the FedEx 800 number for customer service. Making it possible for customers to do these tasks results in great savings to companies. Additionally, customers can become more closely involved with the design and development of products. For example, since Netscape pioneered it, software companies are now much more likely to provide beta, even alpha, versions of their applications for free over the Net. Customers have the opportunity to try out product and provide feedback to the company. This, in turn, helps the company iron out the bugs in the program and develop improvements—in effect a low-cost method of both testing their products and doing market research to determine how a given product matches the preferences of the customers they are targeting.

Web technologies allow companies to off-load information gathering and ordering procedures to their business customers. Business customers can use a company's public Web sites to gather information on its products and history. Companies like Marshall Industries provide online catalogs that include specifications on their products. Business customers can browse through these catalogs to ascertain whether Marshall carries the components appropriate to their own products. This saves Marshall's sales staff the time they would spend explaining and describing such products to customers. Other companies, like Hewlett-Packard, provide customers with limited access to their internal networks of information, to help them track information about HP products that they are incorporating in their own products. Lastly, some companies, like McKesson, allow business customers the ability to tap into their internal databases to check on the availability of and to order products.

Many companies have built internal networks that provide browser-based access to allow their employees to obtain information provided by various departments. By easing access to such information, departments have been able to off-load support for many basic inquiries that they used to have to field. Often, one of the first departments to benefit from these applications is human resources. By placing benefits and other pertinent employee information on these networks, human resource departments have reduced the need to answer the numerous informational queries they get. Some companies have even provided password-protected access to human resource databases, so employees can access not just general information but also track their own confidential information.

Companies have also been able to off-load information access tasks to their business partners. This is usually through limited, browser-based access to a company's own internal information stores. The information provides partners with pertinent information on the activities and products that are shared among the business partners. For example, Ford provides its suppliers with access to its product development information systems. By accessing information on product specifications, suppliers can plan their own design and manufacturing schedules to coordinate with those of Ford. Other companies, like The Gap, have taken advantage of the browser's ability to display multimedia in order to ease communication with suppliers who most likely speak a different language. In the past, miscommunication with suppliers was rampant because most of the instructions for building or altering garments could be sent only in English. Today, The Gap sends these instructions to their suppliers as a multimedia file—including pictures and video that illustrate design and any changes to be made to a garment.

Note that, for the most part, the applications described above have just begun to illustrate the power of the Web for providing value by having users take on tasks once performed within a company. Most companies have developed applications that exploit only the Web's ability to facilitate the transmission of rich information. Companies can gain even more value by taking advantage of the Web technology's ability to support collaboration, its ability to collect customer information and match it to products and services, and its ability to support secure transactions.

Many of the companies cited above have been quite successful in building structural bonds with their customers, precisely because they off-loaded tasks to their customers. Oftentimes, this bond was built through the provision of software packages that facilitated the work of customers even as they took on more tasks. For example, the Federal Express Web site makes it possible for customers to send and track packages. While customers had to take on the task of printing labels and entering package information, they also gained the benefit of convenience—not having to go to a Federal Express office or their companies' shipping departments to send a package, and not having to call and wait on the line to track a package in the Federal Express system. These benefits, plus the fact that Federal Express was first to market with a Web-based system, facilitated the buiding of a structural bond between the company and its customers. As customers use the Federal Express system repeatedly, they become accustomed to its procedures and quirks, and they start to incorporate the Federal Express procedures into their own shipping and reporting processes. At this stage, a structural bond has formed and it becomes difficult for the customer to switch to an online system provided by a rival courier service.

MOVING TO CHEAPER PLATFORMS

Companies can gain value by moving current operations to the cheaper platforms afforded by the Web and Web-based technologies. These include using the Internet as the network for communicating with external organizations using smaller, cheaper machines as clients and servers, and using cheaper software. The culture of the World Wide Web has created an atmosphere that has resulted in lower prices for most of the components that companies use in computerizing their operations. It is entirely possible that this is a temporary situation as many companies sell their products and services at outrageously low prices to gain market share. But it has also resulted in a highly creative atmosphere where companies are trying to do more with less. Furthermore, the strong belief among Web users in the democratic and free access to such products suggests that it will be some time before companies providing components of the Web platform can raise their prices. As evidence of this, consider how much more generous Microsoft has become, with their Internet products especially, since aggressively entering the Web/Internet arena.

Foremost among the cheaper components of the Web platform are the networks that make up the Internet. These networks promise connectivity to both business and individual customers worldwide, at a fraction of the price that companies have paid for such connectivity in the past. At the same time, the presence of the low-cost public networks of the Internet has also placed companies in a great bargaining position to obtain cheaper rates from current network providers, e.g., VANs. Additionally, the Web provides greater independence and flexibility for a company to provide content to consumers. For a long time, many companies have considered sending multimedia content out to consumers via CD-ROM, traditional content providers like America Online, and interactive TV. The advent of the Web in 1994 changed all that. Companies could provide content over the Web. With this option, they had greater control over revenue streams—since they could reach a wide audience without having to commit to the revenue-sharing terms of traditional providers. Thus, no matter which network service they choose to go with, companies are in a position to lower their telecommunications costs and reach companies in an even wider geographic range.

The decision to shift to the Internet, though, should be based on more than just cost. Sending information over the Internet requires that attention be paid to the issues of security and reliability. Companies have to consider the cost of building up the capability for securing the information they send over the Internet, and they have to consider how the possible reduction in reliability that the Internet presents will affect their operations. To date, satisfactory results have been generated from pilot programs by companies who have the highest requirements for security and reliability. For example, Bank of America ran a pilot to test the security and reliability of the Internet for transmitting payment instructions, using financial EDI standards. The pilot results assured the bank that the Internet was a satisfactory medium for transmitting such information and has started to offer the service as an option to its EDI customers (see the case in Chapter 3 for more information).

As companies have matured in their use of the client-server model, they have also realized that there are efficiencies to be gained in shifting much of the processing and file storage to servers, paving the way for smaller, cheaper clients. As discussed in Chapter 3, such clients—called *network computers* or *thin clients*—are built with much less memory and processing power than the personal computers and workstations that sit on today's desktops.

Two caveats need to be recognize with regard to the thin client scenario. First, as of late 1997, there is only a very limited selection of available network computers. More importantly, the first fully functional productivity tools designed to run on these machines are not expected until sometime in early 1998. Judgment on the viability of the thin client platform will have to wait until such a time that these tools become available. A second caveat is that companies have to identify the individuals within their organizations who can perform their job functions efficiently with computers that have these limited capabilities. Significant savings can be realized only if there are a large number of individuals who can do so—and if they can be convinced to give up much of the control over their desktop machines and work files.

Servers, too, could potentially be moved to cheaper workstations. As companies start to parcel out processing in smaller chunks, smaller machines could be used to run these programs. Furthermore, emerging platforms are presenting alternatives to mainframes for the storage of large corporate databases. As discussed in Chapter 3, clustering tools can be used to build heavy-duty parallel processing servers from commodity workstations.

Another component of the cheaper Web platform is software. The Web is currently in an era of experimentation. The Web model is rapidly evolving, and companies and software developers are still trying out different models for playing in this arena and competing for market share. Such an environment has resulted in the availability of cheap software, particularly Web browsers. Following Netscape's lead, much of the basic software that can run on these clients is cheap or even free. Netscape is wont to state that they would like to be the "universal interface," providing a window to corporate information and the full range of application through a front end that functions uniformly across most computing platforms. This interface not only provides value by reducing software costs, its simple, standardized functionality reduces training costs and potentially provides access to valuable information and applications currently provided at very low cost over the Web.

The features of the Web platform result in a situation where companies could stand to realize savings not only in the deployment of Internet commerce applications, but also in their maintenance. The Web platform's emphasis on cross-platform compatibility makes it possible to standardize applications across all machines within an organization. The move to thin clients could potentially make it even easier to control what is run on each desktop, and improve a company's ability to safeguard the privacy and integrity of company data. The centralized nature of this model also simplifies maintenance by allowing organizations to propagate any changes from few servers to many clients. Such simplification, as well as less expensive components, are key to the value derived from moving to the cheaper platforms of the Web.

The advent of cheaper clients as part of the Web computing platform opens up many opportunities for building structural bonds. First and foremost is that cheaper clients can be deployed in greater numbers. A company can thus provide thin clients to many of its customers, and create a channel through which it can provide software, information, and products that encourage the development of structural bonds. Once a company's thin clients are deployed at customer sites, they can provide value-added services to aid customer retention. For example, the company could use thin clients to provide software that organizes the back-office procedures of their customers—e.g., inventory control and supply ordering—much like McKesson's Economost system did for pharmacies. The company could also use thin clients to provide information customized for a given customer. This information could include advertisements geared to each customer's needs, or special guidelines that customers could use to tailor the information, services, and products they obtain from the company supplying the thin clients to their own needs. Value added services and customized services are strong incentives for keeping customers locked onto a given company, thereby encouraging the formation of a structural bond.

INFORMATING PRODUCTS AND PROCESSES

The term *informating* describes the process of increasing the information component of any activity or object.[2] In terms of organizations, informating processes involves changing the very nature of work processes—from one based on approximation and "art" to one based on precise measurements and "science." For example, workers at a paper mill used to know when pulp was ripe by its smell, feel, and color. With the application of IT and informating the pulp ripening process, the workers now sit in a room watching gauges that provide measurements that signal to them when the pulp is ready. The basis for decision-making has moved from one of intuition to one of information, which is explicitly represented in gauge readings and warning lights. Furthermore, not only work processes but also products can be informated. Advances in semiconductor technology and product design have resulted in a strong tradition of embedding computer chips in products. These embedded processors make it possible to quickly change the features of a product to meet contingencies or new customer requirements.

Traditionally, informating has been spoken of in terms of non-Web computing technologies. These technologies have changed the mode of measurement that workers use in performing their tasks to produce goods or provide services. Through such informating, many of these tasks have become digitized, so their attributes are captured with measurements that are in some digital form. Being digitized, these measurements are available for storage and transmission using any computing technologies that come along.

Web technologies allows companies to transmit such information, which facilitates the remote monitoring of processes and products. Within the organization, this provides monitoring capability to a wide range of individuals. Workers who need to keep track of product attributes need not be on the shop floor watching the product closely. Potentially, they could be sitting at home, using an Internet connection to remotely accessing status or exception reports on products. The network can also make the same information available to executives, managers, and quality assurance specialists who might have an interest in monitoring both product attributes and employee performance. Thus, the Web provides access to data on products to a wide range of individuals within the organization.

Perhaps the real power of informating with the Web is realized when it connects customers to the system that determines product attributes. The Internet is one of the cheapest and most direct ways of obtaining information from customers about a given product. One way of looking at it is that the Web allows companies to informate the product design process—in effect, creating a gauge to read customer preferences. Instead of relying solely on sales staff assessments of such preferences, or on slowly produced marketing reports, the Web makes it possible to assess customer preferences in real time. Such information can then be fed back to the product design and production systems to produce a product that meets customer needs most closely.

Realizing the potential value of this application of Web technologies, many companies have devised ways of measuring customer preferences remotely—in effect, creating virtual gauges to informate market research activities. Some of the methods involve repurposing of traditional tools, e.g., customer surveys on the Web or getting feedback on product samples (like when Netscape makes beta copies available for customer tryouts and reviews). Others take advantage of Web software's auditing capabilities to track customer movements through a Web site. Such information is then summarized and processed to extract information on customer preferences. Some of the more innovative market research tools involve the melding of Web and intelligent agent technologies. These tools are most adept at collecting information of which customers might not even be aware, let alone be able to articulate. For example, Firefly uses intelligent agent technology to determine customers' preferences based on their ratings of products they experienced in the past. By closely matching the past behavior of a given customer with that of another customer with similar past behavior, the Firefly system can recommend products and communities of interest to consumers.

The benefits of measuring customer preferences quickly and subtly are further enhanced by the ability to customize products to meet those preferences at the same speed. Quick product customization has generally been seen with products with strong information components. For example, it is much easier to customize the content of an online newspage than it is to customize a car. However, the trend is to continue to increase the information component of all products—information or not. As chip technology improves, we are closer to being able to embed them in almost any item. The microprocessors embedded in these items essentially informate the products so companies can store and react to information collected regarding the user and the environment. Such informating enables greater and faster customization of products; you can alter features by downloading a new program or changing the parameters of the current one.

The Web can impact the customization of products with embedded microprocessors in two ways. First, the Web can serve as the medium for transmitting the programs and information for altering a product. Second, the miniaturization of computing components, the growth of the Web, and a backlash against the unchecked increase in the size of common application programs has fueled interest in the development of small programs. This growth increases the likelihood that we will have the operating systems and programming languages to allow companies to develop small programs that can be transmitted via the Web to the microprocessors embedded in their products.

Within your organization, there are probably opportunities for informating work processes using Web and related technologies. Informating results in many benefits, foremost of which are the cost savings that accrue from the standardization of processes and the products and services resulting from these processes. Computing technologies have strong potential for limiting people performing these processes to a standard set of actions and decisions. At the same time, computing technologies allow greater flexibility within the given set of actions, compared to a situation where an employee does not work in conjunction with a computer.

These benefits make informating an attractive principle for creating value from the application of Web technologies. However, it behooves any manager to be aware of and address the distress that accompanies any effort at informating work processes. Such an effort will involve much persuasion and understanding to move workers accustomed to traditional, intuitive modes of work to the more digitized, remote forms enabled by the combination of Web and non-Web computing technologies.

A company that achieves an efficient way of constantly meeting its customers preferences and keeping pace with the changes in these preferences will increase its chances of building a structural bond with its customers. Customers will tend to stick with a company that constantly provides products that meet their preferences. A company can stay apace of customer preferences by exploiting the information component of its products. This information component can imbue a product with the flexibility to meet the customer's preferences, often in real time. When such components are linked to the company's own systems via a network, it also becomes possible to centralize this customization. This is most readily seen in recommendation systems like Firefly (www.firefly.com). Firefly offers its customers recommendations regarding movies and music products. These recommendations change according to each customer's past behaviors and the behaviors of other customers with similar profiles. Intelligent agent technologies take into account all these behaviors to build a profile of a customer and to provide a recommendation that closely matches the preferences of the customer. The continued accuracy of this match increases the likelihood that a customer will continue to return to Firefly for recommendations.

MOVING INFORMATION, NOT MASS

There are also opportunities for creating value by choosing to move information instead of mass. Mass in this case would be anything that requires the physical movement of a given person or object (e.g., a package). A significant feature of the Web is network links to all areas of the world. Presently, such links facilitate the movement of information worldwide. Because of the ease and low cost of transmitting across the networks that make up the Web, value can be gained by substituting the movement of information for the movement of objects that need to be sent over slower, more costly transport channels, e.g., Federal Express and airline networks.

Companies are already starting to take advantage of moving information instead of mass by linking employees with each other and with the company through teleconferencing and telecommuting—albeit with non-Web-based technologies. The availability of ubiquitous and cheap networks, improvements in bandwidth and compression algorithms, and the multimedia capabilities of many Web browsers portend a platform that easily supports multimedia communications at each desktop. Once the bandwidth is available and Web-based collaboration tools mature, companies can start seriously considering moving their teleconferencing capabilities to the Web platform. When this happens, companies will gain value from using the cheaper networks and equipment of the Web platform. Value can also be gained by reducing employee travel—having them teleconference from their desktops instead of flying to a face-to-face meeting. As with all remote communications technologies, this last value category can be realized only once company employees are comfortable with the new mode of communication. The fact that employees are already teleconferencing and telecommuting suggests that the appropriate comfort level is attainable.

Aside from moving teleconferencing and telecommuting to this platform, companies can also exploit such capabilities for distance learning. Companies can make training programs available to their employees via Web browsers. The files of these training programs can be kept in a central location and, with the Web, employees can download the training programs as needed. Companies save the costs of employees traveling to a central location, or of having to store and maintain duplicate copies of training programs at all locations. Companies can also expect better quality training from such a system. Centralized distribution ensures greater uniformity of training since there is less variation due to differences in trainer skills. Also, centralizing the delivery of training programs allows companies to use the best materials and the best instructors. Browser technology affords additional benefits as well. Its intuitive interface ensures that employees can quickly focus on learning from the training program because they are less distracted by having to invest a lot of time in learning a new interface each time they go through a training program. Additionally, managers can use the auditing features of the server components of browser software to track employee adherence to training requirements and training program procedures.

As Web collaboration technologies improve, companies can use them to build virtual organizations among individuals and companies worldwide. Again, value is gained by saving the costs of having employees travel to meet face to face, as multimedia information sent across the Internet substitutes for these meetings. Furthermore, Web collaboration tools add more value by providing enhanced support for a group's activities. This support includes shared calendars, group process facilitation, and version control for documents developed by the group. Thus, Web-based collaboration is not only less costly, it also is richer in terms of group support.

Web technologies can enable corporate training departments to build strong structural bonds with the customers within their organizations. The use of distance learning applications of Web technologies can enhance the reach and responsiveness of training programs. Lessons can be provided to employees without requiring travel by trainees or trainers. This enables company trainers to reach more employees via videoconferencing and/or computer-based training resources. Additionally, when training programs are provided over the Web it becomes possible to provide just-in-time on-the-job training. Employees could conceivably bring up a training program or lesson most appropriate to a situation they are facing at work, at exactly the time when they are facing it. Thus, the delay involved in waiting for a trainer to come and provide the training is removed, and presumably the learning experience is enhanced for the employees by allowing them to apply the lesson directly and immediately to their own work processes. By exploiting distance learning in the ways outlined above, a company training department can make it inconvenient and/or unnecessary for employees go to third-party vendors for training, effectively building a structural bond between employees and the training department. Furthermore, responsive training programs can also enhance employees' loyalty towards the company—reducing employees' need to transfer to another company to develop new skills in pursuit of their own professional growth.

CREATING NEW MARKETS

Lastly, opportunities can be found in creating new markets. For example, the Internet provides access to unwieldy masses of information—"information overload" is an understatement at this point in time. Current search and information customization mechanisms remain inadequate for parsing this large volume of information and separating the wheat from the chaff. In the absence of a perfect search engine, there is value to be found in packaging the information available from the Internet in a way that makes it useful to given market segments.

Additionally, there are opportunities for facilitating the bartering of information among Web users. For example, Cybergold is attempting to create a market where Web users can barter their attention to relevant advertising for other information of interest. The company pays consumers for viewing ads. These payments could then be used to purchase information from other providers on the Web. In effect, Cybergold seeks to create value by being an information market maker—by providing the mechanism and setting for the exchange of information for attention. Market makers can extract value from such undertakings by either charging individuals for entry into the market (e.g., via subscriptions) or taking a cut of each transaction that occurs in the market, as Cybergold does.

A Los Angeles-based company, Music411 (www.music411 .com), is attempting to create a market for intellectual property. Its vision is to provide a setting where individuals can research and trade investments in various forms of intellectual property. The company is capitalizing in a trend toward the digitization of various forms of intellectual property. In most industries, this digitization is also resulting in a revolution in the way such properties are sold and distributed. This revolution is threatening to change the role that traditional intermediaries like publishers and record companies are playing in these industries. One trend is to remove or bypass these intermediaries completely. For example, some musicians (e.g., Prince and David Bowie) are attempting to sell their music directly to the public via the Web. Music411 is seeking to support and capitalize on such trends by allowing individuals to invest in the production of intellectual property, and then share in the profits gained from its sale and distribution. Thus, investors can eventually visit Music411's trading pit to invest in Prince's next album. When the Prince album is released, all investors gain dividends in accordance with their holdings and the sales of the album.

A company that establishes a new market on the Web can gain a very strong first-mover advantage at this point in time, since these markets are just now being formed. A company can exploit this first-mover advantage to build a roster of buyers and sellers who become used to the procedures and rules of its market. A company that can build such a large roster quickly can make it hard for other players to build a similar market. As buyers and sellers become accustomed to the first market and come to identify it as the primary market for their products, they are less likely to switch to alternative markets that emerge—thus establishing a structural bond with the market established by the first mover.

APPLICATIONS OF INTERNET COMMERCE

A useful structure for thinking about Internet commerce applications is to look at their relationship to organizational boundaries. Although these boundaries are becoming blurred, they are still a convenient way to delineate applications—primarily since it is at these boundaries that organizations are likely to place mechanisms for restricting access in the name of secrecy or security. Thus, the following general discussion of Internet commerce applications will focus on different areas delineated by such mechanisms: those internal to the company, those between a company and its business partners, and those between a company and consumers.

INTRACOMPANY

For years, companies have been attempting to integrate and repackage information in their databases to make it more accessible and useful to their employees. Theoretically, this integration and repackaging has been possible, given the LAN and WAN infrastructures already in place. The stumbling block had always been the difficulty in achieving it with available software packages. For example, sophisticated data analysis was quite difficult when all that was available were repurposed mainframe packages like SAS. Workgroup computing was extremely difficult with complex, highly structured packages like Microsoft Project. In the 1990s, software science and art had reached a point where such accessibility and integration has been eased by cross-platform, user-friendly packages like various Web browsers (Navigator and Explorer) and Lotus Notes.

New networking software (e.g., Notes, TCP-IP, Web browsers, and Windows NT) have fueled a growth in the availability of information within enterprises, in internal networks of information called *intranets*. At this point in time, the most common applications involve information dissemination. For example, human resource departments now generally provide information on benefits, forms, etc., in such platforms. Another common way of using intranets is for software distribution. Because software can be downloaded to clients directly from the server, companies can control the versions and mix of the software that runs on their employees' desktops. Some companies have started using these platforms to support collaboration, by making it possible to share documents worldwide. Eventually, companies might look to intranets for simultaneous communication, essentially having employees teleconference from their desktops. Lastly, companies are using intranets as platforms for experimentation. Since the protocols and software used in intranets often match those on the Internet, companies are finding intranets to be a readily available setting for trying out applications before making them available to the general public over the Internet. Chapter 5 discusses Intranet opportunities and challenges in greater depth.

BUSINESS-TO-BUSINESS

The Internet and other public networks can potentially revolutionize the way business information is exchanged among companies. Already, several companies have experimented with moving the most commonly used standard for business-to-business transactions, EDI, to the Internet platform. Such trials have involved even traditionally security-conscious companies like banks (e.g., Bank of America and Wells Fargo). Other companies are leveraging their strengths in supporting a subset of business operations to provide support for intranet commerce. For example, Federal Express is leveraging its existing infrastructure for the rapid delivery of packages to provide complete order-fulfillment services to businesses who want to transact business over the Web.

The potential of the Internet to connect all businesses to each other presents a huge threat to traditional intermediaries like wholesalers and brokers. Internet connections facilitate businesses' ability to bargain directly with a range of suppliers—thereby eliminating the need for such intermediaries. To address these threats, many intermediaries hope to harness the Internet's ability to quickly collect, package, and disseminate information. These intermediaries see themselves no longer as brokers but more value-added providers in their industries. The value they add comes in the form of information packages, including reports on the business activities of companies and their employees and services that could enhance the products and services of the companies that source through them. For example, McKesson no longer sees itself as a drug distribution company, but more as a value-added provider in the healthcare industry. These days, the company is setting up a network of computers to support its massive sales force and the pharmacies it serves. A sales force application can provide current information on accounts as well as suggestions for products and approaches that might be appropriate for a pharmacy a salesperson is about to visit. For pharmacies, McKesson could provide financial reports suggesting ways in which they could improve the bottom line.

The McKesson application is an example of an emerging paradigm in electronic commerce: the extranet. This paradigm emerged from the realization by companies that the information they provide in their intranets is also valuable for their customers and business partners. These companies have started providing limited access to their intranets to selected customers. The portion of a company's intranet that is made available to these customers is called an *extranet*. Chapter 6 presents a comprehensive discussion of business-to-business applications of Web technologies.

BUSINESS-TO-CONSUMER

Because of its rapid growth, businesses recognize that the Internet could connect them to a potentially large and affluent market. This has fueled a growth in corporate Web sites. For the most part, these sites have been called "vanity pages" or "brochureware" since they are nothing more than the repurposing of company information into a Web format. The infrastructure for secure Web commerce is just now being set in place, and companies are beginning to look beyond these vanity pages to exploit the new sales channels available through the Web and explore new paradigms for marketing.

The most prominent of these new paradigms is that of relationship marketing. Because it is possible to track consumer actions on the Web, companies are realizing that it is a valuable tool for market research—both through moving consumer survey forms on the Web and, perhaps most promising, by taking advantage of the Web's tracking capability and other technologies to make inferences about the preferences of consumers. Once collected, this information can be used to customize products and services, improving the chances of achieving customer satisfaction and creating a lasting relationship between consumers and these products and services. In the case of products and services that have a strong information component, computing technologies make it possible to match consumer preferences and products virtually on the fly—practically providing companies with the ability to segment the market to one consumer at a time.

Relationship marketing involves matching consumer preferences and product/service attributes as closely as possible to create customer satisfaction, which leads to customer loyalty. Relationship marketing itself is not a new concept. Companies have long sought customer loyalty by making sure their products/services match customer preferences. In the past, this has often been done through salespeople. For example, department stores like Nordstroms have generated customer loyalty—despite premium pricing—because of their excellent sales staff. Customers are not only catered to, but sales staff are willing to spend time to find out what the consumers really want, often by trying several rounds of suggestions until arriving at their true preference. The customers leave feeling like they have been valued and that they have truly found the products that they want. Such customers are then more likely to return to the store for similar purchases in the future.

Nowadays, the Web and related technologies make it possible to perform similar functions online. The Web allows companies to track consumer preferences closely—both by asking the consumers directly or by auditing consumer actions as they surf the company Web site. This information can be used as a basis for providing a product or service that is customized to consumers' preferences. Essentially, the Web allows companies to simultaneously perform several key marketing activities that in the past were done by separate groups or intuitively by salespeople: design and development, advertising, distribution, service, and support. Particularly for products and services with a large information component, the Web even makes it possible to do all these activities at once—compressing the process of meeting consumer preferences. With Web technologies, consumer preferences can be polled even as they are sampling an advertised version of the company's product. The polled information can instantly be used to customize the product to meet the consumer preferences—all in the same session.

Currently, companies have only begun to exploit this capability of the Web. Most companies have rudimentary Web sites that provide information on their company, products, and services—essentially moving advertising to the Web channel. Such sites usually offer some customer service online—at the very least through an e-mail link for questions. Often, such sites do not even have a systematic way of tracking customer movement through the site, let alone a way of linking such information to product design.

Another less common way in which companies have exploited the Web is by moving only their distribution activities onto it. For example, JCrew's site allows consumers to order products online.

But the consumer has to have a catalog on hand to enter the correct model number for most products they want to order. Only a limited selection of product information and very little advertising is actually available on the Web (www.jcrew.com).

The company that comes closest to exploiting Web technologies for relationship marketing is Firefly. Firefly uses a Web application, enhanced by intelligent agent technology, for its CD sales service. Consumers join the firefly community and immediately get a list of CDs to rate. These ratings are used to identify other CDs that the consumers might like—based on the ratings of consumers with similar profiles. The longer a consumer stays and rates CDs on the Firefly system, the better the system can predict the consumer's preferences and the better its suggestions. Thus, by moving these design and development activities to the Web, the company's product (a CD recommendation) is being customized to meet consumer preferences. At the same time, consumers can view what are essentially advertisements for the CDs they might want—song snippets, artists' discographies and biographies, etc. Firefly completes the loop by providing its own distribution system and letting consumers purchase the recommended CDs directly on the Web. Customer service is provided through Web links, both to FAQs and through e-mail. Information collected on customer feedback is used to improve the Firefly platform and customer service offerings. Chapter 7 covers the opportunities and issues related to business to consumer applications of web technologies.

IMPLEMENTATION ISSUES

Articulating the key relationships and how they might be transformed with Web technologies is only half the task of building a Web strategy. Equally important is paying attention to implementation issues that could very easily undermine any thoughtfully crafted strategy. Oftentimes the history of an organization, crystallized in current processes and structures, creates the drag that could prevent the successful application of the strategy. Spending time up front to identify these sources of drag helps managers identify the blind spots that could prevent them from preparing for a significant number of possible pitfalls. This up-front work can pay off by prompting the development of action and contingency plans to address key stumbling blocks expeditiously. It includes an assessment of a company's legacies and constraints, building a cadre of key players to push the strategy to fruition, scenario planning, and building an implementation action plan. Chapter 8 covers the details of conceptualizing and building such an action plan.

The cases that end this chapter illustrate how emerging technologies are enabling new ways of building and maintaining relationships. The Cybergold case describes an innovative marketing model that pays consumers for the attention they give to advertisements. A host of measures are used to determine a customer's preferences so they view ads that are presumably matched to their wants and needs. Cybergold and its advertisers are betting that such matching will result in a higher likelihood of a sale and forge a strong relationship among the consumer, Cybergold, and its advertisers. The Inktomi case describes the rapid growth of a small start-up company. The growth was fueled largely by the intelligent formation of relationships among partners with complementary capabilities.

CYBERGOLD: REVOLUTIONIZING EXISTING PARADIGMS OF INTERNET ADVERTISING

Web advertising, like the Web itself, is new. When the Web first began, traditional, mainstream companies had no use for advertising in this medium. The birth of advertising on the Web began with "link trades" whereby two Web sites provided hyperlinks to the other party's site. As the Web grew, link trades proliferated to include commercial advertisers. And since the Web's original population was chiefly avid computer enthusiasts, computer companies were the main commercial presence. Computer companies could place links anywhere and be assured of a targeted audience of computer enthusiasts.

The Web soon reached a wider audience and advertisers from other industries entered the Web advertising fray, paying real money in exchange for hyperlinks. Furthermore, advertising became more formal, with highly designed banner ads replacing simple linked text.

MEASURES AND ADVERTISING EFFECTIVENESS

Widespread Web advertising spawned the need for effectiveness and pricing measures. How much should it cost to reach an appropriate and interested audience, and how can an advertiser be certain the audience has been reached? These issues are far from being resolved. Advertisers are finding that traditional advertising models might not apply to the Web.

Today's dominant pricing model is measured in CPM, a standard advertising industry measure for cost per thousand. This figure attempts to describe the cost of exposing an advertisement to 1000 people through traditional media such as newspapers, television, and radio spots. On the Web, the CPM paradigm is less well understood and explained, but it is an industry standard that advertisers are used to, so CPM on the Internet will not disappear quickly if at all.

Presently, Web CPMs range from around $10 up to $150 for popular sites like HotWired. This fee per 1000 consumers is not small; a CPM of $15 translates to $15,000 for a four-week placement. That wide price range exacerbates the Web CPM confusion because it fails to take into account the quality of how a user relates to a Web site and just who the user is. Lower CPMs generally indicate high-volume, untargeted traffic. Sites with a higher CPM generally have a more loyal following and let advertisers target a more specific audience, such as those reading The Wall Street Journal online.

A less well understood measure of advertising effectiveness is transfer rates. Transfer rates measure the number of clicks on an ad, indicating how many viewers are paying attention to it. Through the act of clicking on the ad, the viewer goes to the Web site to obtain more information about the product or service advertised. Transfer rates might allow advertisers to more effectively measure return on investment.

Other advertising effectiveness rates and advertising models are as follows:

IMPRESSIONS.   The number of users who call up a page with an ad banner. Impressions are also referred to as page views.

CLICK-THROUGHS.   The number of users who click on an ad banner. Click-through rates range from 1 to 10 percent of page views.

KEYWORD SEARCHES.   Search engines sell banner ads for particular, popular searches on their site. Whenever anyone searches for apartments on any of the major search engines, for instance, a rent.net banner appears. Standard rates have been $1000 a month per word, but many of the more popular engines have begun rotating ads for popular keywords.

SPONSORSHIPS.   Sponsors generally obtain prominence or exclusivity in particular areas on a Web site. This category includes entitlements, i.e., getting a sponsor's brand into an area's title.

JOINT DEVELOPMENTS.   An advertiser's brand and products are integrated into the content of the site itself, often in a game or narrative, blurring distinctions between advertising and editorial.

These models and measurements are among those that have been developed for the Web, but no one has been ubiquitously accepted or has gained a firm hold. Furthermore, they have shown that banner advertising is much less effective than many had originally surmised. Many "netrepreneurs" are introducing ways for advertisers to more effectively reach their Internet audiences. A company trying to revolutionize Web advertisement schemes is Cybergold, the concept of which is described below.

THE COMPANY

Cybergold was founded in 1995 by Nat Goldhaber, a well-known Silicon Valley Technology entrepreneur. He derived the concept from a theory of his philosopher cousin, that in our global and information-loaded society, it is people's attention that becomes a more and more scarce and therefore valuable resource. Cybergold matches this concept of attention as a valuable commodity with the interactive, multimedia, and user-tracking capabilities of the World Wide Web.

Nat brought in some prominent advertising and marketing gurus to help direct the company. For the Board of Directors, he hired Regis McKenna and Jay Chiat, and Dr. Peter Sealey acts as adviser to the company; all three are noted experts in marketing and advertising. The company grew to 25 employees by the beginning of 1997, although the concept has not yet been fully implemented.

BUSINESS STRATEGY

In the final stage of the concept's implementation, Cybergold will act as a broker, managing the relationships between three parties of Internet players for whom it will provide a virtual meeting place: commercial companies using the Internet as a medium for advertisers, users, and information providers. The concept simultaneously encompasses a reversion of the existing paradigms of advertising, and a contribution towards improving the information quality to be found on the Internet. The company faces vast challenges since it must demonstrate the viability of both its advertising concept and its enabling technology in order to survive.

As for companies using the Internet as an advertising channel, Cybergold will provide a means of improving the effectiveness of their marketing efforts. In the first place, it strives to enhance the match of advertisers with interested potential customers, beyond current practices. By giving advertisers the opportunity to pay Internet users for focusing on their product information instead of using common broadcasting methods and pushing advertisements onto potential consumers' screens, Cybergold is planning a paradigm shift in existing marketing methods. They envision a situation where advertisements are no longer considered unwanted noise by consumers, who will instead take the initiative and ask for new advertisements. Part of a company's marketing expenses could also go directly to information providers, the third party in Cybergold's concept, who would then be encouraged to improve the quality of the content they share on the Internet. This would again attract users which are currently overwhelmed and discouraged by the vast mass of often poor-quality data.

In order to participate in the game, Internet users will be required to subscribe to Cybergold's Web site, and requested to fill out an initial questionnaire that specifies their profile and areas of interest. Subsequently, they will be provided with advertisements that actually match their personal preferences, and given the opportunity to gain "Cyber gold" via cash, airline miles, or charitable donations.

To improve the consumers' tie-in, Cybergold will harness the interactive and multimedia capabilities of the Web and help companies make advertising more entertaining. Similar to the concept of "edutainment" in today's software learning tools, Cybergold hopes to make advertisements compelling "infotainment" so consumers will want to be involved. Additionally, Cybergold will provide its members with three minutes of information, games, and a quiz about the content of the site they just viewed. This means that consumers will consider Web advertisements to be a fun activity worthy of their effort and attention.

In order to improve the advertisers' buy-in and bring them closer to a situation of one-to-one marketing, Cybergold will track the evolving preferences of a particular consumer through the life of the relationship. Every time the consumer logs onto Cybergold, information will be captured, such as the time spent within an ad, which ads are chosen and in what order, where the consumer chose to click within ads, what time of day the consumer logged in, and whether the consumer answered the ad questions and/or participatory information correctly. Cybergold will combine this information with data from the customer's initial questionnaire and other information on the consumer.

Cybergold will charge advertisers only for consumers who actually view and participate in their Web advertisements. A member must complete an activity or quiz within the Web advertisement to be paid for his or her attention. With this re-quirement, advertisers will be guaranteed a minimum level of consumer involvement in the product advertisement.

Compared to the sites of commercial content providers, the quality of freely accessible information on the Internet is con-sidered to be rather poor in many instances. According to Cy-bergold's CEO Nat Goldhaber, it is most likely to be acceptable only if it is either converted from printed material or is govern-ment sponsored. Consequently, the third part of Cybergold's concept aims at what they call "infopreneurs". The term refers to owners of information and/or intellectual properties who would be willing to publish on the Internet if they receive some sort of compensation in return. In order to solve the dilemma of poor content quality and the lack of compensation schemes, Cybergold is planning a mechanism that would allow for at-taching a set of rules to a piece of information or intellectual property, such as a poem. According to the information owner's specifications, these would specify details, such as the price an interested buyer would have to pay to obtain the poem. The price could also vary, depending on the end user's affiliation, e.g., with an educational or nonprofit organization. Cybergold would act as a clearinghouse for the data and monitor the in-tellectual property transactions.

Cybergold plans to release its initial product—the part centered around online advertising—in the first quarter of 1997. Other parts of the concept, such as the one concerning intellectual clearinghouse services, are not much beyond the pilot stage. This leaves the completion of the full idea at least five years from now, according to CEO Nat Goldhaber. In its final stage, the concept would allow advertisers to customize parts of their marketing expenses directly for the compensa-tion of content providers, which would enhance the quality of the Internet as it is perceived by individual users. The users would in turn act as the central point of the whole idea by giv-ing the advertisers the opportunity to improve the effective-ness of their marketing efforts and creating the demand for high-quality content.

CHALLENGES

Nat Goldhaber's team of prominent advertising and marketing experts complement his own technical and entrepreneurial experience. The team's synergy has increased Cybergold's ability and credibility to market itself as a player in the Internet advertising field. However, Cybergold's group of very well-known experts have an unproven concept that is facing a number of challenges.

Rough competition in an extremely dynamic Internet market environment has increased the necessity for Cybergold to go live in the very near future. As of February 1997, the initial product—centered around online advertisements—was accessible only for a limited amount of Internet users. New users will be added gradually, as capacity allows and remaining technical obstacles are removed. However, this first step is naturally considered as the basis for future products. As it fosters Cybergold's relationship with advertisers and provides it with knowledge about the viewers, the company is about to gain a core competency with online advertising. It is currently exploring the option to offer ad-brokering services, matching up Cybergold advertisements with other sites. However, much competition already exists in the online advertising arena. Firms such as I-Pro and Double Click have already developed strong businesses offering these same services. They have therefore built a loyal customer base with effective processes and strong relationships. Cybergold might, in fact, be entering this field at a considerable disadvantage, with no clear means for future market leadership.

Competition from companies such as Firefly Networks is also emerging. The core of their business is to provide a bank of consumer preferences. This technology and information can be transferred into targeted advertising and gaining a better understanding of consumer behavior in the aggregate. Since the technology concept has many applications, the first mover who can provide users with real value has a clear advantage.

With another "leg" of the overall concept, Cybergold plans to offer its users valuable content. This is actually far from Cybergold's current core competencies. Additionally, there are thousands (if not millions) of content sites already on the Web with which it will have to compete the day it starts entering this market.

While competition issues could be overcome by teaming up with potential business partners, user acceptance might be the most crucial factor to Cybergold's success. The model of being paid to focus on certain advertisements or Web sites is very different from the current paradigm where users freely—and more or less unobserved—roam from site to site, dependent chiefly on the site's content. Users can perceive the model of matching their personal profiles with the advertisements to be viewed or sites to be visited negatively or positively, depending on their trust in Cybergold and advertising in general. Users could perceive it either as a way of providing benefit by showing that organizations want to learn about the users and provide them with exactly what they desire, or as an invasion of privacy whereby organizations can learn more about users than they want.

Additionally, privacy and security concerns for both consumers and third-party sites have to be overcome. Cybergold's database will be a conglomeration of information from all consumers on all sites. Its potential value as a whole will be worth much more than the sum of its parts. Both sites and consumers will have legitimate concerns about their "information rights". Advertisers do not want the consumer information they have generated via their advertisements to be passed on to their rivals, to whom Cybergold might also be offering its services. Users will also not want the information gained about them be passed onto third parties without consent. Therefore, it is important to establish trust among all three groups (Cybergold, partners, and end customers).

Technical issues also abound, even for the parts almost ready to "go live" on a large scale. The central act of tracking usage to measure loyalty is problematic in and of itself. Should Cybergold measure per page, per site, or per hit? Furthermore, Web users often log into their favorite sites from multiple locations and browsers. Dropping a single cookie on the first browser that registers a program might not be adequate. When that registered user logs in from a different browser, that user will not be recognized unless forced to log in, and therefore will not be counted as a loyal customer. The advent of digital signatures will provide an elegant solution to this problem, but this technology is still years away from broad market acceptance.

Cybergold's underlying software is proprietary and, they claim, a source of competitive advantage. Until now, technical flaws have held up the implementation of the whole concept, a dangerous situation in a world where only a few months are considered to be an entire "Web year."

Finally, Cybergold's payment scheme currently lacks flexibility. This could pose a large problem since it will partially determine the consumers that Cybergold can attract to its site. One of its goals is to have its name represent the leading form of online "cybercash" currency. In such a scenario, the company would essentially oversee the currency transaction of all online commerce using the currency medium of "cyber gold." The company had originally planned to roll out this currency along with its "watch an ad, get paid" service, but if customers were paid via its proprietary electronic currency to watch an ad, these users would have few options as to where they could redeem the cyber gold for goods and services. For the currency to be more universally accepted, therefore, more online businesses must accept it as a medium of exchange. To achieve this end, the company must improve relationships with online businesses and commerce sites or, at minimum, create a partnership with a standard online cash company (e.g., DigiCash) to allow cyber gold to be transferred into digicash.

THE BOTTOM LINE

Cybergold's new advertising concept is broad in scope and radically different from other Internet advertising paradigms. Until now, however, its validity has remained unproven. To implement its scheme, Cybergold must overcome current advertising notions and biases as well as potential technological, cultural, and business roadblocks. If the concept works, Cybergold will open up a whole new paradigm in advertising with many potential avenues of growth for the company, and this strategically created entity is sure to draw both publicity and speculators by the droves.

INKTOMI: FORMING NETWORKS OF PARTNERS

Inktomi emerged from the ARPA-funded Networks of Workstations (NOW) project at the University of California at Berkeley. The project was created to find alternative ways of building the capability afforded by supercomputers, which were getting more and more expensive to build. Additionally, because of the length of time required to build such computers, often newer, more powerful chips would be available before they were finished. Users had to always be content with machines running older chip technologies. The NOW project developed a solution to this problem by building computers using commodity hardware, aiming to "harness the power of clustered machines connected via high-speed switched networks." The project developed software that allowed commonly available workstations to work together as one machine.

This solution, aside from being cheaper, resulted in machines that could scale in small increments and had better fault tolerance than mainframes and supercomputers. This type of incremental scalability is ideal for environments such as the Internet, where the pattern of growth in demand is rapid and difficult to gauge. Additionally, the system also improves fault tolerance since losing one node in the network of workstations need not result in degradation of the entire network.

Having built a prototype NOW system, Berkeley NOW project researchers Eric Brewer and Paul Gauthier were approached by venture capitalists who wanted to fund applications of the technology. The two researchers went in search of appropriate applications to harness its power, and settled on a search engine as one of the best applications they could build. As they were looking for an appropriate search engine, Brewer and Gauthier also purchased a server application that they deemed important for making their application unique.

In the fall of 1995, three UC Berkeley students (two from the business school and one from computer science) worked together on a project for a business school computing class. Their goal was to build a Web application that could enable dynamic information delivery. Such an application would customize the content and look of a Web page according to a given user's actions and/or characteristics. This resulted in the Audience1 server, which the team sold to Brewer and Gauthier in early 1996.

Brewer and Gauthier founded Inktomi in February of 1996 with a desire to commercialize the highly effective technologies developed during their research. They licensed proprietary technology based on parallel processing and Web database integration, originally developed at the University of California at Berkeley. Two members of the team that built Audience1 also joined Inktomi: Adam Sah as Technical Director and Kevin Brown as Director of Marketing. Shortly after its founding, other prominent scientists from U.C. Berkeley, MIT, and Cal Tech, as well as alumni from Microsoft, Sybase, Digital Equipment Corporation, Pacific Bell Internet Services, and Silicon Graphics joined the company. This core group of people built a competence and reputation that would serve Inktomi well in its efforts to create partnerships resulting in applications that would demonstrate the capabilities of the NOW paradigm.

From the start, the Inktomi team decided that they would stick to their core competency—intellectual capital in clustering and data flow architectures—and leverage the expertise of its partners. The early months of 1996 focused on efforts at team building, getting venture capital funding, and finding an appropriate partner for a search engine application. The main goal was to find a partner with an established brand name. Wired Ventures, with its strong technology association, trendy "out there" image, and great advertising sales force, fit the bill perfectly.

The partnership launched the HotBot search engine in May of 1996 as the first commercial application of the NOW technology. The two companies have a revenue-sharing arrangement and have clearly defined their roles in the provision of the Hot-Bot search engine. Wired Ventures is responsible for promoting the search engine, managing advertising sales, and designing the look and feel of the site; Inktomi develops and operates the back-end search cluster and advances the core technologies. The search engine benefits from the four technologies combined by the Inktomi team:

· The NOW technology enables low-cost systems with unlimited scalability, allowing the company to increase the performance or database size simply by adding more commodity building blocks (machines, disks, or memory) to the collection.
· User-level networking and application software enables a collection of machines, disks, and network switches to mask the faults of individual components.
· Inktomi's servers provide 100 percent operation even with multiple down machines, since the remaining machines provide continuous backup.
· While primarily using a custom-built database, the company uses traditional database packages, integrated over multiple machines, to track user preference profiles, advertising placement, and accounting.

Aside from allowing incremental scalability to match Web growth, these technologies working together allow HotBot to provide advanced searching capabilities, customized interfaces, and targeted advertising. User characteristics are identified as soon as they hit the site. The database then generates instructions for a Web page to match the user characteristics, including advertising tags. These instructions allow a custom page to be generated for users on the fly. These capabilities have allowed HotBot to offer advertisers the option of selectively showing their advertising material on the basis of attributes like aspects of a user's domain name (domain, country, and company), hardware platform or browser, and the words being searched on.

In mid- to late 1996, the company continued to evolve and grow. In July of 1996, Former Sybase COO David Peterschmidt joined the company as CEO. He proceeded to expand the business team in order to build the company's capability for business development and sales. Having proven the viability of the NOW technology for large applications like a search engine, the company was ready to find new partners and applications, and promote their products for company intranet applications.

As part of his goal of shepherding the company from start-up mode to maturity, Peterschmidt also started programs to help improve the company's communication and coordination activities. He brought in consultants to help structure the company's processes, and weekly reporting cycles were instituted to keep everyone abreast of company activities. He also served as a mentor to company staffers who needed guidance with running meetings, sending e-mail, communicating with strategic partners, and managing projects.

At this point, the company sought to move from being a single-application company to a multiple-product company. Its advertising strategy, borrowed from Intel's "Intel Inside" campaign, was to build an awareness of the Inktomi brand. Every product running on the Inktomi infrastructure would sport the "powered by Inktomi" logo. Additionally, the company hired a public relations firm to build better awareness of its products and involvement with the HotBot search engine. Such an awareness was key to building additional partnerships to develop further applications of the company's infrastructure.

In late 1996, the company was poised to pursue its goal of becoming an alternative infrastructure for building scalable network applications. The company's core technologies were well suited to the computing challenges posed by the Internet's rapid growth. Director of Marketing Kevin Brown likes to say that their technologies help companies avoid the dreaded "fork-lift upgrade," which is basically having to move an old processor out to make room for bringing in a bigger replacement machine. Using the company's NOW architecture (also known as "coupled clusters"), companies need only add or remove commodity workstations from their networks in response to resource demand shifts. Not surprisingly, such an infrastructure paradigm was viewed with much interest by workstation providers like Sun and Intel.

In the area of Internet applications, the company sought to establish more search-engine applications of its technologies. During the first part of their existence, the company's exclusivity contract with Wired Ventures prevented the company from building a direct competitor to HotBot within the U.S. market. Accordingly, Inktomi explored opportunities for building search engines for non-U.S. markets and building smaller specialized search engines on subsets of their database. As a result, the company announced alliances with two partners in late 1996: Nippon Telegraph and Telephone (NTT) and OzEmail. Additionally, HotBot was starting to gain in popularity and application, being listed among the top search engines by Netscape, Cnet, and Microsoft, and becoming the official search engine for MedNet and Bell South's ISP.

When Inktomi started looking at NTT as a possible partner, they were pleasantly surprised to hear that NTT was looking at Inktomi as well. An alliance with NTT was especially important to Inktomi because it was the first major corporation to choose the company, after identifying it as providing the best technology. The NTT/Inktomi alliance created the first large-scale search engine for the Japanese market. Past attempts at building such an engine were hampered by the difficulty of parsing written Japanese text into separate words. The application unites Inktomi's scalable back end with NTT's language processor (InfoBee), which makes such parsing possible.

Furthering its expansion into worldwide markets, Inktomi formed a strategic partnership with OzEmail, gaining entry into a area with the second highest per-capita usage of the Internet. As the leading provider of comprehensive Internet services in Australia, OzEmail had established a track record in marketing and publishing, and generating advertising revenue in a variety of mediums, including print and online publications. The Inktomi/OzEmail alliance involved porting the capabilities Inktomi developed for HotBot into a local Australian search engine called Anzwers. Inktomi also expects that the alliance will help build a global infrastructure comprised of leading regional enterprises focused on each region's unique values and consumer needs.

Meanwhile, Inktomi's own core competency continued to evolve, benefiting from the wealth of intellectual capital afforded by the best thinkers and programmers in the area of parallel and high-performance computing. Key individuals from the NOW project and a crack team of programmers worked on rewriting and reoptimizing the software beyond its original design. In December of 1996, the company announced the release of SmartCrawl technology, a turn-key solution for the rapid indexing of Web site content. With the capacity to intelligently "crawl" more than 10 million documents per day, SmartCrawl became the world's fastest Web crawler. Inktomi's three major search-engine partners—Wired Ventures, NTT, and OzEmail—integrated the technology into their search engines in the first half of 1997.

The hard work of evolving and advancing their search technology paid off in the second half of 1997, with HotBot garnering increased traffic, increased revenues, and a host of awards for being the industry's top search site. Proponents included *PC Magazine*, *PC Computing*, *Internet World*, and *Network World*.

Recognizing Inktomi's leadership in developing search technologies, Microsoft announced in October 1997 an agreement to have Inktomi provide the search capabilities for Microsoft online properties, most notably the Microsoft Network (MSN). With a combination of Inktomi Technology and a Microsoft front-end interface, the two companies plan to provide online users with an index of more than 75 million documents and the freshest information—achieved by refreshing the entire index every three weeks, and subsets of the index daily and even hourly.

In April of 1997, Inktomi announced a new application of its clustering infrastructure, the Traffic Server network cache, designed to improve the efficiency of network usage. The product is designed to reduce network congestion and bandwidth requirements by moving data closer to users within a network, eliminating redundant traffic. Traffic servers placed at strategic points in any network can store recently and/or frequently accessed data so users need not go to original sources each time they need to access the same data.

An audited benchmark test of the software, run with Sun Microsystems, demonstrated that the system could serve over 3,400 operations per second (equivalent to 300 million hits per day) on a 16-node system configured to cache a half terabyte of data. This level of performance far exceeded any published benchmarks, and demonstrated that the product was suited for use in the world's largest networks. According to Ed Zander, president of Sun Microsystems, "With Inktomi's Traffic Server, we can provide the most powerful, cost-effective network caching solution. . . . We believe this technology is the best."

The Traffic Server is viewed with much interest by high-end carriers—e.g., Internet service providers, backbone carriers, and telcos—who are currently testing the product. It has also garnered Inktomi an $8 million investment from Oak Investment Partners, a company that "invests in companies that can become leaders in a high-growth market as a result of a proprietary core technology, product, or service that will create a defensible barrier to entry over multiple product cycles."

In October 1997, Intel and Inktomi announced a strategic alliance to collaborate on porting the Traffic Server product to run on Intel architecture. Making an equity investment in Inktomi, Intel views the Traffic Server product as complementary to its strategy of expanding its networked systems and product offerings. The product is especially attractive to a processor company since it addresses network congestion problems with a solution built on processors, instead of one built on networking technologies.

Inktomi exemplifies a "new age" company that is very aware of its unique competencies, and purposely seeks out alliances with partners that possess the competencies it needs to achieve its goals. It recognized that, with its core group of top computer science researchers, it had the cachet to legitimize and continue to create applications of its unique software products. More importantly, this core group enabled the company to continue its involvement in the evolution of the software product to new applications and greater capabilities. Within its first year, the company was able to leverage this core competence to build high-potential partnerships, either with companies that had proven track records in advertising and sales (Wired Ventures and OzEmail) or with a powerful company that possessed a complementary technology (NTT). In its second year, 1997, it has captured the interest and investments of the dominant players in the information technology industry: Microsoft and Intel. These partnerships provide legitimate and highly visible forums for demonstrating the value that the company's scalable architecture could bring to service providers grappling with the unpredictable and rampant growth of information, processing power, and networking requirements in the electronic commerce arena.

NOTES

[1] Reichheld, F and Sasser, E. "Zero Defections: Quality Comes to Services." Harvard Business Review . September, October, 1990.

[2] Zuboff, S. In the Age of the Smart Machine. New York: Basic Books, 1988.

INTRANETS: BUILDING THE NEW ENTERPRISE

> The intranet allows us, in a lot of ways, to do things we've always wanted to do. It allows us to share the knowledge that's inside people's heads and suggest to other departments ways they can do things differently using the technology available.
>
> —*Bob Walker, CIO of Hewlett-Packard*[1]

Few technologies have been so quickly integrated into organizations as intranets. Compare today's business practices to those of a decade ago and what stands out is the ability of companies to capture, analyze, and act upon information. While intranets are still a very recent means of implementing information management, by late 1997 almost all of the Fortune 500 companies had either deployed an intranet or were in the midst of planning one.

In response to the ever-changing marketplace and increased performance pressure from customers, executives, and shareholders, organizations are seeking new ways to take advantage of information management tools like intranets. Smart employees are leveraging emerging technologies like the Internet and its accompanying tools, and are rapidly developing their own information sources and networks. Several years ago, integrating these various networks into an overall technology architecture would have been a daunting, if not impossible, task for any IT department. Today, the ubiquitous Internet standards—including e-mail, the World Wide Web, and underlying communication protocols like TCP/IP—make it not only possible, but almost easy.

In this chapter we will take a look at what intranets are and at the experiences leading companies have had in designing, building, and managing this new kind of network. We will discuss the various types of intranets and consider some of the surprising variety of uses that companies, groups, and individuals are discovering for them. Finally, we will describe the basic principles that underlie effective intranet deployment.

TECHNOLOGY DELIVERS BUSINESS SOLUTIONS LIKE NEVER BEFORE

Technology is moving at Internet speed on all fronts—hardware, server software, and client software—which is causing an explosion of new ways for people to interact. As discussed in Chapter 3, the set of technologies (the hardware and software that enable clients, servers, communications networks, and database engines) that underlies the Internet is increasingly responsible for the crucial exchange of information, whether through online applications, discussion groups, company-wide e-mail systems, internal corporate bulletin boards and newsletters, and extranets (intranets that grant certain external users access through the corporate firewall). New applications using these technologies provide everything from document management (allowing users to post and manage documents on a corporate intranet) to software that enables companies to order and track supplies and conduct business via interconnected intranets. Even everyday corporate tasks like completing time reports and updating personnel information can be performed on an intranet.

> By the year 2000, smart companies will utilize the Full Service Intranet for all the networking services they used to rely on proprietary network operating systems to provide. Companies that fail to grasp this will be at a significant competitive disadvantage.
>
> —*Forrester Research, Inc.*[2]

We define an *intranet* as the networks, clients, servers, and applications that support an organization's internal operations and communications—when those tools are built with the newly emerging Internet software and protocols in an open systems environment. While many more traditional applications and client/server networks could be construed as being *like* an intranet, we are focusing here on the deployment of these new Internet-related technologies either to build new intranets from the ground up or to provide new kinds of access to older, more traditional applications and databases. (See Chapter 1 for a discussion of the defining characteristics of this set of technologies, Chapter 2 for an overview of the forerunners of today's electronic commerce applications, and Chapter 3 for a more detailed discussion of the architecture of the Internet.)

The borderline between an intranet and the Internet is fuzzy at best, but for our purposes we will focus in this chapter on the *internal* use of these technologies (even though what is internal and what is external is itself getting fuzzier all the time). The impact of using the Internet for external communications and transactions will be discussed in much more detail in the next several chapters.

Intranet technologies are not only revolutionizing business operations, but they also affect the working relationships between IT organizations and end users. Traditionally, those relationships were often very strained—in part due to bad IT report cards and ineffectively managing the resource: a lack of measurable return on IT investments; projects over budget, behind schedule, and off target; and a continuing lack of business understanding among IT professionals. Additionally, end users were at the mercy of the IT organization's information delivery capabilities, which all too often were focused more on technical elegance than on business value.

The very nature of Internet technologies—their ease of use, ease of development, and interactivity—have changed this equation dramatically. The following table compares the information requirements and delivery attitudes encountered in many traditional IT organization with the emerging Internet-enabled environment:

Old Attitude	New Attitude
I know what users need and I'll give it to them.	Users know their mission and audience, and are allowed to create it.
I'm not sure what users need so I'll give them all of it.	Users can make information available on demand.
I don't care if you don't need it, I'm sending it anyway.	Users are allowed to get information from the community they want, in the form they want, when they want.

THE ENTERPRISE TRANSFORMING

But this change in IT delivery capabilities and working relationships is only a small part of the story. What really matters is the way these technologies enable a totally new way of operating a business. When it is easy and inexpensive to capture, process, store, distribute, and access information, it becomes possible to redesign business processes and individual jobs, and to rethink entire communication and transaction architectures. Intranets are reshaping businesses and organizations in very dramatic ways—and this revolution is happening almost literally overnight.

Today's best companies are increasingly pushing decision-making (and the tools for it) out into the field, toward the market-facing edge of the enterprise. And they are putting employees around the world directly in touch with each other, rather than forcing communications to flow from "out there" to a corporate nerve center and then back out again.

The success of these new approaches depends fundamentally on the enterprise's ability to facilitate information gathering, communication, and collaboration. Internet technologies make these information management processes not only more feasible and more cost-effective, but also significantly more dynamic. The traditional business model is changing rapidly as intranet platforms help employees discover new ways to access information, communicate with each other, conduct routine business transactions, and organize into online communities of practice.

To realize the incredible, even transformational, opportunities presented by Internet technologies and network computing, senior executives must think creatively and strategically about how their companies do business. Intranets can do much more than simplify and shorten production cycles; they often lead to the redefinition of roles, processes, and working relationships across the board. Beyond storing and managing data, intranets allow for the creation of collaborative networks across the enterprise, adding value to customer relationships and enabling the enterprise to offer entirely new products and services, as well as new ways to attract customers and better ways to retain them.

An intranet can serve several different functions as an organizational interface to corporate data. Intranets can house internal bulletin boards and corporate information resources such as phone lists, human resource databases, and forms. They can become a platform for sharing best practices—sales presentations, proposals, customer and industry intelligence— as well as a giant search engine and forum for finding and interacting with the individuals who created them.

But these various intranet applications do not just grow up overnight. Indeed, our experience with a number of different companies suggests that intranets develop and evolve over time in relatively predictable ways. Though no two companies' intranets have grown up in exactly the same way, there does appear to be a common evolutionary path. Figure 5-1 depicts the pattern of development we have seen most often.

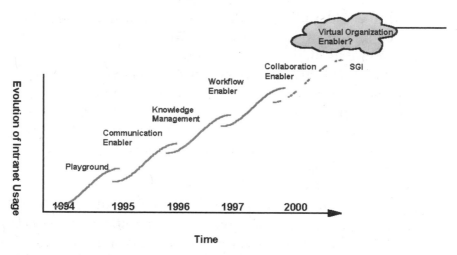

FIGURE 5-1. Evolution of Intranet Usage

THE STAGES OF INTRANET EVOLUTION

While there is nothing absolute or deterministic about the pattern, we have seen this progression (with minor variations) often enough to believe it reflects a natural experiential learning process for organizations.

PLAYGROUND.   Grassroots activities within the organization where individuals and departments experiment by publishing personalized and business-related information.

COMMUNICATION ENABLER.   Use of intranet technologies as a communication and information-sharing tool within the organization (corporate newsletters, contact information, etc.). These kinds of applications help strengthen the corporate community and reduce the cost of communication.

KNOWLEDGE ENABLER.   Employing intranets to capture and disseminate domain expertise to be shared and learned across the organization. These efforts help create a continuous learning environment, and help to reduce the reinvention of already existing knowledge or solutions.

WORKFLOW ENABLER.   Use of intranet technologies to "Webify" and redesign internal transactions such as procurement, management approvals, reports, or access to 401(k) information.

These applications are often "low-hanging fruit" and reduce the costs of bureaucracy.

COLLABORATION ENABLER.   Creation of a collaborative environment where employees can work concurrently on projects, regardless of geographical location. If done properly, such applications can reduce the cycle time of many activities such as product development, public relations, marketing campaigns, team-building, and even customer service.

VIRTUAL ORGANIZATION.   The emergence of a Net-enabled structure that facilitates the sourcing of competencies and skills anywhere at any time for value creation.

As an example, Sun Microsystems is leveraging intranet applications across the enterprise, and has progressed successfully along the described continuum. Employees at Sun essentially live online, using the corporate intranet to process W2 forms, access tax information, receive income summaries and paycheck stubs, and much more. Some of the specific applications used by Sun to streamline the process of information access and sharing include "SunTea," an expense report program through which all Sun-related expense reports are completed and submitted online; "Autoben," which includes weekly updates to 401(k) participation and any changes in allocations; "SunWin," through which every piece of collateral, sales guides, and other presentation information is available online for every employee to access as needed; and "Service-Tool," which provides online processing for all requests for system service. Sun's intranet efforts span across a number of the evolutionary stages. The difficulty, however, is being able to leverage such initiatives for competitive advantage, because many such initiatives are fairly easy to replicate, thereby making any type of advantage difficult to sustain.

Levi Strauss, Ford Motor Company, and Silicon Graphics, described in extended case studies at the end of this chapter, offer additional examples of intranets that have evolved from simple communication enablers to powerful collaborative tools that support a whole range of applications and enable true virtual organizations and meaningful electronic commerce.

MINING FOR INFORMATION

Intranets can also handle more robust information management tasks. Their ubiquitous, flexible architecture allows them to become an intelligent window into the depths of an enterprise's data archives. The current proliferation of so-called "data marts" and "data warehouses" (substantial volumes of highly structured information stored in industrial-strength database software) is an indication of the premium being placed on storing easily accessible information. Accessing information efficiently is as important as sharing it quickly in today's demanding business environment. When an organization attaches intranet access to data warehouses and other sources of corporate information, those intranets often become a universal gateway to crucial corporate information.

A mid-sized West Coast computer systems company specializing in enterprise-wide open computing environments and data warehouses has developed an extensive corporate repository. In 1993, this company began looking at its information management strategy with the specific goal of finding a way to share success stories with and among employees. With a fully automated company-wide e-mail system in place, the next step was to determine how the company could leverage Internet technologies.

The answer was a corporate electronic library, an electronic storage center for all the company's crucial documents. The guiding principle behind the electronic library, as articulated by one of its architects, was to create a data center that contained "everything you need to get your job done." Today, the electronic library is actively used by the company's 27,000 employees, 50 percent of whom are in the field. One of the company's own machines running standard Web server software acts as the repository, and all the electronic library documents are stored on that server. Using a Web browser, employees can access all that data through their individual desktop and laptop PCs. The materials that are available include human resource information, corporate policies and procedures, marketing information, sales presentations, and white papers. Management feels that the electronic library has achieved their vision of it becoming a collaborative information tool. Explains the architect: "It's real and it's working—it's become a very key part of what we do."

Typically, the process of creating such an information architecture begins with extracting value-added data from internal and external sources, and then integrating and summarizing the data as appropriate. This first step is not trivial and could possibly be the most difficult of the entire process. It usually entails much political and managerial work to get various internal and external "owners" of requested data to provide them to the data warehouse. Not only do the participants have to work out the initial access to the data, but they must also arrange for updates to keep the data warehouse current. Furthermore, efforts to integrate data from a variety of sources almost always require significant work in cleaning up the data—making sure that definitions, versions, and formats are all consistent and complete.[7]

Once the structured data has been sourced and checked for validity, it can then be loaded into so-called "subject area" data warehouses or marts. This might include data on customers, products, vendors, human resources, or finance, depending on enterprise business needs and information priorities. Finally, users are provided with ad-hoc query and decision support tools, as well as extensive information catalogs to help them access, query, and analyze the data.

ALL AROUND THE WORLD

Corporate intranets are also emerging rapidly as platforms for multilocation and multiteam collaborative projects. The benefits and opportunities are significant, from both the company's and the employees' perspectives. One advantage of this kind of information and communication is reducing the "wear and tear" on project team members by minimizing the amount of required business travel. Even more significantly, companies can capitalize on the knowledge that used to be concentrated in specific organizational pockets in different corners of the world. Using an intranet, employees from any of these centers of excellence can apply their expertise anywhere, leveraging the company's most important assets regardless of their location.

Many businesses are discovering the power of making specialized knowledge and skills more widely available. For example, realizing the potential of new markets throughout the world for their cars, as well as the increasing demands of consumers in more mature markets, Ford Motor Company launched a globalization program in January 1994. The program goal was to make the company a truly global enterprise, capable of meeting the demands of local markets based on expertise from around the world.

To support the coordination of design activities worldwide, the company installed a product document management system (PDM). The PDM organizes the storage and access of design documents, as well as information on the specifications and availability of various components of those designs. The documents are viewed and marked up with Netscape's browser software running on networked personal computers and workstations around the world. The PDM browser system is integrated into the corporate intranet, which enables product development specialists across the globe to coordinate changes and access information pertinent to the cars they are working on. Moreover, the system also serves as an extranet, providing product design information to major suppliers developing vehicle subsystems for the company.

The results of this major rethinking of the product design process are just starting to appear. Most dramatically, product development times are inching towards 24 months, in stark contrast to the 37-month cycle that had been standard for some time. One new car model has won praise for its engine performance and ride. The company's aim is to launch a new or revamped version of a vehicle every six weeks, on average. Ultimately, the goal is to form a complete product information environment based on process-based, computer-aided design. This system will bring information to both manufacturers and designers at the right time, at the right place, and in the right format (see the Ford case study at the end of this chapter for more detail).

The Boeing Company is another organization that has had great success with a corporate intranet. One of Boeing's major efforts centered around the Wing Responsibility Center. As recently as late 1996, all of Boeing's 747 wings were built by the 747 division. The same wing assembly structure existed for all the different models of the basic 747. The problem was made visible when management realized that there was no need to have five different wings and five different tails being manufactured in such far-flung locations as Washington, Pennsylvania, Kansas, and overseas.

Boeing management decided to consolidate the design and manufacturing of wings and tails under the management of one business unit. This organizational shift, which did not include any restructuring or relocation of the physical facilities, was made possible through the deployment of an intranet. Today, the Boeing intranet provides the general manager with the ability to create policy, know who the employees are and what assignments they are working on, and keep track of parts movement. In other words, the intranet has been used to redesign the organization—without any physical relocations.

Just as e-mail systems no longer limit users to electronic mail addresses within the walls of one organization, groupware products that allow teams or organizations to share both documents and messages have moved from proprietary architectures to intranets. A new class of intranet software takes sharing documents one step further, by allowing real-time collaboration via screen-sharing across an intranet. Diverse constituencies across organizations and continents can now share applications, virtual "white boards," and crucial data in real time.

Consulting firms have been among the leaders in leveraging collaborative technologies. As businesses whose currency is information and people, these knowledge-based service businesses have taken advantage of the communications revolution spawned by the Internet. In the early 1990s, a number of industry leaders began to study ways to harness and share knowledge throughout their organizations. What typically began as a research project frequently led to new organizational positions like the Chief Knowledge Officer, whose charter was to collect the knowledge assets within the firm and determine how best to share them with employees around the globe.

Several consulting firms are now experimenting with approaches to making their corporate knowledge bases directly available to their clients. These so-called "extranets" allow firms to move into the marketplace spawned by the World Wide Web. One consulting firm expresses its goal as using its extranet to build closer partnerships, allowing clients to communicate and share knowledge with the firm and with each other, with the company itself acting as the facilitator (and of course gaining a much deeper knowledge of its clients' needs and interests at the same time):

> Where we see ourselves in the future is helping other organizations identify, capture, and interpret organizational knowledge. At KPMG, our best asset is the knowledge that resides with each of our professionals. With 18,000 employees in the U.S. alone distributed across 120 offices, it's imperative that we share this knowledge to provide the best service possible for our clients.
>
> —*Allen Frank, CTO of KPMG Peat Marwick LLP*[8]

HOW DO YOU MANAGE SUCH SPLENDOR?

As we have seen, the emergence of intranet technologies enables business improvement opportunities throughout the organization. However, with such opportunities come new management complexities. In studying the impact of intranets within companies, a number of crucial issues emerge.

As we emphasize throughout this book, the creation of an explicit strategy and policy is extremely important to the successful implementation of electronic commerce applications like intranets. During your company's initial intranet experiments, however, treat strategy and policy statements as guidelines; it is important that you develop your approach to be right for you, and not just adopt an arbitrary statement drawn without thought from some other company, no matter how well constructed it appears to be. Nevertheless, in the spirit of passing on what we have seen work for others, we believe your intranet strategy/policy statement must address the following two crucial issues:

USAGE. How the intranet is to be used and by whom is often not so much a question of technology as it is of culture—including such themes as what kind of communication or information is encouraged, and what is not allowed (e.g., personal messages, humor, pornography). Who will have access to what parts of the intranet?

DEVELOPMENT/MAINTENANCE. Who is responsible and accountable for the development of intranet applications and associated information? A double-edged sword exists with intranet technologies: on the one hand, their simplicity and ease of use enable virtually all users to create their own applications and databases; on the other, most users have no interest in maintaining such applications, although they often want continuing responsibilities for maintaining the *data*.

Intranet policies and guidelines should include explicit rules on the division of labor among various participants in the development and maintenance of the intranet—allocating responsibility for building and maintaining the technical infrastructure, keeping the content current, building advanced Web applications, and establishing a unified look and feel to the site. This kind of policy is becoming increasingly important as the rising usage and complexity of intranets means that their development and maintenance require significant budgetary outlays from participating departments.[9]

In addition to these two core policies, management and those involved in the development of intranets should also keep in mind the following key issues:

· With every intranet, there will inevitably be an explosion of accessible information. Managing that information, cataloging it, and making it easily accessible is essential. The worst thing you can do is build a tower of Babel—hundreds of unstructured databases including valuable but virtually inaccessible corporate information. For some, an intranet can sometimes be too much of a good thing. With potentially hundreds of sites and thousands of pages of information, getting where you want to go and finding value-added information can become more and more difficult. This experience has led some organizations to adopt "push" technologies that send notification messages and even information downloads directly to individual users based on predefined criteria.

· Do not underestimate the amount of time and effort involved with intranet initiatives. They usually take much longer than expected, and if they are to be useful they will never be "complete" in the traditional application-development sense. A contributing problem is the disembodying effect that corporate knowledge management efforts often create, *disembodiment* meaning an absence of context from knowledge. Information on intranets often lacks a date of origin, an identified creator, and other elements that give "body" or reality to knowledge. Keeping this kind of "knowledge about knowledge" accurate and current is terribly important if the information is to have any value and credibility—and it is just this kind of ongoing data maintenance that is so often not done because it is time-consuming and expensive.

· It is crucial to gain support and buy-in not only from senior management, but also from those who will be most affected by the intranet applications. Otherwise, resistance and lack of acceptance will not only slow down the process, but often undermine its effectiveness. Ultimately, intranets must support and be in concert with an organization's culture.

· Making intranet usage attractive is another key to success. Intranets don't do anything by themselves. Individuals and groups must have a clear understanding of how the intranet will help them, and why they should use it. This perspective is especially important with knowledge management systems, where people must not only access and use the knowledge base, but also be willing to put their own knowledge into the corporate system without necessarily getting anything immediately in return. Several of the most successful organizations have established explicit performance measures and rewards for individual and group contributions to their knowledge management systems.

- In our experience, intranet usage is directly correlated to technical capability and performance. A slow and unappealing intranet will simply not be used. Furthermore, once a company provides intranet access to external users by establishing an extranet, performance expectations rise. At that point, you need to consider building up the infrastructure to provide production-level availability and security. Additionally, planning technical capacity ahead of time and building in enough slack to cover anticipated growth in demand is crucial.

- Keep the customers in mind when developing intranet applications. Ultimately, it is the users who produce organizational value through the intranet. Keeping their needs, desires, and dissatisfactions in mind goes a long way. As we have said often, intranet initiatives are no different than any other corporate IT initiative; they must be aligned with the business goals.

As intranets grow in prominence within organizations, the role of the IT organization also changes. Of course, the IT organization must continue to play the role of basic service provider, but it should also become a mentor and evangelist regarding intranet technologies and their value to the company. To facilitate this expanded role, the formation of a "relationship council" of senior managers from across the organization is often a key ingredient. Such a relationship council can serve as a focal point to encourage cross-learning throughout the organization, identify intranet opportunities, and oversee the establishment of consistent standards and practices.

> The harnessing of Internet technologies within a corporate environment is the most important development to emerge in the computer industry in the '90s. The power of the intranet will transparently deliver the immense information resources of an organization to each individual's desktop with minimal cost, time, and effort.
>
> —*Business Research Group*[10]

LEVI STRAUSS & COMPANY

OVERVIEW

Levi Strauss & Co. is the best-known blue jeans manufacturer in the world. The company was founded in 1853 by Levi Strauss, a German-born immigrant to the United States who arrived in San Francisco at the height of the gold rush in the mid-1800's. Strauss supposedly created the world's first denim pants when he used some canvas-like materials from his dry goods stock to sew together a sturdy pair of pants for some of the gold miners on their way east to the Sierra foothills. The jeans were an instant success, and Levi Strauss & Co. flourished.

In 1902 four nephews of Levi Strauss inherited the company, which by that time had become a highly successful wholesaler of sturdy work clothes and other dry goods. By the 1940's the company, which remained privately held by the Strauss family and company employees, had dropped all its dry goods except clothing and had chosen to concentrate on becoming a manufacturer of high-quality apparel. Over the years the company experimented with a number of other clothing lines, but by the 1990's had chosen to concentrate on jeans, jeans-related apparel, and selected casual sportswear. Today Levi Strauss & Co., still privately owned, is a $7 billion global business with three major brands: Levi's®, Dockers®, and Slates®.

In 1994 the Federal Trade Commission granted Levi Strauss & Co. permission to open and operate its own chain of retail stores in the United States. With a workforce of over 37,000 employees worldwide, Levi Strauss & Co. today is the world's largest apparel manufacturer with one of the most widely recognized brand names in the world. Indeed, one of the company's major challenges in 1997 is coping with counterfeit jeans and black market sales in many non-US markets. The jeans are so popular and so well-known that smuggling, counterfeiting, and under-the-counter sales at deeply discounted prices have become a serious problem—especially for a company that strives to maintain its image of quality, customer orientation, and style leadership.

This case study describes Levi Strauss & Co.'s early experiments and experiences with the Internet, with an emphasis on its development and use of an intranet. The company has made significant marketing investments in its Worldwide Web sites—levi.com, dockers.com, and levistrauss.com, and has focused its energy on making its intranet an internal communications tool. In late 1997, the company was beginning to use the intranet as a business applications development platform as well as an internal communications channel. The intranet was clearly having a dramatic impact on how information is generated, distributed, and managed throughout the organization.

BUSINESS STRATEGY

The company defines its mission as "sustaining responsible commercial success as a global marketing company of branded apparel." Management strives to balance goals of superior profitability and return on investment, marketplace leadership, and superior products and services. The company is well-known for its commitment to conduct business ethically and to demonstrate leadership in its many local communities and society at large. Management wants the work environment to be safe and productive, and to be characterized by fair treatment, teamwork, open communications, personal accountability, and opportunities for personal growth and development.

The company has been owned and managed by Levi Strauss' descendants and their families for its entire history. Management's basic strategy is to maintain tight control of the company, its brands, and its product quality.

TECHNOLOGY AT LEVI STRAUSS

Historically, Levi Strauss & Co. was not an aggressive leader in deploying new technologies. However, over the last several years the company has made major commitments to use technology more effectively, and management has backed that commitment with major investments of funds and human resources dedicated to applying technology aggressively to improve business processes and meet customer needs. Recent initiatives have included a complete overhaul of order entry and customer service business processes and the supporting information systems, and innovative uses of bar coding to enable customized inventory management for selected large retail customers.

This new spirit of innovation and experimentation has carried over naturally into electronic commerce in all its forms—EDI, the Internet and WorldWide Web, and the development of an internal intranet.

ELECTRONIC DATA INTERCHANGE (EDI)

Levi Strauss & Co. pioneered the use of EDI technology over 15 years ago to generate customer orders, automatically replenish customer inventories, provide product information and specifications to vendors, send invoices, and obtain payments. The limitation and complication of EDI, of course, is that it requires reliance on a third party—the VAN supplier—to manage the interconnections and send the data. These arrangements can be expensive; however, they also enable higher volumes of transactions and more secure communications than is currently available from the Internet.

THE WORLDWIDE WEB

Levi's has three separate sites on the WorldWide Web, one for the Levi's® brand (www.levi.com), one for its Dockers® brand (www.dockers.com), and one for corporate information (www. levistrauss.com). The levi.com site is now well over two years old, while dockers.com has been "live" since mid-1996. The corporate site is the newest entry; it "went live" in June, 1997.

The two brand sites were designed primarily to build consumer awareness, enhance the brand images, support regional marketing initiatives, advertise specific products, provide customer services support (product information, frequently asked questions, and email store information), while the corporate side was designed to be less interactive and more information-based.

The corporate Web site serves as a means of disseminating information about the company to a wide range of interested individuals and companies. The site contains company history, press releases, job postings, and other corporate information. Job applicants can also submit resumes, which can then be downloaded to a computer that matches skill sets with job openings.

The company has not yet attempted to measure the success of its Web sites in any quantitative way. Management considers the basic fact that it has a Web presence to be beneficial; it views the three public sites as pilot programs to help identify the potential of this new medium. The two brand sites cost less than the cost of one national advertising campaign to design and launch; the corporate information site cost significantly less. External contractors have done most of the technical development work, while the design concepts were driven by partnerships between the marketing and communications groups and the company's external contractors.

THE INTRANET AT LEVI STRAUSS

Interestingly—and fortuitously—the intranet was originated and funded by the Communications Department as a central repository of company information that could be tapped by all employees worldwide. The intranet actually grew out of a collaborative effort by Information Technology and Communications; it helped almost immediately to reduce printing and distribution costs for employee newsletters, press releases, and other internal documents, even though cost reduction was not its primary goal.

The initial intranet project was implemented by the Information Technology Department, with awareness and content created by a collaborative effort involving the Marketing and Communications, Information Technology, and Human Resources departments. *Eureka!*, as the intranet came to be called, soon became a widely accessible, user-friendly information "channel" that has helped to foster a much stronger sense of community among the company's 35,000-plus employees in 49 countries. In parallel, the IT, Communications, and HR groups realized that *Eureka!* could also be an effective platform for enabling teams and individuals to share all kinds of information within the organization. "We wanted to create a more effective

way for people to share their learnings, their work, and their experiences," said Steve Levandowski, a member of the IT group.[3]

Eureka! was prototyped in late 1994; pilot testing began in
January, 1995. Senior management approved the project in late
1995, and *Eureka!* was almost immediately launched to selected parts of the company. The company's goal was to have
Eureka! on every desktop within two years, and to consider options such as installing *Eureka!* kiosks in all its manufacturing
and distribution facilities.

Eureka! is not managed or controlled centrally; in fact, with
an objective of fostering open sharing and employee empowerment, the company has actively resisted establishing any form
of centralized control over the contents of *Eureka!*. Each department is responsible for creating and maintaining its own site.
However, an Electronic Editors Guild—a cross-departmental
consortium of *Eureka!* editors—has been formed to develop
guidelines, work out problems as they arise, and help introduce
Eureka! to new parts of the company. The company also maintains a Web Development Center to help manage costs and to
leverage new technologies and applications.

In its current state, *Eureka!* is essentially an internal publishing and information retrieval system that is rich with graphics, multimedia, and interactivity. The system is growing
continuously, with new sites being launched and existing ones
being updated and expanded regularly. A wide variety of content
is available on *Eureka!* including information on the Levi's®,
Dockers®, and Slates® brands, a global company newsletter,
company initiatives, and text, video, and audio from key employee meetings.

The most popular applications to date include an Employee
Information Center, a Press Archive, a Global Marketing information project, and personal web pages for individual employees. A brief description of each of these applications follows.

EMPLOYEE INFORMATION CENTER. The first use of Eureka! was as
a repository of product fact sheets, executive biographies, press
releases, and copies of speeches.[4] This type of information was
easy to place on the intranet and of great value to a large num-

ber of employees all across the company. Because it distributes vast amounts of information to all employees, Human Resources quickly became one of the biggest "publishers" and users of *Eureka!*. For example, the employee telephone directory is available through *Eureka!* and is no longer distributed physically.

THE PRESS ARCHIVE. This database is being developed as a one-stop source for all public (and some private) information about Levi Strauss & Co. It will become a comprehensive library of articles, press releases, videos, and audio recordings—all indexed and accessible through a searchable database.

GLOBAL MARKETING PROJECT. This project is compiling and publishing product, brand, and consumer information from around the world, including everything from consumer market trend research to sales data from Levi's kiosks to video clips from television commercials.[5] This capability makes it very easy for company employees anywhere in the world to review products, marketing campaigns, management presentations, and market trend research, and then to download relevant files whenever they are needed. The company envisions that this database will help eliminate duplication of effort and ensure higher levels of consistency in sales and marketing efforts around the world.

PERSONAL WEB PAGES. The company is also encouraging employees to develop individual home pages as a way to help connect names, faces, and expertise. The plan is for each department to publish an organizational chart with hyperlinks to individual home pages.

ASSESSING EUREKA!'S VALUE AND IMPACT

In the early stages of a new effort like *Eureka!* it is difficult to determine or predict its ultimate impact on the company's performance and costs. However, at Levi Strauss & Co. there is little doubt the intranet is providing both significant cost reductions and major improvements in information access and use. *Eureka!* is not only reducing printing and distribution costs, but it is making already-stored information much more accessible—on a global basis. In addition, *Eureka!* has been built with standard Internet interfaces and online help capabilities, which makes it extremely easy for employees to learn and use with minimal training.

Eureka! also enables employees to search for information when they need it, and to do so in a simple, non-judgmental way that does not constrain anyone who may be too embarrassed to ask a supervisor or a colleague for help.

More importantly, management already senses that *Eureka!* is facilitating idea exchange around the globe, helping to create a much stronger, richer sense of community and identification with the company as a whole. In the past, it often took weeks or months for a good marketing idea developed in Europe (or other remote locations) to reach corporate headquarters in San Francisco and then to be redistributed around the company. Similarly, many employees (and outsiders as well) might never see the CFO's speech on the company's latest financial performance. With *Eureka!* these kinds of ideas and information are universally available, almost instantaneously.

These capabilities are gradually shifting the culture at Levi Strauss & Co. from a "push" to a "pull" mentality. Rather than ideas being framed and issued as policies or directives from corporate headquarters, they are now pulled by employees directly from wherever they originated. Thus, a brand manager in Spain who is looking for a new marketing theme might search *Eureka!* and draw on recent experiences in Argentina or Singapore. When a major employee policy or program is changed, everyone gets an email notifying them of the change and telling them where on *Eureka!* they can find the information they need. Subsequently, the information is there when an individual wants it, no one has to wade through piles of paper about things they are not interested in, and frequently asked questions can be answered directly from the databases as often as necessary without tying up expensive human resources.

The net result of this capability has been to support the company's move to a learning organization. As Diane Woods, a Vice President in Human Resources, put it, "In a learning organization, employees capture their knowledge and learnings and make them widely accessible.. . . The result: our employees learn from one another and they work smarter, with an ever-increasing capacity to respond to their environment."[6]

Before *Eureka!*, employees relied on meetings, phone calls, memos, and reports to share information. While those traditional means of information exchange have not disappeared, they were (and are) a very time consuming, costly, and often ineffective way to distribute information widely. *Eureka!* has simultaneously broadened information access and made it far more convenient—ensuring that it happens much more frequently. (Remember that "Eureka" means "I have found it.")

CHALLENGES AND ISSUES WITH EUREKA!

As powerful a tool as *Eureka!* is for Levi Strauss & Co., it also creates a number of new challenges and management issues. For example, widespread information accessibility increases the likelihood that some unhappy or unscrupulous employee might misuse the information or even damage the company's interests by selling confidential information or otherwise making it available to competitors or the general public. Even when loyal employees understand this risk, they may not appreciate the potential value of certain information, or may not realize how it could be misused. Yet the essence of *Eureka!* is to place the accountability for information generation and access on individual employees—which of course means placing a great deal of trust in those same employees.

Eureka! is currently available only in English, which puts many employees outside the United States at a disadvantage. Although there are definite plans to make at least some documents available in other languages, that commitment will add another level of complexity and cost to the system.

As powerful as *Eureka!* is, it is not yet used widely enough or frequently enough to fully justify the time and expense that many departments are incurring to post their important information on the system. However, as more and more employees do turn to *Eureka!* for both their personal and their professional information needs, its value will increase exponentially. With more departments learning to use *Eureka!* over time, it will become more attractive to individual employees and thus even more valuable to the departments that publish on it.

Eureka! is also being used more and more as part of the applications development tool kit. There is already a product development application that uses *Eureka!* to capture and publish product concepts and track the product life cycle changes as they occur. Increasingly, applications and projects that require a broad dissemination of information are relying on *Eureka!* as a vehicle for reporting.

Future plans include using *Eureka!* as the primary vehicle for chat rooms, group meetings, and other similar groupware applications, further enhancing the company's ability to link employees with each other and with the information they need, no matter where in the world they are.

FORD MOTOR COMPANY

Intraorganizational electronic commerce (e.g., intranets) are arguably the hottest electronic commerce applications being implemented today. Whether they are used simply to disseminate information within an organization through a company newsletter or to redesign organizational processes to be more efficient and less costly, companies are using and creating intranets as "on ramps" to the information superhighway and the emerging digital economy.

It's not surprising that companies are experimenting with these types of applications en masse. What's so compelling about them is that they are ubiquitous. Traditionally, the sharing of information within organizations has been quite problematic. Coordinating multiple platforms, data formats, interfaces, and protocols mitigated the sharing and exploitation of knowledge within an organization, but those "fixes" in turn created islands of information that were more often than not redundant and underused.

ORGANIZATIONAL BACKGROUND

What is certainly surprising is when a company like Ford, with all its size, history, and bureaucracy, makes a move to leave behind many of its old computing paradigms and exploits these emerging technologies in the hope of creating a new work environment—an environment that is platform- and format-independent, one where there is one interface and a common protocol.

Realizing the potential of new markets for their cars throughout the world, as well as the increasing demands of consumers in more mature markets, Ford Motor Company launched a globalization program in January 1994. Called Ford 2000, the program aimed to make Ford a truly global company, one that could centralize the development of global product categories that would be customized to meet the demands of local markets. Incorporating lessons learned from its past efforts at globalization, the company's central goals for the Ford 2000 program were:

· A company-wide reorganization that established five Vehicle Centers to take responsibility for the developments of a given class of vehicles, and an Advanced Vehicle Technology center to design, engineer, and test new technologies.

· Shortening new car development times from 37 months to 24 months or less through vertical and horizontal integration as well as by reducing the variety of parts that go into its vehicles.

· Identifying the aspects of any car model that can be developed commonly and those that are best customized for a given market.

INTERNETWORKED STRATEGY

Central to the new organization structure and product development processes is the need to coordinate disparate product development activities. This called for flexible information systems and an application for managing and transmitting design documents across various Ford Centers around the world. Installing such systems quickly meant moving away from the company's traditionally heavy use of in-house developed mainframe systems to more agile packaged client-server software and platforms. This move was met with strong resistance from the company's IS department and led to the reassignment of CIO responsibilities to the company's chief of reengineering in early 1996.

To support the coordination of design activities worldwide, Ford installed Metaphase, a product document management system (PDM) from Structural Dynamics Resource Corporation. The PDM organizes the storage and access of design documents generated by the company's existing computer-assisted design (CAD) applications, as well as information on specifications and availability of various components of those designs.

The documents are viewed and marked up with Netscape browser software running on networked personal computers and workstations worldwide. Expert systems provide design guidelines and advisories that help designers stay within the limits of Ford's manufacturing infrastructure and parts inventory. The PDM/browser system essentially forms a Product Information System component to the corporate intranet through which product development teams across the company and throughout the globe can coordinate changes and information pertinent to the cars they are designing. Moreover, the system also serves as an extranet, providing product design information to major suppliers developing vehicle subsystems for the company.

BENEFITS

From Ford's perspective, the benefits and opportunities were large in scale, including the creation of a collaborative and cooperative work environment and virtual workplaces irrespective of geographic proximity.

Ford's Product Information System has reduced the wear and tear on design team members, eliminating much travel that would otherwise be required to coordinate design efforts. More significantly, it has allowed Ford to capitalize on the expertise that in the past was concentrated at specific development centers in different corners of the world. For example, the European Center specializes in vehicle ride and handling attributes, while the North American Center has expertise on aerodynamics, thermodynamics, and control. With the Product Information System, designers from these centers can apply their expertise to the design of vehicles at any Ford center without costly and inconvenient travel. Furthermore, the Product Information System fully supports the goals of Ford 2000 by facilitating the customization of design to local specifications. Local designers can access the documents that specify the design of common components and mark them up according to requirements specific to their markets. In addition, through the use of a "white board," collaboration between these diverse constituencies can even be done during project meetings.

The results from this major rethinking of Ford's product design process are starting to appear. Most dramatically, product development times are inching closer to 24 months instead of 37 months. The new European Ford Fiesta, although only partly benefiting from the Ford 2000 effort, has won praises for its engine performance and ride. With continued experience with and improvements to its Ford 2000 systems, the company aims to launch a new or revamped version of a vehicle every six weeks, on average. Key to achieving this will be further improvements to the company's Product Information System. Ultimately, the goal is to form a complete product information environment based on process-based computer-aided design. This system will bring information both to manufacturers and designers at the right time, at the right place, and in the right format. By supporting the complete integration of manufacturing and design processes globally, the company is on a track to produce high- quality, realistic yet customized vehicles in a low-cost, efficient, and rapid manner.

CHALLENGES AND LESSONS LEARNED

One of the biggest obstacles to technological change is user reaction, and this also applies to Internet-based technologies. How will people react to the intranet in the different offices/research centers? At first it was a major cultural change, but the training seminars were crucial in helping people understand the possibilities and set expectations. Here are some of the other key lessons learned from Ford's experience:

· There must be standards established for publishing information and hardware.

· Network capacity assurance is vital when dealing with mission-critical processes.

- It pays to be strategic about Internet-related solutions. (What do you want to accomplish?)
- There must be partnerships between different divisions in order to understand business issues and help sell solutions.

SILICON GRAPHICS, INC.

Everyone is talking about intranets. In fact, 1997 is supposed to be the year of the intranet. Ask Mike Graves about the intranets, and a big smile comes across his face. At Silicon Graphics they not only talk about it, but they strongly encourage everyone in their organization to help build it. "Our philosophy is to empower everyone" says Mike Graves, SGI's Chief Information Officer. And empower they have. With this philosophy in mind, Silicon Graphics, Inc., a $3 billion Fortune 500 company, has succeeded in not only building one of the most expansive intranets (Silicon Junction), but also effectively using intranetworking to enable enterprise-wide transformations.

Silicon Graphics, whose headquarters are in Mountain View, California, is a leading supplier of high-performance, interactive, enterprise computing systems. The company's products range from low-end desktop workstations servers to high-end supercomputers. Silicon Graphics also markets MIPS microprocessor designs, entertainment and design software, and other software products.

As a major player in Silicon Valley, SGI was privy to the early boon of Internet and Web innovation. Through their employment of this relatively new technology, SGI has lead by example and successfully improved communication, workflow, collaboration, and reduced cycle times. By exploiting this technology as a change agent, the Internet and intranet at SGI have become key elements to its success and core components of its overall strategy.

WHERE FOR ART THOU, EMPOWERMENT?

Unlike most information technologies, Web-based technologies have essentially enabled lay people to create and build their own applications—a revolutionary concept if you think about it, especially given how technology is traditionally developed and disseminated. Nowhere else did this ring so true as at SGI. At SGI, Intranet development efforts were initially based on the deeds of individuals who created their own Web pages full of very diverse content (some useful from a work standpoint, and some less useful). Employees from various departments took the initiative to create and display department-oriented information to others in the organization.

SGI soon realized that there were opportunities made available through these technologies to improve communication throughout the company. By using their existing network, SGI rapidly developed their intranet, using its existing platforms and applications. They equipped desktops throughout the entire organization with a browser and Web authoring tools. Needless to say, soon after doing so, the SGI intranet experienced an explosion in content. In a little over two years, SGI's intranet has close to 1,000 servers and over 2,500 Web sites, and encompassed 250,000 individual Web pages reaching over 11,000 employees throughout the world. Coping with such a large amount of information is certainly no easy task, but it is also something that has to be done, because not doing anything can have grave consequences.

DEVELOPMENT APPROACH (CHAOS VS. CONTROL)

How does an organization approach developing a useful and efficient intranet, and still maintain its core value of empowerment and creativity? SGI's answer was Silicon Junction, which is the name of their intranet. Silicon Junction is an easy-to-use and enticing set of Web pages with links to internal and external sites. The internal site provides end users with an organized list of items, including news, employee services, special-interest groups, product and sales, and customer and technical support. More importantly, however, it has created new forms of work.

What appears to make this system so powerful is that it was developed and is maintained by the entire organization. No longer do people have to wait for the IT organization to make changes. If you want to add something, then do it. Gone for the most part is the traditional red tape that people have to go through. At SGI, people simply incorporate information themselves. The evolution of Silicon Junction has been as follows:

1. Grassroots development of Web pages: early adopters within company creating and publishing their own individually or departmentally oriented sites.
2. Organizational vision: the organization provides development and authoring tools to all.
3. Silicon Junction is developed: an exponential explosion in information brings about a consolidation and integration effort, where today a small group of people is in charge of standardizing the look, feel, and tool set.
4. Transaction automation: the development of transaction-oriented applications including procurement and employee processing.
5. Work transformation: the creation of "rich applications" such as video on demand and collaborative workspaces.

ORGANIZATIONAL IMPACT

The implications of Silicon Junction have been far-reaching. First, it has helped build a strong culture and sense of involvement, where each employee feels a part of the process of building the organization. Moreover, the collaborative workspaces have effectively increased the strength and concept of teamwork within Silicon Graphics, which is something the company holds very dearly.

The development of instant information and access to product specifications, prices, and the like, as well as rich applications such as video conferencing and training via the intranet has not only enhanced the development of personnel around the globe, but cut the cost involved in training, printing, and distribution. In studying the effects of such applications, SGI estimates that it is saving over $16,000 a month simply on employee training. And with their recent purchase of Cray and their employees, the savings are expected to increase dramatically. The integration should also be much easier.

The payback in terms of cycle-time reduction for internal processes such as purchases, human resource applications, and requests for communication services has been tremendous. More importantly, crucial processes such as software development, which usually involves a long stepwise procedure, has enabled people from different parts of the organization, in different roles and in different locations, to work simultaneously on a project, while lowering the cost and time involved in development and improving product quality at the same time.

WHAT'S AHEAD?

The success of SGI's intranet is more than chance. It is a success driven by innovative employees who are empowered to experiment and build, and an awareness and vision from top management that within these emerging technologies lie opportunities for transformation and competitive advantage. Today, according to Graves, the question is not "whether an intranet can help your organization, but rather how long can you delay building one."

Will 1997 be the year of the intranet? SGI surely hopes so. Having an understanding of and succeeding in answering this question for themselves has created for SGI the opportunity to enter a new market. SGI is known for its specialization in digital media, but they recently made Intranet Junction publicly available as software that can be layered on top of the UNIX operating system. It provides templates and graphics that users can access from a Web browser and use to build and maintain intranet Web pages.

Silicon Graphics is taking its philosophy of empowerment and entering the young and flourishing intranet market. Will they succeed? That will have to be seen in the next months, but SGI is certainly taking an aggressive strategy, pricing their intranet package at about 50 percent of Netscape's.

NOTES

[1] Robert Walker, CIO of Hewlett-Packard, in *CIO Magazine*, January 1997.

[2] Forrester Research Inc., Cambridge, Mass. "The Forrester Report: The Full Service Intranet." March 1, 1996.

[3] Statement made to team of Haas student researchers, October, 1996.

[4] "Eureka! Levi finds Gold Mine of Data." *PC Week*, http://www.pcweek.com/ mgmt/ 0513/13levi.html.

[5] PC Week, op. cit.

[6] Eureka! Promotes Learning. http://gat013/corpcom/whats-new/eureka/lrngorg.htm.

[7] Richard Hackathorne. "Data Warehousing's Credibility Crisis." *Byte*, August 1997.

[8] PR Newswire Association, Inc., January 24, 1997.

[9] Udo Flohr. "Intelligent Intranets." *Byte*, August, 1997.

[10] Business Research Group Report, http://www.pathfinder.com.

INTERORGANIZATIONAL ELECTRONIC COMMERCE: REDRAWING COMPETITIVE BOUNDARIES

In a globalizing, increasingly dynamic, and complex business environment, specialization and collaboration between business partners is gaining in importance. Due to the increased performance and reduced cost of information technology, the part of the value chain covered by the individual company becomes smaller yet gains global reach. The division of labor becomes more and more important, letting the potential playground for business-to-business applications grow.

Companies find themselves in a dense web of economic players comprising commercial as well as noncommercial organizations, government institutions, households, and individuals, and they interact with them in various ways. Business partners take on different roles as they supply input in the form of hard goods, services, or information, act as partners in research and development, or take a company's output as distributors, resellers, or end consumers.

All of these relationships involve information processing and exchange, i.e., communication:

· Information outlining the details of business transactions, such as product data, contract stipulations, or shipment or payment arrangements.

· Information beyond individual transactions, such as customer preferences gathered by customer services that supports or enables future transactions, e.g., by providing input for product development.

· External information used as input for internal processes, collaboration, or enhancing the value of a product.

Information technology offers many ways to support the creation, gathering, archiving and storage, retrieval, exchange, processing, and dissemination of information. As a consequence, it is applicable to all sorts of relationships and, according to estimates, 70 percent of all information exchanged between organizations already involves some form of information technology along with its generation or further processing. But for a large part, information technology is applied *within* organizations. Compared to the complex databases, integrated applications, collaborative tools, and e-mail systems often found inside corporate boundaries, communication and information processing between companies appears to be in a rather prehistoric age. Organizational boundaries still form a major barrier for data and information on electronic media. Since most information is still transmitted or accessed in conventional ways—paper documents, fax machines, telephone, or face-to-face communication—a huge amount of data has to be retyped on at least one side of the communication process. This is not only erroneous, as well as time-consuming and expensive, but it also means that much information is not transmitted or made accessible at all because the effort to do so is simply too great.

Electronic data interchange (EDI) systems connect companies with their business partners, automating the exchange of structured data for order placement or shipping announcements. Although the technology has been in place for more than 20 years, EDI diffusion rates never really met the expectations. The cost related with value-added network services or the lease of private lines, which are currently prevailing for the exchange of data, in combination with a certain inflexibility of the technology itself makes beneficial implementations difficult, especially for small companies with low transaction volumes.

The Internet and electronic commerce technologies, however, offer exciting new and cost-efficient ways for companies to communicate and interact with their business partners. Reaching beyond the mere "electrification" of traditional forms of communication with EDI systems or e-mail, there is the potential to dramatically change methods, purposes, and results of corporate procurement and selling functions, and affect the management of the whole supply chain. In a world characterized by globalization and stiffening competition, innovative business concepts as well as efficiency in performance continue to be major success factors. Although the Internet and World Wide Web are already heavily and in very creative ways used to establish links with households and end consumers (covered in Chapter 7), analysts predict that business-to-business relationships will draw the most significant share of Dollars spent on electronic commerce in the medium term.[1]

In this chapter, we will show how emerging technologies can be applied to interorganizational settings, how they can supplement and improve the paradigm of traditional EDI, and how the deployment of these technologies can reshape business relations as well as eventually change whole industries. We will first outline how the Internet and related technologies can support all phases of business transactions and eventually change the way goods and services are exchanged between organizations. The second part demonstrates some of the ways, innovative information technology supports inter-organizational collaboration and even facilitates new forms of organizations.

EMERGING TECHNOLOGIES IN BUSINESS TRANSACTIONS

A large part of business-to-business relationships evolve around the exchange of goods and services and a resulting form of compensation. These are called *transactions*, and they imply a variety

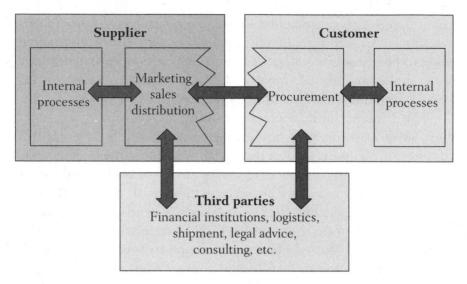

FIGURE 6-1. Transactions, spanning multiple interfaces.

of perspectives (see Figure 6-1). From a functional perspective, you can look at procurement and internal logistics on the buyer side, while on the seller's side transactions evolve around marketing, sales, and distribution (the latter again including internal logistic tasks). In both cases, relationships with external partners have to be established and maintained while service to internal business functions are provided.

Procurement includes all activities involved in obtaining material, and transporting and moving it toward the end user. Positioned between a company's internal customers in need of material to fulfill their tasks and external suppliers providing goods and services, this business function not only has to meet multiple objectives simultaneously, but also needs to establish, maintain, and balance a variety of external and internal relationships at the same time. Its general responsibility is to buy materials of the right quality, in the right quantity, at the right time, at the right place, from the right source, with delivery at the right place. For a long time, procurement focused basically on efficient transaction processing. Today, there is a more comprehensive perspective that also takes into account planning, forecasting, and policy procedures around purchasing, the management of internal and external relationships, and logistics activities. Supply-chain management stands for the integral administration of goods and services from the supply side, through the transformation process and various distribution channels, to the customer and end consumer.

The receiving side of a transaction is also complex. The primary task of marketing, sales, and warehousing and distribution is to ensure that the output of a company's production process not only finds its customer (demand creation), but also has a way to reach it (physical supply). Customer satisfaction plays a major role in today's saturated and highly dynamic markets. *Integrated distribution management*, as it is termed, includes many of the functions that are also covered by supply-chain management: facility location, purchasing, packaging, production planning, material handling, warehousing and storage, inventory control, traffic and transportation, order processing, distribution communications, parts and service support, personnel movement, returned goods, salvage and scrap disposal, customer distribution programs, and vendor distribution programs.[1]

From the perspective of a business partner, a transaction involves not only suppliers and customers on one side and internal processes on the other side, but frequently third parties. Financial institutions such as banks, credit-card companies, and insurance companies offer payment services, consultants, and legal advisers help outline and set up contracts as well as evaluate their stipulations; logistic companies handle shipments and delivery; and industry associations and market research organizations provide additional information.

While these services can also be considered individual transactions, it is important to notice that they evolve around a core transaction with which they are closely interrelated as well as with each other in terms of time, location, and content.

Business transactions consist of three basic steps: information, negotiation, and purchasing and shipment (including monitoring). Buyers identify and evaluate their needs and sources to fulfill them, while potential sellers arrange to provide their goods and identify potential customers. These steps evolve, to a large part, around the exchange of information and are followed by the process of negotiating the terms of a deal finalized by a contract, e.g., in the form of a purchase order. Finally, the purchase is executed and money and goods are exchanged according to the conditions previously negotiated. Some sort of mutual performance monitoring accompanies this step to conclude the deal.

Each transaction involves a large amount of information processing and communication. Additionally, many pieces of the data related to a transaction are used more than once, like product description details, which appear not only in catalogs but also in transaction contracts, on shipping documents, and in insurance policies. Storing and processing data in a way that makes it electronically accessible for every participant reduces communication time and cost, potentially improves efficiency, and adds value to services.

With their high volume of data involved, high task repetitiveness, and fairly easy structurability transactions have been an early field for the application of information technology. Apart from EDI and proprietary systems, which have been around for a while, this has basically meant support for internal data handling and processing. Only in recent years have business-to-business applications gained widespread attention and acceptance.

The following sections provide a closer look at the use of emerging technologies in the stages of information exchange, negotiation, and settlement of inter-organizational business transactions.

EXCHANGING INFORMATION VIA CATALOGS

Before a transaction can take place, potential business partners inquire about the possibility and conditions of procurement, or sales of products or services. In that phase, both parties usually act independently from each other with activities geared toward a large number of potential business partners. Disseminating information about products and services, as well as inquiring about those products and services, comprise the first step towards the establishment of a relationship.

Sellers want to disseminate information on products, services, and the company as broadly, specifically, and accurately as possible to as large and diverse an "interested" auditorium as possible. This includes product and service features, prices, and delivery terms, but also other competencies the company might have, such as the ability to establish ongoing relationships and provide valuable services, comprehensive solutions, and company background to customers.

Catalogs play an important role in business-to-business transactions. Traditionally, sellers (manufacturers, distributors, wholesalers, and retailers) have used paper-based catalogs to disseminate information on products and services to buyers. They are appealing to their readers because of their glossy layout, they allow easy thumbing through the pages, and they provide one or several indexes to locate items. However, they also tend to be costly in terms of production and handling. Furthermore, they provide only a limited form of communication, which is one-way and has no direct feedback possibilities. In case a customer needs additional information on product features or configuration possibilities, catalogs often fall short in providing it. Finally, catalogs usually present information of only a single company, be it a manufacturer, retailer, or wholesaler. To compare competing offers or find complementary products, customers have to consult several catalogs.

Moving paper-based catalogs to CD-ROMs has brought advantages in terms of cost, considering production, mailing, and storage space and the easy deployment of additional search and data-handling capabilities for users. Since they make information available in electronic form, they ease further processing. With a low cost of production, they allow more frequent updates than traditional paper-based catalogs.

Electronic online catalogs make use of Web pages to sell goods and services to members of the Internet via a graphical interface. Alan Cohen, Managing Director for Electronic Commerce of the IBM Internet division, estimates a 10-percent annual growth rate for business-to-business cataloging—twice the growth rate for noncatalog business-to-business ordering and higher than growth in the consumer industry.[2]

Initially, companies moved their traditional catalogs to the Internet primarily for marketing reasons. In that way, they drove their stake in the ground of the online world, established a presence, and showed their technical savvy. The Internet extends the reach of catalogs, while the costs of handling and distribution remain low. Emerging technologies, however, can add a whole new dimension to merely moving traditional paper-based catalogs to CD-ROMs, and they do not have to remain simple electronic versions of their paper-based counterparts, presenting "flat" product displays.

With the advent of the Internet and the Web in particular, catalog designers and providers now have the opportunity to:

- Enhance the catalog's look and feel through graphical and multimedia elements (graphics, sounds, and animation).

- Use cross-indexes to point to additional background information, either within the company's Web site or externally at business partners' sites. The catalog, containing products and services, will eventually be only a part of the comprehensive representation of a company and its field of business. This can also serve as an information repository after sales and for internal staff.

- Support access to product information through different indexes and powerful search tools, e.g., using graphics.

- Interactively guide users through the catalog.

- Link online catalogs with back-end inventory systems to ensure accurate, up-to-date information, accessible 24 hours a day, 7 days a week.

- Design interactive systems that help users find products that best fit their needs, and configure complex systems and solutions.

- Let users make lists of products that are interesting to them while using the catalog. The system can then revert to saved lists later on, gives users the opportunity to obtain automatically updated information.

- Tighten relationships by offering additional support, or alerting customers to complementary products or services and sales campaigns.

· Generate usage reports that track the types of information customers are viewing and selecting, and learn more about their preferences.

By integrating several catalogs, electronic marketplaces can be created that provide links between a large number of potential business partners on either side of a transaction. Customers in search of a particular product and entering such virtual marketplaces can be directed to the shop that provides them with the product that best fits their needs. Possible features are:

· A single point of entry, which brings together a large number of buyers and sellers within a particular industry (e.g., electronics) or environment (e.g., the procurement of supplies for institutions related to the U.S. government).

· An online mall that provides joint infrastructure for underlying catalogs, e.g., search facilities across catalogs and additional industry links.

· A common look and feel for different catalogs—facilitating their use and also improving trust (which is especially important when it comes down to ensuring safe, reliable market transactions).

· Access to a wide variety of stores, which enlarges the number of products that can be accessed without the need for customers to have to leave the common environment.

· Providing a mall targeting a very specific audience, making it attractive to advertisers.

An example is the Defense Logistics Agency (DLA), which developed a customized catalog accessible to the large number of institutions affiliated with the defense sector.[3] The electronic supply center combines parts of electronic catalogs from several suppliers and simultaneously integrates procurement rules into the applications. For example, users of the customized catalog have access to products that they can order at prices that are DoD-specific. They get additional help, such as order forms complying with DoD ordering standards and order-tracking facilities. The Web application actually integrates some of the monitoring and control functions that were traditionally executed manually—current procurement procedures are changed fundamentally as purchasing power is shifted back to end users.

As early as 1992, the University of Utah's Mechanical Engineering Department initiated a project to help engineers and designers locate hard-to-find parts. In partnership with the Defense Logistics Agency, PartNet was developed to directly link customers to supplier databases.[4] It allows engineers and designers to search parts suppliers' product information databases for electronic, electromechanical, and mechanical parts using any combination of user-supplied part names, part numbers, or technical specifications. Besides being provided with access to accurate and up-to-date information around the clock, users can now access several suppliers' catalogs and more than 180,000 parts without having to leave the site.

The idea of creating truly comprehensive marketplaces that provide a certain user community with broad access to relevant information and facilitate links to business partners, which would eventually form industry-wide networks, fostered the creation of several "business supersites." They combine a wide variety of functionalities and have had mixed success.

Cahners Publishing, Reed Elsevier, and Lexis-Nexis teamed up to launch Manufacturing Marketplace,[5] an electronic forum that provides manufacturing industry news and information on products, companies, resources, and trade shows. Additionally, discussion areas, newsgroups, and links to freeware and other manufacturing Web sites are offered.

NetBuyer,[6] owned by Ziff-Davis, a computer magazine publisher, aims at people who purchase computer products "direct"—online or through mail order from manufacturers and resellers. Besides providing online access to more than 100 vendors and their product catalogs, the site also advertises special offers, allows for side-by-side product comparison charts, and offers ordering facilities, links to additional information, technical tips, product reviews, and buying guidelines.

Nets, Inc. created Industry.Net[7], a Web-based marketplace for a business community selling and buying industrial products and, as some claim, an approach that might have been too ambitious for its time. The site offered a combination of online marketing services, commerce opportunities, tools, and information. Initiated in 1990, in 1996 it claimed to bring together more than 275,000 buyers from more than 36,000 companies and 4,500 sellers. Members had access to a wealth of information, including catalogs, corporate profiles, product and service descriptions, demonstration software, application notes, industry news, up-to-date trade association information, career opportunities, and online discussion areas. Industry.Net also aimed to organize online events covering major trade shows and conferences. By creating a one-stop marketplace for a specific group of professionals, Industry.Net also wanted to create a means for highly targeted marketing. Its approach turned out too big and costly, however. By February of 1997, Nets Inc. had more than 260 employees but could not generate enough sales to reach break-even point. The company went bankrupt and was eventually sold to PSC Technology in June of 1997. This subsidiary of Perot Systems now plans to focus the idea behind Industry.Net and partner with clients to create vertically integrated value webs, web arenas consisting of commerce content and collaborative capabilities in more narrowly defined market segments. The case of Industy.Net shows that "a good idea alone does not make a good business case"—the market was not ready yet to adopt Industry.Net's broad and standard-setting approach.

Meanwhile, others are pursuing a more focused strategy.[8] The Plastics Network,[9] for example, hosted by Commerx, Inc., targets a vertically integrated but rather small community: the plastics-industry supply chain. *Focus* and *community* are the key words with which it wants to create a beneficial source on the Internet. So far, the strategy of providing content-rich interactive forums and profound information within a narrow area seems to be successful; its first two years of being online have been characterized by substantial growth. The figures pale in comparison, however, with Industry.Net's broad online community, which in June of 1997 counted 15,000 members. Basically, two features help member companies to create sales: a database, which lets users search by product categories, and online "business centers" (corporate Web sites designed and hosted by Commerx). Apart from selling highly targeted advertising space, Commerx generates a big share of its revenue from the currently about 120 business centers. It plans to extend the network by adding features that let manufacturers submit request bids for parts they need, with automated notification of qualified suppliers and multivendor electronic catalogs.

Although the virtual electronic marketplaces described so far have the potential for making selling and buying more cost- and time-efficient on a large scale, there are some shortcomings. User-friendly and sophisticated applications providing a unique face to a variety of different sources don't come cheap; in fact, the simpler the end-user interface, the more complex and better integrated the supporting applications must be. This adds to the cost. The technology providing payment services and security is just about to reach the appropriate level of maturity.

In one aspect, simple electronic catalogs, as well as most sophisticated online malls and marketplaces, do not differ from their traditional counterparts: they let users basically search through available products one supplier at a time, be it a single manufacturer, distributor, or retailer. Even in cases where there are some overlaying indexes, they mainly lead the user to the right store but do not allow powerful search queries across databases. Users who need to compare and evaluate competing and complementary products in order to configure complex solutions have to browse through a multitude of different sources of information just like in the "old" days of paper catalogs. By actually integrating the content of several catalogs, powerful databases can be developed that allow users to search more than one catalog at a time and easily obtain the product data they need to make informed purchasing decisions. By taking part in this form of interoperable catalogs, sellers would provide additional value to their customers and further expand their reach.[10]

Overall, you would expect that market transparence, fairness, and efficiency would increase in relationship to powerful interoperable catalogs. So far, it is not clear whether these actually have a chance to catch on, since all beneficial effects bear disadvantages for market players who currently benefit from inefficiencies. For instance, improving the fairness and transparency of the market can give companies with small market shares the opportunity to break some of the competitive advantage of established brand names—an experience that "big names" might want to avoid. However, to be successful, electronic marketplaces need to draw in a large number of participants.

Economists predict that transparent markets with heavily competing participants tend to erode profits on the market side of the equation, e.g., by driving down prices or continuously improving other features like customer service. While this kind of situation provides benefits to the customers, it is not surprising that suppliers are hesitating to enter the game. As a solution, the companies supplying information within interoperable catalogs could team up and charge a fee for using the catalogs in order to reap some compensating benefits.

Additionally, the lack of standards for intercatalog communication so far poses a problem when it comes to content description, access, and interoperability. Especially for sellers who are competing on features like quality, delivery times, reliability, or long-standing customer relationships, there is a downside as long as interoperable catalogs hold mainly information on prices and product features, since they cannot adequately represent their core competencies across catalog boundaries.

NEGOTIATION

Following the phases in which buyers identify their needs and potential sources to fulfill them, and sellers arrange to provide their goods and services and locate potential customers, initial contacts are made and the terms of the deal are arranged. Negotiations focus not only on price but frequently on "soft" issues such as quality, quantity, delivery terms, or future relationships. So far, the telephone is still the most important communication channel when it comes to negotiation. Buying companies also frequently solicit competing bids from several suppliers, bargain with many bidders simultaneously, or announce RFPs. Today, by far the most business-to-business transactions are done within relationships where business partners know each other, share some data, and expect to do business in the future. This fact and the complexity of the negotiation process makes automation through IT somewhat difficult.

IT support for negotiation involves the use of decision support systems (DSS), negotiation support systems (NSS), and distributed artificial intelligence (AI).[11] All provide powerful tools to improve the productivity of negotiations or come even close to its automation. So far, they are used mainly as support for one of the negotiating parties or they represent early stages of negotiation automation, sometimes built only for laboratory use. Apart from technology, issues of trust arise. Electronic negotiation is a difficult, complex process that has had limited success. According to a survey on how the Internet affects purchasing practices and supplier relationships by the Fisher Center for Management and Information Technology at the University of California at Berkeley,[12] not more than 10 percent of companies have some type of automated negotiation support system in place.

The Internet can support negotiations in several ways:

- E-mail as an additional communication channel, which supports asynchronous and unstructured forms of communication.

- Information on products or services, corporate profiles, etc., which are readily available and accessible through the World Wide Web. This supports other traditional negotiation processes, e.g., using the telephone.

- Online catalogs, which allow quite complex forms of pricing that adjust to varying conditions in real time. Built-in rules can allow for quantity discounts, reward bundling of certain products, or offer different means of delivery. Additionally, prices can be adjusted even on a short-term basis, which provides high flexibility to react to certain events, like changing weather conditions.

- New ways of pricing. The interactive features of the Internet allow prospective buyers into pricing processes, e.g., let them place an offer to buy supplies at a fixed price that is lower than the one stated in a published price list. After evaluating all fixed-price offers, a supplier can choose which, if any, buyers to sell to at the buyer's suggested prices.

The Internet provides an affordable infrastructure to offer new features like the ones just described, as opposed to the use of bilateral links, which still prevail in EDI systems and private networks.

One form of negotiation, however, seems to be especially well suited to the Internet: auctions (market institutions determining resource allocation and prices according to an explicit set of rules on the basis of bids from the market participants). In the original English auction, bidders participated simultaneously, usually gathered in the same place. Electronic commerce tools eliminate this need and subsequently increase the reach of potential bidders; participation requires not much more than an Internet connection and the time it takes to evaluate the current auction. The auction can also take place more frequently without the penalty of decreasing the number of bidders.[13]

ONSALE provides the most well-known example of an on-line-auction house (see the case study on ONSALE in chapter 7). It's successful concept of auctioning mostly computers and high-technology goods in real time over the Internet, meanwhile has numerous imitators, the most well known being Internet Shopping Network, which started its first auction in June of 1997. Consumer Exchange Network (CXN) plans to sell new consumer products (such as televisions), via a variation of the standard English auction, in which sellers are the bidders (bidding down) and a single buyer is the auctioneer.[14]

Electronic auctions support asynchronous bidder participation and a continuously running auction, and offer the possibility to auction off multiple items in a succession of single-item sales. This allows them to tie together a large group of participants and basically extend the reach of the auction. So far, a large part of the traded goods are electronic and computer products, which are relatively easy to describe and seldom surpass four-digit values. The excitement created by the notion of competition certainly forms one of their major success factors. This aspect might be more relevant in private settings than in today's dynamic and efficiency-driven business environments. Additionally, constraints concerning the product range as well as their random factor prevent auctions from taking over a major part of procurement or selling in a business-to-business setting. However, they do provide a cost-effective "add-on" to established means of price setting and transactions.

These examples show how technology can change the way purchasing processes currently work. The feasibility of their implementation, however, depends not only on the availability of the technical systems, but in some cases even more on the change of established procedures. New technologies provide the opportunity to consolidate small ad hoc purchases that are usually at the discretion of individuals or decentralized departments because they are considered not worth handling on an individual basis. In a large organization, however, these small amounts can add up to significant amounts with consolidation becoming worthwhile. The Internet provides a means to channel these kinds of unrelated, disjointed deals in a cost-effective way, but its realization often requires major changes in established business procedures.

PURCHASING AND SHIPMENT

"Concluding the deal" by exchanging products and services according to the terms contractually stipulated obviously forms a major component of any transaction process. Traditionally, EDI played a major role in automating operations like order processing or the exchange of shipping announcements and invoices. EDI systems tend to be costly, however, because they usually involve the lease of private lines or include value-added network services, and their functionality is rather poor because they are restricted to text-based messages. Additionally, their overall reach is poor: according to Forrester Research, even in the U.S., one of the places with the deepest EDI diffusion, worldwide only 5 percent of companies larger than 10 employees have EDI systems in place. In many cases, their deployment pays off only for large companies with massive transaction volumes. They also tend to have the power to get smaller business partners to comply with their EDI systems and in that way increase the electronic part of overall communication. The U.S. government provides a well-known example of this practice. Especially for the smaller partners, the results are often EDI deployments that merely substitute traditional ways of communication; they do not really pay off in financial terms, but are rather considered a necessity to keep market share.

MOVING **EDI** TO THE INTERNET.   Traditionally, companies rely on value-added networks (VANs) to ship data between more or less private networks. Apart from the electronic linkage, VANs often provide additional services like audit tracking, reliability, archiving, and a certain degree of deniability, as well as a single point of responsibility in case something goes wrong. On the other hand, using these services tends to be costly.

The Internet offers an alternative to this scenario that can help cut costs for access to the network and the transmission of data. Existing EDI-based transactions can be performed at lower cost, while the extension of the number of EDI links is facilitated, making its deployment more feasible for small and medium sized companies.[15] Also, while VANs usually charge on a per-transaction basis, Internet connect charges tend to be fixed. In the "old days," companies usually batched transactions and sent them altogether in one transmission to various EDI partners. Using the Internet, transmissions can be sent whenever necessary at no premium, helping to establish real-time commerce and offering additional advantages in speed and flexibility.

On the other hand, security concerns continue to be one of the big inhibitors for Internet commerce; the network's openness and heterogeneity prevent the control possible in proprietary environments. There is hope, however, as some systems have already been developed offering secure transactions over the Internet, which can help to overcome the concerns. Yet, this solution also tends to be rather costly. In other cases, security concerns might be overstated and will be solved over time as organizations realize their actual security needs in relation to the security threats of the Internet.

Similar concerns apply to reliability. Unlike VANs, which offer centralized management and routing of transactions, the Internet is characterized by a distributed structure that does not permit the prediction or control of the route the data will take across the network. With the lack of a central party of responsibility, concerns about the potential for lost data have to be evaluated in terms of the individual company's requirements. Furthermore, although it is unreliable in theory, pilot projects tend to show that the Internet actually offers quite good reliability.

Since VANs are relatively experienced in providing secure and reliable electronic links, they are predestined to offer such linkages over the Internet. Realizing that some of their traditional domain is crumbling away, they have started to offer new services that include the Internet as a medium for data transmission and, to an increasing extent, Web-based technology at either end of the communication process. Along with this is changes in VAN pricing structures, as well as a certain modularization of their services.

The current situation is characterized by a proliferation of Internet products from VANs as well as software vendors including Premenos, Sterling Commerce, Harbinger, St. Paul Software, GEIS, Oracle, and TCI.[16] More start-ups are targeting smaller trading partners with plug-and-play modules for established software packages, and leveraging commercial partners.

During the first three years of Internet- and Web-based business-to-business electronic commerce, companies have explored the field mainly with prototypes and early applications:

· Bank of America started gathering experience with Internet EDI by taking the initiative for a seven-month pilot with one of its large customers as early as 1994. The project established a link between the bank and Lawrence Livermore National Laboratories, which was able to send payments to contractors over the Internet, thus establishing an electronic triangle relationship. The pilot got much public attention because payment transactions are among the most sensitive electronically processed transactions. (For more information in this, see chapter 2.)

· In late 1995, Avex Electronics launched an EDI pilot with one of its major suppliers, replacing the current VAN solution. The project aimed at saving costs and sharing an already established Internet access, which was later replaced by Avex's own Internet gateway. Today, Avex is well beyond piloting Internet EDI. The Internet is now the preferred communication vehicle for EDI, and the company continues to migrate its EDI links to the Internet. This process is expected to become more productive as a growing number of Avex' trading partners realize the benefits.

· In 1996, McKesson implemented an Internet- and Web-based system to allow the Department of Defense, one of its largest customers, to check its inventory, place emergency orders, and track delivery. The project represents an early application of the first off-the-shelf Internet EDI package: Templar, by Premenos. (McKesson's Internet-EDI project is covered in more detail at the end of this chapter.)

BEYOND EDI: THE "ELECTRIFICATION" OF BUSINESS NETWORKS. The Internet and World Wide Web have much more up their collective sleeve than moving bilateral EDI connections to a new medium. In supporting multiple relationships between business partners within a network and integrating supply chains, they have the potential to kick off major changes in the way companies interact and do business with each other.

In November of 1996, Boeing Commercial Airplane Group's customer service went live with a Web-based online system that enables its customers to order spare aircraft parts, obtain price quotes, check on the status of shipments, and request other information.[17] The system, which makes more than 410,000 different types of spare parts available over the Web, turned out to be an instant success. Within its first six months, more than 200 customers started using the site and generated over 150,000 transactions—"electrifying" about one-quarter of all transactions that were previously handled manually, including those received via phone and fax. Boeing expects that volume to reach half a million after 12 months. "The Boeing PART page provides a quick, easy, economical way for our customers to access the Boeing spares inventory database," says Tom DiMarco, senior manager of spares systems.

"It's intuitive, fully interactive, and lets customers 'pull' information at their option. It greatly reduces the need for hard copies of air bills, shipping schedules, and other documents." Additionally, transactions are generated through conventional EDI systems, in which mainframe computers operated by very large customers are linked directly to the Boeing database.

The DLA procurement Web-site (described earlier in the chapter) annually contracts for goods and services valued at $8 billion. By shifting to Internet applications, the government agency implemented a new business model. It broke traditional forms of communication, where order placement and problem-solving took circuitous routes across different organizational elements. The homepage now provides global information that empowers customers and suppliers to make better decisions, get faster answers, and give constructive feedback. Performance up and down the supply chain was improved by quickly linking supply-chain participants with pertinent information. Additional benefits include the following:

· Customers are quickly advised of product quality situations such as recalls and changes to the application.
· The visibility of surplus goods is increased.
· Customers get an online choice of available support options as well as direct access to customer service.

Fruit of the Loom, Inc. uses an interesting approach to link up with its distributors in the imprinted sportswear market.[18] The Activewear division, which accounts for roughly half of the apparel manufacturer's sales, manufactures blank shirts and sells them to distributors, which again sell them to screen printers and embroiderers, who decorate the items and sell them to retailers, who sell to end consumers. Fruit of the Loom helps its key distributors get started on the Internet, not only by developing and maintaining individual Web sites, but also by providing training for self-administration and links to Internet access providers. Each site displays the distributor's unique Web address, gives customers online access to its product catalog, and allows them to check inventory levels as well as credit limits, and place orders online. The service, which is currently provided free to more than two-thirds of the manufacturer's distributors who showed interest in the system, required Fruit of the Loom to spend $4 million. The investment can be considered strategic, with the manufacturer heading for leadership in the distribution chain by supporting a system that benefits all channel members. By increasing efficiency in the overall channel and tightening customer relations, the company hopes to profit from the goodwill the system will eventually elicit. With the system:

- Distributors save order-entry costs and gain new ways of reaching customers.

- The distributors' value is increased by the fact that Fruit of the Loom lets them include products from other manufacturers into their catalogs, such as leading competitor Hanes, completing electronic covering of their product range.

- Customers get 24-hours-a-day, 7-days-a-week access to distributors' online catalogs, which contain information on products and availability as well as functionality for order placement and status checks.

- Direct links with Fruit of the Loom provide distributors with access to the manufacturer's inventory, avoiding short-term availability problems and eventually increasing sales of Fruit of the Loom products; the manufacturer's inventory literally becomes the inventory of all distributors.

- Activewear Online additionally provides a central location where distributors, customers, and prospective customers can get in touch with each other. Additionally, it gives its business partners access to a wide variety of information to assist in the development and growth of business, fostering relationships between all channel members and bringing Fruit of the Loom closer towards its goal of becoming a channel master.

The Internet and WWW can play an important role in the currently heavily discussed area of supply-chain management.

Although the technology is still relatively new, some companies have it already integrated well into their daily business transactions, with buyers as well as distributors.

General Electric has plans to buy about $1 billion worth of goods and supplies on the Net in 1997, linking up with 2,500 of its largest suppliers through its Trading Process Network[19] within the next three years. Early pilots show reductions in procurement cycle time as well as cost. "Suppliers who know that we need their best and final quote a lot earlier in the process tend to give us lower prices because they may not get a second chance to bid," explains GE Information Services president and CEO Harvey Seegers.

Cisco, the networking titan, represents one of the best examples of how the Internet can be integrated in a corporate-wide IT system, boosting efficiency and competitiveness, and using it to master excessive growth. Cisco moved a large part of their sales to the Internet; within 10 months of its launch in July of 1996, Cisco Connection Online had generated several million dollars in revenue through online ordering and reached $5 million a day. Customers preconfigure customized orders using Cisco's Web site, which are then sent straight to the factory information system. Besides the ability to order products, including online verification of pricing and order tracking, the system also provides help for product configuration and answer inquiry—functions that account managers are now finding indispensable. (For more information on Cisco, see the case study at the end of the chapter.)

Cisco claims their direct salespeople do not feel they are being pushed out of the system, since complex products always need additional information and help in configuring, and they appreciate the opportunity to track user reactions and locate their difficulties. They rather see the Web as a medium to stay in touch with customers. Since online purchasing is available only to existing customers, credit can go to the "right" accountants even when goods are purchased through the Web.

All the systems introduced here involve large companies that can afford to make significant investments. As a manager of Fruit of the Loom explains, one of the lessons they learned was that it is expensive! Cisco has to manage 18 gigabytes of content, a challenge that is compounded by its diverse nature: ranging from simple HTML objects to financial data, with data coming from multiple sources within Cisco. So far, there is no common infrastructure out there that would allow them to establish "electrified" business-to-business links in an easy and standardized way. However, solutions might be just beyond the horizon.

Netscape and GE Information Services founded Actra Business Systems, a joint venture to develop electronic commerce products for the Internet and intranets.[20] Together with MasterCard, Actra has formed a consortium to develop a secure Internet-based purchasing system by bringing together financial institutions, corporations, and suppliers. In May of 1997, it announced a cross-platform family of Internet commerce applications. Successful interoperability tests with leading electronic commerce software providers indicate that the road to a powerful infrastructure for Internet-based electronic commerce applications is open. In November 1997, Netscape bought Actra for $56 million when it realized that not so much the browser was critical to its success as it were comprehensive business applications.

In this chapter, we have so far outlined some of the ways companies can use the Internet to support existing business relationships, examining how the exchange of goods and sevices might be affected, from the procurement side as well as from the viewpoint of sales and distribution. We will now take a look at some more radical impacts the Web and other emerging technologies might have. By enabling new ways of support for collaboration across organizational borders between individuals, teams, and whole companies, industry structures might be affected eventually.

COLLABORATION AND VIRTUAL ORGANIZATIONS: NEW FORMS OF RELATIONSHIPS

Emerging information and communication technologies support new forms of relationships by facilitating the collaboration between autonomous organizational units. In that context the phenomenon of so-called networked, extended, or virtual organizations has recently gained immense attention. We are talking about organizational constructs that consist of small, globally dispersed organizational entities forming a collaborative environment on a temporary basis, with nodes added and removed to the network according to changing customer requirements and environmental dynamics. While to external observers, these networks often appear as whole, "real" organizations, they actually consist of several legally autonomous parts, forming "as-if" organizations, hence the term *virtual organization.*

The concept itself can hardly be considered new; temporary collaboration between autonomous organizational units is common practice in areas such as the film business or construction industry. Usually a coordinating unit "in charge" pulls together individuals or companies with special skills and competencies on a temporary and project-oriented basis. The projected outcome, be it a film or a complex construction site, serves as the common objective, steering activities and holding the group together. A new project frequently means a different set of participants, according to its needs. Traditionally, much of the coordination and collaboration is based on the physical presence of the participants. Nowadays, advanced information and communication systems can be used to coordinate activities between the members. This changes some of the rules and extends the concept of virtual organizations far beyond its traditional scope.

The short-term orientation, especially, distinguishes virtual organizations from longer-term-oriented constructs like joint ventures, coalitions, or strategic alliances. But we also find some longer-term-oriented constructs that relate to the basic idea of virtual organizations. In recent times, a growing number of organizational networks were formed, often around special interests or to deliver complex products and comprehensive solutions, such as the processing of a loan for a house or designing the interior of a shop (CommerceNet's COIN model). In any case, the participants are autonomous units that complement each others' competencies. In the academic world there is no complete agreement as to whether telecommuting should be considered a core characteristic of virtual organizations. For some researchers, virtual organizations could have the organizational structure of traditional companies, as long as there is no single building and the staff is working in dispersed locations, including working from home. We have no intentions to enter the academic "struggle" over definitions here. From a management standpoint and to serve our purposes, it is sufficient to realize that emerging technologies allow innovative forms of collaboration between physically dispersed organizational units, be they legally independent or not. We will consider the impacts of telecommuting and related management issues in greater detail in chapter 7 when we address emerging technologies from the viewpoint of the individual, while in this chapter we focus more on organizational issues.

Participation in and the formation of networked organizations bear potential advantages for organizations of all sizes. Whether they emerge from several small companies intensifying collaboration with peers or from bigger players splitting up into more agile units, adaptability to highly turbulent environments and responsiveness to customers' needs are two of the driving factors. By partnering, environmental complexity can be reduced, while at the same time enlarging the company's competencies.[21]

Pioneers in virtual organizations are found mainly in the information technology industry, yet other areas are also picking up the idea:

· First Virtual Corp., a company based in Santa Clara, Calif. and founded in 1993, realizes the idea of virtual organizations in a two-fold way.[22] First, it specializes in multimedia network products, such as video collaboration tools, that help enable desktop PCs to become high-quality communications platforms, thus providing the technology actually enabling virtual organizations. Second, it operates as a virtual organization itself, focusing on its core competencies: "fast and continuous innovation and building powerful partnerships" and outsourcing all other functions to partner companies such as IBM, UB Networks, StataCom/Cisco, PictureTel, and Bay Networks.

· VeriFone, Inc. specializes in transaction automation systems, enabling computer systems platforms, network systems, peripherals, security products, software, and systems integration.[23] The company is known for its role in payment processing by offering low-cost terminals for electronic credit-card authorization. It consists of widely dispersed geographical units, which globalizes its engineering efforts, application development resources, and manufacturing and distribution operations, with the objectives of minimizing bottlenecks, accelerating product delivery, and improving responsiveness to customer demand. Worldwide partnering plays a major role in application development.

· Inktomi Corp. builds high-performance networked services and systems, such as Internet search engines or IT solutions for enterprise computing, based on a technology that combines commodity workstations and multimachine parallel processing systems.[24] A UC Berkeley-based computer science project provided the prototype, which eventually led to the foundation of the company in 1996. Inktomi managed the rapid growth during its first year of existence, among other ways, by relying heavily on partnering arrangements and thus adding to its basically technical competencies.

· IntellAction, Inc. promises a comprehensive, integrated, and customer-oriented approach to marketing and implementing new materials, manufacturing, and welding technology by combining technical expertise with strategic alliances.[25]

· CALSTART, Inc., a consortium once founded to explore the use of electric vehicles in the military area, uses the World Wide Web to build a knowledge network around "clean fuel" vehicles, available for its now more than 100 industry members and partly to the public as well.[26] It also supports strategic alliances among its participants.

· The Internet-based bookstore Amazon.com, Inc. can be considered a virtual organization, since it gives Web users the opportunity to advertise and actually sell books from their individual Web sites, and collaborates with logistics companies like Federal Express for shipping and handling.[27] Amazon compiles information about products, and provides facilities for searching and online communication among authors and readers.

THE ROAD TO VIRTUALITY

Much has been written and said about virtual organizations gaining major importance as an organizational concept.[28] Our small sample shows already that the phenomenon is "real" and provides participants with the flexibility and adaptability they need to stay competitive in highly dynamic environments. Many more examples exist already, and the number is growing.

Yet, taking a closer look at some of the early experiences also clearly reveals the fact that we are dealing with a complex phenomenon. Meeting its objectives, understanding and managing issues such as communication and trust among the participants, as well as ensuring efficiency, motivation, and corporate identity are absolutely crucial.[29]

Communication processes are at the core of coordinating and integrating a virtual organization's modularized building blocks. Innovative information technologies, particularly the Internet and World Wide Web, clearly bear the potential to make up for physical proximity of the participants. By offering ubiquity, open standards, ease of use, and rich communication schemes, they support the set up of sufficiently flexible structures. E-mail systems and video conferencing support interaction and collaboration, workflow management systems can help streamline process complexity, and EDI links can control for the flow of physical products. Today's technology, however, is still far from allowing easy integration of electronic commerce building blocks, and no generic tools exist that provide easy message passing between multiple communication partners in an ad hoc way. As a consequence, a great amount of coordination reverts back to "traditional" forms like face-to-face or telephone communication. Additionally, in order to be effective, all participants of a virtual organization have to possess or acquire the skills and confidence to work with others to a large part via information networks. With the Internet and World Wide Web still relatively new phenomena, this issue is clearly not a trivial one.

The social integration of the players is another major success factor for virtual organizations, with motivation and trust being on top of the list to ensure efficiency and effectiveness.

Shared visions and implicit rules of conduct need to be established. Developing a unified voice in public statements, avoiding duplicate efforts, and integrating new hires and partners into pure virtual and heavily decentralized environments are far more difficult tasks than in centralized settings.

As it also turns out, performing "mundane" issues such as scheduling meetings and other administrative tasks or making presentations to customers in a decentralized way is difficult, especially in larger settings. The problems gain in weight when you also consider that networking environments can change frequently in terms of the players involved as well as regarding the characteristics of the relationships between them. Any two participants could be knowledge partners today, competitors tomorrow, and involved in customer/supplier relationships the day after that. Accordingly, situations of competition and cooperation can occur simultaneously.

Even today's most sophisticated information and communication systems are still far from being able to compensate for all the features that face-to-face and other traditional means of communication offer. Regular in-person meetings are still absolutely crucial for building up and maintaining a joint vision, trust, and high motivation among the participants, as well as reaching clear task delegation, which is again necessary to establish efficient work environments. At First Virtual Holdings, Inc., a heavily decentralized company best known for its Internet-based payment system, two-day monthly meetings have proven sufficient, yet highly important, for such tasks.

Virtual organizations are frequently characterized by changing structures and blurring boundaries. This increases the importance of the identity of top managers considerably. They are now representing the organization to external institutions, including banks and other sources of finance. At the same time, they have to coordinate and integrate people acting within an otherwise heavily team-oriented environment. These points have to be taken into account when considering compensation of managers and other employees, in order to come to correct incentives.

Furthermore, the blurring and even disappearing of organizational boundaries can strongly influence the motivation of employees used to more stable settings. More research and experience is necessary to identify some of the potential consequences, and to develop measures to compensate for and ensure long-term productivity.

Early examples show that the concept of Internet-based virtual organizations works best in cases where the goals and responsibilities are straightforward and clearcut, such as in creative projects executed by small, strongly motivated, highly skilled teams. Regular meetings and phone conversations can help deal with issues such as employee morale, and avoid the feeling of "being out of touch." It is important to also keep in mind that virtuality is not a virtue by itself. Centralizing what can be centralized, e.g., marketing, operations, or administrative tasks, can still prove to be the most compelling solution.

In this chapter we presented some of the opportunities that emerging technologies offer to establish, maintain, and tighten relationships between organizations, eventually leading to innovative organizational concepts. We also pointed out some management issues, which are crucial for "reaching the goal." The cases below provide more details on how two companies use emerging technologies, and they point out some of the hurdles that had to be faced on the way. McKesson Corp. implemented a sophisticated Internet-based EDI system within 90 days in order to win a major contract, while the Internet and World Wide Web helped Cisco Systems, Inc. in several ways to manage its enormous growth.

Following the cases, chapter 7 provides you with insights on how the Internet can change the relationships between a company and its end consumers and households. We will shift our focus from a rather business-oriented view to take a look at some of the ways in which new technologies can affect social and private lives, and we will point out how companies can make use of, manage, and even foster these trends.

MCKESSON CORP.

With $17 billion in revenues, McKesson is the major wholesaler in the pharmaceutical industry. Maintaining this leadership in an industry that is currently characterized by major take-over turmoil and where average net profits hover around 2 percent requires constant innovation. McKesson has achieved this by growing its generic drug inventories, providing value-added services, and improving the efficiency of its own operations.[30] McKesson's huge inventory of high-margin generic drugs positions it favorably in the cost-conscious managed care environment. This position can only improve as more drug patents expire. Key acquisitions and its own internal development has made McKesson a leader in the provision of value-added services to many segments of the healthcare industry. Many of these services involve the application of information technology to rationalize and improve the efficiency of pharmaceutical and managed care procedures. Not surprisingly, McKesson's early forays into the application of Web technologies affect this aspect of its strategy.

McKesson provides complete information technology solutions to support pharmacy operations, inventory control, benefits management, and supply-chain management to all segments of its customer base. Table 6.1 lists key services and information technology (IT) solutions that the company provides.

Table 6.1   A Sampling of McKesson Services and Products for addressing the requirements of various types of customers.

TYPE OF CUSTOMER	SERVICES	IT PRODUCTS	WEB PRODUCTS
Independent pharmacies	Virtual chain; economies of scale, leverage pharmacy benefits, inventory management (front- and back-office systems), generics management, sales and promotions, and franchising (through Foxmeyer acquisition)	Valu-Rite Omnilink, Caremax, Econolink, POS for Windows (Pharmaserve and Econolink), McKesson Select Generics, HealtyValu$ and Health Mart	Omnilink Value Reports

Table 6.1 *Continued*   A Sampling of McKesson Services and Products for addressing the requirements of various types of customers.

TYPE OF CUSTOMER	SERVICES	IT PRODUCTS	WEB PRODUCTS
Chain pharmacies	Pharmacy, benefits, inventory management (front- and back-office systems), generics management, and sales and promotions	Omnilink, Caremax, Econolink, McKesson, McKesson Select Generics,	Omnilink Value Reports, and InfoLink
Hospital pharmacies	Pharmacy, benefits inventory management (front- and-back office systems), generics management, and sales and promotions	RxOBOT, McKesson, and McKesson Select Generics	InfoLink
HMOs	Patient benefits management, patient history, outcomes research, prescription claims, and benefit services	Caremax, Integrated Medical Systems, Technology Assessment Group, and PCS Health Systems	
Sales force	Customer profiles, salesperson performance reports, promotions, and specials		InfoLink

McKesson systems and programs rationalize and support every aspect of pharmacy operations that affect the delivery of pharmaceuticals to the end consumer. These operations include:

FRONT-OFFICE (IN-STORE) ACTIVITIES.   Physically dispensing products (RxOBOT), promotions (HealthyValu$), point-of-sale applications (McKesson POS), and catalogs of products (Home Health catalogs).

ADVISING ON AND SUPPORTING BUSINESS ACTIVITIES. Support for filling in prescriptions (Pharmaserv), tracking dispensing records (Pharmarserv), advise on drug interaction (Omnilink), generics management (McKesson Select Generics), and monitoring benefits and health plan coverage (Omnilink, Caremax, Integrated Medical Systems).

BACK-OFFICE ADMINISTRATION. Inventory management (Econolink), and store control and pharmacy management (Phamaserv).

FINANCIAL SERVICES. Omnilink financial services provides automated reconciliation and reporting services, advanced payments, and offsets on receivables.

WAREHOUSE ADMINISTRATION. Product supplies to major retailers from currently 41 warehouses nationwide, and warehouse management tools (Acumax Plus).

This list further supports the contention that the company is positioned to operate profitably in a managed care environment, providing the benefits information, product substitutes (e.g., generics), and financial analyses that enable pharmacists to achieve the greatest margins within the limits of their contractual arrangements. These capabilities are achieved primarily through networks that pool information from various players in the healthcare industry—including manufacturers, hospitals, pharmacies, and managed care providers. The networked nature of these applications makes the Web platform a logical infrastructure for them.

THE BENEFITS OF WEB TECHNOLOGIES

The most obvious benefits that McKesson hopes to gain from the use of Web technologies stem from the cheaper infrastructure afforded by these technologies. Currently, there are plans to substitute the Internet for private networks. The company has also investigated the replacement of high-end PC clients that sit in pharmacies with cheaper, low-maintenance network computers running browser software. These clients will be used as the front end for accessing McKesson's current information technology products.

The current push for using Web technologies was fueled by the company's successful application of a high-profile, high-profit Department of Defense (DoD) project. Within 90 days, McKesson was able to meet the DoD's contract requirements for EDI and exceptions ordering over the Internet. The rapid development of these applications was achieved through the use of browser and scripting technology (Netscape and PERL for exceptions ordering) and off-the-shelf applications (Premenos' Templar for EDI). The rapid deployment of these applications, coupled with the magnitude of the contract they won as a result, piqued McKesson executives' interest in exploring the potential for using the Web infrastructure for providing its services. Since early 1997, the Web-based client-server system InfoLink has enabled McKesson to provide customized and current information to both their sales staff and customers. Sales people can now download the most current customer profiles and sales histories in preparation for their sales calls. The use of Internet and Web-based technologies again allowed rapid system development and lead to low maintenance costs.

A sampling of other projects currently being considered include a corporate-wide Intranet, and a version of Econolink over the Web. Additionally, the company plans to extend InfoLink's capability to provide customized promotional and training materials to both its sales staff and directly to its customers.

CHALLENGES AND LESSONS LEARNED

Deploying Web technologies presents special challenges to McKesson's IT department, centered around issues of managing expectations and overcoming the legacies and building flexibility into the infrastructure.

MANAGING EXPECTATIONS.   The rapid development cycles of the DoD project created an expectation within McKesson that Web applications involved short development times. This expectation might be further reinforced by the practice of using rapid application development (RAD) teams to build the front end for current Web applications. These teams have the goal of getting projects done in eight weeks. However, much more time is required to build the back end for these applications—e.g., logic and database extracts/links—with traditional software development methods. Because RAD is still in the early stages of deployment, it is difficult to assess its effect on user expectations regarding delivery of a given application. So far it has helped users form realistic expectations of a given project's time requirements. During the RAD process, users get a better idea and articulation of the application they want and, in the process, appreciate the programming effort required to address those requirements.

Another aspect of expectation management involves McKesson's customers. As more of McKesson's networks are replaced by the Internet, there will be a need to reassure customers and field staff that service levels and security will not change. This is particularly crucial since one of McKesson's key strengths is the quality of its customer service. In an effort to maintain these levels, McKesson has established satisfactory levels of security using Netscape's SSL. Past experiences also show the importance of helping users maintain realistic expectations of the systems. The project team is wont to remind users that although they have to sit and wait a few seconds for a report to download over the Internet, it is still faster than waiting to get the report through regular mail.

LEGACIES AND FUTURES.   Because of its recognized leadership in information technology solutions for the pharmaceutical industry, McKesson has a major investment in traditional mainframe architecture and developer capabilities. While it has been the mainstay of their past success, this infrastructure has also created problems for building a Web-based capability. The problems include not only commonly recognized legacy issues like data integrity and compatibility with Web technologies, but more strikingly it includes a difficult human resources dilemma: how to quickly build competence with Web development tools among the programmer group.

Given their role as the hub connecting a wide range of healthcare constituents, Web technologies clearly have much potential for improving McKesson's ability to enhance the value-added services they provide to their customers. Ironically, the company's past success with networking business partners and customers has created an entrenched infrastructure that presents complications for their exploitation of the Web model.

CISCO SYSTEMS, INC.

"Three years ago we made the decision to consolidate our network by migrating to a TCP/IP router-based implementation. Cisco's products and responsiveness to our needs have played a major role in our network ever since . . . they're part of our team."[31]

BACKGROUND

Cisco Systems (http:www.cisco.com) was founded in late 1984 by a small group of computer scientists from Stanford University. The company shipped its first products, aimed at making it easier to connect different types of computer systems, in 1986. By 1997 the company had grown into a multinational corporation with over $6 billion in annual revenues and more than 10,000 employees. Headquartered in San Jose, California, today it produces a wide range of routers; LAN, WAN, and asynchronous transfer mode (ATM) switches; dial access servers; and network management software. Cisco is in the interesting position of being both a major driver of the growth of the Internet and a major beneficiary of its impact on the economy and on business operations.

Cisco went public in 1990, and by 1997 had become one of the largest companies listed on NASDAQ, as measured by market capitalization (which was in excess of $48 billion in late 1997). Remarkably, in spite of this size, the company has continued to grow at a rate in excess of 50 percent per year.

This case study describes Cisco's growing use of the Internet to support its marketing, sales, and customer service activities. By mid-1997 more than one-third of Cisco's revenues were being generated over the Web (an annual rate in excess of $2 billion, or over $10 million per working day). The company was also saving literally millions of dollars annually in administrative and customer support costs because of its use of the Internet and intranet technologies. In June 1997, for example, the Cisco Web site received over 245,000 inquiries from customers and prospective employees, including over 92,000 order inquiries, and was handling over 130,000 software downloads a month.

The "Cisco Connection Online" Web Site

The "Cisco Connection Online" Web site (CCO) contains typical marketing and product information, but also includes—for registered users with service contracts—powerful additional features such as online ordering, customer support, and configuration agents that enable customers to interact with Cisco electronically for many of their ordering, status-checking, and technical support needs.

Configuration Agents. One of the most impressive aspects of Cisco Connection is that it can configure very complex products electronically. With thousands of parts and software options, Cisco can produce nearly one hundred million different product configurations. The electronic configuration capability enables customers to identify, custom-design, and order the exact combination of hardware and software products they need. Registered customers log into the appropriate section of Cisco Connection and are led through a series of questions about the products they want to order. They can limit or change the configuration as they go, so only currently relevant information appears on the screen. Once the total order is completely configured, the product information can then be fed directly to an order entry system, freeing customers from having to re-enter the data when they are ready to place their orders.

Status Agents. Once ordered, a product's status can also be tracked directly by the customer through CCO's status system. By entering an order number, the customer can identify exactly when the product was shipped and how it is being delivered. In addition, CCO is linked directly to Federal Express's package tracking system, so the customer can locate the shipment within FedEx with a single click.

The status system also includes an online inventory of purchased products and maintenance agreements for each customer, so it is extremely easy to check on licensing arrangements, maintenance, and warranty conditions for any Cisco products at every individual customer location.

Cisco is careful to maintain its relationships with its resellers by offering partner-initiated customer access to CCO as well as direct access. An end customer can use Cisco's Web site to place orders directly, but only with access parameters (pricing, delivery terms, etc.) that are specific to that customer's reseller. Whenever these end customers place an order or download a new version of software, Cisco notifies the reseller, which actually helps the reseller maintain effective working relationships with its customers.

TECHNICAL SUPPORT. Cisco uses several approaches for providing customer-initiated support. Many customer questions are answered automatically, using electronically stored question and answer pairs ranked by relevance to the customer's query. If a question cannot be answered this way, the customer can send the query to a forum where it is researched, answered, and posted back on the Web site. Customers can check the status of their technical support cases, accessing all the text that engineers have written about their case. Cisco also provides proactive support. Customers are notified by e-mail or fax about bugs in the software version they are using as the problems are discovered, and informed about when revisions and upgrades are available for downloading.

INTRANET APPLICATIONS

Cisco also maintains an intranet, the "Cisco Employee Connection," which offers technical support and human resources information to employees. The IS technical response center offers online guides, answers to common questions, product catalogs, technical tips, and training. The center receives nearly 8,000 technical support requests a month.

The human resource management segment of Cisco's intranet contains information on employee benefits, facilities, meetings, and professional development programs. Employees can register for meetings or sign up for training through the intranet. Once they attend a class, attendance is logged and placed in training archives and personnel records. Employees can also access stock quotes, check their benefits, and simply communicate with each other much more easily than they could before the intranet was installed.

Cisco manages its internal network nontraditionally, with systems built on top of traditional network management platforms that interrogate all the company's networks, servers, and applications and then provide needed information back to each network. With this capability, users can get real-time information about what protocols and software versions are running on the network at any given moment. IT managers have "problem dashboards" that alert them to high-priority needs in the organization, such as when a system or network goes down.

GETTING IT DONE

There are two major challenges to building this kind of Web presence: employee education and document management. Employees across the company must learn to prepare Web documents on their own, and the technical support group has to develop the capability to design, install, and maintain the technology platform. Since so few companies are making such extensive use of the Internet and because Cisco is growing so rapidly, it is difficult to find and hire enough new employees with significant Web experience.

Once built, the Web sites, Web documents, and related databases require continual maintenance and management. Manual maintenance of a Web site as extensive of Cisco's would be impossible; there is too much information and too many different departments involved. Cisco uses electronic document management and configuration control systems to cope with this challenge. Everyone who participates must agree to make the move to configuration management, which allows all departments in the company to participate in electronically publishing information. In fact, the system has filters that automatically convert source documents that were saved in a variety of formats and puts them into "targets." One command pulls down all relevant information, giving everyone, not just Web masters, the ability to publish.

WHAT HAS CISCO ACCOMPLISHED?

The company estimates that it avoids over 50,000 customer calls a week as a result of having digital commerce, pricing, and status agents handle the electronic transactions that generate sales and provide customer support. The open forum on Cisco Connection Online handles over 400 questions per week, with an average of only six being sent on to the technical assistance center for human response. The company is now responding to more than 200,000 questions per month, resolving 70 percent of its customers' needs online.

In June of 1997, CCO handled over 600,000 separate logins. One Cisco manager estimated that, without CCO, over 50 percent of those logins would have generated a phone call to Cisco, which in turn would have required well over 300 customer service representatives just to answer the calls and a substantial information system to support the representatives. Before CCO was implemented, Cisco received over 2000 calls a week just from customers checking on their order status. Now, CCO handles more than 70 percent of those kinds of calls, and the support staff can spend its time on more important value-added work.

There has already been extensive public recognition of these accomplishments. Cisco Connection Online recently won the ICEY outstanding achievement award from the Interactive Services Association, and was named one of the top 50 Web sites in the world by Webmaster Magazine. In addition, Cisco was ranked number one in ComputerWorld's "Best Places to Work for IT Professionals" in 1996.

More importantly, Cisco has publically estimated that by mid-year 1997 it was saving at least $250 million per year in administrative costs alone. This estimate includes $85 million in savings on software distribution costs, $125 million in customer support costs, over $8 million in recruiting and hiring costs, and well over $150 million in document production, distribution, handling, and filing costs.[32]

NOTES

[1] James F. Robeson and Robert G. House (eds.) *The Distribution Handbook*, The Free Press: London, New York, 1985.

[2] Alan S. Cohen. "The Coming Revolution in eBusiness." *Journal of Internet Purchasing.* www.arraydev.com/commerce/jip/9701-01.htm.

[3] http://www.supply.dla.mil/emall/homepg_h.htm.

[4] http://www.part.net/.

[5] http://206.128.188.135/.

[6] http://www.marketplace.zdnet.com/.

[7] http://www.industry.net/.

[8] Scott Wildemuth. "Aim carefully for I-net profits." *Datamation*, July 1997, p. 97–100.

[9] http://www.plasticsnet.com/.

[10] "Catalogs for the Digital Marketplace," CommerceNet Research Report, Note #97–03, Palo Alto, March 1997.

[11] Carrie Beam and Arie Segev. "Electronic Catalogs and Negotiations." Fisher Center for Management and Information Technology, U.C. Berkeley, Working Paper 96-WP-1016, Berkeley, August 1996.

[12] Arie Segev, Carrie Beam, and Judith Gebauer. "Impact of the Internet on Purchasing Practices: Preliminary Results from a Field Study," Fisher Center for Management and Information Technology, U.C. Berkeley, Working Paper 97–WP–1024, Berkeley, September 1997.

[13] Carrie Beam, Arie Segev, and J. George Shanthikumar. "Electronic Negotiation Through Internet-Based Auctions." Fisher Center for Management and Information Technology, U.C. Berkeley, Working Paper, 96-WP-1019, Berkeley, December 1996.

[14] Carrie Beam and Gene Fusz. "CXN: A Case Study." Fisher Center for Management and Information Technology, U.C. Berkeley, Working Paper, 97–WP–1025, Berkeley, October 1997.

[15] see Arie Segev, Carrie Beam and Judith Gebauer op. cit.

[16] *Computer Finance*, 1996, ec.com, May and June 1997.

[17] http://www.boeing.com/assocproducts/bpart/partpage/.

[18] Charles Kirk, "Fruit of the Loom's Channel Mastery Strategy," presentation provided at Calico eSeminar Broadcast Site, May 29, 1997 (http://www.calicotech.com/eseminar/kirk/open.html 6/30/1997); Lynda Radosevich, "The Fruits of Their Labors," CIO, *Web Commerce*, Nov 15, 1996, (http://www.cio.com/CIO/111596_fruits.html 6/30/1997); John Kador, "March of Electronic Commerce, Net Development Trends," *Electronic Commerce*, November 1996 (http://www.spgnet.com/NDT/nov96/commerce.htm 6/30/1997).

[19] http://www.tph.geis.com/.

[20] http://www.atracorp.com/.

[21] Judith Gebauer: Virtual Organizations from an Ecnomic Perspective, in J. Dias Coelho, T. Jelassi, W. König, H. Krcmar, R. O'Callaghan, M. Saaksjarvi (eds.): Proceedings of the 4th Eurpoean Conference on Information Systems (ECIS '96), Lissabon/Portugal, July 2–4, 1996.

[22] http://www.fvc.com/.

[23] http://ww.verifone.com/.

[24] http://www.inktomi.com/.

[25] http://www.intellaction.com/.

[26] http://www.calstart.com/.

[27] http://www.amazon.com/.

[28] See for example the enthusiastic plea by W. S. Davidow and M. S. Malone: The Virtual Corporation, New York 1992.

[29] The First Virtual Team: Perils and Pitfalls of Practical Internet Commerce (Part I), 1996 (http://www.firstvirtual.com/company/first_year1.html).

[30] Oswald and Boulton, 1995. "Obtaining Industry Control: The Case of the Pharmaceutical Distribution Industry," California Management Review (38:1, 138-162).

[31] Bob Swithers, VP of Technology Planning, Citicorp, quoted in Cisco Systems, Inc. 1996 Annual Report.

[32] Mark Tonneson, Director, Information System Customer Advocacy, presentation at Cisco Customer Center, August 5, 1997.

CONSUMER-FOCUSED ELECTRONIC COMMERCE

Throughout this book we have stressed the importance of relationships in conducting business, and the impact that the Internet and the World Wide Web are having on the formation, evolution, strength, and value of relationships. Many companies have discovered that loyal customers who feel that they are in a relationship with the company are worth far more than even well-established product brand names. After all, it is customers who buy the products, and it is repeat business from loyal, satisfied customers that turns products into brands. At the same time, customers are demanding more and more individualized attention, as well as customized products and services.

Thus, the new marketing game is to understand your customers and potential customers, build your products and services to meet their needs, and develop customer relationship processes that both fit your customer requirements and your product/service characteristics and enable you to reach the customers you want to reach, whenever and wherever they are. The Internet and the Web are an absolutely perfect way to accomplish these goals.

In this chapter we will first briefly review the basic rules of this new marketing game, and then look in detail at several examples of how companies are using the Internet to reach broader, more diverse, and more individualized consumers on a global basis. We are focusing here specifically on consumer marketing and selling; business-to-business relationships are covered separately in Chapter 6.

The Internet is the essential infrastructure that makes one-to-one, relationship-based marketing and product customization both practically and economically feasible. On a mass basis, you can now present individualized information (product choices, advertising, even prices) to literally thousands of different customers. With Web technology, you can track individual browsing and buying patterns (including the frequency of "hits" on your site and return visits); you can segment your marketplace based on actual shopping and buying behaviors; you can provide highly personalized and very inexpensive customer service on a 24-hours-a-day, 7-days-a-week basis; and you can learn from experience, adapting every aspect of your business to meet customer requirements in real time on an ongoing basis.

The Web is generating fundamental changes in every aspect of consumer marketing, including the marketing and selling experience (for both the consumer and the business provider), the marketing/selling/customer service processes (including all the behind-the-scenes business activities that support the actual transactions), and ultimately the relationship between company and consumer. The Web also offers companies facing intense price competition in global markets a whole new way to differentiate themselves from less progressive competitors.[1]

THE NEW MARKETING GAME

The new marketing game is all about building long-term relationships with customers. Your business challenge is to find the right customers, get your message heard, meet customer demands and expectations, and maintain an ongoing, interactive dialog over an extended period of time.

In this section, we will first examine the concept of customer loyalty and the value of long-term relationships with customers. We will then look at the concept of mass customization, the battle for customer attention, and the many ways the Web allows companies to alter their marketing, promotion, pricing, distribution, and service strategies in pursuit of effective, long-term, profitable relationships.

CUSTOMER LOYALTY AND THE VALUE OF CUSTOMER RETENTION

Frederick Reichheld of Bain & Company, along with a group of researchers at the Harvard Business School, has demonstrated quite conclusively that long-term customers are the key to corporate profitability. In a series of articles in the *Harvard Business Review* Reichheld and his colleagues have demonstrated that improving customer retention rates by as little as 5 percent can almost double a company's profits.[2]

Consider State Farm Insurance. Insurance is basically a commodity business; with only minor variations, a customer can find almost identical insurance policies from any number of different companies. Most forms of insurance are highly regulated at the state level, almost guaranteeing uniform products. And insurance customers are notorious for price-shopping and frequent switching. Yet State Farm manages to retain over 95 percent of its customers, and has agents who are 40 percent more productive than the industry average.[3]

Customer loyalty is obviously important in a business like life insurance, where product differentiation is often difficult to achieve. But it is just as important in more traditionally basic industries, like automobile sales. Car owners typically purchase about seven to ten cars during their adult lifetimes, and switching is common here too. Consider, however, the total value of a loyal customer who purchases each of those seven new cars from the same manufacturer; the total revenue over the lifetime of the customer can easily exceed $250,000 for the cars alone, let alone the services and replacement parts.

But just as important as the revenue potential over a customer's lifetime is the fact that it costs a whole lot less to retain an existing customer than it does to attract a new one. Much of the marketing effort of most companies (especially consumer product companies) focuses on how to create product or brand awareness in the first place. Yet, as Reichheld and others have clearly shown, the easiest (and cheapest) prospects to reach and convince are your current customers. Thus, successful companies today focus on satisfying and retaining their current customers.

THE VALUE OF LONG-TERM RELATIONSHIPS

But the new marketing game goes much deeper than that. As companies shift their focus to retaining profitable customers, they are learning that some kinds of relationships are longer-lasting and more intense than others. As discussed in Chapter 4, customer relationships built on some form of structural dependence or emotional ties are almost always much more enduring and profitable than those built on simple factors like price, convenience, or even quality.

Thus concepts of the "lifetime value" of a customer and the share of a customer's total purchases over time are increasingly replacing the simplistic notion of market share as a measure of marketplace effectiveness. Historically, companies used market share as a measure of marketplace success largely because it was relatively easy to define and capture the data. And companies could track their product sales simply by counting what was going out the door.

It is much more difficult to count repeat purchases by individual customers. First, you have to know who the customers are. Then you have to wait for them to come back and buy again (easy for perishables like beer, toothpaste, or floor wax, but a lot tougher for products like cars, shoes, refrigerators, or lawn mowers that are purchased relatively infrequently). Yet the lifetime customer value, or LCV, can be calculated with some degree of accuracy, and it is an increasingly important measure of a company's future earnings potential.[4]

Focusing on customer retention and loyalty is clearly the right strategy for most businesses; highly satisfied customers typically tell ten or more friends about their positive experiences, in effect becoming a second sales force for the company. And the potential for profit improvement resulting from retaining good customers is enormous.

Product Diversity and Mass Customization

Customer relationships have become more crucial for another reason: the number and diversity of products available in the marketplace has absolutely exploded in the last ten years. The average supermarket now has over 30,000 SKUs, and there are over 600 microbreweries in the United States alone. Remember when there were only three major television networks? Now there are well over 50 cable television channels and at least five major networks, with more on the way. And there are well over 1,000 long-distance telephone companies now operating in the United States.

As Regis McKenna has said, choice has replaced brand in almost every industry.[5] And not only are there many more choices than there used to be, but the economy, as we have noted, has become global. Many more of the choices available to consumers come from outside their own country, further complicating the product selection process, but also of course enriching it immeasurably.

An additional factor affecting the number and diversity of product choices is the movement towards mass customization—the ability of manufacturers to produce many variations on their basic products at very low incremental cost. As futurist Alvin Toffler noted many years ago, companies can now produce variety at virtually the same cost as uniformity. The result is that today you can choose to buy Coke Classic, Diet Coke, Caffeine-Free Diet Coke, Caffeine-Free Diet Cherry Coke . . . and so on. Where there used to be just a few basic flavors and sizes of Jello, there are now dozens of variations (even including special large-letter packaging for senior citizens).

With all the choices out there, advertising has become more important—and more pervasive—than ever. Customers are bombarded with advertisements everywhere they turn: television, radio, magazines, newspapers, billboards, city buses, baseball parks, movie theaters, and now the Internet. The marketing challenge of the '90s is simply to get the customer's attention.

This explosion in choice, while desirable in terms of offering customers the opportunity to find exactly what they want, also means more work for the customer: work to find exactly the right choice, and continual stress worrying that there might be something even better somewhere. So consumers are also looking for long-term relationships as a way to simplify their lives and reduce the number of choices they face in the global, hyperfast, confusing marketplace.

Of course, getting the customer's attention, offering the "right" choice, and then building a meaningful long-term relationship is clearly anything but simple. With all those other marketing messages screaming at consumers, how can you possibly get your message through?

One fundamental principle of effective marketing is to have something to say that individual customers want to hear—to have information that customers are looking for. Or, to put it another way, to send your message only to people who want to hear it and who will respond in the way you want them to.

This is where the power of the Internet (and the customer data it enables you to capture, store, and interpret) becomes truly impressive. By knowing who your customers are, what they want, and when they are ready to buy, you can target your message directly at those individuals who most want to hear it. And with the World Wide Web, you can send your message right to their desktops.

As we have demonstrated, the Web makes it very easy to identify who your customers and potential customers are, to capture personal data about them (including demographic data, expressed preferences, and actual buying behaviors), and to tailor your marketing messages and product/service choices based on that information. Thus, the Web enables you to segment your customers in fine detail, track their browsing and buying patterns, and individualize your Web sites based on who is doing the browsing. The Web makes one-to-one marketing on a mass scale both possible and economic. Consider the two most successful Web-based retailing ventures to date: Amazon.com and Virtual Vineyards. Both companies make extensive use of targeted mailing lists to inform customers of new offers that fit past buying patterns and self-identified preferences.

The challenge, though, is to use the Web effectively, to treat it as a medium for reaching the right customers with the right messages, and to employ the marketing and selling techniques that are most appropriate for your particular value proposition. The relationship matrix, introduced in Chapter 4, suggests how you can use either structural or emotional bonds, or both, to tie your chosen customers to your company and its products/services.

The Web can be an effective medium for either kind of retention strategy (and, of course, many companies use both). For example, The Gap and Levi Strauss both offer several features on their Web sites that appeal to customers' emotions: style guides, samples of print and television advertising that are focused on high style, elegant photographs of models wearing new fashions, and news about the company. The store locator databases offered by each company are good examples of structural techniques; they are easy-to-use information sources that provide real value to customers and are designed to be unique sources of information that will keep customers coming back. Virtual Vineyards makes excellent use of a wine and food information database that offers customers products and information they can't get anywhere else.

THE BATTLE FOR CUSTOMER ATTENTION

Companies use many different strategies to attract and retain customers. Among the classic approaches (familiar to any consumer) are promotions (special-offer discounts, two-for-one deals, coupons, etc.), rebates, "big splash" ad campaigns, unusual ads or campaigns (such as those unveiled at the Super Bowl each January), testimonials by Hollywood stars or well-known athletes, and of course humor.

In the world of the Internet, companies are using all the power and capabilities of the graphical browser format to generate interest. Entertaining logos and other graphics, often with the added power of full-motion video and/or Java-enabled moving cartoons and banners, are the most common eye-catching techniques. Current versions of the leading browsers also allow multiple frames on a single screen, to divide the content and feature eye-catching headlines or scrolling menus. The battle to "capture eyeballs" is on in full force.

But clever and entertaining graphics are only one way to create attention, and they do little to build meaningful relationships. Some companies are also relying on other time-tested techniques, such as lotteries and free give-aways, and are continually changing the content of their Web pages to bring consumers back over and over again. For example, Amazon .com, the highly successful Web-based bookstore, promotes and deeply discounts specific books, but the discounted titles change daily in order to encourage interested consumers to come back frequently. Amazon.com also features a weekly lottery that offers a free book every week for a year. Both of these techniques are time-tested angles designed to generate repeat "hits" (bringing people back frequently), on the theory that some percentage of the time these return customers will actually purchase something.

However, these techniques, as intriguing and creative as they might be, do not generally build either structural or emotional bonds with consumers. At best, they create interest and offer novelty, or a "good deal." But, as we have noted, these strategies by themselves are hardly a basis for developing long-term relationships with customers.

Amazon.com is an excellent example of how to use both structural and emotional bonds to tie customers to a Web site. The company's searchable database of 2.5 million titles is clearly a structural relationship tool; customers discover quickly that there is no other place on the Web (or anywhere else, for that matter) where they can find such an extensive, easy-to-use, and accessible database of books in and out of print. And the fact that they can go immediately from a successful search to placing an order just adds to their dependence on Amazon.com.

The company's ordering process is itself another example of a structural tool; customers can enter their shipping address and credit-card information once, and then place multiple orders quickly and easily (and securely)—another reason for consumers to stay with Amazon.com.

Finally, perhaps the strongest structural bond that Amazon .com offers is the convenience of having orders delivered directly to the customer's home or office just a day or two after the order is placed. Amazon.com's value proposition is thus a combination of accessibility to 2.5 million titles, ease of ordering, and ease of acquiring the books once they have been ordered. For busy, time-starved consumers, this combination creates a significant competitive advantage and a strong tendency to buy again.

Cybergold, described in detail in Chapter 4, is taking the battle for consumer attention one step further by creating longer-term economic bonds with its customers. Cybergold's entire business proposition is based on the concept of delivering information about company products and services to exactly those consumers who are interested and demographically "correct" for your company. Cybergold is paying consumers directly to look at advertisements. It remains to be seen whether this value proposition will create the kind of longer-term structural or emotional ties that, as we have emphasized, are the ones that create mutually profitable relationships.

REAL-TIME MARKETING

Another aspect of the new marketing game is the fact that information, whether it is marketing information, sales transaction data, or post-sale support information, is available to both consumers and providers on a virtually real-time basis anywhere in the world through a local phone call.

The real-time, interactive nature of Web-based information introduces a number of new possibilities and opportunities for companies who want to reach consumers and build customer relationships. As Regis McKenna has pointed out,[6] real-time interactivity enables companies to have ongoing "conversations" with their customers. These conversations can include every aspect of marketing—from product conceptualization and design through marketing and information exchange, the purchase transaction itself, and post-sale support. As McKenna says, "The power of the new media lies in their ability to draw the customer into a conversation with the company."[7] And these conversations can become the basis for building long-lasting relationships with your customers, because they engage the customer in your processes and product design activity, and create both structural and emotional bonds.

The Web enables you to generate and support these "conversations" with individual customers at a remarkably low cost, and in ways that will provide you with even more extensive information about their likes and dislikes as well as their purchasing habits. There is software available today that allows you to build personalized Web pages for individual customers, based on your knowledge of their preferences, demographics, and history with your company. Thus, customers who sign on to your site will see product and service information selected specifically for them.[8]

In fact, the Web is in many ways a better "listener" and learner than a human being; it is always accessible from any location, it "remembers" exactly what the customer said and did in past interactions, and it can "learn" to provide customers with exactly the information they are looking for.[9]

FROM ATTENTION TO INVOLVEMENT

Conversations with consumers provide companies with marvelous opportunities to engage them in discussions about their product wants and needs, their views on current products and competitors' products, and their overall levels of satisfaction. This kind of information is invaluable in helping companies tailor products, processes, and customer support practices even more closely to what their customers want and need.

Netscape provides perhaps the best example of how customers can become an integral part of a company's product development and marketing cycle. Forget for a moment all the hype about Netscape as an Internet company and a Wall Street darling, and just look at how Netscape designs, builds, and modifies products. The company's entire philosophy is aimed at collaborating with customers over a radically shortened product development cycle. This approach has given Netscape a solid hold on the browser market and helped it, so far, to stay ahead of Microsoft in the battle for loyal customers.

Netscape develops its new generations of browser software to only about 80 percent of the design goal before "going public" with them. The whole strategy, as one of Netscape's product managers puts it, is to "get to Beta as soon as possible." The Beta version is made widely available to willing customers (who of course download the software over the Internet with no incremental cost to Netscape). The Beta testers know full well the product is incomplete and might crash occasionally; the "pull" for the consumers is to gain access to next-generation software features well ahead of the general public.

But here is the key to this strategy of distributing "incomplete" products: Netscape asks its customers to provide feedback and suggestions, and to identify all the problems they find with the Beta version. In effect, Netscape has turned its customers into product developers; the company gets a tremendous amount of essentially free product development work and, in return, the customers have early access to the software and a strong sense of making a contribution to an exciting, leading-edge product and a "hot" company.

But that isn't all. Once the Netscape browser is released in its "final" version, Netscape offers a cash reward to anyone finding a bug or a security flaw in the software. Over the first two years after they initially made this offer, Netscape spent more than $100,000 rewarding customers for finding product problems. Expensive? No. It's incredibly cheap for what Netscape got in return: over 100 product flaws discovered and fixed, at a cost less than the annual salary of one good product manager. Netscape also received plenty of favorable publicity in the marketplace by being so open about the imperfections in its core product.

Even more than that, the company also gained hundreds of customers who feel deep commitment to and even "ownership" of Netscape Navigator. Those customers believe the product is theirs as much as it is Netscape's. What more could a company ask for than to have its customers feel ownership and involvement in its products? All the advertising and glitzy trade-show exhibits in the world can't generate that kind of emotional bond between a company and its customers.

Another example of a Web-based business that engages customers in dialog and gains real-time meaningful feedback is Worldwide Music. This company is a Web-based music store that offers consumers database-searching capabilities much like Amazon.com. However, because of the nature of its product, Worldwide Music can actually offer downloadable samples of the music from any of its CDs. But Worldwide Music doesn't stop there; at the bottom of its Web page is a feedback questionnaire that asks consumers to rate each piece of music they listen to. The feedback provides the company with ongoing assessments of the popularity of its titles, so it can do a better job of ordering and stocking titles. Where a traditional company has to estimate future sales from data about current and past purchases, Worldwide Music actually gets information from customers about the products they did not buy.

But Worldwide Music goes even further by tracking the kinds of music that individual customers like and do not like, and comparing this information with the choices of other customers. Thus, the company can actually recommend new CDs to you based on your expressed preferences and the similarity between your preferences and those of other customers with similar tastes.

Similarly, Virtual Vineyards not only offers its wine-tasting advice and judgment, but actively solicits feedback from customers. Wine expert Peter Granoff (The "Cork Dork") corresponds regularly with customers and prospects, a level of interaction that turns product purchasing into an ongoing conversation.

Amazon.com also encourages customer feedback, inviting Web visitors to write their own book reviews and post them for other readers, or even to send e-mail directly to authors.

All of these companies have found ways to use the Web not just to generate dialog, but to conduct ongoing market research with their active customers—to learn from them and to inform them. These are marvelous examples of how the Web can create a type of relationship with customers—deep involvement—that is not possible with any other medium.

FROM INVOLVEMENT TO COMMUNITY

The company that appears to have taken this concept of identifying and exploiting customer likes and dislikes the furthest is Firefly. A Massachusetts-based business, Firefly collects extensive data about consumers, who voluntarily sign up and provide background information about themselves. Then, in reviewing Firefly's various listings of movies, books, and music and answering questions about their preferences, consumers reveal more about themselves and their likes and dislikes. Firefly then uses massive parallel processing computers to relate each individual consumer's preferences to those of other customers, and then that information enables the company to suggest additional movies, books, or CDs that the individual might like, based on the likes and dislikes of others who have similar patterns. Thus, Firefly is creating "communities of interest" among people who have never met; the company essentially generates information for you that heretofore you would have relied on trusted friends for.

But Firefly goes even further, enabling you to get in touch with your cyberspace "soulmates" through a series of chat forums and bulletin boards.

This process often generates surprising and intriguing connections. For example, if you like both the Beatles and Beethoven, you might also like romance novels with a European setting. And if you are a 27-year-old female medical student living in Boston, you might discover a 63-year-old retired aerospace engineer in La Jolla who has similar interests, and develop a wonderfully satisfying "pen pal" relationship through Firefly. Or you might even find someone whose career and lifestyle interests are more nearly identical to yours.

What does this have to do with marketing and selling on the Web? People are at heart social creatures, and they value finding companionship. Many companies have discovered the power of customer communities, and there are certainly many examples of customer communities that do not depend on the Internet or the World Wide Web. But this global communication infrastructure clearly facilitates and leverages the formation of communities that would probably never develop otherwise.

This ability to link like-minded people together can be unbelievably powerful, for both good and bad. For example, Toyota uses its Web site to advertise and foster Toyota owner's clubs. Nike, Levi Strauss & Co., Mpath Interactive, Amazon.com, Virtual Vineyards, and many other consumer product companies also use the Web to encourage and enable the formation of "clubs" and other kinds of customer communities.

At the same time, the Web also gives unhappy customers a place to voice their anger and frustration, and even to find other disgruntled individuals. One Web site (no longer in existence) was called, appropriately, Lemon.org, and was devoted exclusively to telling the world about the shortcomings of the Isuzu Trooper. More significantly, however, it was also a means of bringing unhappy Isuzu owners together and enabling them collaboratively to develop strategies for mass action. This example highlights the value of helping your customers organize to support you, because if you don't, the chances are they will organize themselves, and you will have much less control of the outcome.

Community is another very powerful form of emotional bond. Companies that build genuine communities among their customers have an almost guaranteed base of loyal, long-term, and profitable buyers.[10]

WEB-BASED MARKETING AND SELLING PROCESSES

These examples begin to demonstrate how Web-based marketing and selling is genuinely different from traditional business models. The characteristics of the technology lead to very different kinds of relationships between companies and their customers—relationships that are much more dynamic and interactive, based on structural and/or emotional bonds.

We have previously discussed the core characteristics of the Web that make it a whole new medium and a different kind of marketplace. The Web with its underlying technologies is:

- Interactive
- Immediate
- Interconnected
- Individually addressable
- Cross-platform
- Rich
- Easy to use

These characteristics and capabilities enable fundamental transformations in the way companies design, build, promote, sell, deliver, and support both products and services. To understand these transformations in more detail, consider the sequence of major steps that a buyer and a seller go through for any kind of transaction (see Figure 7-1). From a buyer's perspective, a transaction process includes four basic steps:

1. Identify the need.
2. Find sources for fulfilling the need.
3. Purchase and acquire the product or service.
4. Use, maintain, and (eventually) dispose of the product or service.

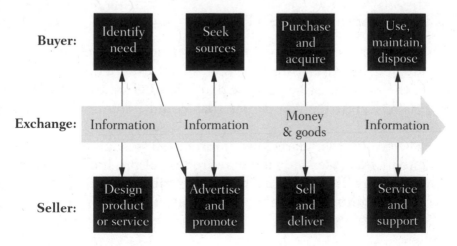

FIGURE 7-1. The transaction cycle.

For the manufacturer or seller, each of the four buyer steps has a mirror-image activity:

1. Design and produce the product or service.
2. Advertise and promote.
3. Sell and distribute or deliver.
4. Service and support the customer.

The Web has a very dramatic impact on each step in this process. First, the buyer and seller can engage in an extended "conversation" about the product or service design very early in the transaction cycle. Second, as buyers seek out prospective sellers, they have a much wider range of choices, and can access all of them from their own desktops. Third, the terms of the deal can be negotiated more broadly, with customers conducting multiple simultaneous negotiations with various providers (with the wider range of choices available to buyers, they are often in a much stronger negotiating position).

We will now briefly examine each of these four basic steps in the transaction cycle, paying particular attention to how the characteristics and capabilities of the Web affect the buyer, the seller, the exchange, and the formation of meaningful relationships between the two parties.

1. IDENTIFY NEED/DESIGN AND PRODUCE

The consumer might have an obvious need, or the need might be created by advertising or other social experiences. In any case, the need must be identified and felt before the customer begins a search for companies that could potentially fill the need.

The Web is a marvelous information resource that undoubtedly increases individual awareness of product or service opportunities. Reviewing a site that describes hot new software or provides information about new mutual funds or new book titles is certainly one way to develop a "need" for a product or service.

The Web can also act as a catalyst, a way for consumers to search for information about products and services before they begin to seek out a specific source or provider. This basic search for information in itself often clarifies needs and generates or increases demand.

Providers also use the Web to conduct market research, determining who their potential customers are and what they want. More importantly, they can actively solicit comments and product requirements from past, present, and future customers, in effect involving them directly in the product design and development process. While the Web might not replace more traditional forms of market research like surveys, focus groups, and interviews, it can certainly supplement them by allowing a company to reach a much larger and more geographically diverse set of prospective buyers at a significantly reduced cost.

2. FIND A SOURCE/ADVERTISE AND PROMOTE

Having decided he or she is "in the market," a customer begins actively looking for the best company from which to buy. At this stage, all the traditional factors in the marketing equation become important: product features, price, availability, etc. Brand name and reputation are obviously important at this point, though more for some kinds of products than for others. In any event, the customer searches through advertisements, goes shopping, talks to friends, observes what others have purchased, and generally narrows down the selection of providers.

Clearly, the Web facilitates the search for a provider of the desired product or service. In fact, the range and breadth of information about potential sources for products and services could be the single most significant value-added element of the Web. Literally millions of Web pages are available to anyone who has a PC and a modem. Powerful search engines help you get to Web sites with potentially interesting and relevant information. The Web puts consumers in a global shopping mall and enables virtually instantaneous shifts from one "store" to another. Comparison shopping is a breeze. For example, if you are in the market for a home mortgage or a consumer loan, you can go right from one bank's Web site to another, and find the cheapest interest rates and the best terms in just a few minutes, without ever leaving your desk.

From the producer's side, the Web is, if nothing else, a worldwide information distribution channel. Companies that establish a Web site and advertise on other sites can reach a much larger global audience at significantly lower price than through almost any other medium. One small, family-run coffee shop in Hawaii closed its shopping center outlet because the rent was too high, opened a Web site, and tripled their business. They are now shipping Kona coffee all over the world out of a garage that has a space cost of literally a fraction of the rent they had been paying in the mall.

3. PURCHASE AND ACQUIRE/SELL AND DELIVER

Finally, when all the choices have been made and the terms agreed on, the purchase transaction is completed. This transaction involves an exchange between the seller and the buyer; a product or service is given in return for a sum of money.

The actual sale (and delivery) of a product or service can be consummated in a Web-based business at a much lower cost than in most retail outlets or telephone catalog operations. After all, the customer does almost all the work, filling out the online order form, indicating a payment method (typically a credit card, which essentially eliminates the seller's financial risk from the transaction), and making the purchase commitment—all without tying up any high-priced labor from the selling organization.

If your product is a "hard good" like books, wine, computers, or home electronics, you will of course need to have some kind of distribution and delivery capability. However, as we have already noted, many Web-based businesses, like Amazon.com, Virtual Vineyards, and OnSale.com, essentially outsource that activity to distribution and logistics firms like Federal Express and UPS.

Some experts have predicted that the whole process of buying will be transformed by the increase in choices available to consumers. The market could become a genuine buyers' market; imagine a customer announcing, "I am in the market for a stereo. Who wants to bid on my purchase?" and then picking the best price from a wide variety of providers who are essentially bidding for the consumer's business.

4. Use, Maintain, Dispose/Service and Support

Once purchased, the product is used or consumed, maintained (where necessary), and eventually disposed of. For many products and services there is little or no interaction between buyer and seller after the sale, but for an increasing number of items there is a very significant level of postsale support required. For example, cars require servicing and buyers of PCs and other consumer electronics products often want training, advice, or assistance as they begin to use the product and later on as they change or adapt its configuration.

The Web paradigm enables companies to provide significant postsale support to customers at an extremely low cost. A Web site with extensive text and graphic information as well as interactive capabilities can often reduce customer calls to service representatives by as much as 70 to 80 percent. Product manuals can be provided online, enabling customers to download current information at a very low cost to the provider organization. Just think of the savings in printing and mailing costs alone, as well as the elimination of out-of-date inventories of catalogs and manuals.

Federal Express reportedly reduces customer inquiry costs by a factor of over 100 every time a customer tracks a package on its Web site instead of calling the customer service center.

Assembling a Business

One of the reasons the Web is so powerful is that it has grown up at a time when many other components of the economy are already in place to enable the development of "virtual businesses." Thus, when someone has an idea of a product or a service that could be sold over the Web, it is possible almost overnight to assemble the functional capabilities needed to produce a whole business model.

For example, Amazon.com put all its creative resources into designing and developing the software that enables it to present a searchable database of over 2.5 million titles to customers, and then to process the resulting orders. All the other major processes in the Amazon.com business model are essentially outsourced. When you place an order with Amazon.com, the company generates an order of its own to a regional distributor, has the books shipped to you by UPS or another carrier, and processes your payment through the banking system and your credit card. Thus, Amazon.com focuses on the customer relationship elements of their business; all the other functions and processes are handled by other companies who are much more efficient and accurate at their distinctive competencies than Amazon.com could ever hope to be (or want to be).

The net result, of course, is that Amazon.com grew from virtually nothing to a full-fledged book distribution business with global reach in a very, very short time. And it did so at much lower cost than anyone had ever imagined would be possible. The real message here is that Amazon.com redefined the economics of selling and distributing books. The company provides its customers with a distinctive value proposition (convenient searching and ordering, discounted prices, and home delivery, as well as extensive, personalized information about books of possible interest to the customer) and does so with a revolutionary cost model that has already dramatically affected the industry and provided stockholders with a handsome return on their investment.

PROCESS TRANSFORMATION

The four steps in the transaction cycle described above, in their purest form, are a chronological progression in the basic set of business processes that any company creates to enable the development, sale, and support of a product or service. In the Web environment, this transaction cycle speeds up and the value chain becomes a "frictionless" flow as the four previously discrete steps blend and merge into each other. The Web enables such rapid and inexpensive communication between companies and their customers, and within companies, that the business processes enabling these communications and their associated transactions must themselves be fundamentally transformed.

To understand the nature and extent of these transformations, let us shift our attention for a few moments away from the customer and look more closely at the business activities and processes that companies employ to create value for customers and to retain customers through continuing service and support. For this inside-the-business perspective, it is helpful to think in terms of a relationship life cycle rather than a transaction life cycle, since the overriding goal is to build and maintain meaningful (and profitable) relationships with customers. Each underlying business process must be examined in terms of how it contributes to this goal.

The decision to build a public Web site focused on customers and business generation almost inevitably raises questions about how the key business processes will operate and be managed. Figure 7-2 highlights our observation that as a company moves toward real-time, Web-based interactions in each of these four steps, the underlying business processes themselves become more and more intertwined and inseparable.

Let's look at this cycle more closely as it manifests itself in a Web-based business, starting with the upper-right quadrant, product design and development. As suggested earlier, companies that are focused on customer retention and ensuring that their products meet customer needs are finding creative ways to engage their customers and prospective customers in defining product requirements, identifying their needs, and reviewing product designs. Remember, for example, the Netscape practice of inviting customers into the very heart of creating and debugging its evolving browser software. Or consider the way

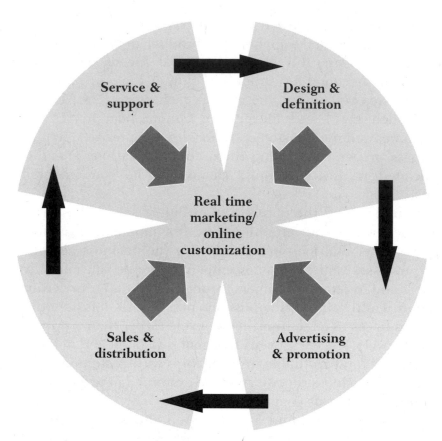

FIGURE 7-2. The relationship cycle.

Worldwide Music treats every customer interaction as an opportunity for feedback and market research, which then influences the selection and packaging of future product offerings.

The most common use of Web sites to date has been for marketing and advertising. The Web, after all, is primarily an information distribution platform, and it provides companies with a relatively inexpensive means of making product information easily accessible to a global audience.

Many companies are discovering that active Web sites can both increase their reach to an important customer base and reduce their marketing and advertising costs. Compared with the cost per reader or per viewer of advertising in more traditional media, Web-based advertising (whether on your own Web site or paid advertising on someone else's site) is a bargain. Not only is the cost often much less than that of a television commercial or print advertisement, but the cost of getting the information to the target audience is orders of magnitude lower on the Web.

Many companies also report a reduction in their costs of printing and mailing catalogs, on the order of millions of dollars annually. And, of course, it is far easier to keep catalog and other information accurate and current; updating it is just a matter of changing the master file on the Web server.

What's more, with a well-designed Web site, a company can get almost immediate feedback on how many "impressions" or "hits" it has gotten, and can even collect information about the people viewing the site, and their reactions to the advertisement or product information (another example of the ongoing conversations with customers enabled by the Web). Thus, information that is incorrect, incomplete, or confusing can be quickly modified, further improving the effectiveness of the marketing effort.

The stage in the relationship cycle that has generated the most public discussion is certainly selling and distribution. It is here, after all, where actual revenues are generated, and when the question "Is anyone making money on the Web?" is asked, it is this step that is the focus of attention. All the discussions about privacy, security, and the size of the Web-based market center around this one step in the total relationship cycle. As important as those discussions are, remember that they deal with only one part of a much more complete and complex cycle of relationship-focused business processes.

Interactive Web sites can be designed to collect all the information needed to complete a transaction. The customer order itself, billing and shipping information, and even market research data about the customer's buying motives and expectations can all be collected at the time of the sale. And, of course, the Web site can be designed to respond differently to different customers, depending on the information they provide.

In addition, your Web page can also inform your customers about follow-up services and launch some form of ongoing interaction, such as a company or product-specific newsletter, or membership in a customer "club" of some kind. These are all examples of how to use the Web as part of a customer retention strategy that makes extensive use of structural and emotional bonds to link the customer and the company.

All of this information, of course, must be compiled, processed, and stored in the company's data files, which typically reside on large mainframe computers or departmental servers. A major part of a Web implementation effort is typically devoted to linking up Web-based applications and files with legacy systems.

The fourth stage in the relationship life cycle is service and support. Many successful companies have learned in the past decade that a sale marks not the end of the customer relationship but the beginning of an ongoing—and hopefully long-term—series of interactions and relationships with the customer. More and more of the products and services in today's economy are complex ones that require regular service, upgrades, or customer instruction to solve unexpected problems with usage. And there are other good reasons to stay in touch, such as providing customers with information about new products, add-ons, or news items of interest.

The Web provides a particularly effective and highly efficient means of staying in touch with customers and providing needed support. Product manuals can be stored on the Web, making them accessible by customers when they are needed. Frequently asked questions can be cataloged and displayed, or placed in a searchable database to enable customers to solve their own problems without placing any demands on company employees.

Here again the cost savings can be enormous, in not printing product manuals, not mailing the manuals (especially to customers who don't want them), not having to send out updated or replacement product information, and not having to employ as many customer service representatives to answer telephone calls. Of course, Web sites will never replace all human-to-human interaction, but they do enable companies to respond to the most common and simplest requests for help at an extremely low cost, saving more expensive human labor to deal with the fewer but more difficult and crucial questions.[11]

The most important aspect of this framework is that it highlights how these four stages of the relationship, each with its own key processes and information requirements, are increasingly becoming interdependent and overlapping. As a business becomes more real-time, the boundaries between these four stages become fuzzier and fuzzier. On a Web site, customers can find the product or service they are looking for, learn about it through promotional information, commit to purchasing it, consummate the purchase, arrange for payment and shipping, and even begin to draw on the company's service and support capabilities—all in one "visit." And if the product is a "soft" good like music, software, or a text or data file, the product can even be delivered over the Web instantaneously. Finally, of course, customer feedback can also be solicited, bringing the customer right into the design and development phase for the next-generation product.

MANAGING WEB-BASED PROCESSES: BECOMING A REAL-TIME BUSINESS

This blending of the entire customer interaction into one seamless, continuous flow creates both marvelous opportunities and difficult management challenges for companies. As the customer interaction becomes real-time and continuous, the company's operational business processes and its management practices must also become increasingly seamless and integrated.

Consider, for example, how Bank of America has organized responsibilities for its Web site. The Web team was established as a special integrated unit reporting to the Senior Vice President for Retail Banking. The team includes both IT and marketing specialists, but it also draws on many other key departments throughout the bank, including legal, public affairs, banking operations, and customer relations. Each of these specialized functions contributes to the design and operation of the Web site.

In many ways, a Web site is a miniature version of the entire company; it is a "store front," but it also requires a marketing department, a sales and fulfillment process, customer service, and all the legal and accounting activities that are needed for any complete business to function. And these functions and processes must operate in real time, which is a marked difference from the way they are normally designed to work.

This real-time operation is also important from a customer relationship and customer service perspective. Customers usually don't know—and they very rarely care—how a company is organized; they just want their problems solved or their informational needs met. With an integrated, real-time Web site, the customer truly does have "one window" into the company.[12]

For many companies, the continuous, integrated nature of these processes enables continuous, ongoing interaction with customers and continuous provision of customer support. Some software companies, for example, provide automatic and automated software upgrades, literally loading software on customer computers as it becomes available (the customer might not even know until after the fact that the software is new, having earlier signed a licensing agreement that includes this kind of real-time support).

Alvin Toffler has suggested that, in the economy of the future, even payments to employees and suppliers might be done on a continuous basis. After all, the tradition of weekly paychecks and monthly billing cycles arose largely because the cost and time involved in calculating payments, withholdings, and payment terms made it impractical to cut checks or issue invoices more frequently. Now, with a comprehensive global communications infrastructure and fully automated business processes, there is no longer any need for delays in completing the financial side of a transaction. And we know that, eventually, virtually all regular transactions will be paid electronically, with e-mail messages confirming that payments have been made or allowing the payer to preview the bill and then simply click a virtual button in the message to authorize an instant transfer of funds.

MANAGEMENT CHALLENGES

No matter how big the consumer electronic marketplace becomes or how fast it grows, the management challenges will be essentially the same:

- Developing a clear customer relationship strategy that is aligned with the capabilities of the Web and consistent with your products, services, and customer value propositions.
- Designing, implementing, and maintaining an effective Web site that is consistent with your company's market positioning and your customers' wants and needs.
- Ensuring that the organization team supporting the Web activity is appropriately balanced between technologists and marketers, and is connected effectively with the senior executives responsible for the business unit.

GUIDELINES FOR SUCCESS

Because the Web and the electronic marketplace are still very new, we offer only a few basic guidelines for successful consumer marketing:

- Develop a Web strategy and design that is consistent with your company's customers, customer requirements, and product/service capabilities.
- Look for ways to use the Web's unique characteristics (interactivity, ubiquity, multimedia, global reach, and individualization) to create preemptive strikes in the consumer marketplace—to differentiate yourself from the competition and to create unexpected value for your chosen customers.
- Actively search for ways to include features in the Web site that create structural and emotional bonds that will keep your customers coming back.
- Be realistic, and learn by doing. Start with a pilot, perhaps aimed at one particular customer segment or supporting one product line. Build a promotional site before you attempt to support an interactive or customized one. Don't wait until the Web design is perfect or super-powerful. Get a Web site up,

encourage customer feedback, and expect to redesign it completely every two to three months for at least the first year.

· Link the Web site to your existing marketing organization and its leaders, but don't let it be dominated by them. The Web represents a revolutionary opportunity that you don't want to constrain, but if the current management team is not actively involved in guiding the implementation and learning from it, they can hardly be expected to embrace it.

These challenges are discussed in more detail in chapter 8.

CASE STUDIES

The case examples in this chapter describe three companies that used the World Wide Web to create fundamentally new consumer businesses. *Virtual Vineyards* is a specialty wine retailer that offers consumers extensive information about fine wines and relies on public shippers like FedEx and UPS to deliver its products directly to their homes. *Mpath Interactive* is focused on the interactive gaming market, offering Web surfers an opportunity to play highly engaging computer-based games in "competition" with other surfers, no matter where in the world they are. *Onsale.com* sells high-tech equipment like PCs and stereos over the Net using an online auction format in which potential buyers can keep raising their bids, based on what others have bid and their own interest in acquiring the products.

All three companies are playing the "new marketing game" extremely well, with a clear understanding of their niche markets and explicit (but very different) strategies for attracting and retaining profitable customers.

VIRTUAL VINEYARDS

Can you imagine buying fine wines without being able to taste them, or even to see the bottle? It is a bit hard to imagine that something as "physical" and unique as an expensive wine could be sold sight unseen (and taste untested) over the Internet, but Virtual Vineyards seems to prove that many of our expectations about what will and what will not sell through this new electronic medium might be wrong.

Peter Granoff and Robert Olson launched Virtual Vineyards (http://www.virtualvin.com) in 1994. Granoff, a highly successful sommelier, and Robert Olson, a computer company executive, blended their skills to create a new kind of business—a "virtual" wine store. Virtual Vineyards sells fine wine and gourmet foods directly to consumers over the World Wide Web; there is no physical storefront facility, and no way for customers to actually taste the wines before buying them. In spite of that reality, the company has been one of the few successful Web-based consumer businesses.

Granoff's desire to build Virtual Vineyards stemmed from two trends in wine retailing that he personally disliked. Recent consolidation among wine distributors meant that a very small number of large organizations were dominating the marketplace. These large firms focused on high-volume, mass-market wines, which made it difficult for small wineries to find profitable outlets for the products, no matter how good they were.

At the retail level, consumers were faced with a related trend towards "big-box" retailing at high-volume, low-margin outlets. These outlets typically competed on price, which made it all that much harder for consumers to find any wines other than the high-volume, mass-market labels. For the same reason, consumers were finding it more and more difficult to get help from knowledgeable wine merchants who really knew the wines and could help consumers make appropriate selections.

Olson had been experimenting with interactive electronic marketing at Silicon Graphics, and he felt that the Web was a perfect environment for selling products like wine that would benefit from being surrounded by an information-rich "package."

Combining their knowledge, skills, and interests, these two men created one of the earliest, best known, and most successful examples of a revenue-generating Web-based business. In the process they developed several crucial aspects of the new business model that has come to dominate the Web: no presence anywhere except on the Web; information-based products and/or information-rich "packaging;" reliance on credit cards and digital cash for sales transactions; a fully integrated Web-based ordering, fulfillment, and customer service systems, the use of commercial transportation companies like Federal Express and UPS for direct delivery; and a distinctive, "personal" relationship with individual customers enabled by the interactive, one-to-one nature of the Web.

BUSINESS STRATEGY

The company markets high-quality wines at retail prices (plus the cost of shipping to the purchaser's home). Most of the wines come from small wineries that typically produce 2000 or fewer cases per year, or from large wineries that sometimes produce small volumes of certain specialized wines that cannot be economically sold through the normal mass-market retail channels.

Virtual Vineyards' basic business is to provide customers with a choice of fine wines and related gourmet foods where convenience and selection are the primary goals rather than price. But the company's differentiation strategy is to enrich the wine-buying experience with information. In Peter Granoff's own words:

> My goal is simple—to find outstanding food and wine selections from superb producers and offer them to you for purchase here at Virtual Vineyards. I also want you to have fun while you are shopping and perhaps learn a little bit about food and wine along the way.

The difference between Virtual Vineyards and any other food and wine store you are familiar with is that the "catalog" includes detailed descriptive information about each wine's taste and its place in a gourmet meal, including not only Peter Granoff's personal commentary but a tasting chart that rates the wine in terms of its intensity, body, dryness, acidity, oakiness, tannin, and complexity. In a very real sense you are buying Peter Granoff's expertise and personal style as much as you are buying the wines he has selected and offered to you. Here is an example of Peter's commentary:

> The 1994 Cigare Volant is deeper and more substantial than the 1993—which was not exactly a lightweight itself. The blend is usually different every year, and this time around it is 41.5% Grenache, 33.2% Mourvedre, 24.7% Syrah, and 0.6% Cinsault. I confess to a snicker as I copied down those numbers—such anal precision is completely out of character for Randall Grahm! My tasting notes make reference to rich blackberry and cherry, white pepper, and smoky, meaty aromas and flavors. These descriptors are all hallmarks of good Rhone style wines, and just make me want to break out the Weber and grill up a leg of lamb. Want to join me? Tasted 7/96.

Just as important as these perspectives is the opportunity for customers to ask the experts anything they want about wines and menus, and to receive a personalized answer within a few days. The company's goal is to provide a "safe" atmosphere where anyone can ask questions without feeling embarrassed, so right on the main Web page is an e-mail link to the "Cork Dork," who responds directly to your individual questions.

The "typical" Virtual Vineyards customer is technologically savvy, affluent, and short on time. Thus Virtual Vineyards' basic value proposition of offering a carefully selected variety of fine wines at full price with virtually no shopping time fits these customers perfectly. Some shoppers make repeat visits to the site and purchase regularly. Some have highly evolved taste preferences, while others know little if anything about wine before they visit. Virtual Vineyards is still developing its knowledge about its customers and in particular who its most profitable customers are.

To date the company has benefited tremendously from word of mouth and highly complimentary articles that have appeared in many of the Internet business magazines and the popular press. As an early entrant in the Web marketplace, the company has been a fortunate recipient of a plethora of favorable publicity, including a number of awards as one the best-designed and most recognized Web sites.

Virtual Vineyards uses online advertising to gain additional visibility and to pull Web traffic to its site. It also uses partnerships with other Web sites to attract potential customers. In addition, the company is making increasing use of newer "push" technology tools to both attract new customers and encourage repeat business.

Revenue growth has also come from expanding the product portfolio to existing customers as well as from an expanding customer base. For example, gourmet foods and a collection of wine/food combination packages were recently added to the site.

Virtual Vineyards enables its customers to pay for their purchases with most major credit cards, offering a fully encrypted information transaction. Interestingly, the company also accepts cybercash, and was one of the first Web-based businesses to recognize this form of currency.

THE WEB INTERFACE AND BACKGROUND SOFTWARE

In addition to their marketing, merchandising, and operations staff, Virtual Vineyards also has a team of engineers dedicated to Web site design and development. Their efforts show, as the site can be a very engaging experience. It is rich with graphics and information that can hold the attention even of visitors who are not planning to buy anything.

The most interactive feature of the Web site is the "Ask the Cork Dork" section, where customers can get one-on-one attention from the sommelier. The company has recently added software that enables it to provide standard answers to commonly asked questions as a means of making better use of its limited human resources.

Customers who want to buy something from Virtual Vineyards browse the site and fill a "market basket" by checking off the products they want to purchase. Customers can change their mind at any time, and a running total of the complete transaction is always available. As noted, the company accepts all major credit cards and cybercash in payment. Billing and inventory management software is fully integrated with the home page and purchase order form.

SUMMARY

While Virtual Vineyards has succeeded in using the Web's information-rich capabilities to create a dynamic sales experience, the company has actually adopted a more integrated organizational model than many other Web-based businesses. Organizationally, the company operates very much like more traditional catalog or direct marketing companies; it just happens to take orders over the Internet rather than the telephone.

Clearly, the company has been a highly visible success model. Virtual Vineyards benefited tremendously from a first-mover or early-adopter strategy, in that it was in place very early in the Web's existence and has been cited frequently as a positive example of how to make money on the Web. The operational model is a compelling one, and depends significantly on the expertise of Peter Granoff. Indeed, Peter's knowledge of wines and his engaging personal style are no doubt the major factors that attract and retain Virtual Vineyards' loyal customers.

In spite of its early success, however, Virtual Vineyards faces significant internal and competitive challenges as it continues to grow and evolve. Will its vertically integrated strategy continue to enable it to operate efficiently and profitably, or will the administrative burdens become too severe for such a small company?

As the company grows, its overhead will be distributed over a larger sales volume, which should increase profitability. On the other hand, expansion will make it increasingly challenging to continue providing the exceptional customer service for which the company is known today.

Will customers remain loyal as competitors move into this attractive marketplace? Can Virtual Vineyards learn enough about its customers both generically and individually to continue to attract and retain their business? And will the company have to expand its customer base beyond the technologically savvy, affluent niche it now dominates?

Those questions will be answered by the company, its customers, and the marketplace in the next few years. In the meantime, Virtual Vineyards is a wonderful example of how to exploit the power of the Web to implement a niche business that leverages specialized knowledge.

MPATH INTERACTIVE

Founded in April of 1995, Mpath Interactive is a privately held online game consolidator. In August of 1996 the company acquired Catapult Entertainment, an organization that provided online capabilities for Sega and Nintendo's console game platforms through special modems. The combined organization, which is headquartered in Cupertino, California, had approximately 80 employees in late fall of 1996.

Mpath focuses on providing interactive entertainment that enables and encourages social interaction on the Internet. In other words, Mpath's games and other entertainment packages are designed to enable many players at different locations to interact with each other—both in real time and asynchronously—as they engage with the game models.

Mpath employs three primary technologies for its various products and services: its proprietary Mplayer product, which supports multiparty online gaming; a cartridge/modem combination that also enables multiple players to interact over the Internet; and a host service that provides capabilities to OEMs and large-scale game developers who want to license Mpath technology for their own games. Mpath's first Internet service was Mplayer, a multiplayer game service that went into Beta testing in August of 1966 and live in November of 1996. Mplayer's user interface allows players to move seamlessly between Mplayer game rooms and in and out of chat rooms. Both the game rooms and the chat rooms support customization of a player's virtual surroundings, as well as live voice chat, text-based chat, and interactive drawing using a shared "white board." These capabilities enable literally thousands of different individuals to interact in ways that seem almost "real" rather than virtual.

Mpath has combined technical and management talent from a variety of industry disciplines, including UNIX system software design, multimedia, personal computer input/output, networking, online services, and game development. This collective base of industry expertise provides Mpath with an understanding of technology trends, and has also enabled Mpath to become the first online game consolidator to solve the hottest problem with interactive gaming today—latency.

Mpath was able to solve this problem through a strategic alliance with PSINet that combined PSINet's ATF circuit-switch backbone with Mpath's proprietary multi-client application protocols (MCAP), which are application programming interfaces that enable multiclient applications on the Web. The protocols are deployed on Mpath Internet servers strategically located around the U.S. and are integrated into PSINet's unique backbone structure to manage traffic dynamically.[13] This partnership seeks to guarantee the quality of the game experience by leveraging the newest backbone technology that other Internet service providers (ISPs) have not yet deployed.

Mpath has also formed a number of other alliances, particularly with software vendors, but almost all of them are nonexclusive. For example, Mpath signed a production and distribution deal with Epicenter, a new gaming company focused on developing content exclusively for the Internet. the alliance will make Epicenter's games available on Mpath's online gaming service.[14] Epicenter might well sign similar distribution deals with other game aggregators. This type of nonexclusive arrangement is reflective of Mpath's philosophy that ultimate value for holders of game rights lies in having as many game players' eyeballs on the game as possible. In addition, Mpath pays generous royalties of 15 percent of the gross revenue for licensed products from alliance partners.[15]

Overall, the company believes that its combination of superior technologies to manage the latency issue, and quality social environment with exciting and widely appealing content, will ensure its success. The company believes that since its technologies can guarantee high-quality game performance, developers will want to work with them and therefore give the company access to quality content. Similarly, gamers will be attracted to sites with low latency and the hottest games. Additionally, the company is distinguishing itself from competitors by broadening its content to attract mass-market game consumers. For example, Mpath is targeting family gamers by putting games such as Monopoly and Battleship online.[16]

THE ONLINE GAMING MARKET AND COMPETITIVE ENVIRONMENT

Although there were somewhere around 40 million Internet users in early 1997, the size of the online gaming market is more like 1 to 2 million hard-core gamers—those who are willing to pay for an online adventure. The characteristics of these consumers is expected to shift over time from a predominantly young male audience to one more representative of the general population.

While much of the existing online gaming content has focused on the more violent action-oriented games attractive to teenage males, the influx of venture capital into the industry and a wider variety of more intellectually focused gaming parallels the expected shift in the characteristics of Internet users. Indeed, one indication that this shift is already occurring is the game Meridian 59, which has a significantly higher percentage of female players than is found in most online games today.

Mpath faces a number of aggressive competitors in the online gaming and entertainment industry. There are at least seven major companies focused on online gaming: Dwango, ImagiNation, Internet Gaming Zone, Kesmai, Multiplayer Game Network, Kali, and Total Entertainment Network (TEN). Most of these companies rely on a combination of access fees and pay-as-you-play pricing mechanisms. However, the companies differ dramatically in terms of their architectures, customer acquisition and retention strategies, and advertising revenue-generation techniques.

In addition to this direct competition, Mpath also faces competition from other kinds of online entertainment companies, such as Interactive Imaginations. Interactive Imaginations, a leading Web-based entertainment and marketing company, produces Riddler, an intellectual game channel with over 100,000 registered users. Riddler offers prizes and cash to its registered customers while simultaneously providing an effective and unique platform for advertisers. Riddler receives over 1.2 million "impressions" or "hits" per day. The games available on Riddler include word games, trivia contests, and brain teasers. Riddler's strength lies in its ability to provide highly targeted marketing information and a broad base of Web sites to advertisers. One indication of its strength is its strategic relationships with Microsoft, NBC, Random House, Toyota, Snapple, Encyclopedia Britannica, Atlantic Records, PC Flowers, and Royal Caribbean.

Online gaming revenues are growing. In 1995, online game companies were a $50 million industry. However, almost all this revenue came from commercial online service providers who were happy to offer this content as part of their subscriber retention strategies because game players are loyal, repeat customers. Bernard Yee from Jupiter Communications estimates that the average online game session lasts 75 to 90 minutes, or about six times the length of a typical nongame online session.[17] Market estimates for online games for the year 2000 range widely from $500 million to $1.6 billion.[18]

However, the composition of these revenues is changing in ways that might make life for Mpath and its many competitors much more challenging. Many industry analysts believe that online service subscriptions will become an increasingly less important source of revenue over the next several years. For example, Jupiter Communications forecasts that by the year 2000 only 40 percent of Web surfers will pay for subscription services.

Future Internet revenues are more likely to come from direct and indirect advertising, as the Internet and the World Wide Web migrate more and more toward the television and print media business model, and away from the subscriber-paid approach that is most common today.

This projection generates a serious challenge for Mpath and its competitors, as the online gaming and entertainment industry seeks to develop viable revenue-generation techniques. As a company increasingly dependent on advertising, Mpath must develop a strategy that will effectively deliver a demographically desirable group of consumers to appropriate advertisers, and do so in a cost-effective manner that will not "turn off" its game players.

Thus, Mpath is actively exploring several different approaches to advertising, with the goal of continuing its growth through the creative delivery of valuable services to its players, while at the same time attracting and retaining the advertisers who are willing to pay for access to those consumers.

DETERMINING AN ADVERTISING STRATEGY

Mpath's advertising strategy must resolve two basic questions: first, who are the most promising potential advertisers and, second, what kinds of advertisements would be most effective?

Although prospective advertisers are increasingly turning their attention to the Web, most remain highly skeptical—even critical—of "new media" advertising and are actively searching for more innovative ways to take advantage of this new information distribution vehicle. A 1996 study by Jupiter Communications indicated that Web-based advertising, by industry, was distributed as shown in Figure 7-3.

The marketing challenge for Mpath is a traditional one: determining which industries and companies will be most interested in reaching the audience that Mpath can deliver. Given the distribution of advertisers shown in Figure 7-3, it would be natural for Mpath to target other Web-based businesses, computer products companies, consumer goods, and automobile manufacturers.

The more challenging and more recent advertising strategy question involves choosing the proper kind of advertisements and placement strategies. Here, the interactive, individualized, and graphic nature of the Web introduces a new set of choices for Mpath and other Web-based companies who want to develop advertising-based revenue streams.

There are basically three types of advertising available on the Web:

· Banner and frame ads
· Tournament and event sponsorship
· Embedded ads

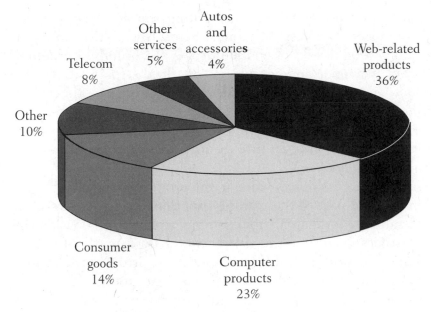

FIGURE 7-3. Web-based advertising, by industry.

Each of these approaches has its own strengths and limitations. Banner ads are simple block images containing an advertising message. The images typically contain a "hot link" that a viewer to click on to go directly to the advertiser's Web site for more information. With software like Java, banner ads can include simple moving and changing images, and can be made to scroll across the page—all techniques that increase the likelihood of capturing the viewer's attention.

Tournament and event sponsorship on the Web works just like it does in real life; Mpath could develop large online game events and offer sponsorship to potential advertisers, in the same way that the Super Bowl, the World Series, and other major sporting events are funded through television and print ads. Of course, generating the volume of game players required to justify the sponsorship fees would require Mpath to spend some advertising money itself to hype the events. Nevertheless, an event-oriented marketing strategy can bring in revenue from both sponsors and advertisers and the game players themselves.

Embedded ads involve incorporating the advertisers' products and logos right into the games themselves, in the same way that Hollywood movies often include specific brands of products like cars, personal computers, or soft drinks (paid for by the product manufacturer, of course). For example, in the movie *Mission Impossible*, Powerbook laptop computers were used in several key scenes. Apple Computer gained significant exposure for its Powerbook product line through this targeted or embedded product placement.

In a similar fashion, a video-game product placement would be an integral part of the gaming experience. In the persistent world game[19] Meridian 59, for example, a player could visit a virtual restaurant and ask the virtual waiter for a bottle of virtual Jolt cola. The waiter would then deliver the virtual bottle of Jolt, including the product's distinctive logo right on the bottle.

Embedded ads can have genuine appeal for Web advertisers because the messages are subtle but powerful. The products are seen as part of the game context, which actively reinforces their role in the real world. However, there is virtually no experience with this approach in the industry to date, and the cost of programming the embedded products into the games, and then maintaining and changing them as contracted advertising expires or is renewed, is still very difficult to estimate.

Lessons Learned

Advertisers in 1996 generally agreed that, although Web-based online gaming has great potential, they are still very unclear about just how effectively it can deliver specific advertising messages. Before committing major promotional expenditures, advertisers are demanding proof of the exposure, or number of impressions, their ads are actually generating.

It is precisely because the Web is still so new and is changing so rapidly that the marketing and advertising choices confronting companies like Mpath are complex and filled with uncertainty. Nevertheless, the basic decisions are in reality little different than those facing marketing and sales executives in more traditional companies. While the cost equation is different in the Web world, and the support requirements are often technically much more sophisticated, the business ingredients are essentially the same: delivering a demographically predictable audience of a given size to an advertiser, creating an effective advertising design and placement strategy, and determining the value of the exposure.

Mpath is a good example of a Web-based business that looks very different from a traditional company on the surface, but the fundamental business issues, challenges, and choices facing senior executives are really no different than they have always been.

Note: This case study was written by James Ware and was based in part on research conducted by Michael Kan, Marcell Typrin, and Anjali Vichare.

ONSALE, INC.

The past two years of commercialized activity on the Web have brought about leaps in the technology required to conduct electronic commerce. As emerging technology enables new forms of exchange, many innovative solutions found online belong to those who exhibit a sophisticated strategy rather than just sophisticated technology.

Innovative business models are crucial for success in this new environment, and ONSALE is such a model. Whenever anecdotes of success on the Web are cited, ONSALE (http://www.onsale.com) is often used as the carrot. They have successfully created a marketplace for not only selling online, but also exploiting organizational opportunities afforded by emerging technologies by building a truly virtual organization. With knowledge and information of the auctioning process being its primary resource, the relatively small company has gained significantly in size and functionality by partnering with other organizations and outsourcing nonessential activities.

The recipe for success is not easy and includes numerous spices. Selling online is no easy feat, as many companies have had to find out the hard way. In fact, a successful selling environment must include the right mix of leadership, value propositions, tenacity, strategy, and luck. ONSALE has effectively brewed these ingredients to establish a compelling marketplace for a target set of consumers. Not only have they matched their target audience with a large proportion of the actual Internet community, but compliance with already well-established "remote" forms of buying and selling in the area of electronic goods has further enhanced the acceptance of the new channel. The concept gained its unique flavor with a rigid exploitation of some of the Net's special characteristics, such as its ubiquity, interactivity, playfulness, and communalism, which ultimately brought the newly founded company positive net returns within less than a year of its inception.

THE COMPANY

ONSALE, Inc. is an online auction house that sells, for the most part, computers, chips, peripherals, and other computer-related add-ons through the World Wide Web. As CEO Jerry Kaplan put it, the focus of the company was on "end-of-life" products, encompassing anything below a Pentium 133 in mid-1996. Today, ONSALE characterizes the focus as "excess inventory," which encompasses end-of-life, close-out, refurbished, and manufacturers' overrun inventory. While excess inventory is frequently at the end of its life, a lot of computer gear is manufactured with certain expectations of demand that turn out not to be true. In July and August 1997, for example, most major disk manufacturers overproduced 9GB disk drives, leading to a glut of these high-capacity devices, and hence fodder for ONSALE.

Most ONSALE goods have been pushed out of retail channels by newer models, and come from dealers who face a steady progression of upgrades that perpetually devalue their existing inventory, as well as OEMs faced with liquidating discontinued hardware.

The company was created in October 1993 by a handful of entrepreneurs who early on envisioned the capabilities of emerging technologies. They evolved the business concept, built prototypes throughout 1994, and went live with the site in May 1995.

Since 1992, Alan Fisher and Razi Mohiuddin, two of the developers of Streetsmart, a package for Charles Schwab customers, were looking for new applications for their product. In 1993, they contacted Jerry Kaplan, founder of Go Corp., the pen computer pioneer that went out of business in 1994. A take-out food-ordering system was among the early ideas that the new team came up with, yet there seemed to be no easy way to bring customers online. They quickly realized the necessity of combining unique features of the new technology with the needs of the people making up the demographics of the Internet. Fisher, Kaplan, and Mohiuddin based their idea on enticing Internet users who were in search of a bargain and aware of constantly changing products. They created a highly interactive marketplace that bundles information on products, as well as market participants. Fisher describes their concept of buying and selling products on the Internet as "part Las Vegas, part QVC." (QVC is a U.S.-based retailer that enables people to purchase goods over television: see http://www.qvc.com.)

Several circumstances pushed their ideas towards the realization of an online auction: as a coin collector, Fisher was familiar with the auction format; the team believed that the auction format was a good match for the technical capabilities of the Internet; and they took the chance to orchestrate an online benefit auction for the Boston Computer Museum. Held in May of 1995, the charity event was a great success and gave the newly founded company a major PR kick-off.

ONSALE began selling a broad variety of items such as sports and rock-and-roll memorabilia, computers and electronics, last-minute vacation packages, special wine collections, tickets to events, and vintage watches. Among those, computers and computer-related products turned out to sell so well that the originally eclectic mix of products soon gave way. After a year and a half of business, the company was now booking over $1 million of weekly sales from three auctions closing on Monday, Wednesday, and Friday. Most recently it made an initial public offering. By early 1998, they conducted five auctions per week (every weekday) with plans to switch to daily auctions and booking sales exceeding $3 million per week. In October 1997, ONSALE completed a secondary offering, raising an additional $45 million.

Business Model

The company remains small at about 112 employees, of which over 30 are devoted to merchandise acquisition (sourcing supply for the daily auctions). Their source of supply continues to be a constraint to their growth. Excess merchandise acquisition is a relationship business, and these relationships usually take a year or two to build. In fact, one of company's biggest challenges has been a lack of retail and distribution experience at the partner level. They have just recently begun to hire in this crucial expertise. On the other side of this incredibly lean, flat organization are the eight customer service representatives who deal with shipping problems. ONSALE is, in essence, in the asset management business—moving towards becoming a truly virtual organization where inventory is minimal, geographical proximity has less import, and information and partnering are king.

From day one, ONSALE's strategy was and is to create a dynamic selling environment by using a highly participatory auction format. The computer market was not the original segment targeted, but—depending on how it is defined—refurbished computers and peripherals is a $7 to $15 billion market. The ONSALE management team made a conscious decision to serve only the domestic market, and thereby avoid extravagant shipping expenses.

Dozens of other auction companies exist and could be described as direct competitors. For the most part, however, they are regional liquidation auctions that advertise in the paper and seasonally flood the market with cheap PCs. None has the vibrancy and activity of ONSALE.

What makes this situation even more compelling is the fact that the target customer is a good fit with prevailing Internet demographics. In the words of Jerry Kaplan, "Instead of running around to the usual retailers—Land's End, Tower Records, Sony Music and Tapes, whatever you see everywhere all over the Internet—we have targeted the demographic on the Internet with a very particular class of goods: items of discretionary interest, primarily, to relatively well-off technical males." According to Fisher, 10 to 20 percent of customers buy goods in quantity. In other words, they are resellers or purchasing agents for organizations.

The true value of ONSALE has been less with the proverbial "coolness" of their site and more with sound business. The Web site for ONSALE is relatively simple and stresses functionality over creativity. The back-end functions, however, including all sales and log file information of every registered user, are sophisticated, often proprietary, tools. All of the development, including their substantial EDI applications, is handled in-house by Software Partners' engineers. As of late 1997, ONSALE still had its own engineering staff of 31 engineers, of which about 5 originally came from Software Partners.

The strategic impact of their approach has been far-reaching to say the least. ONSALE not only has gained a first-mover advantage, but with 20,000 to 25,000 logins per day, has been able to bring people back. "We are the place where this happens. We have brand loyalty," says Kaplan. Moreover, ONSALE has been able to create exclusive relationships with suppliers, thereby locking out other auction houses. Suppliers cannot afford to not do business with ONSALE as it is the largest online computer auction house. Ironically, Fisher reported that the company is supply-constrained and could easily sell more product to their existing customers.

ONSALE has also created a competitive advantage by increasing the barriers to entry through innovative technology such as their proprietary server software and EDI tools that have been developed over the past 10 years in the business. The start-up costs to potential new entrants are large; it would take them some time to catch up. Alan hopes to win exclusive rights to online auctions, with five pending patents.

Inventory and shipping are structured in a very advantageous manner. First, there is currently little channel conflict to speak of since the closest direct competition, the roving auctions, operate only regionally. ONSALE and their manufacturers enter into either an *agency transaction* or an *in-principle transaction*. The former is the traditional auction-house model whereby ONSALE takes a predetermined percentage of the good's sale price. With the in-principle transaction, ONSALE takes title to, although not necessarily possession of, the goods before the auction. ONSALE actually prefers in-principle transactions because they can realize higher margins.

Whenever possible, ONSALE does not take possession of their goods as they would like to avoid the additional expense and headache. Instead, they let the manufacturers and merchandisers maintain the inventory and manage the shipping of goods. ONSALE submits orders to the merchants within one to two days following the close of the auction. Most merchants require an additional four to seven business days to process and ship the goods. Recently, ONSALE has preferred to "take title" to a computer before selling it without actually taking possession. The benefit of this arrangement to ONSALE is that they can participate more fully in the upside of transactions, rather than just taking a straight percentage. While this has margin benefits, it often requires the company to take physical possession of the goods it sells. Consequently, ONSALE tried using Federal Express to handle all such shipping fulfillment and logistics, switching to the Michigan-based Gage Corporation in 1997 because of performance.

So WHERE NEXT?

The company captures a great deal of customer information in the course of the auctions and sales, and they plan to use this knowledge to create customized e-mail letters notifying users of "hot deals" in which they might be interested. Registered customers currently receive generic twice-weekly e-mails announcing the upcoming auction's product mix.

In addition, ONSALE plans to exploit its ever-greater exposure by exacting a premium for featuring products on high-traffic "hot deals" pages. By differentiating this space on the site, the company hopes either to generate additional revenues in the form of advertising, or to induce OEMs to include extended warranties on the products.

AND WHAT DID WE LEARN?

The case of ONSALE demonstrates vividly how a small start-up company can successfully create an Internet-based online market and become a leader—i.e., gain first-mover advantage—by pairing a good business model with strong entrepreneurial spirit, the necessary technical skills, and a portion of luck. The ability to react to customer preferences in a fast and flexible way proved to be a crucial success factor. After the initial start with an eclectic mix of products, the company soon found out more about the preferences of its online audience and subsequently targeted them more specifically. The items that are auctioned now are relatively easy to describe online, i.e., ONSALE does not differentiate products by their features. In fact, this standardization could be considered a benefit since buyers know what they can expect—especially since the target is an audience that is already "in the know" and used to buying and handling high-technology goods. Additionally, customers who are already familiar with the online world are provided with a convenient way to shop.

The application of an auction environment to an electronic commerce site was not ONSALE's brainchild, but they have executed the form more effectively than any others. They appear to have reached a certain critical mass after which the auction creates its own momentum. Furthermore, by establishing a brand name, they have managed to overcome barriers of trust that otherwise often prevail in the rather anonymous online world. Trust is also fostered by clear rules of the game, a strong focus on customer service that lessens the anonymity of the Net, and rigorous quality criteria for participating manufacturers and resellers. In 1996, ONSALE was able to auction a $12,500 IBM mainframe—a transaction that was conducted entirely over the Internet.

It appears that the auction environment is an effective agent rather than the strength of the deal, combining the ease of purchasing over the Net with the expectations of cutting a good deal and the excitement of competition. ONSALE successfully created an engaging and entertaining retail space where the customer's value proposition derives not only from convenient access to close-out prices but also from the thrill of the chase. This is evident by the fact that, by setting a low minimum bid, the ensuing bidding frenzy often drives the sales price higher than the merchandiser could typically realize.

ONSALE has cleverly dodged direct competition by being a national reseller in a market that seems to be regional. In an environment that is commonly seen as threatening to the position of intermediaries, they have successfully positioned themselves and created formidable barriers to entry based on both intellectual property, capital investment, and the notoriety of being the first mover. By teaming up with business partners such as merchants and shipping and logistics companies, the small start-up remains agile and focused on its core competencies while appearing bigger from the outside and able to cover a larger proportion of the value chain—the case of a truly virtual organization. Its challenge in moving forward will be to stay ahead of new entrants into the online auction arena (e.g., ZAuction and WEB-Auction), and deal with the margin pressures they will encounter in the PC market as companies like Compaq, HP, and others come out with sub-$1,000 computers.

NOTES

This entire chapter draws significantly on research conducted by Wendy E. Ware of Cambridge Management Consulting, San Francisco, as reported in "Web-Based Customer Service for the Telecommunications Industry," 1997.

[1] Wendy E. Ware, "Web-Based Customer Service for the Telecommunications Industry." Cambridge Management Consulting White Paper, May 1997, p. 3.

[2] Frederick F. Reichheld and W. Earl Sasser, "Zero Defections: Quality Comes to Services." *Harvard Business Review*, September–October, 1990; Frederick F. Reichheld, "Learning from Customer Defections." *Harvard Business Review*, March–April, 1996.

[3] Riechheld, 1996, op. cit.

[4] Ware, op. cit., p. 31.

[5] Regis McKenna, "Real-Time Marketing," Harvard Business Review, July–August, 1995.

[6] McKenna, 1995, op. cit.

[7] McKenna, 1995, op. cit.

[8] Ware, op. cit., p. 21.

[9] Ware, p. 22.

[10] For a more extended discussion of customer communities and the power of enabling them, see John Hagel III and Arthur G. Armstrong, *Net.Gain*. Harvard Business School Press, Boston, Ma., 1997.

[11] Ware, op. cit., p. 24.

[12] Ware, op. cit., p. 30.

[13] "Let's Play Games." *Red Herring*, April, 1996.

[14] *Variety*, September 23–29, 1996.

[15] "Slashing On-line Gaming Clutter." Information and Interactive Services Report, October 11, 1996.

[16] Interview with Debbie Pinkston, Mpath, November 1996.

[17] "Kesmai is fighting to control the industry that it created." *Marketing Computers*, September 1996.

[18] "Game Playing Web Surfers Get a Wave of New Choices." *Investors Daily*, June 19, 1996.

[19] A persistent world is a continuously developing virtual world that a player can enter or leave, but that develops its history as the game is played.

PLANNING AND MANAGEMENT OF INTERNET-BASED TECHNOLOGIES

Throughout this book, we afforded you a number of examples demonstrating various ways in which companies develop a vision and define key relationships using the unique features of emerging technologies. At the end of chapter 7, we provided you with some guidelines to consider on your way to success. Eventually, you will arrive at the point where you want to leave the 30,000-foot level of visioning and shaping an Internet strategy, and come down to the task of "putting it all together" and implementing the projects. This process frequently turns out to be complex and cumbersome. It includes a variety of different management tasks and evolves around organizational as well as technical questions:[1]

· What types of projects will be involved with your Internet strategy, and what are the expected benefits?

· What are the resources needed to put the strategy into reality and how does the Internet fit into the existing structure?

· Who will bring the new applications from concept to market and how will necessary resources be structured, including project approval and funding?

- How will projects be coordinated that have scope across multiple departments or business units, and how will the projects be managed and executed?

- How will you get the project working, i.e., how will you select service providers, address security and privacy issues, and use internal policies and documentation, statistics, and overall evaluation from a business perspective?

- Which parts of the project can you execute internally, and which parts does it make sense to get support for from outside?

- How will the new applications be managed though their life cycle once they are deployed? Who will be responsible for Internet management, administrative coordination, support, training, "technical" connections, evaluation, and expanding or upgrading decisions?

These are some of the questions we will address from different perspectives throughout this chapter. As is the case in most projects, the management of Internet- and Web-based strategies encompasses planning and specifying requirements, as well as implementing and monitoring project success. However, with Internet- and Web-based technologies still being relatively new phenomena, the ways in which companies make use of them differ greatly regarding scope and underlying experience; no widely accepted best practices have been established so far.

In this chapter we will first give you an overview of different levels of Web usage, defining the scope of your Internet and electronic commerce project. Even in rapidly changing environments, true revolutions are seldom achieved overnight. We will explain why you might want to take a stepwise approach on your way to becoming Web-centric. Subsequently, we will outline some of the requirements necessary to make it happen. By identifying the gap between your goals and your current status you will be able to determine your requirements, e.g., concerning the project team and the IT system. As your applications become more sophisticated, systems connecting back-end systems with your Web front ends (middleware) and security issues will gain in importance. Requirement definition also provides a basis to make the business case. With electronic commerce strategies competing with many other projects and ideas in an organization, you will always want to be able to somehow justify the efforts and expenses related to it. We will give you an overview of the issues to be considered, before we address the decision of whether to buy or make your Internet portfolio. Finally, we will point out some barriers to success, namely in terms of legacies and the task of getting buy-in from management and end users.

CHOOSE A STEPWISE APPROACH

Although you should have a fair understanding of the things that are possible with a Web site by now, you do not want to try to create a full-blown Web site immediately. While you clearly have enough knowledge to avoid many of the mistakes of the earliest pioneers, and enough insight to short-circuit the long learning cycle that many organizations have had to go through, you nevertheless will be more successful in the long term if you recognize and plan for significant organizational learning along the way.

To demonstrate the different ways many organizations apply Web technologies, we identified four basic levels of Web usage intensity. They also show different stages of Internet maturity, i.e., some sort of learning curve that many players go through:

- Organizations often start by becoming familiar with the basic features of the Internet in a rather passive way by exploring it as a pool of information. Often initiated by technological savvy members of the IT section or outward-oriented business departments, or by some sort of external pressure, online access is established and ideas slowly evolve of how to use the new technologies for the business. External information sources, such as the press, peer reports, and external consulting services, frequently play a major role here.

· Issues around becoming an active "netizen" evolve as soon as a Web presence is established. Usually relatively simple and cheap promotional sites are developed in the first place, presenting basic information about an organization and its tasks and products, posting employment opportunities, press releases, and perhaps links to additional information, either to the outside world or internally in case of an intranet. As the size of the site grows, crucial issues include keeping a consistent look and feel, especially if content is provided by different sources, and maintaining up-to-date content.

· Linking the Web site to business operations and integrating it with back-end systems leads to more sophisticated Web sites/intranets, enabling transactions and a tighter management of business relations through interactive links with partners, customers, and internal staff. This significantly rises the level of complexity and cost, but offers in return an opportunity to track individual user requirements, interests, or inquiries; offer individualized content; and let customers place and pay for orders.

· As an organization becomes Web-centric, major business functions are built around the Internet and Web technologies. To date we find only a few examples of companies willing to make the commitment and bear the risk of integrating new technologies deep into their business strategy. Cisco Systems represents one of these few examples, managing its excessive growth to a large extent through the application of innovative technologies and business pratices (see case study in Chapter 6). At this level we tend to find highly tailored systems. The need to comply with individual strategies and specific situations again raises the level of complexity and cost.

Throughout the book we provided you with many examples of how the incorporation of the Internet and the Web into businesses can lead to significant changes in the existing way of doing business and interacting with business partners; in some cases it even changes industries. Organizations entering the on-line world must be aware of this and, ideally, implement their general vision right from the start. However, given the complexity and newness of the field, the potentials that emerging technologies already offer, the volatility with which new developments evolve, and the large number of unknown variables, there is no way of becoming Web-centric in one go. It also requires experience and knowledge about the technology and about changing relationships, which can be acquired only over time. Additionally, although improving at rapid pace, Internet-technology itself is still currently far from mature, leaving many questions open. As a result, organizations have to compromise between gathering experience by "jumping into the water," which gives them hands-on experience and lets them shape out new ideas, and, on the other hand, developing a vision and pursuing the big picture.

Instead of providing a simple management guide with steps to be taken sequentially, one at a time, we therefore suggest taking an evolutionary and rolling approach with an initial vision that will be implemented in small steps. This is somewhat similar to a technique called *evolutionary prototyping*, which is commonly used for software development. Here, an initial application is developed as fast as possible, and then subsequently tested and refined as soon as flaws and requirements for its usage become obvious. By dividing the whole task into digestible pieces and repeating project management phases of planning, implementing, and monitoring success on a smaller scale, you can constantly learn and improve your Internet maturity.

When we walk you through some of the issues that will come about with the management of your Internet projects, keep in mind the art of balancing the pursuit of the big picture and refining it according to lessons learned on the way there. This might not always be as easy at it sounds. To avoid becoming tangled in details, remember that the success of any Internet project ultimately depends on its compliance with your organizations general strategy and priorities and combining immediate communication needs with long-term strategic goals for network participation.

REQUIREMENTS

In Chapters 2 and 3 we walked you through the process of planning the scope of your Internet projects, and provided you with an overview of basic types of Internet applications: those supporting relationships within companies (intranet), between companies (business-to-business), and between companies and consumers, which we covered in Chapters 5 through 7. Use the examples we have provided throughout the book as food for thought and a starting point to develop your very own vision of where you would like to go. To put it into practice, explore the gap between your goals and your current position. This will help you to define your requirements, e.g., in terms of skills and technology, and to address cost issues.

GAP ANALYSIS

It is important to not only understand where you want to be positioned within different time frames concerning Internet commerce and Web presence, as well as general business strategies, but also what is achievable within a reasonable time frame given your company's current position, resources, and budget restrictions. In other words, you have to perform a gap analysis, i.e., identify requirements to realize wishful thinking and compare them with the reality in terms of technology, skills, and cost from where you start. Determine your current Internet maturity in terms of technology that is already in place and skills that are available throughout the company, and also take current developments on the market into consideration. Additionally, this process will help you to identify legacies that might turn out to be hurdles on the way to project success.

The application of Internet success stories always need to be adapted to an individual company's situation. To be able to "sell" the project to management and within the rest of the company, you need to be very clear about the reasons why you want to use the Internet and how it can fit into your own organization and existing IT infrastructure. To make a business case, you need to address the needs of your business and expected benefits that innovative technologies can provide at the various levels of adoption.

Set milestones and measurements to monitor the success of your project. Given the dynamics and pace of development currently experienced by the world of electronic commerce, a feasible time frame is no longer than one year, especially when you are still in the early stages of Internet maturity. To foster the learning process, articulate your vision and revisit it on a regular basis (e.g., every three months).

PROJECT TEAM

In many organizations, the first initiatives to explore the Internet come from lower management levels and independently from institutional assistance. The initiators are usually technologically savvy and able to configure systems that are already in place. While they can be found among members of the business community, especially in areas that are dependent on communication with the outside world, such as market research or corporate communications, in many cases the information systems department has the strongest skills.

In order to move beyond grassroots initiatives, however, a project team with clear-cut responsibilities has to be established. According to the location of the first kick-off, Internet projects are often initially owned by the IT group. With growing experience, it makes sense, however, to split up responsibilities of the Internet project according to content, look and feel, and technology between business functions, corporate communications, and IT.[2]

It is important to identify and recruit a project team that understands the project parameters and key objectives. This means that the team must encompass a wide variety of skills and knowledge in the following areas:

· Technology
· Content crucial for the Internet commerce applications
· Users' needs and preferences

Especially regarding technical skills, companies currently experience a serious shortage of and problems finding, training, and keeping the right people—a situation that cannot be solved by compensation alone.[3]

You have to determine a project team leader and provide him or her with sufficient backing from top management. One of the most important tasks the project leader has to face is coordinating all the parties involved, ensuring that they work collaboratively towards a common goal. In most cases, you will need cross-functional teams combining management, technical, and business skills, both from inside the company and in many cases leveraged by outside contractors, service providers, etc., to provide start-up, short-term, specialized technical expertise. Cultural differences, e.g., between business and technical people, and power issues, e.g., in relation with budgeting, will typically aggravate the task of team coordination. Keeping the project team small but diverse can help to reveal these issues early on and to ensure acceptance across a wide variety of "home departments" while still being effective.

Each of the different phases of an Internet project (developing the vision, implementing and maintaining it, and monitoring its success) requires a unique mix of expertise and skill sets:

· Senior managers point out the direction and provide sponsorship throughout the organization.

· Network and messaging architects design the network infrastructure and plan message roll-out throughout the company and with external communication partners.

· System and database administrators install and manage the Internet applications and provide database access.

· Interface designers and application developers design and implement applications in terms of look and functionality.

· Web content providers and Webmasters design, implement, and manage the Web "front end."

· Users articulate their needs and learn how to use the new applications.

The exact composition of the project and support teams depends on specific implementation requirements. The combination of skills is usually more mixed across business and technology in the early phases of the life cycle of a distinct application, whereas close to implementation technical skills become more important—a perspective that is in line with a classical notion of application development.

THE SYSTEM

In order to get started, you have to determine the requirements for the basic network infrastructure necessary to get online access to the Internet. We can categorize these into network requirements and application requirements.[4] Network requirements comprise hardware in terms of server machines and client workstations that, in the case of the Internet, are connected via the TCP/IP protocol, the network backbone (LAN/WAN), and basic network services for authentication, file transportation, remote login, hypertext transport protocol (HTTP), etc. You have to decide on the Internet tools you need, such as e-mail, access to the World Wide Web, files and applications on remote systems, usenet newsgroups, list servers, etc.

Application requirements for designing your front ends and connecting them to existing systems include publishing services (tools to create, edit, and administer content), tools for communication and collaboration (to develop network applications), and tools for network management (directory services, information access controls, replications services, and network administration).

When choosing the products you want to implement, evaluate their features in relation to your requirements. Here are some criteria you might want to consider:[5]

· Performance and scalability
· Access control and possibilities for user authentication and encryption
· Interoperability with existing systems, applications, and data

- Availability and robustness
- Manageability and ease of handling
- Efficient use of network resources
- Cross-platform support

Determine your system's requirements not only in terms of bandwidth necessary to handle anticipated data flows, but also in terms of necessary server CPU and disk space, and identifying which platform is most adequate to deploy your system.

When designing the network topology, implement open standards and protocols whenever possible to maximize interoperability with other systems and applications, ensure scalability, and avoid vendor lock-in. The new applications should be leveraged and seamlessly integrated with existing resources to minimize additional cost and changes to the underlying data infrastructures. Also carefully consider the placement of the new servers within your network topology to maximize efficient use of bandwidth and ensure high application performance. High availability and reliability is essential, especially for transaction and mission-critical applications.[6]

While addressing these issues sounds complicated, not all of them are equally crucial right at the start of your online presence.[7] Carefully ensuring scalability and avoiding early lock-ins will provide you with the flexibility to grow your Internet resources according to changing needs.

Many organizations start by connecting just one department to the Internet and World Wide Web, focusing on one implementation of immediate interest, e.g., market research or improved support from system vendors. This could be the beginning strategy, eventually involving the whole company, but also the end of the efforts until another priority comes up. Requests for more connectivity should be handled from an overall strategy viewpoint. Cost benefit analysis will help to determine the most beneficial applications. Access to e-mail and newsgroups might immediately prove to be useful to a large number of company members because it makes current external information available, such as trends, activities, innovations by competitors, active participation of customers, evaluations of products and vendors, and information on potential future business fields. According to a study conducted at the Fisher Center for Management and Information Technology, UC Berkeley, many companies start out by connecting distribution-oriented functions such as market research, marketing, and customer support to the online world.[8] Although the Internet offers a wealth of opportunities for sourcing (see chapter 6), procurement and purchasing departments are often equipped rather poorly with Internet access and browser stations.

After the first steps, it is crucial to foster a momentum. Sharing information internally is a possible first action, e.g., through implementation of a central "library" function.

The process of moving from first experiences with a mostly promotional Web site to more sophisticated sites and eventually allowing transactions means having to address increasingly complex issues. For example, electronic catalogs can be transformed into full-service order-entry and fulfillment systems including order tracking and payment functions, while Internet mail can help to improve customer service and support. Finally, customers and suppliers can be given access into previously forbidden inventory, production, and sales as well as marketing systems via private intranets. This last task, especially, is leveraged by the possibility of using already existing databases, tools, operation systems, and hardware technologies. Several issues have to be overcome, nevertheless: you have to establish links between Web front ends and your existing system, while security issues gain in importance.

MIDDLEWARE

By the time organizations move away from simple point-and-click informational and promotional Web sites and start incorporating the Web into their business, the issue of linking its legacy systems to Web applications becomes crucial. Eventually, some mechanism to guarantee financial transactions is needed. Both tasks are performed by a form of software called *middleware*.

Generally speaking, the term *middleware* names any software that connects two machines, and starts out when a single database server is accessed from a single client. It is thus a key element in all client/server environments and has been an issue for several years now.[9] As long as the overall task stays simple, requirements are not too complicated and the systems to be connected are not too heterogeneous, most middleware is written in-house. As soon as multiple database servers are to be connected to a variety of clients operating on various platforms, using different languages and operating systems, manageability becomes more difficult, however. Some companies find themselves in a situation where 40 percent of the IS department staff is writing middleware in some form. This is where commercial middleware comes into play, which may solve the problem of two- and three-tier client/server integration.

The type of middleware a company uses depends on several things, such as:

- the complexity of the back-end systems to be connected in terms of heterogeneity
- the volume of database requests to be handled
- security requirements, e.g., in the financial industry, guaranteed transaction processing is crucial, as is the guarantee that it is processed only once.
- speed of message delivery

In recent years, the growth of client/server applications as well as the diffusion of the Internet have pushed the general middleware market to a current volume in the range $100 to $200 million, as have development tools for middleware. Traditionally representing a niche market for small companies, in recent years big players also hit the market: IBM offers its MQSeries very successfully, as does Digital Equipment with its DESmessageQ.

The Internet and World Wide Web are currently reshaping the middleware market. Especially by addressing the Web with the "universal" browser interface, the task of linking heterogeneous clients to database servers is greatly simplified, reducing it to establishing the link between the Web server and the database. IBM, for example, allows their mainframe databases now to be accessed through Web technology, facilitating the integration of dispersed data and eventually allowing the development of comprehensive data warehouses with reasonable effort.

Linking Web sites with legacy systems is usually done by using Common Gateway Interface (CGI) scripts (e.g., written in Perl, tcl, also C and C++) coupled with procedures stored in the database management system or Application Programming Interface (API) calls. Overall, however, the technology is not yet very advanced.[10] On one hand, we find HTML and multimedia tools for content creation that were developed originally as authoring environments for CD-ROMs, etc., and that are now targeting the Web. Compared to "traditional" middleware, both are limited in terms of the functionality they are offering, especially when it comes to sophisticated database manipulations, handling complex data, and ensuring transactions. Also, there is still a lack of tools that provide simultaneous performance measurement for data bases and Web sites. Companies willing to use the Internet and Web-based technologies for mission-critical business applications often have to develop the tools required to bridge legacy systems with new technologies, in-house or with help from outside contractors. Companies without the necessary skills and resources to do so will have to keep a close eye on the currently rapidly changing market developments.[11]

SECURITY

There are several reasons to take a closer look at security issues these days.[12] More and more computers have become part of larger networks and, with the Internet growing, more and more machines are connected to public networks, directly increasing the exposure of corporate data systems to security threats. On the other hand, there is a trend toward deploying open computing systems, including diverse and inconsistent security products with little standardization of security solution across different solutions, let alone platforms. The Internet offers little security if any by itself; with telnet and ftp, for example, user names and passwords are effectively transmitted in the clear, communications via e-mail are not strongly protected from tampering or exposure to third parties, and identities can be forged. The lack of confidentiality and integrity protection, digital signatures, and nonrepudiation services, therefore, can be seen as a major inhibitor to the wide acceptance of electronic commerce over the Internet.

While secure systems are available (see Chapter 3), their deployment is basically a cost issue in most cases. This leaves companies with the task of evaluating cost and risk factors and determining the correct amount and quality of security for their businesses, i.e., establishing a security policy. Knowledge about the threats as well as the measures to overcome them is necessary in order to assess the economic value, determine the correct level of security, and perform this inevitable risk analysis in a beneficial way. Additionally, cultural issues have to be considered. A sound security policy identifies general rules of who should have access to a company's electronic resources and under what circumstances. In the rush to establish an Internet presence, companies have a tendency to overlook this issue. However, determining the appropriate level of security for a business and choosing the policy accordingly is an inevitable prerequisite to establishing a sound security system in an efficient way.

According to BBN, a firewall provider, security policies fall along a continuum that ranges from promiscuous at one end to paranoid at the other.[13] In a *promiscuous policy*, the organization's internal network can be accessed by everyone on the Internet unchecked, while a *paranoid policy* prohibits any access between the private network and the Internet. In between these two extremes, however, the permissive and prudent policies are two more palatable alternatives.

The *permissive policy* allows all traffic to flow between the internal network and the Internet except that which is explicitly disallowed. Permissive policies are implemented, for example, through packet-filtering gateways. These prevent individual packets of data from crossing the network boundary if the packet is coming from or going to a specific computer, network, or network port. There are two major drawbacks to a permissive policy, however. First, in order to cover all possible addresses and ports that should be denied access, an exhaustive set of filters is necessary. Second, static filtering methods are problematic in the case of dynamic network environments where network port numbers change depending on the protocol state.

A *prudent policy* disallows all traffic to flow between two networks except that which is explicitly allowed. Prudent policies are implemented by a set of application proxies that understand the underlying application protocol and can implement a set of state-maintaining filters, allowing application-specific data to pass from one network to the next. Because the filters follow the state of the protocol, they can change dynamically when the protocol changes state. This way, rules allow only properly authorized data to flow across the network boundary. Prudent policies are implemented, for example, through application proxy firewalls.

Oftentimes, organizations allow some flow of data from the inside out and let their members access outside locations, but they do not allow outside access back into the system and internal servers. With strong security tools in place, access to a part of the internal system might be provided to dedicated business partners. These solutions are called extranets, referring to the part of the intranet that is accessible to the external world.

After selecting the appropriate security policy, the policy has to be deployed with a set of procedures and supporting software systems that should address all types of security violations, including accidental administrative mistakes, human factors, and unauthorized modifications to the security policy. The security procedures should include and document rules for the management and administration of the security system and its generated events, record a trail of all modifications to the security system and signal alarms when someone attempts to violate the policies.

Additionally, it is important not only to focus on the outside of a corporation, but also to consider the risk of break-ins from inside. This applies both to end users within the company and to security system personnel. Their backgrounds should be checked, and security management and auditing functions should be separated in order to prevent an administrator from altering the audit of management actions.

Make sure to consider security issues from the beginning when designing a system, not as something to be implemented after the fact. There are numerous examples where applications had to be rewritten in order to match security requirements that came along with going online. Determining the sensitivity of your data and finding the right balance between the security level necessary to protect your business and the cost and performance issues related to it is crucial and complicated because of the general trade-off between security on one hand and issues like convenience and performance on the other.

The exposure to potentially malicious intruders will always go together with Internet connectivity, and accessing internal data from outside will always be a delicate issue. More and more often, companies want to give business partners with which they have close relationships access to their internal data. In that context, two general issues must be kept in mind: first, even with cost issues left aside, complete protection is virtually impossible; second, since a certain amount of trust is the prerequisite for any long-lasting relationship, the need to provide systems that are 100-percent secure is probably lowered in such situations.

As mentioned earlier, the general approaches that companies take to address the issue of Internet security can be ranked between extremes paranoia and complete openness. When implementing your security strategy, keep in mind that it should serve the community as do the other functions of Internet connection, in the sense of providing services while ensuring security.

Finally, there is a need to consider intranet security. Both Internet and intranet systems can use similar (or the same) networking and client/server components. Both might use components from the TCP/IP protocol suite as well as browsers and Web servers. The general assumption that all insiders are good and all outsiders are bad can be a very dangerous one![14] Rather, the same innate vulnerabilities that exist in IP networks exist within intranets and the Internet. In some situations, the vulnerabilities of an intranet are even greater; the physical security of an intranet is often less robust than that of the Internet and WAN connections can be broken into as easily as can Internet connections, but attacks on an intranet can be better planned by insiders. This means that it is not sufficient to simply install a sort of corporate gatekeeper, i.e., a firewall that protects internal data from external attacks. You might want to consider a second firewall around your most sensitive data, or encryption.

MAKING THE BUSINESS CASE

Cost Assessment

It is difficult give general cost estimates for building a Web site. On one hand, there are no established measurement methods; on the other hand, even simple promotional Web sites differ greatly in terms of functionality, size, and looks. The cost of maintaining a site after its launch depends on how fast the information provided changes, i.e., business dynamics and also the initial efforts determining the scope of the site. Additionally, in cases where Web sites are built in-house, different levels of available skills contribute to the variety in estimated costs.

To assess costs, you must include all the direct and indirect costs factors, such as:

· Technology in terms of hardware, software, and network components
· Additional related fees
· Maintenance
· Database and legacy system integration
· Network security
· Management
· Skills, training, and the learning curve

In 1996, Forrester Research estimated the cost to launch and operate a relatively simple Web site advertising a company's products and services over the period of one year, at $304,000.[15] Estimations for more sophisticated sites providing updated news, weather, or entertainment reach up to $1.312 million, and transactional Web sites that allow viewers to shop, bank, or get customer services average $3.368 million. According to

Josh Bernoff, senior analyst at Forrester, "it's only do-it-yourself hobbyist sites that are inexpensive." (See Table 8–1). While the technologies to build a site are becoming commodities and hence cheaper, the costs of implementing superior solutions are actually still on the rise.

Table 8–1   Costs for set-up and 12 months of operation of different types of Web sites.

	PROMOTIONAL WEB SITE, PROMOTING A COMPANY'S PRODUCT AND SERVICES	CONTENT WEB SITE, PUBLISHING CONSTANTLY UPDATED NEWS, WEATHER, OR ENTERTAINMENT INFORMATION	TRANSACTIONAL WEB SITE, LETTING VIEWERS SHOP, BANK, OR GET CUSTOMER SERVICE
	$304,000	$1,312,000	$3,368,000
Content and service: Content/program Management Sales and support	$237,120 (78%)	$813,440 (62%)	$1,919,760 (57%)
Marketing: Advertising/PR Paid links	$15,200 (5%)	$249,280 (19%)	$774,640 (23%)
Platform: Hardware Software Connections Hosting	$51,680 (17%)	$249,280 (19%)	$673,600 (20%)

Source: adapted from Forrester Research

To just dip one's toes in the water and to see if it works for your business, you can start your Web presence by setting up a virtual server (renting space on somebody else's server) for about $30 per month. This does not require much more than a computer and a high-speed modem in the first place, which can also be rented. The provider can set your system up so it looks to the rest of the world like a separate server. Usually, offers include some megabytes of storage space for Web pages, which should be heaps to start off with. Setting up a mailing address, a list server, or an auto responder might comprise additional features of the package.

While getting online and establishing a Web presence can be quite cheap, building more sophisticated applications and linking them to existing systems augments the amount of necessary resources as well as the risk of failure almost exponentially.

The biggest bulk of the cost, one to two thirds, is for hiring people for tasks like generating computer code, designing graphics, providing content, promoting the site, and eventually interacting with the Web site's visitors. The cost for hardware and software accounts for a smaller share and also tends to decline every day.

While Forrester's figures can give you some idea of the dimension we are talking about, be aware that the cost for building and maintaining a Web site for a year, tend to vary significantly. The application of these results to your own situation might lead to very different estimations. NetMarketing, an Internet consulting company based in Hamden, CT, recently sent out bids for three prototypical sites to 21 Web developers and ad agencies. Each participant received a site description and was asked to submit a bid for a small, 20-page site, a medium-sized 100-page site, and a large site that included custom programming, a database front end, and secure transaction capability. Bids for the large site ranged from a rock-bottom $15,000 to a heart-stopping 42.8 million.

In fact, many Web sites go up for considerably less than $205,000. ActivMedia reports that typical site development spending by companies with more than 500 employees is in the range of $10,000 to $100,000. Only 5 percent of a survey sample of 1,000 mentioned spending more than $300,000 on a site.

ESTIMATE IMPACT AND BENEFITS

While estimating cost is already a difficult undertaking, addressing the impact and benefits of Internet and Web applications turns out to be even more problematic. Most technological changes have indirect or unintended consequences that defy measurement, since they do not show in terms of direct cost savings or sales increases. Many impacts are not foreseeable and show only after the fact, as usage patterns evolve and processes and relationships change. Obviously, the complexity and interdependence of effects grow as companies become more Web-centric.

You might want to start out by picking a single business process that has a high priority for your business and outline a Web-based application that you would like to implement. Alternatively, you could take the "low-hanging fruit" approach and start with a process that allows easy deployment of Web technologies.

In order to determine the effect of the new application, consider the way the process is currently performed and answer the following questions:

· What is the current activity breakdown (value chain) of the process?

· How much does the current process cost?

· How often does the process occur?

· To what extent is this process crucial to the organization?

· What other alternatives are there to performing this process?

Determine the likely quantifiable impacts in terms of cost savings, e.g., from reduced paper, postage fees, data entry, and errors. Intangible effects include improved communication and intensified relationships, increased speed of business, shared knowledge, and cultural unity. Decide the relative importance of cost effects vs. performance improvements. There is often a leap of faith that needs to be taken for Internet commerce solutions, and this faith is difficult to find in American business. Making them visible by listing them might provide justification for the project in some cases.

BUY IT, MAKE IT, OR RENT IT?

In addition to evaluating hardware, software, and staff costs, it is crucial to evaluate whether to make or buy an Internet commerce portfolio and how much external support is needed, in technical as well as management issues. All options yield potential advantages, but also bear risks. In any case, the decision to make or buy your Internet commerce portfolio should not be based on short-term financial incentives; rather take issues of core competency and competitive advantage into account. However, a closer look at the issues often reveals that the task is even more complex.[16]

If you are going to buy your portfolio, virtually every component you need can be rented or outsourced. Internet service providers can give you access to the online world via dial-up lines, SLIP accounts, or high-performance leased lines. Some also provide content, like AOL or CompuServe. Component programs, such as Java applets, can be purchased over the Net, a rather new phenomenon with great potential to catch on in the future. Outsourcing the design and hosting of external Web-sites is a quite popular choice in order to get access to technical knowledge as well as the art of creating a compelling site in terms of look and feel. Beyond that, you will find outsourcers for every other task, from linking your Web sites to internal systems to managing your advanced e-mail and network systems, even to the development of entire Internet strategies. And in every case you need not outsource a task in its entirety; you can hire consultants on a temporary or project-related basis to add specialized knowledge to the skills that are available in-house.

Outsourcing usually aims not only at achieving cost benefits but also toward more strategic effects:[17]

· Less internal overhead.

· Free compensation schemes—with salaries for the Internet knowledge skyrocketing, many companies experience difficulties in recruiting staff to fit into their compensation schemes. Hiring outside contractors on a temporary basis can alleviate this problem.

· Temporary involvement at point of need, and the ability to cope with workloads that vary seasonally or changing technologies.

· Flexibility to adapt new technologies, which allows for building an infrastructure quickly and integrating it with existing technology.

- Fresh knowledge and expertise in a quickly changing technology, and the ability to compensate for a lack of in-house knowledge.

. The opportunity for executives to concentrate on providing information to keep an up-to-date technology infrastructure, improve management, and respond better to market changes instead of responding to changes in technology.

- Hedging the risks of difficult technology decisions, e.g., moving to a client/server environment or implementing enterprise-wide network solutions. This might also speed up the transition to new technologies.

Companies that make the decision to make their own Internet commerce portfolios want to own the knowledge and leverage the organizational learning. However, it also means a relatively high cost of acquiring hardware, software, and netware components. The major benefits of building your own portfolio include:

- Knowledge ownership and better understanding of your internal needs
- Keeping "control" over the in-house systems
- Ability to develop and implement a long-term strategy
- Hardware and software ownership (which can also be a drawback)
- Fewer security problems

An evaluation from a cost perspective has to include obvious cost components such as hardware, software, network components, human resources, and consulting fees. But also consider factors that create a more hidden cost, e.g., Internet access, system maintenance, and security.

ACCESS

When choosing an Internet service provider (ISP) or a company to host your Web site, a crucial issue is evaluating the connection speed that is provided. This has a major effect on the response time that your end users experience. The choice depends on the type of access your targeted users usually have as well as on the sophistication of the Web site you are planning, i.e., you have to match your bandwidth requirements with what is available for your end users and balance this with your budget restrictions.

MAINTENANCE

Maintenance includes several technical issues, such as updates, system support, and network reliability (up time), as well as content-related issues.

Managing consistency in terms of software versions and updates not only poses a considerable management problem, especially in client/server environments with many users, but it can also be a cost issue. This is one reason for deploying thin clients and network computers, which allow for centralized version control. When deciding on outsourcing IS functions, ask how frequently software updates will be provided and in what way version control will be ensured.

An Internet presence that seriously promotes your organization, that goes beyond the development of nice-looking pages and tries to generate money, most likely requires ongoing support. Outsourcers don't always provide 24-hour-a-day system support. Often a help desk can be reached around the clock, but the technical staff has to be paged when problems are detected.

In terms of network reliability, big differences prevail among different outsourcers. Going with the big players might be the safest bet; with other companies, at least ask for uptime records and inquire about average outage lengths.

Keeping the content of your Web site up to date is an issue that you must consider when outsourcing the development of your external Web site. In principle, management issues are the same whether you go with a vendor or decide to keep the task in house. You have to think about many things beforehand and eventually include them into the contract in order to avoid problems later on.

SECURITY REQUIREMENTS

When choosing an outsourcer, it is important to ask how the firm manages security issues and to match them with your own requirements, which will depend on the sophistication of the Web site, especially how much it will be integrated with your internal system. Evaluate the importance of protecting your data against accidental loss and theft, unwanted manipulation, etc., and determine the risk related to outsourcing the functions.[18] When beginning to use your Internet presence for electronic commerce, you must first make sure a secure server is in place, enabling the transport and processing of sensitive financial and other business data. Companies that outsource their external Web sites to protect their internal systems from outside access have to keep in mind that they will have complete segregation of data only as long as they provide no links to their internal systems; in other words, outsourcing first of all affects pure informational sites and is not feasible when real-time online transactions are needed. Sometimes it is even important to ensure security of Web sites that are not connected to in-house systems. In case of poor protection at an outsourcer's network, for example, someone might load a server with sniffer software that could monitor data traffic. Then the intruder could steal sensitive information, particularly names and passwords, if servers on the outsourcer's network aren't isolated from another.

When choosing an outsourcer, two things have to be considered, in particular. First, evaluate its experience; second, carefully set up a contract.

EXPERIENCE

There are literally thousands of outsourcers out there offering services around Internet and Web technologies. They differ significantly in size, scope of services offered, and, maybe most importantly, experience and capability in Internet projects. In order to choose one or several vendors, determine the scope of the project and your requirements in technical terms. Ask if the outsourcer is experienced to actually provide these services by questioning reference projects. Gartner Group segments the market into three levels according to the complexity of the projects that companies undertake in terms of business value:[19]

- At level one, companies are experienced in exploiting the Web for marketing purposes. These companies often come from the area of advertising or electronic media design. Companies of that level, e.g., agency.com, DimensionX, Organic Online, and TVision, provide static HTML pages, searchable sites, forms to simply capture client information, and multimedia data types (sound or video).

- Level-two companies focus on building business solutions using stable technologies with existing standards and applications, as opposed to newer "bleeding edge" technologies. Their representatives, such as EDS, Hewlett-Packard, IBM, SHL Systemhouse, and Unisys, provide services for publishing, online catalogs, and basic interaction with legacy data.

- At level three, forms are focused on providing services to organizations who want to use the Internet to attain a competitive edge. Projects at this level usually combine building mission-critical applications that use the Internet with business process reengineering and change management as part of an overall corporate transformation initiative. Most large consulting firms are expected to be present on that level in the future, such as AMS, Andersen Consulting, Cap Gemini, Ernst & Young, and KPMG Peat Marwick. They provide secure data exchange, secure electronic commerce (e.g., electronic banking), and are involved in large projects that transform the whole enterprise. However, given the newness of the Internet, not many companies have significant project successes in that area so far—which makes the task of selecting a company more difficult.

CONTRACT

In general, the success of outsourcing projects hinges to a large extent on the underlying contracts.[20] Every contract should first of all meet individual requirements, and not all issues are crucial for all companies. However, accepting a vendor's standard contract might lead to difficulties later on. Before setting up a contract and negotiating the details, carefully define all aspects of the outsourcing arrangements. This should include issues such as growth rates, baseline measurements, and nonperformance clauses. Getting a second opinion might be well worth the effort. The additional cost of hiring external technical experts to help measure baseline services and performance levels, as well as legal experts to write the outsourcing contract and negotiate it with the vendor, might pay off in the long run. Given the dynamics of the field, you should build a renegotiation option into your contract to be able to cope with unforeseen changes in prices or workload. In order to eliminate or reduce problems from conflicting goals, establish partnerships and "win win" situations, e.g., via profit sharing.

It is crucial to simultaneously consider the right mix of decision factors, in addition to cost factors and simple rules such as "never outsource core competencies." Also keep in mind that outsourcing need not be an all-or-nothing decision. In some cases it can be advantageous to establish relationships with several vendors, which might prevent you from getting locked in with one vendor, provide you with better deals by way of the competition it provokes, and enable you to get the best of each vendor. Also, considering the time factor, outsourcing can be a viable option to gain first-move advantage, followed either by an internal catch-up in knowledge or by micro-managing your outsourcer and then establishing regular benchmarks to make sure your partner remains up to snuff.

As a rule of thumb, you might want to keep the functions that you are good at, especially if you consider them to be mission-critical or to provide strategic advantage. In that case you would outsource other functions in order to allow your people to spend time with crucial tasks. However, a well thought-out and tight contract possibly even allows the outsourcing of core competencies, or at least some of them; even in cases where you consider your Internet strategy at the core of your plans, you can still outsource part of it, such as the design of your external Web site.

SOME BARRIERS TO SUCCESS

Throughout the book, we have pointed out many opportunities for the development and deployment of Internet- and Web-based strategies. A comprehensive strategy, however, involves more than just identifying the opportunities for transforming a company with emerging technologies. In order to eventually put the vision into reality, it is important to a) identify potential hurdles to the changes that come about with each project, and b) get management and end-user buy-in.

IDENTIFYING LEGACIES

As with every attempt at change, a comprehensive Internet strategy involves more than just identifying the opportunities for transforming a company with Web-related technologies. As with every attempt at change, the success of a strategy implementation hinges on the ability to address or bypass a company's legacies. Oftentimes, the history of an organization, crystallized in currently institutionalized processes and structures, creates a drag that could prevent the successful application of the strategy. Spending time up front to identify these sources of drag helps managers identify the blind spots that could prevent them from seeing and addressing a significant number of possible pitfalls. This up-front work can pay off by prompting the development of action plans and contingency plans to address key stumbling blocks expeditiously.

   In the case of the Internet and related technologies, legacies include:

· Information technology infrastructure

· Current workforce skills

· Organization's culture

· Past experiences with change attempts

· Resources available for the effort

INFORMATION TECHNOLOGY INFRASTRUCTURE. Building rudimentary Internet and Web technology capability is probably cheaper than most IT projects attempted in the past, but ramping up to conduct production-level transactions often means integrating heterogeneous and dispersed systems, that have been developed more or less "in isolation." Although open standards and significant improvements in middleware technology facilitate this task compared to the old days of mainly proprietary systems, it should not be underestimated in terms of time and cost.

CURRENT WORKFORCE SKILLS. Internet commerce technologies require the development and maintenance of skills that are rather scarce, both within most IT departments and the programming community. Companies are faced with the dilemma of having to train their IT staff, pay them off-scale salaries, or outsource development and maintenance. While cheaper, the first option does run the risk of building skills that become quickly obsolete, leaving the company with overpriced IT programmers. Companies are addressing these risks not only by outsourcing, but also with the creative use of bonus schemes, allowing base salaries to remain at reasonable levels while compensating their best talent at or above market rates.

UNDERSTAND THE ORGANIZATION'S CULTURE AND ANALYZE PAST CHANGE EXPERIENCES. An important legacy to attend to is your organization's culture and history—what the employees think the company stands for and what they think are its values. It is helpful to understand how your organization's culture might clash with the emerging Internet commerce implementation, and also how aspects of the culture could intensify or mitigate resistance to change in general.

AVAILABILITY OF RESOURCES. An accurate assessment of the available financial and human resources is vital. The level of available resources has a bearing not only on the magnitude of change you can effect, but more importantly on how much risk can be tolerated during the change. A huge store of resources allows large organizations to weather and recover from failures and misjudgment, and it also allows them to accrue the organizational knowledge that comes from exploring risky options.

GETTING MANAGEMENT AND END-USER BUY-IN

The best Internet commerce strategy will never be implemented without the commitment and dedicated resources of top management, and it will never be a success without the support and acceptance of the end users affected by the system. As we pointed out earlier, many Internet initiatives start out at lower management levels, which means that to ramp up to production-grade applications, successes have to be communicated to top management for overall approval and funding, and subsequently to the rest of the organization. Key activities related to getting management approval are as follows:

IDENTIFYING KEY PLAYERS. An effective approach to get organizational buy-in is identifying the individuals who will have the greatest involvement in implementing the strategy. Implementing an Internet strategy involves change and, as in any change process, the real key to success is identifying the key players who can provide the resources and influence to make it all happen.

IDENTIFYING RESOURCE-HOLDERS. These are sources of finance (capital), information technology (equipment), and human resources (organization-wide) that are necessary to implement an Internet strategy.

IDENTIFYING OPINION-MAKERS. Successful Internet projects involve everyone in the organization. Top-down initiatives most likely won't work. Opinion-makers are needed to influence employees at every level in order to have a winning strategy.

IDENTIFYING DECISION-MAKERS. You might have a popular idea, but only a decision-maker can make it happen. At Microsoft, it was Bill Gates who gave the two teams responsible for MSWeb, Microsoft's intranet, the go-ahead.

IDENTIFYING CHAMPIONS. You might not have the clout to reach your CEO directly. Seek a champion who has the ear of top management.

EVANGELISM

Securing commitment from management as well as the end-user community requires a broad-based knowledge and ability to communicate effectively. This combination of knowledge and communication is often called *evangelism* in technology circles. In order to spread the news, an evangelist has to keep up with rapid changes in information technology, whether or not he or she manages this function directly.

In some cases, top management initiates the first Internet project. A large wholesale company experienced a situation where the incentive of winning a major contract forced the (at the time) Internet-inexperienced company to develop a rather sophisticated Internet-based system within a very short time frame. While top management's commitment to the project faciliated its realization immensely, it did not necessarily include all resources needed to actually carry it out. The project team still had a tough time educating the business and IT community in order to gain their acceptance and convince department managers to provide part of their budget for the implementation of the system.

The difficulty of selling an Internet vision to top management depends heavily on the company's individual situation and also on the IT culture of the industry in which it operates, i.e., the perceived need to deploy IT in general and to connect to the Internet specifically. Looking at industry competitors with the objective of realizing the role IT could play within the organization or industry can provide a starting point. From there, the next step would be to realize that the Internet "is here to stay."

Management, on the other hand, should listen to what their people are coming up with and realize the strategic role that IT can play. Industry leaders are more and more often characterized by an intensive use of IT (e.g., IBM, Federal Express, and

Charles Schwab).[21] In order to circumvent the cost problems that this might cause, especially for small- and medium-size enterprises, they often team up with business partners—a structure that can be supported by the communication capabilities of the Internet.

"Spreading the news" throughout a company requires the ability to manage customer and management expectations, balancing such factors as:

· The burden of success. Early-success applications, be it because they were pushed heavily by top management or because they are "low-hanging fruit" (easy projects), can create the impression that it will all be cheap and easy.
· The speed of development.
· Performance perceptions.

An effective evangelist must understand what end users want, and communicate what customers can do to be more successful with Internet commerce. This information is communicated by:

· In-depth knowledge of applications.
· In-depth knowledge of information, which is the product of Internet commerce that can be mined and segmented in different ways to provide more value to customers/users.
· In-depth understanding of top management goals and strategies (the ability to translate key applications to solutions and green lights for management goals and objectives).

In order to be effective, evangelists have to pay attention to the perceptions and biases of the people they are trying to convince: top management as well as end users. These perceptions and biases result from:

· Resistance to change and entrenched traditional operating models
· Inflexible funding strategies

- Poor information technology report cards and previous failures
- Bureaucracy
- Not understanding true project costs

Major challenges often revolve around people and the need to reengineer processes, rather than on the drawbacks of technology. Overall, getting buy-in, be it from management or end users, always means the integration of technical and business knowledge with creativeness and communication skills.

WHERE NEXT?

IMPLEMENTATION AND ACTION PLAN

Creating an implementation plan enhances your ability to estimate time, resource, and effort requirements. More importantly, it could help you to foresee possible contingencies and plan for them. And you will need to set clear progress milestone parameters. Monitoring progress includes collecting data on your success indicators and tracking the planned timeline and budget. Such information could be used not only to judge the current strategy but more importantly to suggest whether a revision of the strategy is merited.

CREATING SUCCESS CRITERIA AND KEEPING THE SPIRIT ALIVE

Identify success criteria relevant to the process or application you have selected. Establishing a framework for regular evaluation promotes more sophisticated planning for new applications and ideally incorporates expectations for performance improvements as part of the planning process. Success can be gauged by a wide variety of measures, including:

CYCLE TIME.   By measuring product development, order processing, and delivery.

CUSTOMERS.   By measuring the number of customers serviced and improved satisfaction, e.g., through interviews and surveys.

EMPLOYEES. By measuring satisfaction and productivity, e.g., by monitoring usage and internal surveys.

BUSINESS MANAGEMENT. By measuring process improvement and better decisions.

IT ORGANIZATION. By measuring number and type of skills.

BUSINESS PARTNERSHIPS. By measuring number of partnerships and relationship improvements.

MARKETING. By measuring channel expansion, CPM, response rates, and lead conversion.

SALES. By measuring cycle time, number of sales, and dollar amounts.

COMMUNICATION. By measuring increased and improved communication.

COST. This might be the right thing to measure when the short-term objective is improvement of connectivity and lowered telecommunication costs.

In the increasingly dynamic environment of the Web, establishing an infrastructure that enables and fosters the continuous development process is crucial. One way to achieve this is forming a cross-functional team that will meet on an ongoing basis. Its task would be to explore flaws in and the success of existing applications and identify opportunities for improvement as well as new applications. This implies not only a close collaboration with end users inside the organization, but also an open ear for customers and external end users who connect to your system. Besides watching business trends, you need to closely monitor technology developments and apply them to your individual environment. At the end of the book, we will give you some references that can serve as starting points to doing so.

The complexity and newness of the electronic commerce arena, as well as the speed with which new technologies and business practices evolve and only recently evolved ones change, make the task of simultaneously staying focused and not losing the overall picture absolutely crucial. Developing a clear and valid vision of where you want to go and how you want to make use of the opportunities offered by the new paradigm requires the input of many different voices and views. It needs integration across business and technology functions, from top management to the user group on the production level or the sales force staff out in the fields. Carefully balancing the comprehensiveness of a broad vision and consistency in pursuing it, with the flexibility to revise and fine-tune the path every couple of months, helps to avoid losing it as well as becoming locked into the wrong track.

With the cases in this chapter we will demonstrate how two companies managed the task of establishing a Web presence. We will first describe the stepwise approach that The Gap took, by first establishing an internal information pool and then "going public" with an external Web site, carefully drawing on its experiences. Pacific Bell Internet Services, a spin-off of Pacific Bell, was able to gain second-mover advantage with the launch of its Internet access service by following on the heels of its arch rival AT&T and by carefully adapting AT&T's experiences to its own strategy.

The following two chapters address some of the further reaching implications that come along with the shift towards the Internet and Web's computing paradigm. In Chapter 9 we outline some of the impacts of this shift on organizations and their structure. We will then take a look at political and social issues before we provide you with a reivew on the most common mistakes that we see managers making and give you some guidelines for success.

ELECTRONIC COMMERCE AT THE GAP, INC.

The Gap, Inc. is an international specialty retailer offering casual apparel, accessories, and personal care items for men, women, and children under five brand names: The Gap, GapKids, BabyGap, Banana Republic, and Old Navy.

From its beginning in 1969 when the company was founded as a jeans-only store, its history has been one of consistent growth and development. As of late 1997, The Gap, Inc. operated more than 2,000 stores in the U.S., Canada, the UK, France, Japan, and Germany. While the majority of sites are located in North America, international expansion is underway. Net sales reached over $5 billion in fiscal 1996, leading to over $450 million in net earnings, or $1.60 per share.

Two characteristics distinguish The Gap, Inc. from its competitors. First, the company covers a broad spectrum of consumer segments, with apparel offerings from the low end of the price spectrum with Old Navy, all the way to the "destination" high end with Banana Republic. Secondly, it features nearly complete vertical integration, with product design, sourcing, advertising, distribution, and sales all done by or under the supervision of Gap employees. This approach gives the company flexibility to react to changing business requirements, as well as the ability to ensure quality at a relatively low cost and uniformity in all of its brands. The vertical integration strategy plays a crucial role for this highly visually oriented company, which considers its brand image to be a key success factor.

The Gap, Inc. epitomizes the modern-day global organization, not only with its worldwide dispersed stores but also with eight distribution centers that serve as centralized shipping locations for their stores around the globe. Corporate headquarter facilities are spread over several locations in San Francisco and nearby San Bruno, with the data center consolidated in tectonically more stable Rocklin, California. International sourcing offices are located in the United Kingdom, Hong Kong (which alone employs over 300 people), and Singapore. The Gap, Inc.'s product design center is located in New York City, which allows the company to be where the action is in the fashion industry.

INFORMATION TECHNOLOGY AT THE GAP

The company's IT organization, under the direction of Mick Connors, Senior Vice President and Chief Information Officer, has developed a very effective partnership with the business.

Through this partnership, the company has deployed many technology solutions that keep its expansive organization running smoothly on a 24-hour-a-day basis. Formally, an Executive Steering Committee that is composed of members of top management decides the overall IT budget (e.g., the percentage of sales to be spent on IT) and sets priorities in different areas, such as sourcing and distribution of goods, stores, and corporate support. Informally, however, many decisions are made up front through the "preselling" discussions that precede the quarterly meetings of the Executive Steering Committee.

The majority of initiatives are driven by business sponsors and elaborated in close cooperation with the IT department, which provides technical consulting and support. Project evaluation (cost-benefit analysis) is crucial in order to get approval from top management. It also illustrates a general rule of the company: that technology has to serve business needs and must not be deployed for its own sake. After the general budget allocation, the figures and plans are further elaborated on a project level.

To address the range of application solution opportunities, Mick Connors established a Business Partner Computing Group to complement traditional application development. While the traditional Application Development Group addresses broader-scale problems, the Business Partner Computing Group focuses on "quick hits." In its entirety, the IT department consists of some 400 Gap employees, supported by outside contractors for specific tasks.

Starting four years ago, the company replaced its former mainframe connections by a private routed network that includes a mainframe, UNIX systems, and PCs. The company's main offices are connected via T1 (or faster) domestic connections, with more varied international connectivity. E-mail is the company's self-described "glue" in all of this, with Lotus Notes having recently replaced cc:Mail. The Gap, Inc. has a full complement of applications to support all aspects of its vertically integrated business. Room-based and desktop videoconferencing systems facilitate collaboration among geographically dispersed groups, e.g., for visualizing design or discussing styles and fabrication.

Electronic communication between the geographically dispersed stores and headquarters is crucial. Headquarters closely monitors daily sales and inventory figures from each of the stores. At the end of each day, report information such as work hours and sales reconciliation data are uploaded to the headquarters data center, while at the same time new pricing tables, inventory figures, and new software releases, such as basic business applications used for store operations, are downloaded.

For communicating with suppliers, such as exchanging information and supporting discussions, The Gap, Inc. has traditionally relied on VANs, using EDI functions and e-mail. Here, the Internet is playing an increasing role, helping to lower connectivity costs and offering new means of communication.

INTERNET STRATEGY AND MANAGEMENT

The Gap, Inc. recognizes that innovative technologies can change the way business is done, but with every new project the company sticks to its motto: "Use technology to fit the business; don't change the business to fit technology." There are several current uses for the Internet and related technologies, such as the World Wide Web—unique features of the new technologies enable support of internal business needs as well as interaction with the outside world.

For cost and other reasons, the company has replaced VAN-based e-mail with the Internet. Also for economic reasons, EDI links will be moved to the Internet in the future, too, replacing costly VAN connections. The company uses ftp to exchange files between headquarters, vendors, and agents, and Web browser applications will be deployed to simplify the distribution and maintenance of software applications with trading partners.

The company's Web strategy goes well beyond cost issues. Since mid-1995, it has had an intranet in place that serves both as a tool for information distribution and as a test-bed for the external Web presence. The external Web site, which was launched in December of 1996 after a thorough planning process, is considered to be another form of advertising, supporting general marketing activities. Besides creating an Internet presence for

The Gap, Inc., its main function lies in brand establishment and the provision of information, such as store locations or financial data geared to investors. Plans were underway in late 1997 to add a transactional sales capability to the public Web site, which until then had been a purely marketing and information site.

The distribution of information to manufacturers, many located in non-English-speaking countries, provides an interesting example of how the company uses technology to fit its business. In order to improve the fit of the garments to be sewed, designers formerly sent out a combination of sketches and a narrative description. However, the vendors often relied solely on the sketches, ignoring the written instructions—sometimes producing less than satisfactory results.

Today, fit sessions can be taped on video and supplemented with an easy-to-understand narrative description. Together with an embedded player, the files are compressed and can be stored on a dedicated ftp server, ready to be accessed and downloaded by the business partners. In a similar way, images of garment specifications and sketches are exchanged between New York-based design groups and California-based technical services, new logos created by the designers are sent to the legal department for approval, and collaboration among different groups working on store construction is facilitated.

SECURITY ISSUES

The Gap, Inc. management is aware of the security flaws posed by the Internet, but also evaluates the company's requirements in a realistic way. The company's security strategy seeks to balance needs and threats on an ongoing basis. Currently, a firewall is in place to protect internal data from the outside. Access from and to the Internet is managed through several servers for e-mail, ftp, and the external Web site. For file transfers, the company uses a secure ftp server that works with rolling keys, in order to keep anyone from being tempted to "pick up all the designs." New security issues will evolve when the company starts using EDI over the Internet, which will include the transfer of financial data.

TAPPING INTO THE WEB

The Gap, Inc.'s history of using the Internet is one of small yet consistent steps, always keeping the company's strategy and needs in mind. Management feels there are currently three areas in need of Web-based technologies: accessing the outside world via the World Wide Web, exploiting the existing wide area network via an intranet, and using an external Web site as an alternative channel for advertising and sales.

While the Internet has been growing over the past few years into one of the largest and most efficient resources of information on basically every topic known to humankind, some employees at The Gap, Inc. discovered that access to the Web could directly improve their productivity. As a result, some divisions and a number of individual employees convinced management to provide them with direct desktop access to the World Wide Web. For instance, key strategic planning employees use the Web to track down market research data, and the legal department uses the Web to do copyright work.

While access to the World Wide Web was deemed important to some, it has by no means reached every desktop within the company. Manning Sutton, a lead technician in Business Partner Computing, explains that linking every desktop to the Web would not make business sense; it would be too expensive and possibly even counterproductive. The conventional concern is, "If we give Internet access to folks, will they just surf all day?" As a result, the company has established some controls of Web access. Specifically, management has developed a means for monitoring Web usage and, before anyone can even get access to the Web, their request must be deemed necessary and approved by a vice president. This desire to ensure that access to the Internet is used both effectively and efficiently is in direct contrast to the company's intranet strategy.

INTRANET: THE FIRST MAJOR WEB-BASED PROJECT

The intranet project started as a partnership between Business Partner Computing and the Corporate Communication department. Corporate Communication is responsible for dispersing a variety of information, ranging from policy changes to merchandise updates to The Gap, Inc.'s daily newsletter, *Dateline*. The original objective for the intranet was to find a way to distribute *Dateline* directly to everyone's desk. Ideas about what else could be distributed followed. cc:Mail, the prevailing e-mail system at that time, was not robust enough to support daily "global" or broadcast e-mails to all headquarter employees. A Web-like intranet offered a more user- and network-friendly alternative, requiring only the installation of one server and equipping each desktop PC with a browser.

Building the business case, however, turned out to be a real challenge. While addressing the cost in terms of hardware, software, service needed, etc. was a manageable task, quantifying the tangible benefits was nearly impossible, apart from the cost of paper to be saved. Most of the intended benefits were intangible, such as improving employee access to accurate, up-to-date business information, and educating and motivating employees. The project was eventually approved by top management because it supported their strategy of improving internal communication and distributing information efficiently. In addition to the daily newsletter; reference information, corporate and financial news, the employee telephone directory, human resource information, and the company calendar of events are all part of the intranet. There were also aggressive plans in place to add divisional and departmental data to the intranet site.

The intranet project began with a prototype, developed by a small team of people from Corporate Internal Communication and the IS department's Business Partners Group. The team decided to start with a "proof of concept" site that was accessible by a small group of employees. Approximately 100 people were chosen as the initial pilot group. This group included a wide variety of employees who were representative of the needs of the company's workforce. They also represented different levels of technological skill and different computing platforms. In order to get the feedback necessary to make the intranet a success, the project included an online feedback tool and an informal network of initial users. Success with the first group allowed the project team to expand to a larger pilot group. At that time the project team also provided intranet access to other employees who specifically requested it. In addition, anyone who already had approval to access the World Wide Web automatically had their browser configured with The Gap, Inc.'s intranet site set as the default homepage.

After their first experiences with the new system, the project team started marketing the intranet more extensively throughout the company's headquarters. Team members also pitched the site to senior executives during monthly technology briefings. Furthermore, they conducted brown-bag informational meetings to educate employees and create a grassroots demand. To gain top-level support, a presentation was also conducted at a director's meeting, illustrating potential benefits to employees. All of this work contributed to the eventual acceptance and success of the intranet. Remarkably, the users considered the technology to be very intuitive, and, unlike other systems, it did not require any classroom training.

To date, the Corporate Internal Communication group manages the intranet site and maintains ownership of the intranet's content. However, with the network growing, it began to make sense to shift responsibility to the departments that actually provide the information, moving to a "distributed authorship" model. In order to do so, guidelines, standards, and templates are being developed by the project team to ensure compatibility with the company's high visual standards. In addition, everything added to the internal Web site must offer some sort of business value, helping employees to be more productive or effective in their work.

To ensure distributed authorship, a Lotus Notes-based system was created in late 1997. With this tool, Web authors throughout the organization can create and maintain their own subsites without needing to know specific technologies like html, ftp, and so on. In this way, content authors can focus on the *information* they want to communicate, not the underlying technology. A variety of programming tools are being built to support this goal, including an online newsletter template, a calendar template, and other similar "standard" formats. Information that is posted on the intranet will be automatically added to a corporate database, allowing it to be archived and searched.

THE PUBLIC WEB SITE

Gap.com—the public Web site—"went live" in December of 1996 after being in development for over a year. The site initially focused on providing product and store information, and it included several interactive components designed to simulate the in-store experience that is so important to The Gap, Inc.'s retail success.

From its inception, Gap.com had six main content areas: *gapnews* (new product and current promotion information); *gapstyle* (specialized product information, including "get dressed interactive," a software package that lets customers "try on" different combinations of clothing and accessories); *stores* (a store locator search engine); *denim* (specialized information about jeans, including size guidelines); *advertising* (information about recent campaigns, including copies of billboards, examples of other illustrations, and viewable video samples from television ads); and *company* (a corporate history, current financial reports, employment information, and other general company information).

Each of these sections is filled with colorful, high-quality photos of Gap products, models, and stores, as well as with highly compelling graphics. The site's basic graphic design is highly consistent with the company's strong emphasis on style and fashion.

MARKET POSITIONING STRATEGY

The Gap, Inc. is a market leader with a high-profile, high-design retail store image and a large number of well-placed retail locations. When Gap.com was launched in 1996, senior management viewed it primarily as a means for learning how the Internet might become a valuable marketing and sales channel. At that time there was plenty of hype about the Internet, but very little evidence that it could become a profitable vehicle for selling consumer products. Management wanted the Internet to complement and enhance the company's retail stores, but not to weaken or compromise in any way its strong presence in shopping malls and other high-traffic locations (historically, the in-store experience had always been a key component of the company's market positioning and differentiation strategy).

In addition, management knew that selling products over the Web would require new processes for order-taking, fulfillment, shipping, collections, returns, and customer service, and they were clear that the company had to be able to deliver the same high level of customer service over the Web that was already available in the retail stores.

Once those core business processes were adapted to handle Web-based transactions, the company began offering selected products for sale over the Web in November of 1997. After almost a year of experience with Gap.com as a marketing and informational tool, management was confident that the organizational capabilities to handle Web-based sales were in place, and that the challenges posed by this exciting new channel would be met successfully.

Note: This case study draws heavily on original research by Haas School of Business MBA students Breitbard, Cain, Fernandez, and Liu. Special thanks also to Mick Connors, Dan Joaquin, and Debbie Gardner of The Gap, Inc. for their assistance.

PACIFIC BELL INTERNET SERVICES

Pacific Bell, the regional Bell operating carrier operating in California, considered two options in shaping its entry into the brave new world of online and Internet services in 1994: make it part of their core business or establish a separate subsidiary. Pacific Bell managers chose to go with the latter option and founded Internet service provider Pacific Bell Internet Services (PBI) in July of 1995. Managers expected the spin-off to provide greater agility and competitiveness in forecasting and adapting to changing market requirements, particularly in comparison to a unit embedded in a traditional RBOC organization. Specifically, it isn't tied to the regulatory restrictions in pricing schemes as its parent—an important contribution to flexibility, which is required in the new and quickly changing market of the Internet. By being self-sufficient in terms of customer support, marketing, human resources, accounting, finance, etc., it gains additional agility and responsiveness. Yet, there is still significant interchange with the parent: The board of directors consists primarily of Pacific Bell management, and the subsidiary leverages some Pacific Bell sales channels. Thus, PBI benefits from the experience of its RBOC parents while possessing the capability for agile reactions to market conditions.

In September of 1995, PBI (with headquarters in San Francisco) started business with high-speed services dedicated to large- and medium-sized commercial users. The consumer and small-business dial-up service, which we will focus on in this section, was launched in May of 1996. Within less than five months, more than 50,000 users had signed up for the service, and the company had grown to around 300 employees and contractors.

MARKET SEGMENTATION AND PRODUCT DESIGN

Prior to launching their service, PBI had to design the Internet-related products and services they would be offering. Key was the realization that fast and reliable Internet access is the *sine qua non* of all Internet activities, preceding all content and customization issues. With less than 20 percent of the U.S. population over the age of 16 having access to the Internet at that time, PBI managers recognized the significant market potential for increasing this percentage by stretching the Net's reach into private homes. Incidentally, this task leveraged PBI's core competencies as the spin-off of a major telecommunications company: The ability to run and manage large networks, and long-standing experience in customer service and support.

PBI started off with the mission of providing fast and reliable Internet access in California and Nevada. Additionally, the company developed navigation guides for their subscribers, but deliberately refrained from offering original content or providing Web hosting. Instead, it formed partnerships with Yahoo! to assist customers in finding valuable content, and with content providers such as the *Los Angeles Times*.

Three groups of market players made up the company's major competitors: "traditional" Internet service providers, online service providers, and other local or long-distance carriers. Among those, AT&T, with its nationwide reach, was considered the number-one competitor. The strategy PBI took when launching their service three months after AT&T's own launch will clearly show how they tried to outperform this major rival.

After defining the general area of business and determining the competitive environment, the start-up addressed the issues of segmenting the consumer Internet market and identifying the groups to be targeted. The sophistication of online users was considered a key differentiation, a factor correlated to the number of hours users spend online. Three major groups were identified: novices on the low end, "power users" on the high end, and PBI's target group—"knowledgeable pragmatists"—in the middle:

- "Knowledgeable pragmatists" spend 10 to 30 hours online per month. They tend to be medium-volume users with some online experience, e.g., from using America Online or other services, and know the very basics of setting up and using their computers and getting online. They are self-sufficient enough to cope with basic obstacles. They consider an online service to be a useful tool, adding value to their everyday lives, but are not overly dependent on it. Especially in terms of customer support and necessary network infrastructure, this group promised to be the most attractive market segment, and subsequently became the number-one target of PBI's services.

- Novice users (people with no or only a little experience online or with a PC at all) tend to demand extensive customer service, providing them with plenty of "hand holding," as well as extremely simple-to-use access tools. Given the fact that they are prone to lose interest in the service at all after a while, or switch access providers, PBI decided not to focus on this segment initially. By the time users get acquainted with the system and eventually start using their e-mail address on business cards or letterhead, the cost of switching to a different provider is much higher.

- "Power users," as PBI calls people who spend more than 30 hours online per month, are also not targeted for several reasons. Not only does their extensive usage pattern require high network capacity, but they also tend to have higher expectations of network reliability, speed, and instant support for sophisticated technical problems. They also tend to be less forgiving when their expectations are not met.

The features of the Internet service that PBI launched in May of 1996 closely matched the preferences they assigned to the targeted "knowledgeable pragmatist" market segment.

At the launch of their services, PBI offered Internet access via a modem at a speed of 28.8 kbps. Shortly thereafter, facilities for access via ISDN connections at a speed of 128 kbps were added. Subscribers were provided with a customized version of the Netscape browser, which is available for most common PC platforms. The software gave users access to the World Wide Web and also served as an e-mail tool and newsgroup reader. Users were provided with free access to 24-hour-a-day customer service and support, online as well as through toll-free 800 numbers. Additionally, the close link of PBI with Pacific Bell allowed it to give customers the choice of being charged for the Internet service on their telephone bill. Deliberately, telnet functionality was not included in the range of services, i.e., PBI did not allow their users to access remote computer systems, a feature that high-volume users would usually demand.

PBI's tactical marketing approach prior to and upon launching the service in May of 1996 clearly reveals a focused assault on its major rival, AT&T.

HOW TO BUILD UP SECOND-MOVE ADVANTAGE

PBI started out preparing for the launch of service in the traditional way: building the business case as well as developing the systems, product, and channels (usual activities prior to launching any product). Estimates were based on some rough predictions of how many Web subscribers they would have by the end of 1996.

In January 1996, when AT&T came out with its Internet service, PBI realized that it might have to refine its approach. It soon turned out, however, that AT&T had problems with handling the several hundred thousand orders they got during the first weeks, which far exceeded their expectations. Their marketing efforts had produced a splash that far outpaced the capacities of technical operations in terms of software delivery and customer service handling.

Estimating optimal capacities for order taking and handling, as well as technical support, was crucial. What the marketing team finally came up with turned out to be an interesting and rather unusual approach: they planned their capacities on a week-to-week basis by adjusting AT&T's adoption rates based on their own characteristics. The company was able to do so, first, because AT&T made its figures public and, second, because PBI's launch followed its rival's closely in time—only three months later.

How Did the Approach Work?

- First, PBI adjusted AT&T's nationwide figures to the geographical area that it would actually service. Twenty percent seemed to be the right estimate, representing California's share of the U.S. Internet market.
- The second point was brand image. Clearly, freshly founded PBI started off with the image of Pacific Bell. The telephone company scores high as a player that is reliable, stable, solid, and well-known to the customer. Compared to AT&T, however, it falls short in terms of leading-edge technology and innovation. While the spin-off of PBI as a "cool little subsidiary" could somewhat compensate for the image of Pacific Bell as a stodgy old company, at least in the longer run, the innovation factor was considered to be crucial in the highly dynamic world of the Internet. Based on this brand image differential, the project team decided on a discount of about 10 percent off of AT&T's adoption numbers.
- A look on PBI's pricing plans clearly shows their response to AT&T's scheme, and reveals how they went after the "knowledgeable pragmatist" (medium-volume user) market. Besides offering unlimited access for $19.95 per month, AT&T had a second plan that gave users free access for the first five hours

per month, followed by $2.50 per additional hour. The word "free" was an essential part of AT&T's promotional activities. PBI's marketing team had spent a lot of time figuring out a plan that would give users a cost advantage over AT&T's rates just in the 10-to-30-hour segment, leaving the nontarget segments to its rival. Like AT&T they came out with two different plans. One gave users 10 hours of access a month for $9.95, followed by a charge of $1 for each additional hour; the second plan, called the Carefree Access Plan (CAP), offered users 20 hours of monthly access for $14.95 a month, with a .50¢ charge for each additional hour, "capping out" at $19.95 a month. The graph in Figure 8-1 depicts the hourly fees users had to pay in each of the four plans offered by the two companies, depending on their monthly overall online time. It shows clearly that PBI would be the company of choice for the medium-volume market segment in terms of

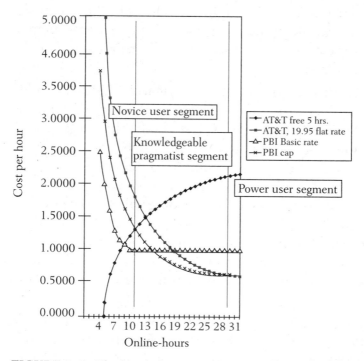

FIGURE 8-1. The hourly fees users have to pay for each of the four plans offered by both PBI and AT&T, depending on their monthly online time.

price. Adjustments were made according to estimations of the percentage of users attracted to each of AT&T's plans. PBI reduced expected adoption numbers, particularly in the low-usage segment, because their promotional strategy did not target this group (ads did not include the word "free"). Because they expected to reach more of the mid-level users, they increased the adoption numbers for this segment.

· Initially, PBI considered AT&T's first-move advantage as an important factor for discounting, given the possibility that AT&T could have "sucked up" a considerable part of the overall market by the time PBI entered it. However, AT&T's difficulties with fulfillment led to a situation where many of its customers were getting their software at the same time PBI launched their product. Also, it turned out that barriers to consumer switching were fairly low. Since AT&T offered 30 days of free access, customers had time to switch to PBI.

· Last but not least, estimating the effect of their own promotion activities also played a major role in the analysis.

PBI's promotional strategy involved three major factors:

· As AT&T had done before, PBI planned to launch its service with a big splash, called a "surround launch." Major advertising campaigns and press coverage were expected to give the service an initial lift, eventually kicking off a snowball effect and leading to a situation where a major part of subsequent customers would be brought in through word of mouth.

· The approach PBI took, especially with regards to newspaper and radio ads, is called *targeted messaging*. On one hand, PBI's advertisements contained e-mail addresses without further explanation, meaning they were digestible only to those already "in the know," i.e., somewhat experienced with the online world. On the other hand, one objective of the strategy was to add a human face to the campaign as well as to create some sort of community, something that medium-volume users expect—in contrast to high-volume users. A number of characters were created, such as an old lady with the user name Cyberpunk, a young skateboarder named Shredder, and a group of "mudders" socializing in Calistoga's mud baths. The target message to customers was "If I can do it, you can do it." PBI also broadcast ads featuring the characters sending out amusing e-mail messages to each other, telling about their favorite Web sites and leisure activities. The ads also invited customers to get in touch with the characters themselves.

· Additionally, PBI made use of Pacific Bell's already established sales and support channels, leveraged its brand name, and completed the concept with activities such as direct mail, appearances at trade shows, and partnering with the retail industry.

Taking all promotional factors into account and balancing them with AT&T's figures led to a forecast, on a week-by-week basis, that was accurate to approximately 90 percent for the first four weeks. The forecast itself was built within six to eight weeks. Given the innovation of the service that was launched, this result is quite astonishing. Unlike AT&T, PBI did not experience major order-taking or delivery problems during the initial phase. As it became clear that the demand would surpass in-house resources, order taking was outsourced to an outside vendor. Building up enough capacity for technical support posed a more difficult problem in terms of short-term scaling. The exact forecasts, however, facilitated early preparations for increasing technical support capabilities.

THE RESULTS

After four months, PBI had 50,000 subscribers. By that time, capacity forecasts no longer had to rely on AT&T's figures, but could rather be based on PBI's own customers' patterns of adoption. This was facilitated by a sophisticated mechanism of keeping track of customers and learning about their reaction to different promotional activities. Each time a new customer registered, the order-taker asked how the customer learned about PBI's service (from a newspaper, radio, or online ad, PBI's Web site, direct mail, flyers distributed at trade shows, retail, word of mouth, etc.). The answer, which was encoded with an assigned customer number, allowed for tracking the performance of promotional activities throughout the course of a customer relationship. It also helped to predict the effects of future activities. In the long run, such a tracking mechanism could also help PBI identify different user profiles, allowing the company to customize services for them.

Twenty percent of the customers in its first months were on the Internet for the first time, suggesting that 80 percent were somewhat experienced and didn't fall into the novice segment—a result very much in line with the objectives of the marketing strategy. By September of 1996, the word-of-mouth rate had climbed to 40 percent, leveraging marketing expenses. PBI also experienced a rather low churn rate, showing rather high customer satisfaction. The majority of users chose the CAP pricing plan, PBI's high-end plan.

In spite of all its marketing success, PBI has not yet reached break-even point. In fact, the company considers their first couple of years as investment years, as do other industry players. Getting a foot into the "Internet door" is a strategic decision for both AT&T and Pacific Bell, and eventually a means of keeping their telephone customers by offering them one-stop shopping for their telecommunications services.

LESSONS LEARNED

· This case provides a good example of how an established company can turn entrepreneurial and become a successful player in the fast-paced world of the Internet. By spinning off PBI, Pacific Bell founded a highly flexible and responsive company that is not constrained by regulatory rules, but at the same time is backed by the assets of the larger parent.

· Making the first move does not always guarantee a means of controlling a market. A clearly defined and focused "follower strategy" might prove to be just as or even more effective.

· Product cycles on the Internet are fast, and strategy development has to adapt to that pace. PBI's six-week forecasting effort shows how quickly reactions to changing market requirements can affect the results of a product launch as a whole.

- Internet consumers are not "sticky" yet. While they tend to give anybody a chance, they also switch companies when they are not fully satisfied. Stable relationships are not easy to build.

- The losses that both AT&T and Pacific Bell take into account show the fierceness of competition that characterizes today's Internet service market. The number of Internet service providers, numbering about 3,000 by early 1997, is expected to drop significantly due to consolidations over the next couple of years.

NOTES

[1] See Cronin, Mary J, *Doing More Business on the Internet: How the Electronic Highway is Transforming American Companies*. New York, 1995, p. 249ff. See also Gualtieri, M. "Grappling with EC: It's Hard to Define, So Where Do You Start?" *ec.comm*, November/December 1996, 5–6.

[2] See the *Netscape's Intranet Deployment Guide* appendix (Intranet Team and Applications). Netscape Communication Corporation, 1997 (http://home.netscape.com/comprod/server_central/query/idg/appendix.html).

[3] See "Building and Information Systems Infrastructure: Avoiding Skill Legacies," Fisher Center for Management and Information Technology, U.C. Berkeley, threaded discussion 96–TD–001, Berkeley, 1996 (http://isr.berkeley.edu/citm-s/discussion/skills.html).

[4] See *Netscape's Intranet Deployment Guide*, Determining Systems Requirements. Netscape Communications Corporation, 1997 (http://home.netscape.com/comprods/server_central/query/idg/requirements.html, 04/17/97). Other useful sources are Jill H. Ellsworth and Matthew W. Ellsworth's *The New Internet Business Book*, New York 1996, and Rob Kolstad's BSDI white paper "Becoming and ISP," Berkeley, 1997.

[5] See *Netscape's Intranet Deployment Guide*, Determining Systems Requirements. Netscape Communications Corporation, 1997 (http://home.netscape.com/comprods/server_central/query/idg/requirements.html, 04/17/1997).

[6] For more detailed information, see *Netscape's Intranet Deployment Guide*, Designing your Intranet. Netscape Communications Corporation, 1997 (http://home.netscape.com/comprod/server_central/query/idg/design.html, 04/17/1997).

[7] Cronin, op. cit., p. 249ff.

[8] See Arie Segev, Carrie Beam, and Judith Gebauer: "Impact of the Internet on Purchasing Practices: Preliminary Results from a Field Study," Fisher Center for Management and Information Technology, UC Berkeley, Working Paper 97–WP–1024, Berkeley, September 1997.

[9] See Eva Freeman, "Middleware: Link everything to anything," in *Datamation*, October 1996 (http://www.datamation.com/PlugIn/issues/1996/oct/10cs1.html). For a more in-depth overview, see Philip A. Bernstein, "Middleware: A model for distributed system services," in *Communications of the ACM* v39, n2 (Feb 1996), 86–98.

[10] See Gartner Group, "The Internet and DBMSs: What is Real?" Strategic Data Management Research Note SPA/180/193, November 26, 1996 (http://www.gartner.com/webletter/article9/article9.html).

[11] See Michael Jay Tucker, "Managing your Web-to-database performance," in *Datamation*, January 1997 (http://www.datamation.com/PlugIn/issues/1997/jan/01dbstor.html), Patrick Dryden, "Middleware management muddle," in *Computerworld*, 03/03/1997 (http://www.computerworld.com/search/AT-html/9703/970303SL9bmc.html).

[12] Vance McCarthy, "Web security: How much is enough?" *Datamation*, January 1997 (http://www.datamation.com/PlugIn/issues/1997/01secur.html). Also Dean Adams, "Securing your business," a white paper by The Open Group, 1996.

[13] BBN white paper "The Managed Internet Security Solution: Internet Site Patrol" (http://www.bbn.com/doc/white_papers/secwp/managed.htm).

[14] Gartner Group research note "What Makes Intranet Security Different," 1996.

[15] See Julia Angwin, "Building a Web Site" in the "San Francisco Chronicle" September 6, 1996.

[16] Mark Gibbs, "Buyer's Guide: Internet Outsourcers." *Network World*, v13, n5, January 29, 1996, 53–56.

[17] Carol Saunders, May Gebelt, and Qing Hu, "Achieving Success in Information Systems Outsourcing." *California Management Review*, v39, n2, Winter 1997, 63–79.

[18] "Building a Business Case for Outsourcing: Risk Analysis," Gartner Group Research Note ESP, TU-OUT-185, September 1996.

[19] "Can a Firm Really Do Internet Consulting/SI? (Part 1)," Gartner Group Research Note INET, KA-ICN-051, July 1996.

[20] Saunders, Gebelt, and Hu, op. cit.

[21] "IT in the Spotlight, Information Week 500," *Information Week*, September 22, 1997.

ORGANIZATIONAL IMPACTS

The full organizational impact of the Web computing paradigm is yet to emerge. Three years since the emergence of the Web as a business platform, companies are still working out how they might exploit the platform and what it all means for their businesses. In this chapter we will explore the impact of the Web paradigm on organizations, in terms of both their structure and the work lives of the managers and employees who populate them. We will start with a discussion of how the Web paradigm affects organizational structures, and then move on to a discussion of how it affects individual work lives within such structures. The final section of the chapter covers managerial issues created by these organizational impacts.

ORGANIZATIONAL STRUCTURE: THE CORPORATE WEB AS A REFLECTION OF COMPANY RELATIONSHIPS

The impact of the Web paradigm on organizational structures can perhaps best be summed up in its ability to map and then transform the various relationships that constitute and involve an organization. Many of the relationships that sustain the ongoing conduct of any business today are supported at least in part—and sometimes replaced—by some form of computing technology and a network link. For example, electronic data interchange (EDI) has allowed digital transmissions to substitute for the flow of paper tracking a variety of transactions (e.g., purchases and payments) between trading partners.

As to be expected, this digitization of relationships has also resulted in their transformation. The most obvious transformations come in the form of increased articulation of organizational knowledge, as well as the increased fluidity of such relationships and the configurations they constitute.

ARTICULATION OF ORGANIZATIONAL KNOWLEDGE

The enthusiastic adoption of corporate intranets has led to an increase in the amount of information and knowledge that is digitized and accessible to a wide audience both inside and outside the organization. Digitization essentially results in the articulation of knowledge at the organizational level. Once knowledge is in the form of a file, it can be transmitted, stored, processed, and accessed by anyone in the organization. At this point, the knowledge becomes articulated at the organization level—where previously it was articulated at the individual level only, if at all. Sometimes, the process of digitization articulates knowledge that was previously tacit, even to the individual using it, e.g., knowledge on which intuition is based.

While some of this digitization occurred through the repurposing of printed material, often the most valuable digitized information has resulted from either new work done within departments or the publication of files previously kept private by individuals or departments charged with creating and/or managing them. Notably, such individuals or departments are usually happy to part with such information because they would like to highlight them in their department's Web page. Also, they expect savings to accrue from reducing their involvement in providing this information; once it is published in the departmental Web page, employees and managers can simply access the information without having to call the department and take an employee's time to search for and transmit the information.

A less innocuous avenue fueling the articulation of organizational knowledge is the advent of sophisticated monitoring systems. As corporate computers have become networked, it has become possible to track the activities related to, and products of the knowledge-making activities of employees. Some of the more common knowledge elements tracked are e-mail messages and computer screen captures. Files and databases generated by the collection of such elements further digitize the knowledge that was previously the sole property of the managers and employees creating and disseminating it.

INCREASED FLUIDITY OF RELATIONSHIPS

One of the most compelling impacts of the Web paradigm is the enhanced flexibility it has enabled. As more and more relationships have become digitized—mapped into organizational networks and databases—they have seemingly become much easier to reconfigure into new sets of relationships in order to meet the requirements of new opportunities and problems an organization might face. Although relationships by definition are much "stickier" than the digital networks that reflect them, the fact that they are digitized has created at least an aura of flexibility. Relationships mapped onto digital networks seem to take on some features of the digital network itself—in this case, the ease with which linkages can be created, dropped, and re-linked. While relationships will never reach the level of fluidity displayed by digital networks, the aura of flexibility can still persuade the people involved in such relationships that reconfiguration is possible, if not easier. This influence, coupled with an actual increase in flexibility, has fueled much discourse and interest in flexible organizational configurations.

Perhaps the most popular manifestation of this is the virtual or networked organization. In their most idealized forms, these organizations constantly and fluidly attach and shed business partners and personnel to match the changing demands of the market and other environmental factors. The proliferation and linking of computing networks has reduced the cost of linking and unlinking new elements to an organization. The aggressive worldwide dissemination of such networks means the search for appropriate partners and personnel need not be bound by geopolitical borders. Furthermore, the digitization of organizational knowledge makes such knowledge not only replicable but also portable. Thus, more and more knowledge appropriate to any situation is much more easily stored and transmitted to the locations where it is required—independently of the people who create the knowledge.

As is to be expected, the emergence of Web technologies and the concomitant transformations in organizational structures have much import for the lives of the people who populate these structures. The most obvious impact is the transformation of the way work is performed within organizations. The digitization of organizational knowledge enables informating—an increase in the informational content of most organizational work. This increase has resulted from and results in major changes in the environments and tools that constitute our everyday work lives. Even more compelling is the evolution of the social contract among workers, management, and an organization. While not the only or first factor causing this evolution, the application of Web technologies is one of the most compelling catalysts for hastening this evolution. Essentially, Web technologies can potentially enable the agile, adaptive organizational transformations essential for success in the current business environment.

CHANGING WORK LIVES

The emergence of cheaper network computers in today's computing environment portends a trend toward the increased computerization of our workplaces. As the cost of computerization decreases, we can expect that more and more of today's work will be moved onto digital platforms. Work itself can be transformed as we gain the ability to replace intuition with digital indicators of progress and accomplishment. Cheaper workstations suggest the potential for the pervasiveness of this phenomenon.

Yet the current computerization trend is markedly different from past efforts at achieving such ubiquity. It is possible to achieve a much wider application of this technology much faster than any past efforts—thanks to the low cost of such efforts, the potential savings to be achieved, and the easy transfer of programs developed on the Web platform from one setting to another. This situation has obvious benefits over efforts at the wide adoption of the microcomputer. Networked configurations (NCs) are much cheaper than microcomputers, albeit less capable as stand-alone machines. They are also projected to be cheaper to maintain, giving information systems personnel the ability to standardize configurations, monitor, and repair workstations remotely over the networks that link them to their servers.

The same networked configuration that makes remote system maintenance possible also increases management's ability to enact the surveillance of employee activities. These include capturing a range of employee activity indicators: e.g., e-mail messages, keystrokes, and screen captures. Such measures could enhance management's ability to keep track of the efficiency and effectiveness with which company resources are being used. The presence of these measures, however, does not resolve the need to carefully consider what management is trying to measure. Managers still need to determine whether they will measure process or outcomes, how they will enact these measures, and what incentives they will link to the measures. The effectiveness of a monitoring system built upon a network platform is dependent on the care managers have taken in addressing these three issues. We will discuss these issues further in the next section of this chapter.

Another factor that managers need to take into account when wielding this newfound ability for surveillance is the effect it might have on employee morale. Employees are likely to find the presence of constant surveillance an unwelcome and unacceptable intrusion into their privacy. Furthermore, constant surveillance might cut into the amount of nonprescribed activity that employees might need to engage in. Such nonprescribed activities are usually key to generating creative solutions that benefit the company.

Aside from clear-cut policies regarding privacy, the negative effects of surveillance can be mitigated by the increasing availability of products for protecting the privacy of individuals. These fortuitous by-products of a strong Web ethos against domination make it possible for individuals to control access to information about their identity and/or activities. They include powerful and increasingly easy-to-use encryption methods that allow individuals to render e-mail messages and other private files virtually unreadable to most unauthorized viewers. As more sophisticated means of monitoring become available, we can expect that more and more products to protect personal privacy will also become available for individuals who want to have greater control over the dissemination of information they deem personal.

The network computing paradigm is emerging against a backdrop an increase in the movement of personnel across companies. The rise of a contingent workforce and high merger and acquisition activity, along with the high mobility of employees possessing skills in high demand, has resulted in an increased need for facilitating the constant reconfiguration of company systems. The cross-platform nature of Web technologies promises some relief in this domain. Additionally, the networked nature of these new configurations allows for the inclusion of workers in organizations—regardless of their geographic location. This feature not only enables companies to build workforce configurations that achieve their goals at the lowest cost, but also allows companies to offer nontraditional work arrangements, e.g., telecommuting, which enhances their ability to attract and retain some of the most highly recruited personnel.

This last work arrangement—telecommuting—has strong implications for the lives of workers. A key dilemma today is where to draw the line between work and home or work and play. As the traditional indicators of these lines are blurred, it is tempting to spend a disproportionate amount of time on one side of the line versus the other. Workers can no longer rely on the clock, their bosses, or coworkers to draw that line. In the overwrought workplaces of the '90s, workers have to contend with more projects than they can handle in a traditional workday. This has led to much burnout as workers struggle to get ahead of their commitments at work, while falling behind in their home commitments. The recent move towards early retirement, part-time work, and socially meaningful work suggests that workers are starting to push back and reclaim some of their nonwork spaces. It is well worth noting that the network computing model both facilitates these new work arrangements and could stretch work hours to unreasonable levels—if workers and managers are not aware of the risk and make an effort to address it.

MANAGERIAL IMPLICATIONS

In this section we will discuss several key dilemmas that can help you think about how to manage or at least account for some of the effects we have discussed in the previous sections. These dilemmas can be summarized as follows:

- Balancing the standardization and customization of client configurations

- Encouraging employees to share information they deem private

- Determining measures to use in monitoring the workforce

- Designing human resource policies to support building and maintaining an agile workforce

BALANCING STANDARDIZATION AND CUSTOMIZATION

As previously discussed, networked computing facilitates standardization like never before possible. Information systems personnel can remotely download configurations and check whether given machines on the network adhere to prescribed configurations. At the same time, client machines are becoming more and more able to support custom configurations. As programs written in Java or ActiveX become more and more available, users can build custom configurations based on personalized combinations of these smaller programs.

A management dilemma involves determining how much of a configuration the IT organization must prescribe. It behooves any IT manager to recognize that the network computing paradigm is not a return to the mainframe days. The clients in this new network model are much more capable and customizable than the dummy terminals of the mainframe era. Users, particularly more sophisticated ones, will likely try to exploit such capabilities once they become more familiar with their client machines. Management has to consider whether and how much they are willing to allow such client customization, and the costs of doing so.

An important consideration is the level of sophistication of the user base and its tasks. The more sophisticated the task and/or the user, the more likely there will be demands for customization of client machines. One solution would be to have different machines for different types of users, providing more powerful, customizable machines to more sophisticated users. Thus, most common discussions of the uses of network computers suggest that their deployment should be limited to individuals who perform simple, repetitive tasks, like data entry.

However, managers might want to consider the additional savings they might reap by deploying network computers to other personnel, including knowledge workers. Such workers might be persuaded to move to less capable computing platforms such as network computing by a computing policy that recognizes their need for customizable platforms. One way to build this case is to determine what functions such workers are willing to give up. A survey will surely suggest routine tasks such as backing up and archiving files, upgrading rapidly evolving applications, keeping track of system configurations, lugging laptops around, and security. These services can very well be centralized so the IT department takes care of the routine tasks and keeps track of configurations, allowing knowledge workers the freedom to leave their laptops behind and travel anywhere around the globe, pulling up their own configurations at a network computer installed at their destination. This can make a compelling case for the use of network computers, but only if it is coupled with guarantees that workers' data will remain private, and that they will have unencumbered access to the applications and files they need.

ENCOURAGING EMPLOYEES TO SHARE INFORMATION
THEY DEEM PRIVATE

In the early, heady days of Web computing, employees—caught up in the excitement of it all—were quick to share data they were storing. After almost three years of such activity, many of the less sensitive and carefully guarded data stores are probably accessible through company intranets and even on the Internet or extranets. At this point, managers need to tow the line between ensuring employee privacy and making sure that pertinent information is shared across the network among people who need it. This task is complicated by the fact that workers will very soon be able to easily encrypt and potentially hold valuable corporate data hostage if they feel threatened by managerial coercion.

Managers need to build a policy about privacy that ensures that every worker has the right to personal data, but identifies information that is deemed public in a given workplace. But perhaps even more importantly, they must control the interpretation of such policies. It is very easy to fall back on the explanation that a company is overly intrusive when such policies are announced—no matter how generous they are toward a worker's privacy.

Personal privacy is one of most people's cherished and vigilantly protected rights. Managers need to be sensitive to the potential explosiveness of this issue and seek to mediate employee interpretations of such policies. Information sessions, forums, and other forms of communication are necessary to build an acceptable shared interpretation for such a policy. Managers will do well to stress the benefits of such policies to both the corporation and individuals, as well as acknowledge that the policy is imperfect and might not sit well with the values of every person within the organization. Such attention to building a shared understanding will be valuable in pushing the acceptance of any policy on privacy that managers might build. Managers can also fall back on any established history of trust between workers and management—perhaps asking for an endorsement of the policy from trusted individuals in the corporation after they have had a chance to review the policy.

DETERMINING MEASURES FOR MONITORING THE WORKFORCE

As previously discussed, the ability to monitor employee actions has been greatly enhanced by the networked computing platform, but this capability does not do away with the need for managers to carefully design the measures they will deploy with these monitoring systems. A key dilemma is whether the measures should address process or outcomes.

Most commonly described monitoring systems focus on process. For example, capturing computer screens can tell you what an employee is doing with the computer during the day. But it is an imperfect measure because there are many productive—as well as unproductive—things an employee could be doing that do not register on the computer. More importantly, there is a tenuous link between the actions that employees take in their day-to-day jobs and the actual outcomes of those actions. An employee could be busily scanning the Web for information that is valuable to the company, but this information could become valuable only when the employee provides a product such as a report or presentation that summarizes the information and its implications. Outcomes such as reports and presentations are less likely to be detectable in monitoring systems that focus on process. Since outcomes directly affect organizational effectiveness more than process, managers need to build measures of outcome into their monitoring systems, or at least enhance monitoring systems with measures of outcome.

Having determined whether they would like to focus on process or outcomes, managers should then focus on how they will implement the measures and what incentives they will link to the measures. There are a whole slew of measures for the various processes and outcomes that are important to an organization—from highly simple counts to sophisticated biometrics. Paying careful attention to their validity and non-intrusiveness can contribute much to the soundness of a monitoring system.

Another consideration is the ability of employees to adapt to any measures used, so they can make themselves look good in a monitoring system without necessarily being productive for the organization. Building dynamism into the monitoring system allows managers to not only guard against this phenomenon but also further refine their measures. For example, as more measures of process and outcomes are taken, it will be possible to start correlating these measures to determine which process measures might have the strongest relationship to the desirable individual and organizational outcomes.

DESIGNING HUMAN RESOURCE POLICIES

It is no surprise that there is so much movement in the current workforce. The difficult times of the '80s and early '90s have weakened individual loyalty to companies. The current economic boom has lead to low unemployment and is fueled by a rise in the numbers of contingent workers. Employees can move from one job to another and command higher salaries and benefits at every move. This focus on mobility has detrimental effects beyond the disruptions of employee turnover. Employees who move from job to job are likely spending more time on their own job searches than in getting the job done in the organizations where they are currently employed. Organizations suffer not only because of this but also because they lose the benefits of a strong culture, which must be built on many years of stable personal relationships among employees, managers, and co-workers.

Recognizing this dilemma has fueled much discussion of solutions for stemming turnover and giving employees an incentive to stay in their jobs. Many of the preferred solutions give corporations some flexibility for dealing with market changes and skill demand changes that seem to happen at an increasing pace in today's business climate. Chief among compensation strategies is providing bonuses for various achievements (e.g., signing and completed projects). Such strategies allow companies to bring employee compensation in line with market rates without needlessly raising the more structured salary-scale schedules of the company and without making a long-term commitment to a salary level that might seem inflated when skill demands change in the near future. Companies also recognize that compensation need not mean only money. Often times, conditions other than salary keep workers in a company. While these conditions can translate to simple yet extremely useful concierge services, they also include benefits that link closely with the networking technologies that we are highlighting in this book. Chief among these perks is offering employees the option of telecommuting. Also, the cross-platform nature of Web technologies facilitates the movement of employees and contractors across different organizations. It is entirely possible to hook individuals and any devices they might bring into the corporate network. Now more than ever, networking and browser technologies are making it possible to get new employees quickly up and working on organizational tasks. Managers might consider using the same systems to hasten the integration of employees into the corporate culture and way of doing things. Activities such as new employee training and FAQs on the company can be delivered quite easily and effectively over browser-based systems. Such activities can go quite far in facilitating the rapid integration of new employees and other individuals into the organization.

The two cases that end this chapter, Marshall Industries and MCA, illustrate the impact that Web technologies could have in two companies that distribute contrasting products: electronic components and entertainment. The cases present contrasting ways in which Web applications were introduced in the companies. At Marshall, there was a top-down effort with much support and strategic direction from senior management. At MCA, exploiting Web technologies required the ingenuity and efforts of forward-thinking individuals within the information technology group who recognized the impact that such technologies could have for the distribution of entertainment products.

MARSHALL INDUSTRIES

Marshall Industries was one of the first companies in its industry to recognize and take advantage of the opportunities offered by emerging information technologies. The company is the fifth largest domestic U.S. distributor of industrial electronic components and production supplies, employs around 1,600 people, and achieved net sales of over $1 billion for the first time in 1995 and a net income of $40 million. Their 31 sales and distribution facilities and three corporate and distribution centers in the U.S. and Canada serve over 30,000 customers. Why the need to enter risky ground?

PUSHING TOWARD THE INTERNET

Contrary to the situation in most companies, the idea behind collective tools, intranets, and the Internet did not have to be sold to top management. The idea originated from the CEO himself, Rob Rodin, who is a keen believer in information technology and in its possible commercial applications. Rob Rodin was highly interested in Dr. Deming's total quality management ideas and the potential that information technology could have in improving service. Top management attended a series of seminars held by Dr. Deming and were then put in charge of communicating these ideas down the hierarchy, so each person within the organization became involved and understood the importance of the changes. Formal groups were also created to discuss specific organizational and technological matters.

From the start, the objectives behind the changes were to serve the customer better, to become more efficient by reducing costs, to open up market places where Marshall was not present, and to lead the industry. Rob Rodin clearly wanted his company to be seen as an innovator, ahead of its competitors. All these objectives of course were superseded by the need that the changes generate revenues and new customers.

Vice President Bob Edelman points to the fact that Marshall does not focus as much as its competitors on financial targets at the individual activity level. Instead, it is more interested in the global effects of the company. Incentive schemes play a key role, so projects such as the redesign of information systems and the introduction of groupware, intranets, and Internet were not sold on the basis of a predicted fixed ROI. Top management was, however, convinced (and remains convinced) that electronic-based applications would significantly contribute to the company's financial results.

Before implementing electronic-based applications, Marshall carried out some basic market research. It organized focus groups with customers (who would be the future users of the systems) and employees (who were the most familiar with the legacy systems). Marshall also organized surveys and asked outsiders to give them feedback. These preliminary steps, however, more validated existing ideas than served as the basis for real decision-making. The results were not too compelling, as many engineers declared that they did not see a use for electronic-based applications. However, Marshall believed that these results were due to generational differences among engineers, since a 25-year-old engineer most likely has a mindset completely different than a 50-year-old engineer. In addition, most customers could not foresee the potential of IT to serve their needs better.

In the beginning, therefore, Marshall made the decision for its constituents: customers, suppliers, and employees. Marshall did not clearly respond to a need, but it had a vision that electronic-based applications would be valued by its constituents. Marshall understood that customers do not always know what they want in advance. Once Marshall had established the electronic networks, and direct feedback from customers was made possible, the systems could be refined to meet customer (and other constituent) needs more accurately. The systems could evolve in sync with customer needs.

MARSHALL'S CUSTOMERS

Most of Marshall's customers are OEM's (original equipment manufacturers) in major industries such as producers of computer mainframes, office equipment, or communication hardware. Marshall distributes semiconductors, connectors, passive components, computer systems and peripherals, production supplies, tool kits, instrumentation, and workstations. These products are sourced from 150 suppliers, mainly brand names. The products include over 170,000 individual part numbers.

Marshall distinguishes between two different kinds of customers: design engineers, who constitute its core customers, and purchasing departments of manufacturing companies, who are negotiating long-term, high-volume, high-price contracts with Marshall.

Design engineers look for technological specifications and want to know what is out there and how it all compares. Although they said they would not use billboard advertising on the Web during the original focus groups, in reality they make extensive use of these, and advertising has become a major source of revenue for Marshall. Purchasing is almost spontaneous. The Internet has given these customers a vehicle to facilitate their purchases. They are given information concerning price, availability, and product characteristics. Marshall does not carry all product lines; for example, it does not distribute Intel products in the U.S. although it does in Europe. However, Intel products are commodities; engineers are interested in getting information on complex products and systems, and this is what constitutes Marshall's distinctive offering, compared to its competitors.

Marshall offers a virtual search feature that enable customers to search for information on products. Marshall has chosen to provide a continuous search method throughout a customer visit to the Marshall virtual store, which means that each supplier site accessible through the Marshall site has the same form. Marshall was actually forced to create sites for more than 50 of its suppliers, which did not have a Web presence. Suppliers provided the content and Marshall converted this content into a harmonized site. Some suppliers showed strong resistance and invoked all kinds of reasons for not wanting to prepare such sites, such as there possibly being a mistake in the specifications. Marshall convinced them by proving to them that there was little difference between information on the Internet and information on paper, that the problems in the real world were the same as the problems in the virtual world.

Purchasing departments of manufacturing companies care more about prices, lead times, ordering forms, out-of-stock items, etc. Although their relationship with Marshall continues to be mainly based on direct, telephone, or face-to-face interactions, they have begun to discover the benefits of electronic-based applications. Price negotiation occurs outside of intranets and the Internet, but these systems can be used once a price has been negotiated for a specific time and volume.

RESHAPING RELATIONSHIPS THROUGH THE INTERNET

Marshall has developed what its chairman, Rob Rodin, calls virtual distribution, which aims to provide access to products, services, and information at any time from any place. This is a service now open to companies across all industries.

Marshall's network solutions are tailored to the specific needs of different constituents. The company could not provide numbers of how much these networks are actually being used, but they believe they have had a great impact on the overall structure of the company. They understood from the beginning that they could not meet everyone's needs using a single model, so they set up separate networks and separate Web sites (and Web subsites) in order to give its constituents what they were looking for. Over time, Marshall has been refining its services to meet the needs of subsections of its constituents (for example, it is currently launching a specific service for a specific category of customers, namely design engineers).

Marshall's Internet solution was launched in 1996. It contains areas protected with passwords and SSL (secure socket layer, Netscape's standard for secure online transactions) that contain customized information for specific classes of users, and the new service specific for design engineers should soon be introduced. It is used by suppliers to find information about sales volumes, design registration activity, pending sales opportunities, and quotations. Customers use it to find information about backlog, credit limit, work in progress, purchases to date, pricing, and inventory.

The Internet has enabled Marshall to change the nature and frequency of its contacts with both customers and suppliers. In the past, Marshall had only occasional contacts with its customers. Now the plug-in feature enables customers to receive the newest information on products that interest them. In addition, a weekly newsletter is sent to them via e-mail.

The nature of Marshall's relationships with its suppliers used to depend on the sophistication of the suppliers. The least sophisticated waited for monthly paper reports on the state of business. However, suppliers realized that they could not afford to wait 30 days to get the information and that constant, up-to-date information was necessary. Marshall undertook an aggressive campaign to move its suppliers over to electronic-based solutions. It organized interactive multimedia seminars over the Internet, in which over 100 suppliers participated. Suppliers understood that they needed to follow in order to remain competitive.

Marshall is currently running a pilot program to test the potential for EDI over the Internet. As there is too little demand yet from suppliers, Marshall prefers to wait until suppliers integrate this technology into their workflow before it starts pushing the feature.

The company claims that corporate redesign has been a phenomenal success. From 1993–1996, employment has decreased 16 percent while sales have doubled. The company grew from a $575 million sales figure at the end of 1992 to $1 billion in 1995, and employee productivity increased from $360,000 to more than $800,000 in 1995. This figure is high for the industry. The company has operating profit margins that are among the highest in the industry; in November of 1995, this number was 7.9 percent, compared to a range from 5.4 to 7.4 percent for its competitors. Marshall also has one of the strongest balance sheets in the industry and a solid track record of consistent earnings growth and above-average profits.

The company also claims that the Web site has produced 125,000 new customers since 1994 and that 10,000 new addresses are logged on each month from 67 countries. A reliable cost-benefit analysis is difficult to carry out. On the cost side, the company says it has invested $1 million in development of the Web site since 1994. Revenues from the use of the intranet and online presence are more difficult to estimate, but management claims that the Web generates over 1,000 leads a month. Generally, productivity per employee is used as a measure of the success of a new internal policy. By this measure, the success of the new technology is immense.

In addition, Marshall reports changes in customer purchasing; for example, at a recent online seminar involving 87 engineers from 12 countries, two or three development tools were sold, an event that rarely occurs at a normal seminar.

Marshall Industries was one of the first companies in its sector—the distribution of electronic components—to recognize and take advantage of the opportunities offered by information systems, computer networking, collaborative tools, intranets, and the Internet. These new technologies have played a key role in helping Marshall differentiate its offerings from that of its competitors and establishing a competitive advantage in what is basically a commodities market. Marshall has capitalized on the success of the applications it has developed to meet the needs of its customers, suppliers, and employees (e.g., with interactive online seminars), and extended beyond its traditional activities to become a provider of high-technology applications. It has also developed new competencies beyond its usual core (distribution), which it now uses to compete in new markets.

Marshall, however, faces two challenges today. It needs to maintain the first-mover advantage it gained through using the new technologies to improve and optimize its relationship with constituents, as competitors follow in its footstep and start offering similar services; this can be achieved only through constant innovation. In addition, it needs to learn how to compete in a new market, the interactive and entertainment services industry, which will mean developing new skills beyond technological competencies. The two activities will increasingly be run as separate entities; the challenge will be to continue to share the technological competencies developed between the two.

MCA/UNIVERSAL: THE EVOLVING ROLE OF THE CIO

In 1993, there were numerous, uncoordinated efforts within MCA for building interactive applications for direct-to-consumer platforms. At that time the company started negotiating with America Online (AOL) to provide multimedia content to AOL members. During negotiations, it became apparent that using AOL as the distribution medium for MCA content would reduce the company's control over the material and make the timing of online events more difficult. The fact that

AOL would be doing some of the work of formatting and publishing the content meant that additional time and effort would be expended for coordinating between MCA and AOL. Furthermore, any contract with AOL would cut into any profits that MCA might generate through the provision of such content.

Fortuitously, the Netscape browser was released in the middle of negotiations and development of the MCA content service. Seeing the potential to gain wider distribution and obtain greater control over the publication of their content, MCA decided to port the service over to the WWW platform—a feat they accomplished in two days. MCA CIO George Brenner aggressively moved to build up the company's capability to have a reliable and significant Web presence. Using a combination of discretionary funds from the Information Technology and Marketing budgets, Brenner purchased the hardware to create a new media room to support the service. He also obtained servers on loan from Sun Microsystems. The site went live in August of 1994.

Building up content for the Web site was a joint effort between the Marketing and Information Technology departments. The Information Technology department provided the platform expertise and was responsible for posting Web content onto the site. Key project leaders from the Marketing department promoted and guided the development of various content products for the Web site. Third-party vendors like Digital Planet and ZM Productions were hired to help with the presentation of the Web content. Funding for these early campaigns came out of the Marketing budgets of the various projects being promoted. Some of the first campaigns were the *Junior* film premiere, a *Back to the Future* ride, a *Waterworld* attraction, and a *Jurassic Park* ride.

To coordinate these efforts and promote a unified feel for the Web site, all divisions involved with Web projects were represented in monthly Internet committee meetings. The meetings were also used to share information on technological advances that could affect the type and design of the content that MCA could offer over the Web. The Web site evolved from providing event-based promotions to building a new image for Universal Studios, and from being just a theme park to being a virtual park as well. The site thus included not only introductions to new movies and attractions, but also featured interactive tie-ins to park attractions, e.g., a behind-the-scenes tour of Dr. Brown's Think Tank. It also sold tickets to the park as well as vacation packages.

The Web site has exceeded the expectations of MCA management and everyone involved in its development. In their first year, the site got 100,000 hits, way above the 10,000 expected. As of September of 1996, just barely over two years since going live, the site had logged 100 million hits. This was especially notable because of the relatively minimal amount of money the company invested in the site. MCA spent a total of 4.5 million on infrastructure and content, way below the investments of some of their competitors (e.g., Time Warner invested $30 to $40 million in Pathfinder).

MAKING MONEY ON THE WEB

The impressive performance of the public Web site made a strong case for the viability of the Web as a distribution and marketing vehicle for MCA products. To integrate more fully and focus resources on capitalizing on the Web as a revenue-generating channel, the company formed a new group in 1996, Universal New Media. The new group is composed primarily of the individuals who led the development and promotion of the early campaigns on the Web platform. The group has the task of bringing MCA's Web efforts to the next level: partnering with various MCA groups to leverage existing content in order to build innovative "interattractions," coordinate all Web efforts, and develop revenue-generating products. To this end, CIO George Brenner saw the role of MCA's Information Technology department as essentially a service utility—providing the platform to meet performance requirements of each group, and helping each campaign come up with realistic performance and infrastructure requirements.

The Universal New Media group has aggressive goals for the next three years. It expects to spend its first year setting the ground work for future applications by building its Web infrastructure and forming strategic partnerships with content suppliers, e.g., UPN and NBC. The group seeks to build advanced Web capabilities, including the ability to host online chats, track customer demographics and movement through the site, and customize Web content on-the-fly based on customer characteristics. At the end of the first year, the group expects MCA's online site to be among the top 25 to 50 sites on the WWW, offering a better-quality Web experience to a greater number of users than it does currently. Such a rating positions the company for generating revenues through transactions as well as advertising. If they are successful, the group expects MCA to break even on its Web investment by the end of the second year, and turn a profit by the third year.

As of late 1996, several months into its inception, the New Media group was experiencing tremendous support from various MCA groups. The technology was seen as providing many advantages for the company. Overall, the entire enterprise was given much leeway to be in a learning mode, with limited pressure to generate profits immediately. Members of the group, though, struggled with the most pressing issues of Internet commerce: what infrastructure to build and plan for, given the available resources; how to measure the level of interest from and characteristics of their users; and determining the model for generating profits on the Internet platform. They also worried that there were many issues brought on by the applications they were developing that had not been resolved by their legal department. For example, who would own the rights to any script ideas that might be generated from online discussions hosted by MCA?

CONTINUING THE QUEST TO LEVERAGE NEW TECHNOLOGIES

Having seen his efforts at promoting a new technology result in the creation of a new business group within MCA, CIO George Brenner continued his quest to transform MCA's business with advanced technologies. This time around, he set his sights on applying the same technologies in-house, primarily by building MCA's corporate intranet and by exploring opportunities for cost reduction.

Brenner envisioned the corporate intranet as a "window into company databases and files." He saw this application as moving his organization beyond data processing and into information processing. Unlike most company intranets, MCA's intranet did not start off by repurposing human resource policy manuals. Rather, the technology saw the first application in the Corporate Communications department. With this first application, employees in this department would scan press articles mentioning MCA, instead of clipping them. Next up are intranet sites for human resources and a sales staff intranet for Geffen World. Also under consideration are extranet applications including a marketing and promotions site that the Marketing department could use to exchange edits of movie posters and ads with advertising agencies, and an application that would allow authorized parties to view daily rushes on films in production.

Internet technologies have also afforded the opportunity to reduce the cost and effort involved in developing and maintaining the hardware and applications supported by the Information Technology department. The ability to provide browser-based interfaces to legacy systems reduces pressure to change legacy systems. For example, instead of a major revamping of MCA's highly successful executive management system, the Information Technology department plans to build an intranet and Internet extension of the system. Given the simplified development tools available for browser-based systems, Brenner expects a shortened development cycle: 3 months to prototype the screens and 18 months to build a fully operational link to the legacy executive management system. He is also extremely vocal about the savings to be gained from substituting network computers for the personal computers and workstations sitting on the desks of MCA employees. He expects to save up to $6,000 a year for every replacement he makes by using a cheaper box and centralizing configuration and maintenance. Although the systems themselves will not be appropriate for every employee in the company, he sees much use for network computers among employees doing simple, nonknowledge-intensive tasks.

The MCA case illustrates the typical evolution of electronic commerce applications within companies. Most companies start out with inexpensive forays into applying the technology—often funded by discretionary funds and/or grants from infrastructure companies who expect to benefit from the widespread adoption of such applications. Such experiments are often promoted, almost with evangelical zeal, by individuals who have recognized the potential of the applications early on—in this case the CIO George Brenner and individuals from the Marketing department. As companies see the value of the technology for the business, they start bureaucratizing the development of its applications. While this shift often brings with it an influx of funds for production-level applications, it also often comes with higher expectations of returns, e.g., profits from the sale of products over the Web. Many companies today are at this stage of the game: one to two years into a full-scale application of electronic commerce technologies, and trying top managers' patience over tangible returns on their investment. It is an intriguing situation that is perhaps much more appealing from the vantage point of an outsider. As George Brenner, having moved on to promoting intranet applications of the technology, puts it:

> We don't want someone calling us up in the morning and we're getting a couple of hundred thousand dollars per hour and the network's down. I don't think I want to be that person being yelled at for destroying a revenue stream . . . the CIO is not necessarily empowered to be a revenue generator/originator. The CIO and his team and his organization usually serve as support. Even though we're linked strategically at the hip when it comes to the creative content side of the business, I think you're gonna find that we're in the background.

C H A P T E R

T E N

SOCIAL IMPACTS
AND POLICY ISSUES

This book focuses on how to manage Web-centric strategies within a company. As a manager, you are rightly interested in how you and your organization can take advantage of these new technologies—how you can gain a competitive advantage by applying the technologies and management principles we have been describing to your marketplace, your customers, and your organization.

However, your company obviously exists within the larger society, and within a technological context that is largely (but not completely) beyond your control. Other businesses and government agencies are making decisions daily that dramatically affect your ability to apply these technologies to your business. The core technologies, the Internet infrastructure, the economic and regulatory environment, and the social and political perspectives that result from these new technologies—all these factors directly affect you and your company's success in the marketplace.

None of these broader social, economic, and technical issues can be controlled at the company level, yet their direction and resolution is crucial to your future. Historically, the public debate and decision-making about these issues has been driven almost exclusively by the "policy wonks" and domain experts in Washington, D.C. and other national capitols around the world. However, we believe it is essential for business executives to play a much more active role in these discussions, and so we include in this chapter a brief summary of the most important political and social issues surrounding the Web and its evolution into a global information infrastructure that is fundamentally redefining our society.

We will also provide you with a few suggestions for becoming a more actively involved and influential participant in the policy arena. There are certainly many ways to make your views known, whether letters to your congressman, testimony in Washington or your state capitol, active participation in industry and professional associations, or simply voicing your opinions at neighborhood picnics. We want to encourage you to become more active in the political and policy-making process, because you can make a huge difference to your company's future business success by influencing the debate around these crucial issues.

In this brief chapter we will summarize the major social and political issues that affect your business, whether or not you want them to. In addition, we will suggest some specific ways you might be able to influence legislation and the direction of national policy in these important areas.

We will discuss the Web's social impact and policy issues in terms of three broad themes:

THE CHANGING LEGAL LANDSCAPE. How Web technologies are redefining fundamental concepts like privacy, security, identification, money, ownership, copyright, and freedom of expression.

GOVERNANCE. How you can (and must) work with ISPs and various government organizations to resolve questions about taxation, conflicts between local community interests and a global infrastructure, information pricing and access, protection from various forms of digital crime, and differing national laws about privacy, copyright, intellectual property, taxation, decency, and the like.

POLICY. The social issues that legislators and regulators are concerned about that will affect the way your company operates in the future—issues like telecommuting, the redistribution of jobs and facilities, environmental impacts, changing patterns of transportation, the redefinition of work, and labor laws that either support or constrain the development of the new economy.

THE CHANGING LEGAL LANDSCAPE

The Internet and the Web have brought our society right up against the fact that digital information—especially information that is globally and easily accessible to anyone with an inexpensive personal computer and a modem—is unlike anything in our past experience. Digital information (whether text, data, video, or sound) is almost ridiculously inexpensive and simple to create, store, transmit, and copy, and every copy is identical to the original. Furthermore, you can give away or sell any information you have without losing possession of it. Information, especially digital information, is a strange beast indeed.

Information, even when it is not stored or transmitted digitally, has the interesting aspect that it can be given away without its owner losing possession of it. If I sell you a car or a chair or a bag of groceries, you take possession of the goods from me and compensate me with some form of cash or other economic value. I then have the cash but not the goods. On the other hand, if I sell you a digital copy of a book or an article, I still have the original and I can sell someone else another, identical digital copy at virtually no additional cost (and each copy is indistinguishable from my original).

We have not yet come to grips with this reality. The computer enables almost anyone to copy, reproduce, reuse, modify, and transmit digital information to almost anyone else, and to do it at extremely low cost. Our legal system, based as it is on precedent and an accumulation of principles and agreements over many years, is having a tough time dealing with these new conditions.

The characteristics of digital information challenge many of our customs, expectations, and laws—ways of thinking and resolving disputes that have evolved over centuries—to deal with the ownership, property rights, and compensation for physical things.

To be specific, we will consider what these characteristics of information mean in five specific areas:

- Copyright and intellectual property rights
- Pricing, costs, and payment systems
- Privacy and security of information
- Identity (authentication of the owner or originator of a document)
- Freedom of expression

COPYRIGHT AND INTELLECTUAL PROPERTY RIGHTS

The control and ownership of content is hardly a new issue; many people first became aware of the messiness of copyrights and intellectual property when the audio tape recorder and the video cassette recorder first put copying capabilities in the hands of average citizens. Both of those technologies, however, produce less-than-perfect copies (although good enough for most purposes, whether legal or not). Now, with the advent of the digital audio cassette and recordable compact discs, intellectual property issues go well beyond the Internet.

With the Internet and the Web, however, the issue is much more profound. Now, anyone with a personal computer, a modem, and Internet access can make perfect copies of literally millions of image, text, video, and sound files. In fact, it is literally impossible for an Internet service provider to give you access to anyone else's Web site without making temporary copies of the original files and transmitting them to your hard disk. This basic aspect of the way the Web works introduces several thorny legal issues surrounding the ISP's liability for content, even when (as is usually the case) the ISP is just acting as a common carrier in transmitting information from one individual to another.

Of course, universal access to information is at the very heart of the Web. Most if not all information providers want you to access the words and images on their Web sites (and those of their other subscribers); that is the whole idea. However, our society is also built on the premise that the creators of content—sounds, images, and other forms of intellectual creativity—should be compensated when their intellectual property is used by others (especially if that subsequent use generates revenues for the individual or organization that uses it).

There are a number of attempts currently underway to either protect original images or provide adequate compensation to the content creators. For example, most stock photography outlets on the Web show only images that have a distinct embedded digital "watermark" (now there is a term whose meaning predates digital technology by several generations!). Only after you have opened an account with the photo supplier and ordered specific images for a fee can you access the original. (Of course, once you have paid for and received the original image in digital form, there is no practical way that the owner of the copyrighted image can stop you from reusing or redistributing it. Much of our society still depends on the good faith of individuals to behave honestly and fairly, and no laws will ever completely replace the foundation of trust on which society is built.)

The digital compensation schemes that have been developed to date often include some kind of encryption system that prevents people from actually viewing the contents of encrypted files until they have paid an access fee. One such approach developed by IBM is called a "cryptolope" (a combination of the words *encrypted* and *envelope*). Before you can read the contents of any files contained within a cryptolope, you must first pay a specified access fee.

Similarly, there is work underway to define a standard header protocol for digital images that would clearly identify the copyright owner, terms and conditions for use of the image, and other pertinent information that will help deal with intellectual property issues. And the industry standards will require that the header always remain attached to the digital file.

Other possible approaches being discussed in various arenas include mechanisms or software embedded in PCs and other digital recording/display machines that would limit the number of copies that could be made of any single file. This rather extreme measure might include provisions for making additional copies after the payment of some kind of licensing or registration fee to the manufacturer (which would then have the very difficult and messy task of redistributing those fees in some equitable fashion to the many producers of the digitized intellectual content).

The most definitive legal statement on these issues, which includes policies regarding fair use, legal penalties for stripping off header information or otherwise using digital content inappropriately, and formal definitions of temporary copies, rights management practices, and related policies, is the White Paper on Intellectual Property and the National Information Infrastructure that was prepared for the United States' participation in the World Intellectual Property Organization Conference in Geneva, Switzerland, in December 1996.[1]

PRICING, COSTS, AND PAYMENT SYSTEMS

Three fundamental economic issues are central to the future of the Internet: pricing of Internet services; cost sharing and allocation among the various Internet service providers, long-distance carriers, and consumers; and payment systems that enable content providers to capture value from consumers.

PRICING AND SERVICE GUARANTEES.   This is not so much a question of national policy as it is business strategy for the ISPs and other providers of services over the Internet. Current ISP pricing practices typically offer unlimited Internet access for a relatively low fixed monthly price (currently approximately $20 in most U.S. consumer markets for basic, low-bandwidth access, with higher rates for ISDN lines or higher bandwidth services). Some ISPs have stopped offering such a low price to new subscribers, claiming they cannot earn a profit at the going market rate, but competitive pressure seems to be holding most providers to these fixed-rate pricing strategies.

This pricing scheme is essentially a one-size-fits-all approach, and it provides the same level of service to all buyers. There has been much discussion recently about alternative pricing strategies, such as priority services (higher bandwidths, priority access to transmission lines, priority treatment of messages and files) for a premium price, or per-message rates for both very heavy and very light users of the Web.

A discussion of pricing strategies would not be complete without a comment on service guarantees. Remember what happened to America Online in the winter of 1996/1997 when it switched to a fixed price for unlimited Internet access after many years of time-usage pricing. AOL could not meet the demand, and thousands of its customers experienced busy signals for hours on end. The company quickly became known as "America On Hold" and "America Offline," and suffered severe image and credibility problems. Class-action suits were filed in over 20 states as subscribers demanded refunds and other forms of compensation for being denied access to a service they had paid for.

The AOL lesson is simple but important: As the Internet expands its presence and importance in the economy, customers and ultimately the government develop a serious interest in its performance. More importantly, companies that charge for Internet or other electronic services, whether they are basic access providers, content services, or other providers (such as private networks, procurement systems, payment systems, or just plain retailers), must provide those services at the promised level, or they will suffer loss of credibility (and thus market share), and be subject to civil or criminal penalties if they are found guilty of failing to fulfill their contractual obligations.

Because of the history of regulation in the telecommunications industry, these pricing and service issues will most likely be strongly affected by legislation and regulation aimed at creating an equitable distribution of Net access and legitimate delivery of services for all customers.

ALLOCATION OF COST AMONG INTERNET PROVIDERS. The telecommunications industry is one of the most heavily regulated industries in the United States. One of the major reasons that basic Internet access charges are so low is that the FCC some years ago determined that Internet service providers, as a new industry, would not have to pay basic access charges to long-distance telecommunications carriers—charges that local telephone providers have always paid and continue to pay today.

Because the Internet was originally conceived of as a way to transmit data from one computer to another, the FCC considered it to be a distinctly different service than voice telecommunications, and exempted ISPs from these access charges.

Now that the Net has grown to such a large, visible, and highly used carrier of all forms of digital content (including voice, of course), there is increasing public pressure to restructure the entire access charge system (especially from the telephone companies, who quite rightly see the Internet as a distinct threat to their long-distance business).

As more and more homes order second and third lines for faxes and computers, there is also increasing interest in pricing these additional lines differently from the first or primary line. The FCC is currently studying a wide range of proposals for changing its approach to access charges and the universal service concept.

You can expect significant and continued public debate on these issues in the foreseeable future. We encourage you to stay well-informed about the issues and the options, and to keep your own organization's interests in mind as you formulate positions or attempt to influence legislation or the regulators.

PAYMENT SYSTEMS. One of the thorniest problems on the Internet today is how to enable micropayments so that the creators of content can be easily and efficiently compensated for their creations. The difficulty is that the dominant payment systems in place today just don't fit the cyberspace environment. Cash transactions essentially require the two parties to exchange their goods and cash in a face-to-face interaction. Checks require an elaborate and expensive banking system that includes remittance processing, clearinghouses, and account reconciliations; and the exchange of value takes several days to be completed. Credit cards certainly can (and do) work for Web-based transactions (although there are still major public concerns about authentication and security). However, like checks, credit cards are far too expensive for the kinds of micropayments that many people see as necessary to make Web-based commerce really take off.

The difficulty lies in the fact that—even though there is still a strong culture in cyberspace that believes "information wants to be free"—there is a growing (and soon to be dominant) view that the only way electronic commerce can work is for the creators of intellectual content to be properly compensated for their efforts. The vision driving many Netrepreneurs is that the creator of a poem (for example), or of an elegant piece of software, will make the file available to anyone who wants it, but only for a fee, which might be on the order of a cent or even a fraction of a cent for each access (this vision is behind IBM's development of cryptolopes, discussed in the previous section). Making this kind of system work requires an accounting and transaction system that is capable of transferring value from the "reader" account to the "author" account at an incredibly small transaction cost. A per-use system for prices below a penny has to be able to record and execute millions of transactions at fractions of a cent per transaction.

There are various efforts underway to build such micropayment systems, such as ecash and cybercash. To date, however, none of them have been widely enough accepted to become a dominant standard.

One approach that might eventually be workable is to use smart cards, or stored-value cards, which are credit or debit cards with an embedded chip. As the use of smart cards grows in the United States, it is highly likely that computer manufacturers will begin to offer PCs and keyboards with smart-card readers and recorders in them. Once that technology becomes common, it will then be feasible for Internet shoppers to insert their smart cards in a PC-based reader to fund Internet purchases. The value of the purchase—even if it is only a fraction of a cent—would be deducted from the card as the purchase is made.

No matter what micropayment system becomes the standard, however, we will be faced as a society with a number of new and very perplexing public policy and regulatory challenges. For example, the federal government regulates the banks and controls the supply of money through the federal reserve system. What role should it play in the regulation of electronic cash? Is ecash, or smart-card cash, a form of money? Can it be created only by a chartered bank, or could other businesses offer digital cash directly to consumers? How could any central government possibly control, let alone monitor, the amount of ecash in circulation? And, given the global nature of the Internet, will ecash be denominated in dollars, yen, pounds, or some new form of international currency? And—toughest of all—how will taxation be handled for international payments (or, for that matter, even for interstate transactions)?

These questions will be part of the electronic commerce landscape for some time to come, and their answers will make a profound difference for every individual business.

PRIVACY AND SECURITY OF INFORMATION

Public concerns about privacy and information security are perhaps the biggest constraint today on further growth of electronic commerce. These concerns take several forms, but usually include the following two issues:

- Fear that personal information will be sold or otherwise made public, beyond control of the individual
- Unwillingness to purchase products or services over the Internet, because of concerns about the security risks involved in transmitting credit-card information over a public network

These fears are not unfounded, but they tend to be larger than the real risks. Nevertheless, perceptions are the only reality that counts in the marketplace, because it is perceptions that drive individual and group behavior.

PRIVACY. As we have pointed out in several different chapters of this book, the Internet and the Web allow an unprecedented level of target marketing, enabled by the ability of the technology to capture unique information about individual browsers or Web site visitors. When individuals are willing to share information about themselves and their preferences, companies like

Amazon.com, Virtual Vineyards, and other similar businesses can provide them with highly tailored (and often highly valued) individualized services. However, the flip side of that coin is that individuals must be willing to reveal certain information about themselves. The choice between anonymity and personalized service is a very real one that both sellers and buyers face constantly.

In addition to these kinds of voluntary disclosures, there is also the potential for retailers, credit-card companies, credit bureaus, and market research firms to amass and combine their records with publicly available data on consumers to discover buying and preferences patterns. Current information technology has an extraordinary power to enable the compilation and analysis of data, and the public has developed a genuine, if somewhat uninformed, fear of "big brother." This public fear is in many ways more important for policy-makers and strategists than the technical reality, because it can drive legislation and public debate almost independently of what companies are really doing.

SECURITY AND ENCRYPTION.   In many ways, the technologies that enable data encryption and other forms of security are inextricably intertwined with concerns about privacy and control of personal information. When transactions are reliably and clearly secure, people are generally far more comfortable about transmitting private data like credit-card numbers, bank accounts, and social security numbers. Thus, the extended public debate in 1997 about encryption has generated a healthy increase in public awareness and understanding, although it has probably also (unfortunately) heightened the fears of a significant minority of consumers.

Not all those fears are unfounded, either. There are almost daily news stories about bugs in popular software like Web browsers that enable hackers to gain access to personal files. In mid-summer of 1997, one expert who was being paid to test the security protocols at a regional Internet service provider actually found his e-mail account flooded with password information from literally hundreds of individual accounts. The fact that he was testing the system legitimately and received the individual passwords only because of a programming glitch on his client's computers did not reduce the significance of his experience. The story made the national news[2] and only served to reinforce the concern of the general public that the Internet is still a long way from being genuinely secure.

In spite of these continuing concerns, by mid-1997 there were a number of relatively effective encryption packages on the market, and most companies engaged in actual business transactions on the Internet (including all the banks offering online services) were using secure servers and assuring their customers that transmitting personal data like credit-card numbers was much less risky than giving your credit card to a minimum-wage server in a restaurant and having him or her disappear with it for five or ten minutes.

In addition, all major credit-card issuers have essentially offered their customers the same liability protection they currently get when their cards are lost or stolen. While companies like Visa and Mastercard are not yet publicly or actively encouraging consumers to use their credit cards for Internet purchases, they are reasonably confident that their financial risk on the Internet is not measurably greater than it is in "normal" transactions. As one credit-card company executive commented to us, the most serious risk with credit cards is not when the numbers are being transmitted on the Net; it is when an employee in some product company steals or copies a database of customer records that includes credit-card data—and that risk really has nothing to do with the Internet per se (nor does it have more than a minor connection to technology; most fraud and theft of this type relates far more to dishonest employees and lax corporate operating procedures than it does to the Internet or other computer technologies).

Another major part of the encryption debate has centered on the United States federal government's concerns that if encryption becomes too effective and too widespread it will prevent or at least curtail what the government considers necessary and appropriate surveillance of terrorists, drug dealers, and other criminals. For that reason, the government has been attempting to limit the export of encryption software to at least increase the difficulty of non-U.S. citizens to protect themselves from government surveillance. However, by mid-1997 there were many effective software encryption products available outside the United States developed by non-U.S. companies, and the government itself was relenting somewhat in its attempts to prevent the export of U.S.-produced software.

IDENTITY AND AUTHENTICATION

Another difficult problem that the Internet introduces is the identification of the author of any particular content or message. Our society operates in large measure on trust; we assume that the writers of our daily newspapers and radio/television news stories are honest people honestly reporting what they believe to be the truth (leaving aside for the moment the continual debate about reporters being politically biased).

In most cases we rely on the "brand name" of the newspaper or the network to, in effect, warranty the validity and accuracy of the information we receive. We also become familiar with individual news anchors, reporters, and other public figures whose track record and public presence gives us some degree of confidence in what they say and write. Of course, with television and radio personalities, we actually see and hear the individual. With newspapers, we make the reasonably safe assumption that if a column carries a certain name on it, then that person is in fact the author of the column and the source of the content.

But with the Internet we have to operate much, much more on faith. In the first place, there are only a limited number of well-established news and information sources publishing over the Net, and even then we simply have to assume that the Web page that claims to be ABC News or Public Television or CNN is in fact produced and controlled by that respective organization. In fact, on the Net it is much easier, and still somewhat common, for anonymous individuals to impersonate well-known individuals or organizations, and it can be relatively difficult to determine whether they are in fact who they say they are.

Of course, literal, fraudulent impersonation is relatively rare, even at the wild frontier of cyberspace. What is more common is for information to be presented as fact in newsgroups or on Web sites that is either deliberately or unintentionally erroneous. That information then often gets picked up, copied, forwarded to others, and is soon being repeated as gospel truth by completely honest, well-intentioned people who have no direct connection to the original source.

The point is that it can be dangerous to rely on information sources when you don't know who the source is—and the Internet is full of unauthenticated, poorly informed sources. Moreover, it is very simple (and very common) to create false or fictitious identities on the Internet, either maliciously or in jest, and the Net seems to have more than its share of people with either misguided or criminal intent. Since the information we receive from Web sites or through e-mail or newsgroups all comes to us in the form of digital bits, we have to either assume that the sender is who he or she claims to be, or we need some form of digital authentication.

In one well-publicized case, a woman who had lost her job at a high-tech company claimed she had been sexually harassed and presented copies of e-mail messages from the company's Chairman as evidence. It turned out, however, that she had composed the messages herself and only made them look as if they had come from his e-mail account. The lesson, of course, is that it is extremely simple to create counterfeit documents when everything comes from digital files and can be copied and manipulated at will.

In an even more public event in late 1996, Pierre Salinger claimed to have clear evidence that the TWA flight 800 explosion was caused by a missile, not recognizing that the story he had read on the Internet had been proven to be a hoax several months earlier.

These examples might seem somewhat trivial, but they do serve to highlight the importance of authentication. In fact, digital authentication is absolutely central to the growing use of the Internet for EDI and other forms of financial transactions. One of the core concepts of electronic transactions is nonrepudiability, which makes it impossible for either the originator or the recipient of a financial transaction to deny that he or she either sent or received a message.[3] This capability of authenticating the senders and receivers of message is central to using the Internet—not only for financial transactions, but for all forms of communication and information access.

The most common solution for this requirement is the use of public key cryptography, discussed in more detail in Chapter 8. These keys—which make real the concept of a digital signature—enable recipients of messages to decode them using a public key that is identified with only one sender, thus verifying who the message actually came from.

While public keys and digital signatures do not solve the problem of verifying the kind of informational accuracy that got Pierre Salinger in trouble, they do provide Internet users with the ability to verify who the source of the information is, and that goes a long way towards creating a more reliable and more useful information network.

FREEDOM OF EXPRESSION

The Net is fostering a communications explosion. It is essentially a do-it-yourself publishing medium. As we have said repeatedly, the dramatically reduced costs of developing a Web page and putting it up for the world to access have brought literally millions of new users onto the Net, both to seek and to publish information.

While this open forum for information and ideas generates volumes of new, creative ideas and information for public consumption, it also creates a glut of material, much of which is either offensive or boring (and sometimes both). The Net is in many ways challenging our society's commitment to freedom of expression, because it is such an open communications medium. Anyone can create and publish almost anything, and make it instantly available to anyone else—including, of course, minors, who most of us want to prevent from accessing pornography and other forms of expression that we consider harmful.

The Communications Decency Act of 1996 included specific provisions prohibiting the distribution of sexually explicit materials to minors over the Internet. However, in June of 1997, the Supreme Court upheld an earlier decision by a federal court in Philadelphia that the provisions of the 1996

Act were an unconstitutional limitation on freedom of speech and amounted to illegal government censorship.

As a society, we have not yet fully come to grips with the nature of the Internet. In many ways it is a broadcast medium, like television. Individual "broadcasters" publish material that is then accessible by anyone and everyone. But in other ways the Net is more like the telephone system, in that it enables point-to-point communication (like e-mail) or one-to-many messages to a selected (often a self-selected) group of individuals (newsgroups, for example). Of course, one of the more frustrating aspects of the global communications infrastructure today has been the rapid growth of junk e-mail and "spamming" (intentionally barraging e-mailboxes with unwanted and often offensive messages, many aimed at selling something, others containing editorial point-of-view messages designed to influence recipients to vote or act in alignment with the author's objectives, and some simply intended to harass the recipient).

As a society we have chosen to regulate and control the content of broadcast media like television and radio far more than we have the telephone system. No one seriously expects to be able to control or limit the content of the millions of telephone conversations that take place daily, but we do worry a lot about television content that is simply tossed out into the ether and available to anyone with a receiver (yes, there are adult cable television channels that are available only to customers who pay a premium price, but the pricing mechanism also tends to limit their availability to adult audiences).

Our difficulty with the Internet is that it has characteristics of both the telephone and the television system,[4] a fact that generates confusion in many people's minds about just what it is and how to treat it. Some of the "infoglut" problem relates to the fascination that many newcomers to the Net have with the opportunity it gives them to broadcast their ideas or creations, artistic or otherwise. It can be a very heady experience to have a global audience for your ideas, and many people are creating things for fun and ego gratification rather than to generate revenue (the author James Gleick commented in a *New York Times Magazine* column that the Internet seems to be characterized by a prevailing attitude of "enough about you, let's talk about me"). Of course, others are actively experimenting with new businesses and other new kinds of revenue-generating schemes. Over time, much of the trivial and superficial stuff will fade away. But, given the core economic nature of the Internet, don't expect it to ever go away completely.

Just to complicate the issue a bit more, different countries and even different states within the U.S. have both differing community standards and differing laws regarding freedom of expression. CompuServe, for example, has been embroiled in a dispute with the German government for several years over decency issues. Germany's laws are much stricter than those in the United States, and Germany has taken CompuServe to court over the availability of some sexually explicit materials in Germany—content that was created by CompuServe customers, not by CompuServe itself, and which is completely legal (though not necessarily respectable) in the countries where it originated.

The same kinds of issues are also generating some perplexing cases in the United States. One couple, residents of California, was indicted in a Tennessee court for selling materials over the Web that Tennessee considers obscene, even though they are legal in California.

This question of whether and how local governments can control a medium that is completely global in scope is being actively debated right now. And its resolution will affect a lot more than decency questions. Taxation, for example, is another huge area fraught with difficulty. When someone buys something over the Internet, where does the transaction take place? At the computer of the buyer, or at the seller's computer? Where should taxes be levied, and by what government body? And how is the government ever going to be able to identify the fact that the transaction took place at all?

There are an increasing number of software programs and services available to help parents and corporations block access to undesirable or unwanted Web sites. Packages like NetNanny and others contain predefined lists of sites the owner wants to block, and most also allow the user to add other sites to the list.

These approaches have begun to put control back in the hands of the message receivers without in any way intruding on the first-amendment rights of the creators and broadcasters of the content.

COMMENTS

These are difficult issues, and we are in still in the midst of sorting out how we will respond to them as a society. Our legal system, based so extensively on precedent and case-by-case resolution of conflicts, is being sorely tested by the scope, structure, and characteristics of this new medium.

The consequences of this shifting legal landscape are not just broad, social ones that are "out there" somewhere. They also affect corporations and individuals directly, and on a daily basis. Managers have to be concerned about copyrights and intellectual property, both as consumers of information created by others and as creators themselves. When logos, photographs, and other images can be copied by anyone at anytime, and easily reused, ownership of images, brands, logos, and slogans becomes a major concern of every corporate counsel. All property owners want to control their property, and they must expect to pay for the use of images and ideas created by others.

But these legal issues surrounding information and its use are only one piece of the puzzle. Let us now turn to the broad questions of governance. How will the Internet itself be managed, controlled, priced, and made accessible to the general public?

GOVERNANCE

The Net is a bit like Gertrude Stein's well-known (and horribly unfair) comment about Oakland, California: "When you go there, there isn't any 'there' there."

The Net's greatest strength—and, according to many, its greatest weakness—is that it is essentially unmanaged. It has no single center, no controlling body, not even a central "brain." Of course, it was designed to be exactly that way, to have built-in redundancy and no single center, precisely to make it an indestructible communications network in the event of a major war, a nuclear attack, or some major natural disaster.

The Net has grown rapidly in the last few years precisely because there is no central organization planning its growth, raising funds, recruiting staff, and doing all the other things that most corporate groups do (sometimes well, but often very poorly). The Net is a "network of networks," and it grows whenever someone sets up a new server, registers an IP address, and goes online. (The Network Solutions company does manage the master IP address registry under a contract with the National Science Foundation, and there is a coordinating committee that creates protocol standards and worries about the Net's future, but neither Network Solutions nor the coordinating committee acts as a senior management body charged with managing or operating the Net in any fundamental way.)

In fact, the future of the Net might well be even more chaotic than its past, since there has recently been a decision to open up a number of new domains (.stores, .firm, .computer, .news, .bank, .brokerage, etc.) and the directory service that Network Solutions provides is also being opened up for competitive bid.

This diverse nature of the Internet means there is no one place or organization you can go to with complaints, suggestions, or conflicts. It also means that there are many different entities, with vastly differing interests and objectives, that are attempting to influence policies, practices, standards, and future directions.

At the same time, as we have said frequently, the newness and differentness of the Internet creates some conditions and conflicts that our society has almost no experience dealing with. In this section, we will describe very briefly some additional issues that are particularly difficult to resolve because the Internet is so distributed and uncontrolled.

This is not to say that certain component parts of the Net are completely uncontrolled. The long-distance telephone carriers, for example, are heavily regulated. Both the FCC and the 50 state PUCs (in the United States) are actively engaged in sorting out the pricing and cost allocation mechanisms, and will continue to be for many years.

In fact, the different regulatory bodies that are attempting to control parts of the Net are a major part of the governance problem that managers of individual companies face. They sometimes have to live with directly conflicting laws coming from different jurisdictional bodies, all claiming to have "the" charter for control.

We have already mentioned many of these issues: conflicting taxes and differing tax codes, differing decency standards, and differing laws regarding intellectual property and privacy. The plain fact is that the Net will continue to evolve as it began: in an organic, often-redundant fashion. These differing views will be worked out through some undefined combination of market-place actions and various administrative and legislative actions.

PUBLIC ACCESS TO THE INTERNET

One difficult political issue that crops up frequently in discussions about the Internet is how to ensure that access to the Net will not be limited to those who have high disposable incomes. PCs are still relatively expensive; they have been purchased by only about one-third of American families, and many of those home PCs do not have modems. Thus, there is still a rather large majority of the population that does not have access to the Net, and all the talk about electronic town meetings and real-time democracy is just that: talk.

There is great fear in many quarters that the marvelous information resources available on the Internet will lead to a society split into "information haves" and "information have-nots." Indeed, this concern is high on the list of issues for such disparate organizations as the Federal Communications Commission, the Electronic Frontier Foundation, the Progress and Freedom Foundation, the Internet Society, Computer Professionals for Social Responsibility, and many individual corporations with an interest in seeing the Internet grow and thrive.

There have been a number of efforts launched in the past two years to "wire up" public schools and libraries around the country, and the FCC is exploring ways to extend its universal access concept to include the Internet. It is considering creating a special government fund to provide the financial resources needed to link schools, libraries, and local government offices to the Net. The FCC wants to designate a specific percentage of the access fees paid by telecommunications carriers for redistribution to public schools, libraries, and local governments for the specific purpose of installing data lines, purchasing appropriate computers, and paying for Internet accounts. The FCC is also discussing mandated discounts of up to 90 percent of ISP fees for such public institutions.

The specific nature of this universal Internet service plan had not been completely determined by late summer of 1997, but there is little question that increasing public access to the Internet will be high on the FCC's agenda for some time to come.

FRAMEWORK FOR GLOBAL ELECTRONIC COMMERCE

The federal government certainly appears to be embracing the Internet as the most important basic national infrastructure investment since the interstate highway construction program that began in the 1950s.

In early July of 1997, the Clinton administration released a white paper and policy statement defining its views on how the Internet should be governed and regulated in the future. The statement, called A Framework for Global Electronic Commerce, was generally well-received by the cyberspace community, largely because it calls for minimal government involvement and actively supports entrepreneurial efforts as the best way to foster continued growth. The Framework provides a basic foundation and direction for federal government policies and practices with respect to the Internet, and is thus a crucial document for anyone concerned with the future governance of the Net.

The Framework is notable for its explicit recognition that the role of governments should primarily be to create conditions that support growth, equity, and competition, and to prevent fraud. It fully supports the decentralized, bottom-up nature of the Internet, and it calls for international cooperation to make the Net a truly global information infrastructure.[5]

The Framework begins by endorsing five general principles and then makes nine specific policy recommendations. Because of their importance, we are reproducing here all five principles and nine recommendations from the Executive Summary to the white paper:[6]

Principles

- The private sector should lead. The Internet should develop as a market-driven arena, not a regulated industry. Even where collective action is necessary, governments should encourage industry self-regulation and private sector leadership where possible.
- Governments should avoid undue restrictions on electronic commerce. In general, parties should be able to enter into legitimate agreements to buy and sell products and services across the Internet with minimal government involvement or intervention. Governments should refrain from imposing new and unnecessary regulations, bureaucratic procedures, or new taxes and tariffs on commercial activities that take place via the Internet.
- Where governmental involvement is needed, its aim should be to support and enforce a predictable, minimalist, consistent, and simple legal environment for commerce. Where government intervention is necessary, its role should be to ensure competition, protect intellectual property and privacy, prevent fraud, foster transparency, and facilitate dispute resolution, not to regulate.
- Governments should recognize the unique qualities of the Internet. The genius and explosive success of the Internet can be attributed in part to its decentralized nature and to its tradition of bottom-up governance. Accordingly, the regulatory frameworks established over the past 60 years for telecommunication, radio, and television may not fit the Internet. Existing laws and regulations that may hinder electronic commerce should be reviewed and revised or eliminated to reflect the needs of the new electronic age.
- Electronic commerce on the Internet should be facilitated on a global basis. The Internet is a global marketplace. The

legal framework supporting commercial transactions should be consistent and predictable regardless of the jurisdiction in which a particular buyer and seller reside.

Recommendations

Tariffs and Taxation.   The Internet should be declared a tariff-free environment whenever it is used to deliver products and services. The Internet is a truly global medium, and all nations will benefit from barrier-free trade across it. No new taxes should be imposed on Internet commerce. Existing taxes that are applied to electronic commerce should be consistent across national and subnational jurisdictions and should be simple to understand and administer. State and local governments should cooperate to develop a uniform, simple approach to the taxation of electronic commerce, based on existing principles of taxation.

Electronic Payment Systems.   The commercial and technological environment for electronic payments is changing rapidly, making it difficult to develop policy that is both timely and appropriate. For these reasons, inflexible and highly prescriptive regulations and rules are inappropriate and potentially harmful. In the near-term, case-by-case monitoring of electronic payment experiments is preferable to regulation.

Uniform Commercial Code for electronic Commerce.   In general, parties should be able to do business with each other on the Internet under the terms and conditions they agree upon. Private enterprise and free markets have typically flourished, however, where there are predictable and widely accepted legal principles supporting commercial transactions.

The U.S. supports the development of an international uniform commercial code to facilitate electronic commerce. Such a code should encourage governmental recognition of electronic contracts, encourage consistent international rules for acceptance of electronic signatures and other authentication procedures, promote the development of alternative dispute resolution mechanisms for international commercial transactions, set predictable ground rules for exposure to liability, and streamline the use of electronic registries.

INTELLECTUAL PROPERTY PROTECTION.   Commerce on the Internet will often involve the sale and licensing of intellectual property. To promote electronic commerce, sellers must know that their intellectual property will not be stolen and buyers must know that they are obtaining authentic products. Clear and effective copyright, patent, and trademark protection is therefore necessary to protect against piracy and fraud.

The recently negotiated World Intellectual Property Organization (WIPO) treaties for copyright protection should be ratified. Issues of liability for infringement, application of the fair-use doctrine, and limitation of devices to defeat copyright protection mechanisms should be resolved in a balanced way, consistent with international obligations.

The government will study and seek public comment on the need to protect database elements that do not qualify for copyright protection and, if such protection is needed, how to construct it. The administration will promote global efforts to provide adequate and effective protection for patentable subject matter important to the development of the Global Information Infrastructure (GII), and establish standards for determining the validity of patent claims. The Administration also will work globally to resolve conflicts that arise from different national treatments of trademarks as they relate to the Internet. It may be possible to create a contractually based self-regulatory regime that deals with potential conflicts between domain name usage and trademark laws on a global basis. The administration will review the system of allocating domain names in order to create a more competitive, market-based system and will seek to foster bottom-up governance of the Internet in the process.

PRIVACY.   It is essential to assure personal privacy in the networked environment if people are to feel comfortable doing business across this new medium. Data gatherers should tell consumers what information they are collecting and how they intend to use it. Consumers should have meaningful choice with respect to the use and reuse of their personal information. Parents should be able to choose whether or not personal information is collected from their children. In addition, redress should be available to consumers who are harmed by improper use or disclosure of personal information or if decisions are based on inaccurate, outdated, incomplete, or irrelevant personal information.

The administration supports private-sector efforts now underway to implement meaningful, user-friendly, self-regulatory privacy regimes. These include mechanisms for facilitating awareness and the exercise of choice online, private sector adoption of and adherence to fair information practices, and dispute resolution. The government will work with industry and privacy advocates to develop appropriate solutions to privacy concerns that may not be fully addressed by industry through self-regulation and technology.

SECURITY. The GII must be secure and reliable. If Internet users do not believe that their communications and data are safe from interception and modification, they are unlikely to use the Internet on a routine basis for commerce. The administration, in partnership with industry, is taking steps to promote the development of a market-driven public key infrastructure that will enable trust in encryption and provide the safeguards that users and society will need.

TELECOMMUNICATIONS INFRASTRUCTURE AND INFORMATION TECHNOLOGY. Global electronic commerce depends upon a modern, seamless, global telecommunications network and upon the "information appliances" that connect to it. In too many countries, telecommunications policies are hindering the development of advanced digital networks. The United States will work internationally to remove barriers to competition, customer choice, lower prices, and improved services.

CONTENT. The administration encourages industry self-regulation, the adoption of competitive content rating systems, and the development of effective, user-friendly technology tools (e.g., filtering and blocking technologies) to empower parents, teachers, and others to block content that is inappropriate for children. The government will seek agreements with our trading partners to eliminate overly burdensome content regulations that create nontariff trade barriers.

TECHNICAL STANDARDS. The marketplace, not governments, should determine technical standards and other mechanisms for interoperability on the Internet. Technology is moving rapidly and government attempts to establish technical standards to govern the Internet would only risk inhibiting technological innovation.

The full report also designates lead government agencies with responsibility for oversight and, in some instances, regulatory authority for these various areas of concern.

Keep in mind that this white paper is only a statement of intentions, and the details of putting those intentions into practice will be worked out over many years, by several future presidents, and by a wide variety of legislative bodies and regulatory agencies at the state, federal, and international level.

It is worth noting that, in many areas like taxation, security, technical standards, and intellectual property, the federal government interagency team that drafted this white paper recognized that the issues are truly global in scope and cannot be resolved at the national level. The debates, discussions, and experiments about how to "govern" something as distributed, chaotic, and organic as the Internet will go on for many years. Be sure to stay informed, because how these issues play out will surely determine the shape, economics, and value of the Net to you and your business.

SOCIAL POLICY AND PLANNING ISSUES

Like any new technology, the Net is being assimilated into our economy and our society over an extended period of time. And like all other new technologies, the Net affects the way we work, live, think, and act in both predictable and unpredictable ways. These second- and third-order consequences have raised a number of important challenges and opportunities for individuals, companies, communities, and society as a whole.

Our purpose here is primarily to identify the most important and most obvious of these extended consequences of Net technologies and Web-centric organizational practices. We want to help you think constructively about what existing national and local policies might need to be modified, and what new policies might be needed.

It is helpful to consider the social consequences of the Internet at four distinct levels of analysis:

· The individual

· The company

· The community

· Society at large

However, it is very difficult to discuss the policy issues and implications within any one level without considering the others as well. After all, as individuals we are simultaneously members of companies, of communities, and of society at large, and our actions (and reactions) are not normally confined to only one of those levels.

Thus, we will focus on each of the first three levels, and then pull it all together by discussing the broader policy implications that cut across all levels and affect us as a larger society.

THE INDIVIDUAL AND SMALL GROUP

Web technologies clearly enable individuals and small groups to work and interact in radically new ways. The concept of "any

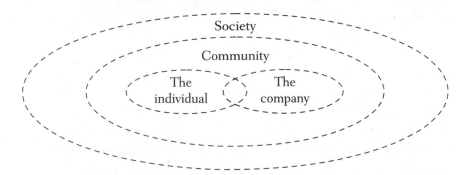

FIGURE 10-1. The four levels of interaction with the Internet: individual, company, community, and society.

time/any place" is becoming a reality for more and more workers. There is a whole body of research and literature on the nature of distributed teams, and there are now hundreds of software products developed specifically to support collaborative work by groups and individuals who are located all over the globe.

At the most basic level, the Web supports the kind of individual work that requires extensive information search and access. But it is not just a matter of enriching current jobs; the characteristics and capabilities of the Web actually enable organizations to redesign individual tasks and work flows or business processes around totally new concepts.[7] Knowledge workers can access, generate, process, format, and distribute information in ways never before possible, and groups of knowledge workers can collaborate across time and space far more efficiently and more effectively than they could with earlier generations of technology.

These new approaches to work and work design mean that the individuals involved must master a whole set of new core skills like information search, problem-solving, collaborating, and knowledge-sharing. Both individuals and the companies they work in and with are faced with dramatic changes not only in tasks and skills, but in work habits, working relationships, management practices, and compensation and reward schemes.

In addition to these changes in the nature of work, the mix of jobs in the economy is also undergoing dramatic change. As discussed in Chapter 2, one of the basic consequences of the "Webification" of the economy is the transformation of the extended value chain and the changing nature of many businesses. The Web is bringing buyers and suppliers much closer together, both in business-to-business transactions and in consumer markets. One result of these shifts is the elimination of many "middleman" jobs, and the creation of new value-adding roles. In this Age of the Consumer, many companies are significantly increasing their customer support staffs, while in other industries whole new intermediary roles are taking hold.

Another change affecting millions of individual workers is the increasing practice of outsourcing many jobs to specialty companies and/or individuals working as independent contractors. The Web facilitates these diverse working arrangements by making it extremely easy for individuals to work from their homes or from small local offices. This changing pattern of work location, of course, has major implications for communities and society as a whole. We will discuss these factors in more detail later in this chapter, but just consider how these new patterns of work affect things like:

· Commuting patterns
· Clothing styles and purchases
· The need for in-home childcare
· Individual needs for continuing education
· The design and construction of home offices
· Furniture and equipment purchases
· Opportunities for social interaction

For individuals, this changing labor market means both new opportunities and new challenges. For some, whole job categories are disappearing, while for others the digital economy provides marvelous opportunities to start new businesses, work independently, and adjust working patterns to personal circumstances.

THE COMPANY

For the company, new configurations of work create new managerial challenges. As more and more knowledge workers take advantage of the power of the Web to work out of their homes, hotel rooms, and airplane seats, companies must develop infrastructures to support them and to leverage these new practices.

As more and more work becomes "anytime/anyplace," many companies are actively redistributing office facilities, in effect relocating jobs (and the taxable income associated with them) to regions with a lower cost of living, more desirable climate and recreational possibilities, and more extensive communications infrastructures, such as fiberoptics and adequate phone lines.

Another major impact on employment and jobs has been the dramatic downsizing that so many companies have gone through in recent years. Business process reengineering has enabled companies to dramatically increase worker productivity, and to redesign work flows to enable distributed teams and remote workers to operate as though they were physically together. Web technologies have been instrumental in making these changes possible.

One of the natural side effects of downsizing and reengineering has been the growing practice of outsourcing. More and more companies now choose to hire specialty companies and individual contractors to carry out many of their noncore work processes—buying products, services, and processes rather than making them. Outsourcing gives companies much more flexibility to grow or shrink depending on their economic success, and it enables them to draw on specialty talent that they could not afford to hire on a full-time, long-term basis.

This phenomenon also owes a great deal to the increased power of computing and communications technologies, which enables individuals and teams to operate from many different locations almost as effectively as if they were all in one place.

This capability has in turn enabled many individuals to restructure their working arrangements with their employers. Many people choose to work part-time, some to work full-time from home, and many decide to become independent contractors or consultants who work for several clients at the same time.

Anytime/anyplace work and an outsourced workforce generates many organizational efficiencies, but it also introduces a whole host of new managerial challenges. While sales managers have known for years how to supervise and monitor the work of individuals they don't see every day, now managers in every functional area are confronted by this necessity. Once again, new skills are called for, as are new measurement and control systems that focus more on evaluating the results of an individual's efforts rather than on the specific techniques for achieving those results.

One large manufacturing company we worked with chose to outsource both the manufacturing and the engineering design of many core parts and subassemblies. While buying parts from suppliers was not new, entrusting those suppliers to create and produce their own product designs was a difficult managerial decision to implement effectively (after all, each part and subassembly still had to fit and work perfectly with all the other parts and subassemblies).

The company built an extranet and equipped its suppliers' engineers with the same CAD software it used internally. But what it had not expected or understood was how difficult it would be for the "inside" engineering managers to manage engineering instead of engineers.

The managers were uncomfortable with assessing only the final results of the suppliers' work without being able to peer over the shoulders of the individual engineers or to check progress along the way, as they had been able to when all the work was done inside the company. The head of Engineering and the head of Purchasing discovered that this change was much, much more complex to implement organizationally than it was technically.

These new managerial challenges are paralleled by new and more complex social policy issues. Labor and tax laws that were created in a simpler time when virtually everyone was a full-time employee working in a company-owned facility are just not relevant to today's digital economy. In fact, they are often counterproductive; consider the obvious example of how Congress recently reduced the tax deduction for a home office, just when PCs were making it much more feasible for people to work at home. The use of outsourcing and part-time labor, while economically and managerially sound, results in the shifting of costs, management time and decisions, and even core competencies across organizational boundaries, which introduces a whole new level of complexity in the legal relationships between buyers and suppliers.

And all this because of Web technologies! Well, maybe not all, but you get the picture—Webifying your business changes virtually everything, not only inside an organization but in the outside world as well. The impact of these changes on local communities, regions, and the country as a whole is equally important.

THE COMMUNITY

Local communities are also experiencing change: in traffic patterns, land use, educational needs, infrastructure requirements, and even local business demands. When companies spread their work out over more but smaller offices, or encourage telecommuting, or shift whole business units to different regions of the country, local economies are dramatically affected.

For example, even a moderate number of telecommuters can dramatically affect transportation patterns. Telecommuting can reduce highway congestion significantly; at the very least, it spreads daily traffic jams out over longer time periods as telecommuters adopt atypical working hours. In fact, national policy already promotes telecommuting, because the federal government's Clean Air Act Amendments of 1990 require many heavily polluted metropolitan areas to discourage unnecessary auto use and encourage efficient commuting. One of the goals of the Clean Air Act is to reduce the number of employees commuting to work in single-occupancy vehicles.

Affected corporations are required to reduce the average number of commuter trips per employee through a combination of car-pooling, public transportation, telecommuting, and other actions. Encouraging and supporting telecommuters (individuals who work at home or at a local satellite office at least one day a week) can be a very effective way of reducing the total number of commuting trips, so the Clean Air Act has been a very positive force in increasing corporate interest in telecommuting.

Less traffic also means less air pollution and energy consumption, since it takes far less energy to move bits than it does to move atoms (it has been estimated that moving an electronic message across the country consumes less than one-seventh the energy it takes to move the same message on paper through the U.S. mail or a service like Federal Express). While this environmental impact seems like a free bonus resulting from our move to a Webified society, it also suggests an opportunity for local and regional governments to pass laws and establish regulations that in fact encourage and reward telecommuting and other forms of moving work to workers rather than the other way around.

There are still other social consequences of telecommuting that often get lost in discussions of the technology capabilities and traffic congestion issues. When individuals work at home, they typically seek out local neighborhood restaurants for quick meals and for brief meetings with colleagues or customers. They usually patronize local cleaners, grocery stores, and quick-print shops as well. So local communities often find themselves faced with new zoning issues and shifting local land use. While these kinds of developments often mean new sources of income for the community, they can also require changes in local neighborhoods that might not always be viewed as desirable by local residents.

Remember, too, that as jobs and office facilities are relocated to new areas, land values are directly affected, and when land values change there are always winners and losers. And losers usually go down only with a fight, whether in the courts, the legislatures, or City Hall.

And City Hall could lose big if telecommuting and other elements of Web-based businesses really take off. Remember that most local tax revenues (especially those that support public schools) are based on property taxes. When a substantial number of employees are telecommuting and sharing offices, companies can operate with significantly less floor space per person, and thus pay much lower property taxes. In addition, many Web-based businesses generate significantly higher revenues per employee than traditional businesses, have relatively little plant and equipment, and virtually no physical inventory—all factors that further reduce the amount of property taxes they will likely pay. This intangibility of the digital economy has the potential to create a genuine crisis in local government.

As these massive shifts in jobs and living patterns continue to evolve over the next several decades, we are likely to see many fundamental changes in our urban and suburban landscapes. Not only will commercial buildings and residential neighborhoods look different, but life in cities and towns will no doubt feel different too. While we do not pretend to know what cities will be like in 20 years, we can hazard some educated guesses:

· There will be fewer large office buildings.
· There will be fewer large shopping malls and traditional department stores.
· Urban transportation systems will deploy smaller, less expensive buses, relying more on shuttles that can move a few people at a time economically.
· There will be more local shops and small neighborhoods.
· Fewer people will commute long distances.
· There will be many smaller, regional office parks where "semi-commuters" will go for a day or two to link in to their corporate offices.
· There will be more conference and convention centers where groups of professionals will gather for short one- and two-day face-to-face meetings (sometimes everyone will work for or consult to one corporation, and sometimes there will be representatives from many organizations gathering for collaborative work).

To the extent that the Internet facilitates shifts in where and when people work, it will dramatically affect all local communities:

· The demand for some jobs (and related skills) will go up, while for others it will go down.
· Some communities and neighborhoods will gain in population and local income-producing jobs, while others will lose.
· Transportation needs and patterns will shift.
· The demand for local services will be transformed.

Society at Large

Many of these issues can be resolved only at the national level (and some, including the opportunity to locate work anywhere and to order and pay for goods and services no matter where you are, will require international attention). To date, the national agenda in the United States seems to include the following four crucial topics:

- Funding the national information infrastructure
- Establishing national standards for Internet access in the schools
- Ensuring that labor laws take the new working conditions into account
- Adapting tax laws to the new realities of cyberspace

At an even broader level is the whole question of what role government can and should play in regulating activities in cyberspace. For example, what if any role is there for government to play in certifying identity, in enabling nondeniability in financial transactions, in protecting electronic messages (much as the postage stamp guarantees the delivery of secure paper-based mail), and in regulating electronic commerce (protection from fraud, price discrimination, service guarantees, taxation, etc.).

Finally, there is also the whole subject of electronic democracy—what do these new technologies mean for how public debate takes place, how we select our legislative representatives, how they communicate with us, and how legislative decisions are made? Should we consider holding national "town meetings?" Should our legislative practices change to take advantage of this new information and communications infrastructure? Consider, for example, that it is now possible for all citizens (at least those with access) to view and interpret the same information, to participate in discussion and debate on matters of national interest, to express their preferences, and to cast their votes in a national election. Could we establish a national electronic democracy? Should we? Is direct democracy preferable to representative democracy? These are questions that need to be asked and debated, for the simple reason that technology now presents us with alternative forms of national governance that were simply unimaginable a few short years ago.

RESHAPING SOCIETY

These questions about the shape of our society, which we can only begin to frame today, raise once again a theme that has run throughout this book, that digital excellence is not about technology, even though technology is clearly its foundation. Rather, the search for digital excellence is a search for a whole new way of thinking, living, working, relating, and creating value. The Internet and the World Wide Web are the foundation of a radical new economy, a whole new social and political structure, a whole new way of life. The search for digital excellence is nothing less than a massive social revolution.

Marshall McLuhan once commented that "we shape our tools and our tools shape us." This book reports on the search for digital excellence; although that search certainly includes understanding and shaping our new tools, it is really all about reshaping ourselves.

NOTES

¹ See http://www.wipo.com for more information about the World Intellectual Property Rights Organization.

² Jared Sandberg, "Accidental Hacker Exposes Internet's Fragility." *Wall Street Journal*, July 10, 1997, p. B1.

³ Arie Segev, Jaana Porra, and Malu Roldan, "Internet-Based Financial EDI: The Case of Bank of America and Lawrence Livermore National Laboratory Pilot." Fisher Center for Management and Information Technology Working Paper #96-WP-1018, University of California, Berkeley.

⁴ This ambiguous nature of the Internet was first identified by Alvin Toffler in a private conversation with one of the authors.

⁵ It is interesting to note that it has been just two years since Vice President Albert Gore was leading a national debate on the development of a "national information superhighway," and now the Internet is clearly seen as a "global information infrastructure."

[6] The Executive Summary and the full text of A Framework for Global Electronic Commerce are available on the Net at: http://www.whitehouse.gov/WH/New/Commerce/ and http://www.whitehouse.gov/WH/New/Commerce/summary.html.

[7] See, for example, *Reengineering the Corporation* by Michael Hammer and James Champy, HarperCollins, 1993, and *The Process Edge* by Peter Keen, Harvard Business School Press, 1997. Though many of the examples in these two books predate the Web per se, the underlying technologies and process designs are clearly very similar.

GUIDELINES FOR SUCCESS

Throughout this book we have suggested how to be successful at transforming your company into a Web-based business and organization. We have looked at many different companies across a wide spectrum of industries to learn what has worked for them, what has not worked, and what difficulties and unexpected challenges they confronted.

In this summary chapter, we will review the common mistakes that we see managers making, and suggest how to think both constructively and comprehensively about integrating your Web initiatives into the mainstream of your company's business.

First we'll look at the five most common mistakes: examples of overly simplistic thinking that will be easy to avoid after reading this book. Then we will discuss what we call the basic realities: the core characteristics of the Web, Web-based economy, and underlying technologies that you must take into account as you build and execute your Web-based business initiatives.

Finally, we will provide you with a catalog of guidelines for success, beginning with a core set of "first principles"—something like the ten commandments for thriving on the Web. We will also go beyond this list to describe in more detail the core strategic and tactical directions that are essential for any business to follow if it expects to win the digital revolution.

So let's get started. Here are what we call the "Five Big Ones"—five very common mistakes that companies make as they move towards Web-centric strategies.

THE FIVE MOST COMMON MISTAKES

MISTAKE ONE: FAILING TO LINK WEB INITIATIVES TO THE EXISTING BUSINESS STRATEGY AND FOCUS

In the excitement of jumping on the Web bandwagon, many companies have "followed the crowd" and, in knee-jerk fashion, simply built a Web site because it seemed like the cool thing to do rather than because it made strategic or economic sense. The typical result is easy to predict: little or no Web traffic; weak or nonexistent sales; heavy investment expense with no hope of a positive return; and a cynical, unhappy senior management team.

The unfortunate consequence of these failures is, predictably, management's reluctance to move ahead even when a more rational, more carefully constructed follow-up strategy has been defined. The initial failure creates an atmosphere of distrust and lack of confidence that leads to unrealistically high standards before management is willing to try again.

The failure to align a Web initiative with existing strategic direction and focus usually occurs when the Web team has not thought through basic marketing concepts like "Who are our customers and why do they buy from us?" If your typical or most important customers are not Web-savvy or are unlikely to use the Web at all, then the best Web design and the heaviest advertising in the world won't help.

MISTAKE TWO: ASSUMING "IF WE BUILD IT, THEY WILL COME"

What if the Web is just another distribution channel? Granted, it is something new and different, with characteristics unlike anything we have seen before (that is, after all, the fundamental theme of this entire book). But if you think of it as "just" another distribution channel, you realize quickly that it will work only if you treat it that way. This means you have to give your customers a reason to seek out your Web site: by making it a "cool" place with interesting and unusual graphics or information, by offering prizes, special prices, or otherwise valuable information, or in other ways making it a compelling place to visit.

Most managers believe (for very understandable reasons) that their products and services are the best there are, and that customers will naturally want to buy them. But the world does not beat a path to your door or to anyone's door unless there is something behind the door that the world wants and needs. And even if there is, the world has to learn about that door—through advertising, public relations, word of mouth, etc.—and they have to want what is behind the door.

Many businesses have gotten so caught up with the Web craze that they let the technology overwhelm their existing knowledge about their current (and prospective) customers and why customers buy their products and services. If your customers are older, for example, what are the chances that a high percentage of them will use the Web at all, let alone do business with you that way? More to the point, even if your current customers are highly computer-literate, if your Web site does not provide them with the information or the interactions they want, it will almost certainly fail.

For instance, Volvo launched an informational Web site that included the e-mail address of the Webmaster because the company wanted to solicit feedback about the homepage design. However, Volvo's customers saw the site as a point of contact for getting questions answered about their cars and service needs. The Volvo Webmaster was overwhelmed with e-mail full of questions from customers about things like brake performance, engine characteristics, service requirements, and new models, plus complaints about specific dealerships. Because the Web support organization was not capable or qualified to answer these kinds of inquiries, Volvo turned off the e-mail account. The tragedy here is that Volvo had inadvertently created a potentially marvelous customer service and feedback channel, only to find itself unable (or unwilling) to take advantage of the opportunity to build constructive, interactive relationships with its customers.

So don't expect your Web site to be successful just because it exists. Remember the discussion of the new marketing game in Chapter 7, and think through in advance what your value proposition is. Give the public reasons to visit your site, offer them something of value, do it in compelling ways, and recognize from the beginning that you have to spend some time and money telling them about the site and its value before you can expect them to show up.

MISTAKE THREE: FAILING TO PROVIDE ADEQUATE RESOURCES TO
MANAGE THE WEB

One of the most compelling aspects of the Web is its basically low
cost. Relative to other means of conducting business or advertising, it is remarkably inexpensive. However, many companies,
again, are seduced and misled by their incomplete understanding
of what it takes to design, launch, and maintain an adequate Web
site. Just like earlier IT architectures, the major costs of Web
technologies are incurred in maintaining the site, upgrading the
technology platforms, and updating the contents.

The basic danger of underfunding your Web initiative is that
a "halfway" Web site can be worse than none at all. Don't start a
Web-based business unless you are prepared to fund it adequately
(for ongoing maintenance and enhancements) and to adapt to the
new requirements it places on your organization. Once you "go
public" with your Web site, you had better have it working properly or your customers might have such negative experiences that
all the advantages of having the site will be dissipated.

For example, one particular bank was one of the earliest to
develop a sophisticated Web-based banking application that allowed customers to access their accounts and account histories, transfer funds, pay bills electronically, and conduct other
basic banking business from any PC anywhere in the world.
However, the server supporting the application initially lacked
the capacity to support the growing number of customers who
tried to use the service. As a result, access was very limited, response time was horribly slow (often taking more than five minutes simply to display a new screen), and many customers quit
their online banking sessions in frustration. Some of them
never signed on to the service again, and there is evidence that
some previously satisfied customers actually closed their accounts and took their business elsewhere as a result of their
negative experiences with online banking.

The bank has since beefed up its technology platform and
added some screens to the Web site to inform customers that
their accounts are in the process of being accessed and to tell
them how long they might have to wait. Wait times are down
significantly, and the overall performance of the site is now
fully competitive.

However, the bank's general reputation might have suffered as a result of its launching the online banking service. Ironically, rather than enhancing its reputation as a technology innovator and a market leader, the bank was seen for a time as an organization that could not match its advertising hype and was incapable of managing technology effectively.

The moral is clear: if you want to be a technology leader, do it right and do it completely, or don't do it at all.

MISTAKE FOUR: FAILING TO LEARN FROM EXPERIENCE

If one message is clear from our research and consulting about the Web, it is that things are changing. The Web itself is continuing to evolve, and the lessons from the pioneers are piling up daily.

As we noted at several points throughout the book, the worst thing you can do is to fool yourself into thinking that a Web site can go up and stay up without continued maintenance and enhancements. The need for resources to maintain the accuracy and currency of the information on the site is only part of the reality of learning from experience. You should expect to be updating the core structure and design of your Web site on an ongoing basis for at least the first several years, as you learn from your successes and failures; as you get feedback from customers, employees, and business partners; and as the technology itself continues to evolve.

Consider again the lesson that Volvo did not learn (at least initially) from its customers. They wanted answers to basic questions about their cars and service requirements; Volvo failed to "hear" what its customers wanted, and missed an important opportunity to adapt to the marketplace.

Like every other new technology, the Web itself is evolving through a basic innovation cycle, and we are still very, very early in the cycle. As Paul Saffo of the Institute for the Future puts it, "Never mistake a clear view for a short distance." While most of us think of the World Wide Web as a very recent phenomenon, the Internet has of course taken over 20 years to become an "overnight success." We have commented frequently about the dizzying and accelerating pace of change that characterizes the Web. This is completely normal for something as new as the Web, but it means that you simply cannot expect things to be stable for some time to come.

But it is not just the Web that will evolve. Your own understanding of what your Web site means and how it can support (or lead) your business strategy will develop rapidly if you pay attention to what actually happens to your organization. What parts of the site do your customers go to first? What pages do they return to over and over? Who are your Web visitors? What sites do they come from when they land on yours? Where do they go from your site? What kinds of questions do they ask? What information do they seek?

Your Web site is a living experiment, an opportunity to engage in interactive dialog with current customers, prospective customers, the general public, investors, prospective employees, and suppliers—in short, everyone who is interested in your company, your products, and your services. Every interaction with every interested site visitor is a chance to learn how you are perceived, what your public wants and expects from you, and what kind of interactive capability is right for your business. Be sure to pay attention to learning opportunities about both content and process.

Recognizing a Web site as a dynamic learning vehicle requires that you not only commit enough human and financial resources to keep the site current and responsive, but also develop mechanisms for learning from your experiences. Plan on regular, major overhauls of your Web platform and its design every two to three months for at least the first year, and every six months after that.

MISTAKE FIVE: DEFINING THE WEB SITE AS AN INFORMATION TECHNOLOGY RESPONSIBILITY

It should be very clear by now that we view the Web as a business venture that just happens to rest on new information technologies. The leadership and accountability for launching a new business venture—even one dominated by technology—must reside in a business unit, not in the IT organization.

It is certainly natural and understandable that the early initiatives for exploring and employing Web technologies come from the IT organization. After all, that is where both the awareness of new technologies and the ability to make them work should reside. But your IT organization is at best a support unit for the rest of the business. Its role is to inform the organization of what is available on the technology frontier and to help the company think through the opportunities and challenges of every new technology.

Once your organization commits to using Web technologies, whether for an intranet or a public Web site, it is imperative that a business executive take responsibility for the success of the effort. For example, the marketing Web sites at Levi Strauss are managed by the Marketing department, with support from a Webmaster. But there is no doubt that the Web site is a marketing tool. At Bank of America, the online banking Web site is managed by a team that reports directly to the head of the retail bank. The team certainly includes technical specialists, but it is headed by a banker with strong marketing experience, and includes legal, public relations, and communications experts.

THE BASIC REALITIES OF THE WEB WORLD

These all-too-common mistakes help to highlight the "simple" fact that the Web is different (actually, it really isn't simple at all; the differences are complex, profound, and terribly important). The basic realities of successful Web-based businesses and organizations are so distinctively different from those of a traditional business that we want to highlight them here before we move on to define the core principles that are essential for ensuring success.

THE WEB IS EVOLVING AND WILL EVOLVE FOR THE FORESEEABLE FUTURE

You must make all your business and organizational plans with this basic fact clearly in mind. The technologies that form the foundation of the Internet and the World Wide Web are still being developed and improved—and at a frenetic pace. The core telecommunications platforms, bandwidth, access speeds, browser capabilities, Internet service providers' value propositions and offerings, content providers, regulatory environment, pricing schemes—every aspect of the Web—are all undergoing continuing change. While most of these technical and economic changes are for the better, they might not all be positive for you, and they will affect different businesses in different ways.

The only way to survive in this environment is, as they say, to "stay tuned." Pay attention, read the news (both print and electronic), attend conferences (selectively), and learn from your competitors and business partners.

A WEBIFIED BUSINESS REALLY IS DIFFERENT

Among the most important characteristics of a Web-based business is its ability to:

· Radically lower the cost of reaching and serving customers

· Increase global reach with virtually no incremental cost

· Support multiple steps in the transaction life cycle with a single Web site and a single customer interaction (see Chapter 7 for a discussion of the transaction life cycle and the impact of the Web on customer relationships)

· Reach millions of customers with individualized information at virtually zero incremental cost

· Update basic product and company information and have the current information instantly available to all customers and employees regardless where they are physically

· "Hotlink" customers and suppliers with each other to facilitate the completion of transactions (and in some instances to take yourself out of the middle of the transaction)

· Interact directly and individually with each Web site visitor

WEBIFYING YOUR BUSINESS MEANS CHANGE—BIG CHANGE

This assertion is patently obvious, but important to state and to emphasize. For all its uncertainty and continuing evolution, one thing about the Web is very, very certain: it means massive change for individuals and organizations, and massive change is never easy. As discussed in Chapter 9, individuals and groups in organizations can find many ways to resist and reject change when they don't understand or like it. Leaders who want to ensure the success of Web-based business ventures will do well to carefully think through how they introduce these new technologies, who they involve in planning and implementation, and what messages they send out to the organization and its customers.

Organizations are complex, adaptive systems. Unlike simple machines, organizations react to and actually initiate actions to change their environment. Of course, an organization is not a unitary thing that acts on its own. An organization is made up of people who interact with each other in a variety of ways to convert raw materials into finished products and services that can be sold to customers. Organizational members use tools, technologies, money, and ideas/information to produce a product or service that provides value to a customer. Managers oversee the use of these tools, design processes to link them together, and use various measurement and reward systems to track performance, allocate resources, and prompt individuals and groups to behave in ways that further the achievement of their organizational goals.

These various components of an organization—people, processes, tools, and management practices—combine to create a complex, internally consistent, and homeostatic business system. And when you change something as basic as one of the core tools of the business system—which the Web certainly is—you upset the equilibrium. The system and the people who comprise it generally resist that kind of disequilibrium, especially when they believe the changes have been imposed on them.

You Will Make Mistakes and Change Your Strategy Frequently

As we have just pointed out, one of the biggest and most common mistakes that Web pioneers can make is to assume that they know everything they need to know up front. Building and executing a Web-based strategy is all about learning from experience. In any new arena like this one, the only feasible approach is to recognize at the outset that, no matter how carefully you think things through before you start, you will discover new ideas and new approaches along the way. To be successful, you must be willing to embrace those discoveries and go with them, even when it means throwing out significant investments or reversing direction. It is far better to risk being seen as undirected than to stubbornly stay on the wrong path just because it once looked right.

GUIDING PRINCIPLES

Given these basic realities, we can describe a clear, simple, straightforward set of guiding principles, and then—finally—define specific guidelines for ensuring that your Webification efforts will produce the results you want. Our guiding principles are simple to state and easy to remember:

MANAGE THE ENTIRE BUSINESS SYSTEM

Ignore the business system at your peril. Whenever you introduce Web technologies, whether for a public site or for an intranet, you must plan for and expect to manage change along all four of the key dimensions of a business system: people, processes, tools, and management practices. Healthy organizations have business systems that are well-aligned, where the characteristics in each dimension are compatible with and mutually reinforced by each of the other dimensions.

SWEAT THE DETAILS

Achieving digital excellence isn't easy, and it isn't simple. The incredible variety of topics we have covered in this book should make that clear. The task is not beyond doing (witness all the success stories we have included), but it does require you to pay attention to a lot of details, to manage complex, multidisciplinary teams, and to orchestrate change in large organizations. Any one of those tasks is difficult on its own, but you have to do all of them if you want to be successful. Effective "change masters" worry the details, become obsessive about their principles, and care deeply about making everything come together the way they know it can.

LEARN BY DOING

We have said this so often that you are probably shaking your head and rolling your eyes by now, but we say it only because we know it is true. Webifying your organization is a long journey down a new path. Pay attention to what works, stop doing what doesn't work, and keep trying new ideas.

LEARN BY LISTENING

As that great American philosopher Yogi Berra once said, "You can see a lot just by watching." We recommend that you not only watch and study other companies' Web sites, but listen too. Go to a few trade shows and conferences, and listen to the pioneers. Listen critically, constantly asking yourself what worked for them, and—more importantly—why. Did they:

· Enlist senior management support?
· Ensure that their Web marketing efforts were consistent with their corporate strategy?
· Round up enough resources?
· Build enthusiasm and support across the company?

Remember, too, that learning by listening can be a whole lot less expensive than learning by doing. It might cost you a plane trip and a conference registration fee, but that is a lot cheaper than buying the wrong hardware or software, or—worse—launching a Web site that not only fails on its own, but brings down the entire company.

With these general principles in mind, at last we offer you the following specific guidelines. We won't repeat the many specific suggestions we have made throughout the book; rather, we have boiled them down to a manageable set of crucial things to remember.

SPECIFIC GUIDELINES FOR SUCCESS

We have found it useful to think of these success principles in two broad categories. The most important principles are the strategic ones—those that deal with intentions, priorities, and focus. But tactical principles—guidelines focused on effective execution rather than intention—are just as crucial.

We also find it helpful to think separately about the business, organization, and technology platforms. The business is the set of decisions and actions you take in the marketplace, aimed at providing value to customers. The organization is the set of practices, procedures, policies, and processes that you design and deploy to carry out the business (where the business issues center around "what," the organizational issues are focused on "how"). The technology issues have to do with the tools you select, how you fit them together, and how you deploy them across the organization to meet your business goals.

Of course, the most crucial guideline of all is to be certain that your strategies in these three broad domains are aligned, consistent with each other, and mutually reinforcing.

With these ideas in mind, here are our guidelines for building a successful Web-based business:

IMPLEMENT A WEB STRATEGY THAT SUPPORTS AND REINFORCES YOUR CORE BUSINESS STRATEGY. Of course, the unique characteristics and capabilities of the Web might well lead you to transform your core business strategy over time. However, we know of no company that has successfully launched a Web-based business that was fundamentally inconsistent with its existing strategy and current marketplace strengths. Your business strategy reflects your organization's core competencies, its knowledge of products and services, its existing customer relationships, and its marketplace image and credibility. Ignoring those powerful resources when you launch a Web site is not only silly, but it can lead to outright disaster.

TAKE ADVANTAGE OF THE WEB'S UNIQUE CHARACTERISTICS AND CAPABILITIES TO DEEPEN YOUR RELATIONSHIPS WITH CUSTOMERS, SUPPLIERS, AND BUSINESS PARTNERS. We have repeated over and over that the Web is about relationships. It helps you reach new customers on a global basis, but more importantly it enables you to customize your information, products, and services to each individual customer (whether that customer is another organization or an individual). The Web enables you to reach out proactively to customers, to engage in interactive dialog with them, to build communities of interest with and among them, and to learn from them. Failure to take advantage of these capabilities amounts to ignoring the core strengths of the Web.

KNOW YOUR CUSTOMERS, AND DESIGN A WEB STRATEGY WITH THOSE CUSTOMERS AND THEIR SPECIFIC NEEDS CLEARLY IN MIND. As we have pointed out previously, it makes sense to invest in a promotional or sales-oriented Web site only if a significant proportion of your target audience (customers, suppliers, investors, employees, etc.) are in fact regular users of the Web and will be comfortable using your site the way you want them to. Otherwise, you are just throwing money and human effort into a very big black hole.

UNDERSTAND YOUR BUSINESS ECOSYSTEM, AND FIT YOUR WEB STRATEGY TO IT. By *ecosystem* we mean the extended network of customers, suppliers, venture partners, investors, shareholders, regulators, and employees who have some interest in your firm. These individuals and groups form the network of relationships and transactions that is central to your existence. Think through the important processes that connect all these entities together and enable them to create and exchange value, and you will have a much better understanding of how the Web can be used effectively to reduce costs, shorten cycle times, focus efforts, and enhance the entire ecosystem.

JUST DO IT. As should be eminently clear by now, we are strongly biased towards learning by doing. We certainly recognize that there are some businesses and customer segments that are simply inappropriate for the Web. And, as we noted earlier, launching a Web site just because it is "cool" or technically interesting is hardly a wise business move. However, the opposite is also true. If you wait until the concepts are "proven" or until the technologies settle down, it will be too late. The Web rewards innovators and risk takers; the only really effective way to learn what the Web can do for your business is to experience it.

Of course, the trick is to develop your Web site in a rational manner, and to invest in it at a level appropriate for your particular business. That means spending enough planning and preparation time to think through what messages you want to send to which customers and prospective customers, how to present your products and services and other information to the public, and how to interact with your various constituencies through the Web. But don't think for a minute that you can work out all the details before you "go live." It is this waiting for perfection that leads to inaction and loss of leadership. While you don't want to do anything rash or do it just because everyone else is, you also don't want to miss out on the learning and market leadership opportunities just because you are unsure about the eventual payoff.

The following are guidelines for building a successful Webified organization:

DON'T DO ANYTHING WITHOUT ADEQUATE SUPPORT FROM SENIOR MANAGEMENT. In an ideal world, senior management would actively lead the efforts to build a Web-based business, would be actively involved in strategy formulation, would review and approve the business plans, and would regularly monitor progress. However, as we all know, that ideal world exists only in the fantasies of middle managers. Senior executives should certainly be aware of your plans and progress, but if they are too closely involved too early on, their attention could actually be harmful in that they might want visible signs of progress unrealistically soon, or they might suggest inappropriate tactics that actually delay success rather than enhance it.

There are a number of techniques you can use to build top management support and understanding. First, of course, is basic education. Communicate the vision of what the Web-based business could become, and use lots of examples of what other companies are doing or have done (few topics get senior executives' attention more effectively than information about what their competitors are doing). Engage the executives in discussion about their strategic goals for the business, and explore with them how a Web capability could support achievement of those goals.

Once you have achieved basic consensus about the business vision, be sure to link the Web initiatives to that vision and ensure understanding of what resources you will need (funding, technology, people, cooperation from other parts of the business) to achieve the results the executives want.

Chances are you will be most successful if you position the Web initiatives as a pilot or an experiment. This approach helps keep expectations reasonably low, and ensures that the whole organization is in a learning mode as the venture is launched.

One highly effective way to get the right level of executive involvement is to establish a steering committee or advisory group to work with the Web team. This kind of structure is something that senior executives are familiar with, and it provides them with a forum for convening regularly to learn about issues, challenges, and progress without becoming too deeply involved on a day-to-day basis. Once you have established the steering committee, be sure to produce the promised progress reports on a regular basis. At the same time, don't wait for scheduled committee meetings to discuss your progress with key executives. Make a point of sending messages or notes about crucial events or important milestones to key members of the committee, and go to them for advice before making major decisions or commitments. This way you are in charge of the volume, frequency, and type of communication between the Web team and senior executives, and you can manage their understanding and their perceptions of progress to ensure continuing support.

ASSEMBLE A MULTIDISCIPLINARY WEB TEAM AND LOCATE IT AT A HIGH LEVEL IN THE ORGANIZATION. Whether you are focusing on a public Web site or an intranet, your Web team will need a combination of technical, organizational, and business skills. And the team should report to a senior business executive who has an appropriate level of authority and expertise to ensure that the Web initiatives receive the right level of attention, and are adequately linked to other business improvement efforts. In addition, be certain that the sponsor of the effort is well-informed and actively involved in both the strategic and technical decisions the team must make.

PLAN FOR DRAMATIC ORGANIZATIONAL CHANGE AND BE SURE YOU HAVE THE OD SKILLS TO SUPPORT THE CHANGES. Selling your products and services over the Web is not just an additional channel or a storefront with no space costs. Yes, the Web is a whole new channel and, yes, it does provide you with an outlet that has virtually no rental costs. However, as most businesses with Web sites have already discovered, the Web introduces all kinds of unexpected changes into a business and its organizational practices.

The most obvious change is having your "storefront" open to the marketplace 24 hours a day, on a global basis. Customers and prospects all over the world can access the information you have created at virtually no incremental cost to you, and provide you with instantaneous feedback about what they like, what they want, and how they view your site. Recognize that you could be faced very quickly with a need to offer versions of your Web pages in languages other than English.

However, the most important thing you can do is to build understanding of how the "simple" characteristics of Web technologies that we have identified (interactivity, ubiquity, individualized response capability, ease of use, and global access) introduce the potential for dramatic change in every component of a business system.

As we noted in Chapter 7, the Web transforms the whole customer relationship process, introducing opportunities for direct, one-to-one interaction with thousands of individual customers. Companies that launch a Web site without understanding how profoundly it will affect their marketing and sales organizations are doomed from the beginning to be forever reacting to unexpected demands and unexpected pressures from both customers and employees.

The core business processes of a Web-based organization also operate very differently than those of a conventional business. For example, with a Web-based order entry process, the customer completes the order information, including all the basic facts about product codes, order quantities, destination address, and shipping arrangements. Your order entry process must have built-in filters to verify the accuracy and completeness of the customer-entered data, and to guard against both fraud and inadvertent mistakes (such as ordering 100 cases of wine when the customer really wanted 10).

In addition, many Web-based processes involve links to other companies' processes, whether it be a distributor who stocks the items you are selling, a shipper like UPS or Federal Express, or a credit-card organization like Visa or Mastercard. Ensuring that these electronic linkages are working properly and are secure is a crucial step in launching a sales-oriented Web site.

The technology tools for a Web site are obviously different from those that support more traditional business processes, and they require different kinds of planning and operational support. Your Web site must be operational 24 hours a day, seven days a week, and it requires backups and overflow storage capacity in the event of software or hardware failures, unexpected demand, and other unforeseen events. Failing to take these needs into account can create all kinds of problems.

The area most often overlooked in Web implementations is the skill required to build and support the Web site, including all the affected business processes. As suggested in Chapter 9, Web-based organizations operate very differently from traditional ones, and the core skills—both business and technical—are very different as well. Organizations often initiate Web projects without understanding what new skills are required, or they get partway into implementation and discover that they are very short of necessary skills.

Finally, it is common for organizations to almost completely overlook the necessity for new management systems to measure, monitor, and evaluate the Web-based activities. Since the business processes are often embedded directly within the Web application itself, performance tracking requires new kinds of management systems. The actual performance measures themselves must be redefined, and capturing them is also different.

These examples just highlight the basic differences in Web-based business practices and the business system in which they are embedded, but the impact of moving to a Web-based business goes much deeper. Most significant is the way your organization relates to its customers and other constituencies. As described in Chapter 7, the entire marketing process shifts from a broadcast to an interactive model. Failing to understand how this changes the marketing function and its activities can be catastrophic.

Remember, too, that a Webified organization operates very differently from a traditional, hierarchical, command-and-control organization. Transitioning from one style to another is no simple task. To take full advantage of the power of intranet technologies, you must supplement your technology capabilities with a first-class organizational development team. Some of the crucial skills needed are:

· Basic knowledge of how networked organizations operate
· Interpersonal and team-building skills
· Change orchestration
· Stress management
· Communications and PR skills

CONFRONT ISSUES OF INFORMATION SHARING AND OWNERSHIP AGGRESSIVELY AND DIRECTLY. Everyone has the heard the phrase "information is power." Sharing information is not natural in most organizations, which typically promote and reward individuals rather than teams or groups. A Webified organization is built around a very different value system—that information belongs to the organization, and that the organization will be more effective, more efficient, and more responsive to customer needs if information is widely shared and easily accessible.

Moving to a widely used intranet means confronting this value-laden and cultural issue head-on, and it is one more reason you will need all those organizational development skills described above.

And here are our guidelines for building a successful Web technology capability:

ASSEMBLE AN EFFECTIVE WEBMASTER TEAM. A good Web team will have a diverse mixture of technical and organizational skills (and we believe the organizational skills—including change management—are just as important as the technical skills). There are four broad skill sets that are crucial to the success of a Web team:

· Core Web technology capabilities (HTML, TCP/IP, and other telecommunications technologies; database design; legacy systems knowledge; and security)
· Project management

· Communications media and design skills
· Knowledge of the business processes that will be affected

Build a Robust Web Platform.   Time and time again we have seen companies fail to anticipate the volume of activity that their Web site will generate. And nothing can hurt you more with customers and prospects than slow response time—or, worst of all, having potential customers turned away from your site with the familiar message "The URL is not responding. It may be down or experiencing overload. Please try again later."

Remember that the pace of change in the Web world is several orders of magnitude faster than it is in the rest of the world. If your site is even moderately successful, we can almost guarantee that you will be scrambling to add servers, modem ports, and related infrastructure components. While it can be costly to invest in excess capacity ahead of need, doing so is probably cheaper than the negative publicity or reputation you will develop if customers cannot access your site—to say nothing of lost revenues when capacity constraints prevent customers from buying your products and services.

Match Your Web Technologies and Design to Your Business Strategy and Customer Requirements.   In spite of our fascination with the power and relatively low cost of Web technologies, we want to remind you that not every business needs all the bells and whistles of the Web. If your Web site is a static one, you don't need a secure server and you might not want to invest in capturing individual data about your site visitors. If you know that most of your customers and prospects are individual consumers or small businesses with low bandwidth access to the Net, don't load up your homepages with lots of graphics requiring long, slow downloads.

If, on the other hand, you are a bank or other kind of financial institution, then security is a crucial issue and you have no choice but to invest in technologies that will provide you and your customers with the necessary privacy—not only secure servers and communications lines, but password protection, notices, and all the other peripheral materials that convey to your customers that you do indeed have a secure site.

One other very important principle: make sure that your Web business, organizational, and technology strategies are aligned and mutually reinforcing. There is nothing more counterproductive than internally generated conflict or friction among these various components of your overall Web strategy.

SOME FINAL THOUGHTS

Webifying your business is not simple, but it isn't rocket science either. In fact, we believe that too much has been made of the Web's underlying technologies and not enough of its core characteristics—the ones that affect basic management strategies like understanding and catering to your customers; matching your organizational capabilities and processes to customer needs; recruiting, retaining, and managing skilled professionals; encouraging innovation and growth; and paying attention to things like cash flow, earnings, profitability, return on investment, shareholder value, and growth.

In the end, the search for digital excellence is a search for managerial excellence. It just means taking advantage of powerful new tools: being aware of their existence, recognizing what they can do, and learning to apply them to your business—as it can be, not as it is today.

WHAT'S NEXT?

"Prediction is very difficult, especially about the future."

Yogi Berra

This book has taken you on a quick tour of the Internet and the World Wide Web. More importantly, we have shown you how dozens of companies are taking advantage of the Web today, adapting their strategies, organizations, and management practices to the new realities of this global information and communication infrastructure. We have focused on what it takes in leadership, strategy, organization, and management to be successful in the digital economy.

The new economics and value propositions enabled by the Web are truly exciting and revolutionary. There is little question that our society is in the midst of a powerful transformation in the way we learn, do business, communicate, create knowledge, and even build and maintain personal relationships.

The one "big question" everyone asks us—and the one we desperately wish we could answer—is "What's next?" In other words, where is all this going? Will we all someday be perpetual Web surfers, doing all our shopping on the Web, using it as our primary news and information source, conducting all our business and storing all our knowledge on it? Some so-called experts really do believe our future will be a purely digital one, while others assert—just as persuasively—that real life (as opposed to cyberlife) will continue almost unchanged. They remind us that only a very small percentage of the world's population has ever connected to the Web, and assert that all this exponential growth in Internet use is just a temporary phenomenon in a very minor sector of the overall economy.

On the other hand, many other technologies that we take for granted today were just as revolutionary, and took significantly longer to gain widespread acceptance. Consider developments like electricity, telephones, television, the automobile, commercial jet airplanes, fax machines, VCRs, automated teller machines, personal computers, and credit cards. Every one of these technologies grew slowly at first. Then, when they hit the inflection point in the assimilation curve, they not only swept into widespread "overnight" use, but, more importantly, they launched profound transformations in our way of life—transformations in our daily experience, in neighborhoods and cities, in economics, in the marketplace, in our social, economic and political lives, and in the products and services available to us.

But the question before us, the question we are devoting this final chapter to, is "Where is the Internet going, and how will it affect our lives?" Realistically, no one knows the answer to that question, because the Internet isn't "going" anyplace on its own. We as a society—all of us together—will invent the future of the Internet, just as we invent our futures in other spheres of life.

Nevertheless, we are going to speculate a bit, and offer some ideas about what to look for: what signs, signals, and clues you should pay attention to that will tell you something important is happening. The challenge for any futurist is to know what events and patterns serve as early warning signals—indicators that things are changing, and pointers towards how they are changing.

As we have done throughout the book, we will look at the Internet and its consequences along four basic dimensions: the technology itself, its economic impact, its social impact, and the political/regulatory environment that will likely result from the convergence of the other forces.

We will also point you toward a number of other sources that will enable you to pursue specific threads toward the future in more detail. We are not suggesting that you go read several more books, but rather that from now on you make it a habit to regularly peruse key Web sites, attend industry conferences, and read both the general press and focused publications. Ultimately, the only way anyone can successfully navigate the future is to be in touch with it on a daily basis.

TECHNOLOGY TRENDS

The trends in network commerce technologies generally point towards massive cost reductions coupled with improvements in capabilities, ease of use, and development, along with the increasing integration of previously unconnected means of communication and information processing. These trends bode well for predictions of widespread and ubiquitous application of these technologies. The expectation of continued and accelerated growth in the percentage of the world population that is hooked up to a digital network is not far-fetched when you consider the emergence of cheaper access devices (e.g., thin clients), cheaper servers (thanks to clustering), and cheaper bandwidth (with soon-to-mature broadband technologies like cable modems and xDSL combined with greater use of caching and compression technologies). We expect the widespread application of these technologies to enable the far-reaching networks and multimedia communications essential to the sweeping social, economic, and political impacts we will discuss later in this chapter. In this section we will discuss these technology trends in terms of the basic building blocks of network commerce: clients, servers, and networks.

CLIENTS

The major trend in clients is a movement to smaller and cheaper devices. Fueled by a quest to break the industry dominance of Microsoft and Intel (a.k.a. Wintel), IT vendors led by Sun, IBM, and Oracle have proposed scaled-down devices for desktops. Generally called *thin clients*, these devices portend a revolution at the desktop: moving processing and storage off the desktop and onto centrally located servers, and running Java-based software rather than Windows. Although the final mix of industry players is uncertain, one thing is clear: the threat and attractiveness of such devices has resulted in much anticipation over useful changes happening at the desktop. Clearly the savings in total cost of ownership and centralized maintenance of these machines have been great selling points. Most of the estimates range from 15- to 60-percent reductions in costs, even after upgrades to servers and networks. These numbers, along with the potential increase in demand for centralized IT services, have fueled much interest in thin clients among IT executives.[1]

This level of interest in cheaper desktop devices has moved Microsoft and Intel from denigrating the machines to announcing development of their own thin client, the NetPC, which will run the Windows operating system and software. Microsoft has also announced an initiative to simplify the maintenance of Windows-based systems with "zero administration." Because Java-based thin clients from vendors like Oracle and Sun are just now appearing in the market, it is quite possible that the dominant thin client will be a Wintel device, which will most likely be available soon and be promoted very heavily by the marketing machines of Microsoft and Intel. Furthermore, products such as Citrix Winterm are making it possible to run Windows software at Pentium performance levels even on Macintosh and 80286 machines![2]

The entry of the NetPC and products such as Citrix Winterm could prove the death knell for non-Wintel devices, particularly because the success of these latter devices is dependent on user acceptance of new productivity software developed using the JAVA programming language. The widespread adoption of Windows software results in inertia that might make it impossible to shift users to the Java-based software. In the end, though, users and corporations will likely benefit, no matter which scaled-down devices become the standard. The overwhelming hype and interest in cheaper, scaled-down client devices in the last year or so will guarantee their realization, although it might not change the balance of power in the software and hardware industries. The presence of such machines and the possibility of reusing old PCs and Macs as scaled-down client devices means that corporations could deploy more machines and get more of their employees hooked into the information networks within and outside their corporate firewalls. On the consumer front, scaled-down inexpensive devices that hook up to the home TV are likely to result in an accelerated growth in consumer connections to the Internet. Both of these trends suggest an expansion in the markets available for business-to-consumer applications.

Another major trend is the movement towards embedded clients. These clients (usually a common device like a car, copy machine, or clothing) benefit greatly from the computing power provided by microchips embedded in them. Such embedding augments the functionality of a given device by allowing the storage of rules and procedures that make it more responsive to changes in its usage or environment. Some of these embedded microchips are also assigned IP addresses. These IP addresses allow the machine to be addressed over any IP network—including the highly ubiquitous Web. The IP-addressable parts can then be monitored, repaired, even modified remotely. Thus, these parts act as loci of customization within the machine, allowing the transmission and processing of information that enable the machine to transform itself in real-time to meet changing demands of users or any given situation. A striking example is a prototype car built by Daimler-Benz.

Daimler Benz has built a car equipped with an on-board, integrated wireless communication system and the computing infrastructure to provide multimedia Internet connectivity while stationary or in motion.[3] Besides giving its driver and passenger access to real-time information, e-mail, and voice-mail support, the prototype might soon be enhanced with integrated GPS and mapping technologies. The car itself might feature "location awareness" for services such as remote diagnostics, or even for locating a teenager who has missed curfew. With help from increasingly sophisticated traffic sensors, it will become possible to obtain real-time information on construction, accidents, and other everyday traffic snarls.

Lastly, software and applications designed to run on clients are being used to enhance the ease of use, functionality, and customizability of these devices. Many of the new and proposed client software systems incorporate browser technologies into the operating system, creating a seamless environment for data access and processing. The software systems allow for the viewing and use of rich multimedia content and work consistently over a wide range of hardware platforms. This multimedia capability enables rich communications over the internet: from telephone calls to video-conferences to television and radio programs. The integration of these methods of communication with the Internet further widens the usage of its networks. Additionally, artificial intelligence applications are easing the interface between client devices and users, and improving the security of such devices. Voice recognition software, already available on the market in mid-1997, is reducing the need to type in command or document text, which eases the adoption of computing by individuals who can't—or won't—type. Advances in biometrics foreshadow a future where we can finally give up our reliance on easily misplaced or stolen passwords and "smart cards," gaining access to devices by flashing the unique patterns of our ever-present eyes, hands, voices, or even body odor.[4]

These new client software systems provide users capabilities that could conceivably offset the loss of control they might feel when moving from relatively independent personal computers to networked thin clients. First, the ability of these applications to handle multimedia content and their customizability will allow users to build environments that are best suited to their working styles. Such environments can be frozen in their current states and retrieved quite readily in a thin client environment. Second, new client software packages are making it increasingly easier for users to manage their own personal privacy. As encryption and authentication technologies become wrapped in user-friendly interfaces, more users will be encouraged to use them and thus take personal responsibility for the stewardship of their personal and most private information.

SERVERS

A major trend among servers is the move to Windows NT and clustering. More and more organizations are migrating and standardizing by using Windows NT as their enterprise operating system. It is now common to hear the phrase, "No one ever got fired for recommending Windows NT." Although part of this mass migration could be a manifestation of the risk aversion among IT managers, a large part of it can be attributable to the clear benefits that Windows NT offers. Aside from making system administration easier, NT provides the capability for clustering machines—a trend that managers will surely want to track.

Clustering servers has gotten a lot of attention in recent years because of the major benefits it provides in scalability and cost savings. Clustering makes it possible to add processing power in much smaller increments than was previously possible. In the past, companies had to replace an overused mainframe with an even larger mainframe. These upgrades necessitated the major effort of physically moving very large machines, as well as large sums of money. With clustering, companies can build servers incrementally by adding common workstations, or even obsolete workstations and PCs, to the cluster. Such clusters are made possible by the network operating system and high-speed networks. In late 1997, Microsoft is planning to ship a version of Windows NT that includes the capability for limited clustering—essentially allowing two machines to be clustered with one machine serving as the backup for the other machine. Future versions are expected to allow clustering of more machines and true parallel processing. While many other vendors provide clustering, having Microsoft's market clout and marketing muscle surrounding such a capability again suggests that this is going to be a viable configuration for servers in the near future.

A growing trend is to build a middle layer of servers to act as bridges between legacy systems and the new client software and models of network computing. In the past, this middle tier was used to support Internet services like e-mail, newsgroups, and Web access. The middle tier is being used for more and more sophisticated processing, from data warehousing to information caching to collecting data on visits to company Web sites to preprocessing files that enter the protected networks of a given company. This type of processing could be, for example, identifying who can access files or preprocessing files into formats to ease their accessibility over a corporate network (by changing their formats or making them smaller).

NETWORKS

Bandwidth to support efficient transmission of rich multimedia content and operation of high bandwidth applications (e.g., Internet telephony) is likely to be available quite soon, especially within the U.S. Trials of cable modems and xDSL technologies have suggested that such broadband technologies will have widespread application by the turn of the century at the latest.[5] In addition, other technologies ensure much more efficient use of any bandwidth available. Compression technologies make it possible to reduce the size of files that traverse such networks. Caching reduces network traffic by bringing files closer to clients and reducing the number of times that clients have to access the files from their original sources. The emergence of thin client devices has prompted the development of software that minimizes the flow of information between clients and servers, reducing such communications to low-bandwidth levels.

The Internet's ubiquity and low cost, and the prospect of high-bandwidth services, has fueled interest in using it as a transmission medium for business-to-business communications. There is much consideration of using the Internet to replace WANs, VANs, etc. to transmit documents using either the EDI standard or other format. With the application of encryption technologies, it is possible to build virtual private networks on the Internet. This prospect raises issues regarding the measurement of service quality and the pricing of different service levels. Such quality of service standards and protocols are presently under discussion by some of the leading players in the Internetworking arena.

Outside the U.S., prospects for network availability are less clear. Many countries outside the U.S. and Europe are just forming their own versions of the Internet. Thus, while they might have decent levels of access to the U.S., many of these countries do not have the ubiquitous networks that the Internet has provided to the U.S. This greatly limits the communications and network commerce opportunities within each country, since it is oftentimes more difficult to connect two local entities than it is to connect out of the country to the U.S. With the increasing worldwide deregulation of telecommunications industries, competition is growing from wireless networks—both in the U.S. and in many countries where cable, copper, and fiber networks are not quite as well established. Already, wireless access at T1 speeds (1.5 Mbps over the UHF spectrum) is available for about a sixth of the cost that phone companies charge for dedicated lines, at a fraction of the time it takes to establish service. Cheap, global wireless communications are much more tangible when you consider the amount of entrepreneurial activity involved in harnessing every band of the wireless spectrum—including a Bill Gates venture to launch hundreds of satellites dedicated to high-speed data transmission.[6]

The development of network commerce in most countries will likely follow a much different path than in the U.S., where network commerce took off at a time when there already existed an extensive network of high-speed links crisscrossing the country (at the time, mostly serving government and university users). Such a ubiquitous network made entry into the network commerce arena relatively cheap: basically, purchasing an account with a local Internet service provider and building a Web site. The low cost of entry fueled much interest in using the Internet as an alternative and less costly transmission medium for existing dial-up and WAN communications, e.g., to transmit EDI documents or to facilitate communication between business partners. Even in Western Europe, where networks are quite developed, there are often gaps in service. Outside the U.S. and Europe, where such a ubiquitous network does not exist, the price of entry into the network could be prohibitive and thus not much better than purchasing traditional network services like digital subscriber lines. Fully developing network commerce within such countries is dependent upon lowering the cost of entry into existing networks—a possibility that will be delayed by the persistence of telecommunications monopolies and infrastructure limitations within each country.

The client-server-network systems described in this section are already very much a part of current discussions among

vendors, industry pundits, information technology professionals, and experienced users. As such, they will most likely be
available for application in business and home settings quite
soon, providing far-reaching networking and multimedia communications. Already, the San Francisco Bay Area, where many
information technology vendors are located, is teeming with examples of what work and home life might become, given the
application of such technologies to build platforms of ubiquitous and rich networks. This hotbed of experimentation and
hype serves as a rich source of ideas for understanding where
this new world might take us. In the next sections of this chapter, we will discuss some of the economic, social, and political
impacts suggested by these exemplars.

ECONOMIC TRENDS: A NETWORKED
BUSINESS WORLD OF TOMORROW

As the technologies discussed previously continue to engender
the evolution of a global and truly multimedia networking infrastructure, revolutionizing impacts on the business world are
looming on the horizon: information handling will become increasingly efficient and provide fertile grounds for innovative
types of products and organizational forms, such as virtual organizations and online communities. As a consequence, changes
in market structures, e.g., triggered by an altered role of intermediary market players, will continue to be interesting to ob-
serve, but hard to predict.

EFFICIENT INFORMATION HANDLING

Perhaps we are not far from the ultimate scenario, where each
piece of information needs to be stored permanently in only
one place after having been created. In some cases the most
convenient location might be the physical place where it was
created; in other situations it will be the one where it is most
heavily used. With a ubiquitous network infrastructure, information will become accessible from anywhere around the world

in real time. Consequently, with powerful tools to capture, aggregate, and analyze data that today are usually spread across many locations, data warehouses will become a more common option. They will help organizations tighten the relationships with their customers by constantly keeping track of their activities, learning about their preferences, and steering marketing and service activities accordingly. The notion of real-time marketing might actually not be so far away.[7]

INNOVATIVE PRODUCTS AND SERVICES

We will see a whole generation of new and more sophisticated products emerge as computer chips find their way into products and manufacturing processes. Connecting more of their parts will lead to smarter goods, factories, and homes that can send out or retrieve information, as well as act (or react) according to it. The Internet car built by Daimler Benz, discussed earlier in the chapter, is a good example.

Reduced cost and improved information handling and communication (increasingly over wireless networks) with humans, databases, and all other objects and machines that can carry computer chips could lead us to a completely networked economy with everything being linked to everything else, information becoming globally accessible in real time, and electronic communication becoming truly multimedia.[8] This will, for example, enable the remote performance of tasks that are dangerous, such as cleaning contaminated areas, or that require experts, such as in medicine.

INNOVATIVE FORMS OF ORGANIZATIONS

As we have outlined throughout the book, the networked economy is already significantly changing business and organizations—a trend that we expect to continue and even intensify. Traditional, hierarchically structured firms with well-defined boundaries are giving way to highly specialized, autonomous organizational units that form tight but in many cases temporary relationships to perform specific tasks and projects and offer highly customized products and services in a highly efficient way.[9] As a consequence, competition between companies is already being replaced by competition between networks.[10] Their success is based on a global and readily accessible information infrastructure, as well as sophisticated communication systems enabling communication links. Throughout the book, we have already touched several times on the notion of these networked organizations—also called *extended* or *virtual organizations*— that are, it seems, increasingly becoming the standard, allowing market players to react to business requirements with a flexibility not previously possible. At least in the service sector and apart from the production of hard goods, we could envision an economy that consists of mostly self-employed specialists forming short-term contracts on a project-by-project basis.

Since its founding in 1987, the Berkeley-based Dynamic Software Company has relied heavily on its network infrastructure to connect its diverse group of mathematicians, scientist, educators, artists, and programmers. Through its telecommunications collaboration efforts, Dynamic Software has been able to attract needed specialists to its projects, many who might not have been willing to join a project if they had to leave their current position with their present employer or place of residence. For example, to develop one of its graphic design software packages, FractaSketch, it integrated the input of experts separated by vast distances: a computer science professor in Belgium with expertise in linear fractal designs, a leading fashion designer based in New York known for producing Jacquard fabrics, and an algorithms specialist in Berkeley developing for the Windows platform—not to mention the necessary support staff of artists, programmers, and writers.

ONLINE COMMUNITIES

Business processes will continue to change from sequential step-by-step manufacturing to nonlinear and heavily information-based networking, improving efficiency and flexibility simultaneously. Additionally, long-term relationships will play an increasingly important role in an ever more complex and fast-paced business world. Knowing your business partner not only helps you cope with uncertainties, but also eliminates the risk and expenses involved with having to set up clear-cut and complex contracts. A growing number of online communities—evolving around business tasks as well as private life issues—document this trend.

A major community redevelopment initiative underway as part of the San Francisco Giants' stadium construction triggered the formation of an online community and information pool that would bring together government, private industry, and neighborhood groups. Besides offering information about premises, such as digital photos of individual buildings and streetscapes, zoning records, building permits, and business and residential environments, the network could also include real-time information about street excavation activities and construction progress. By integrating a comprehensive number of services, online building permit granting will become possible, enhancing the efficiency of development project logistics.

CHANGING ROLE OF INTERMEDIARIES

Reduced communication costs generally enable better and cheaper coordination of business players. Consequently, we see a major change in the traditional role of intermediaries and markets, namely bringing together buyers and sellers of goods and services. Even if the ubiquitous information space that is the Internet would ultimately automate the matching of buyers and sellers, an increased need for new types of intermediaries will probably more than outweigh this "loss." They will help companies shape Web business strategies, get started and establish a presence in the online world. Even more importantly, they will help businesses and users cope with a more and more complex world, e.g., as information brokers or ensuring trust among market players and protecting sensitive data.

Again, we come across the networking paradigm. Today's intermediaries often offer comprehensive, yet geographically limited services. Real estate brokers, for example, help home owners sell or buy houses not only by matching offers with applications, but also by providing market information, advice on investment opportunities, and guidance for closing deals. Again, with the

Internet and World Wide Web, we see intermediaries offering highly specialized services on a global basis, teaming up with providers of complementary products.

Abele's Owners' Network (http://www.owners.com) permits Internet users to act as their own real estate agent and advertise their homes for sale. This publicly accessible database contains more than 30,000 properties nationwide and lets users search by price range, number of bedrooms, and region.[11] And the Web site provides additional value: visitors can check comparable home sales while looking at a listing, find school information and property mapping for most listings, and get financial advice. Although accessible from its Web site, these services are not provided by Owners' Network itself, but by equally specialized business partners. By teaming up with business partners offering complementary services, Owners' Network establishes a network that provides a comprehensive real estate service on a global basis, just as a nationwide association of traditional real estate brokers would do.

You probably realized by now, that we do not expect that the Internet will eliminate middlemen on a large scale, but that it will find its place among many things that characterize everyday life.

Research by International Data Corporation suggests that the level of electronic commerce conducted over the Internet will increase to more than $200 billion by the year 2001, from an estimated $10 billion in 1998. As much as 80 percent will supposedly come from business-to-business transactions. The numbers seem credible, maybe even conservative, given the fact that leaders such as Cisco Systems already report reaching an annual sales rate of more than $2 billion over the Web, and announce a share as high as 60 percent as their mid-term goal for online ordering. With the emergence of increasingly secure and innovative payment schemes, such as smart cards or micropayments, this development will get an additional boost.

Multimedia capabilities of the Internet and World Wide Web will continue to transform the world of entertainment, blurring the boundaries not only between vast areas such as the television, music, and movie industries, but also with software and manufacturers of hardware and network components such as cable modems. While the redefinition of business areas is obvious, the outcome of the struggle is still unclear.

Businesses have to become and remain increasingly aware of potential changes, as well as to stay realistic; so far, the Internet is still a very long way from reaching into every home or onto every desk! It surely creates competition, but in most cases creates new opportunities at the same time. Consider newspapers— while the Internet certainly threatens the traditional paper-based version, we don't believe paper will ever go away completely. How would you use your laptop to read the news in the tub, or prevent the oil of your leaking engine from staining the floor in your garage?

There are other "buts" and limitations that have to be overcome for the whole new networking world to be fully realized: to name a few, the necessity of an adequate communications infrastructure, potential impacts of an online availability that is coming close to 24 hours a day, and cost issues.

COMMUNICATION INFRASTRUCTURE

An adequate communication infrastructure is an inevitable prerequisite to make it all happen. With different applications requiring different levels of bandwidth, security, service reliability, and multimedia capabilities, some people envision a number of distinct yet interwoven networks of different qualities and prices. These could range from simple structures supporting newsgroups and chat rooms, to more sophisticated but easily accessible education networks, to entertainment networks providing high-bandwidth and full multimedia capacity, to electronic commerce networks enabling highly reliable and secure transactions. However, the realization of this scenario is definitely still some "Web years" away.

24/7 AVAILABILITY

The 24-hour-a-day, 7-day-a-week availability provided by modern technology does not come without obvious downsides. Wireless, speech-operated, "hands-free" Internet access, for example, will allow online connection not only from everywhere but also in ever more different situations, like while driving a car. The question arises whether we will end up as complete workaholics.

Could anyone manage with zero downtime? Or will we soon be living in a world where work and spare time become so much intertwined that they can barely be distinguished. Imagine you could be reached by friends as well as business partners all around the clock. Reachability management, i.e., helping users filter out unwanted calls, control their level of accessibility, and simultaneously maintain a high degree of privacy, might ultimately become an inevitable task to cope with such a situation.[12]

COST ISSUES

Web-centric applications don't necessarily come cheaply, as we have pointed out throughout the book. Ultimately, the economic value of the Internet will drive technology development. Only if economic value is created will companies be willing to pay what it takes for technology suppliers to bring new products to market. In addition, the successful realization of some of the scenarios detailed in this chapter depends not only on the effective reduction of production cost, but in some cases also on the further miniaturizing of devices. In 1997, the Daimler Benz Internet car still needs a trunk full of technology equipment in order to connect to the Internet.

Despite some obstacles along the way, there is strong evidence that the business world is already marching towards the networked world of tomorrow. A look at the revolutionary potential that emerging technologies bear for our private and social life will show some interesting parallels mirroring and reinforcing many of the trends that we expect to see in the business world.

THE SOCIAL WORLD OF TOMORROW

The picture we are painting is of a world with almost infinite bandwidth; low-cost PCs, NCs, and workstations; public Internet kiosks; full multimedia (including video); widely used global Internet telephony; and almost universal information access through workstations, PCs, network computers, and kiosks in homes, schools, libraries, bookstores, cafes, airports, shopping malls, and even cars, planes, and trains. With the whole economy operating like a gigantic network, with everything connected to everything else, what will our personal lives be like?

The most effective way to imagine such a future is to consider what it will be like to be in what Michael Dertouzos of MIT's Laboratory of Computer Science has called "electronic proximity," with literally millions of other people and virtually any piece of information you need, whenever and wherever you need it.[13]

While the Internet of 1997 is still limited by bandwidth and CPU processing capabilities, we are fully convinced that the Internet and the Web of tomorrow will provide rich communication experiences that are very nearly as complete and as satisfying as face-to-face interactions are today.

Given those technology capabilities, the essential reality of the Internet is the elimination of physical geography as a barrier to communication and the formation and maintenance of relationships.[14] Today, millions of other individuals, anywhere in the world, are no more than a keystroke and a few pennies away. We believe that, eventually, virtually the entire population of the world will have some form of Internet access (though we also recognize there will be a period of distinct differences in access among various groups and countries, a period of "haves and have-nots" that will be highly stressful on all sides).

As Dertouzos points out, virtual proximity means that we can (and will) extend our personal networks not only in space but in scale. We will be in easy and frequent communication with literally thousands (or even millions) of other individuals and groups: family members, personal friends, professional colleagues, employees, customers, or, if you are in or seeking political office, constituents and prospective voters.

Some of those relationships are more personal than others, of course, but the point is that our personal and professional networks, our spheres of influence, and the number of people who try to influence us will explode by several orders of magnitude. And like all social transformations, this change will bring with it both positive and negative consequences.

First, we must learn to manage a much larger number of relationships. The sheer number and variety of communications will most likely be overwhelming; many people will find this new richness stressful, while others will thrive in it. Surely some individuals and groups will retreat from open and diverse contact, while others will reach out for it.

People are also likely to become even more impatient with delays, whether in communication interactions or in finding and getting the information and products they want. The Internet enables almost instant gratification, which in our time-constrained lives we value highly. (In our own experience on the campus at UC Berkeley, we have online access to all the university libraries. In our haste to find relevant information, we often find ourselves resenting the need to walk the 50 yards or so from our offices to the Haas School library to find a book or journal, and get irrationally frustrated when the full text of the article or chapter we need is not available online for instant downloading.)

This new richness of electronic proximity and extended electronic communities will enable a much richer two-way dialog and broader debate of major social and political issues. It can bring people closer together, but it can also generate higher levels of confusion and could even create a climate ripe for a demagogue who promises to bring people back together around simple or even oppressive social principles.

At the same time, the opportunity to hear from and interact with people from all walks of life, all ages, and all ethnic backgrounds on a more or less open and equal basis might well create much more openness and tolerance for diversity.

In fact, we believe the likelihood of some national or global demagogue succeeding in a world where millions of individuals can freely exchange information and ideas is relatively low. The Internet has created a world where millions of "publishers," millions of sources of information, and millions of decision-makers can engage in open debate and discussion, mutually influencing each other. Thomas Jefferson once said that given a choice between a powerful government and a powerful press, he would choose the press every time. Assuming for the moment that it remains the open, pluralist, organic entity that it is today, the Internet might be the best protection we will ever have from tyranny and oppression.

However, our experience with Internet newsgroups suggests that, as in other areas, this freewheeling, open debate is a two-edged sword. We don't want to be Pollyannas about a completely free and open society, because individuals with strong opinions often dominate newsgroups and chat rooms, and it is of course much easier to be obstinate, stubborn, single-minded, and even malicious when you are anonymous or using a fictitious persona. While anonymous and distributed groups often act more democratically and make more effective decisions than face-to-face groups, they can also be even more subject to domination by individuals or coalitions. Much more research is needed on the effects of these technologies on group behaviors and decision-making.

The risk we face is that society will become so overwhelmed with information and opposing viewpoints that it might look for simple answers as an antidote to all the complexity and multiplicity of choice.

LIFE AS A CONSUMER

In a world of universal access to information and other people, the scarcest and most precious resource will be time, and the battle in the marketplace will be for attention. We will be bombarded more than ever with advertisements and commercial gimmicks designed to generate interest and capture both our minds and our wallets.

People will use the Internet to shop for commodities and hard-to-get items, relying on UPS and FedEx to deliver physical goods directly to their homes and offices (information, music, software, and other "bits" will of course be directly downloadable). But we don't expect the general public ever to give up shopping in person for clothing and other more personal items where they want to touch, see, try on, or even smell the product before committing to buy it. And for many consumers, shopping is still a social experience. "Hanging out" at the mall, or just getting out with friends and combining shopping with a meal and a movie, will remain a popular activity for millions of people around the world.

For millions of other shoppers, however, for whom time is in short supply, the opportunity to save time and increase choice by using the Web and personal delivery services will be very, very compelling. And, of course, real-time Web-based interactions might also serve as substitutes for physically "hanging out," at least for some individuals and groups (it is worth noting that in 1997 the American Psychological Association officially recognized Internet Addiction Disease, IAD, as a serious and real affliction).

Already, interactive games and sports-oriented Web sites on the Net are bringing people "together" for social experiences, and virtual shopping malls are emerging that offer cybershoppers various kinds of both real-time and asynchronous interactions with other consumers—including chat rooms and newsgroups where discussions about the latest fashions, rock stars, automobiles, and electronic equipment help consumers make up their minds about what to buy (and no doubt encourage larger and more frequent purchases). Amazon.com, for examples, offers space for readers and prospective book buyers to leave each other and authors personal notes about what they liked or disliked about any given book.

In a very real sense, this kind of communication with fellow shoppers can serve as a meaningful substitute for exchanging comments or raised eyebrows among the shelves in real stores. In addition, of course, it provides you with a whole new source of information about the products and services you are interested in, including recommendations for new products that others who think like you do have already bought and "endorsed."

As in so many other areas, the Internet is not replacing other forms of shopping as much as it is complementing them. In the process, consumers gain yet more variety and more choices, not only in what to buy, but in where and how they shop.

LIFE AT WORK

We envision organizational life becoming much more fluid and dynamic, with almost no "standard" work day or working pattern. The Internet and intranets make very real the promise of "anytime/anyplace" work. We will see much more variety in patterns of work and physical office environments. More and more people will work in multiple locations: in the main office a few days a week, at remote office locations, at home, in multicompany satellite offices, in hotel rooms, in airplanes. Fewer people will work in only one location, with the dominant pattern being flexibility and change—a few days in the company office, a few days at the home office, a business trip, and so on.

This kind of flexibility is of course already enabling millions of individuals to work part-time or on a self-employed basis. More and more people are holding down two, three, or even four part-time jobs, all from their homes or personal offices. The elimination of geography opens all kinds of new forms of employment and contractual work, and also encourages more people to live where they want to live, whether in balmy climates, on mountaintops, at the shore, or in the woods.

This opportunity to blend work and personal life, unfortunately, has its dark side too. Many individuals are working longer hours, taking PCs and pagers with them on vacations, on outings with their children, to dinner parties, and on the golf course. As Internet access becomes more widespread through smaller, cheaper, wireless devices, the ability to be in constant touch will become more and more seductive. We expect a significant increase in stress in personal and family life, and more and more examples of individual burn-out before we learn as a society and as individuals how to control our need for access and accessibility.

These diverse and varied patterns will also necessitate much more highly developed interpersonal skills. Not only will people learn to be flexible and adaptive, but they will learn to form new working relationships quickly, and to work effectively with many other individuals and in teams with people who they don't know very well.

Trust will be crucial to the new digital economy, because there will be so many instances of transacting business with firms or individuals you have never met before. As we pointed out in Chapter 10, an individual or a company Web site is no guarantee of reliability, or even that the site is genuine. With such a fast pace of business on a global scale, there will rarely be enough time for even mundane credit checks, contracts, or other more traditional forms of guarantees.

In fact, the most important enablers of electronic commerce might well be Visa, MasterCard, American Express, Discover, and other universal credit cards, because the firms behind those familiar names serve the increasingly important function of validating or certifying that the parties in a given transaction are both who they say they are and good for the economic exchange. For an individual consumer, knowing that a Web merchant accepts a Visa card means that the merchant has been "preapproved" by Visa as a valid place of business. And for the merchant, the fact that a consumer has a credit card means that he or she has passed a basic test of credit worthiness (or at least the bank that issued the credit card will stand behind the transaction and guarantee payment to the merchant).

But the issue of trust is not restricted to economic transactions. It also surrounds interpersonal relationships and the credibility of information sources. We expect new mechanisms to be developed in order to verify identity and guarantee accuracy of information. Yet the issue of trust will remain a major concern.

As discussed in Chapter 10, digital images can be enhanced, distorted, or just plain invented (whether used openly in advertising or entertainment situations, or fraudulently in business transactions). Millions of unknown individuals post "facts" in newsgroups every day. More and more individuals take on false or fictitious identities (as the famous *New Yorker* cartoon points out, "On the Internet no one knows you are a dog"). How can we know that the information we acquire is "true?" How do we know the individual on the other end of the e-mail or in the chat room is honest and ethical if we have never met face to face or shared a common real-world experience?

The Internet is in some sense a new frontier, and it is still just as wild and woolly as the American West was 150 years ago. It provides individuals and groups with an unprecedented opportunity for experimentation, whether with new personas or new business propositions. There is room for wonderfully imaginative creativity, but there is also room for incredibly devious and malicious fraud.

With all of these new behaviors and no new "rules" to govern them or provide us with predictability, society could end up becoming much more fragmented and less trusting overall. At the very least, it will be some time before new cyberspace rules are developed and widely accepted. Until then, it is more than simply "buyer beware;" you must truly look out for yourself.

LIFE AT HOME

Some so-called "visionaries" see a home of the future with each family member glued to his or her individual monitor, sending e-mail messages to each other and rarely, if ever, doing anything together. Others predict a return to a more "normal" family life, as telecommuting and video-conferencing actually reduce the amount of time family members are away from home.

In the area of education, we also expect the notion of networking and interactivity to have a major impact. Here, it will lead to new forms of knowledge creation and representation, virtual classrooms, and increasingly permeable geographical borders.

Students will be able to do more learning from home, reducing the amount of time they spend in libraries and classrooms. But more importantly, they will learn in new and very different ways. Students of tomorrow will learn from online "books" assembled in "real time" from information brought together from all over the world (indeed, the students themselves will be doing the assembling). Students will form personal and educational relationships with other students, business experts, scientists, and other experts from all over the world. Learning will not be confined to the classroom; already many elementary school children have "visited" undersea exploration vessels and actually directed experiments with remote controls in the same way that NASA scientists controlled the Sojourner vehicle on Mars in 1997.

Students as well as other citizens will regularly visit the great museums and libraries of the world, using the Internet as a window on works of art, poetry, literature, and other forms of knowledge no matter where they are physically located.

Electronic proximity will also enable all kinds of new and existing personal relationships to flourish as never before. Personal relationships will not be limited by geography; with e-mail, we will be able to communicate with friends and relatives literally all over the globe as easily and as frequently as we interact with our next-door neighbors. Senior citizens and home-bound invalids are already corresponding regularly with each other and with remote family members, exchanging digital photos and videos, and engaging in two-way video conferencing. There are already many "cybercafes" whose patrons communicate in real time with similar individuals in other cities around the world. We fully expect the same kind of electronic interaction to spread to all citizens in all walks of life over the next decade.

In addition, as more people discover special-purpose newsgroups, chat rooms, and other specific interest groups that maintain Web sites, individuals will form friendships and formal affiliations with other people with similar interests no matter where they are located physically. Michael Dertouzos has even suggested that the whole concept of a nation and nationality might break free of physical boundaries: Greeks, Germans, Koreans, Malaysians, Bosnians, and Israelis will form extended communities and share in national holidays, ethnic rituals, music, and even theater performances—to say nothing of common political causes—no matter where in the world they happen to live and work.[15]

All around the world, online communities of all kinds are already thriving. "City networks" such as Pasadena-based CitySearch, Microsoft's Sidewalk, and the German Stadtnet provide information to local citizens and tourists about issues of local interest, events, movies, restaurants, and other activities.

Indeed, one of the open questions about the Internet is whether it will foster some new, hybrid international culture—a homogenization of culture around the world—or whether it will enable communication and contact for special-interest groups of all kinds, which will contribute to an even greater fragmentation of our society. Will we become one global society or thousands of intersecting and overlapping tribes? Will electronic proximity bring us together or tear us apart?

The answers to those very profound and very crucial questions will not be found anywhere in cyberspace—though they

are already being debated and acted out in numerous newsgroups and Web sites—but rather in the halls of government
and in living rooms and board rooms all over the world. For
these questions are social and political, not technical.

POLITICAL ISSUES

From a political standpoint, there are numerous issues that will
be given attention. Broadly speaking, these issues fall into two
areas: government's role in developing and managing these
emerging technologies, and the issue of governance within organizations and society in general, which will both be affected
by these technologies.

GOVERNANCE OF THE INTERNET AND ITS EMERGING TECHNOLOGIES

The goal of Internet governance is to ensure that these emerging technologies are designed and implemented through competition among a diversity of providers. The government's role is
to promote private-sector investment consistent with the dereg-
ulatory language of the Telecommunications Act of 1996, but
also to ensure that competition is fostered among a diversity of
players alongside the nation's largest media, phone, and cable
operators. Also, the government agenda for a "national" infrastructure will be conscious that the digital environment is a
global concept that cannot be managed by any one country.

The government must also promote a diversity of content
and information consistent with the vision and promise of the
Internet technologies as a public good and a fully interactive
medium of communication.

Universal access and connectivity by users and institutions,
including private, public, and nonprofit, will be ensured. Another assurance for users will be that the Internet technologies
develop guidelines for the secure transmission of content, as
well as respect for the privacy of users of electronic information
and communications.

Consumers will be seeking more assurance. Whether
through habit or otherwise, people have a sense of assurance

with traditional forms of commerce. The move toward electronic commerce will create an added burden of trust on the part of the merchant. And what better way to make consumers and businesses feel more comfortable with Internet transactions than to have trusted intermediaries, perhaps a government body or public accountants, bless Web sites with a seal of approval?

The American Institute of Certified Accountants has identified this need for trust-building, and an opportunity for themselves to capitalize on the need for assurance. The group has convened a committee of roughly 20 accountants throughout the "Big Six" and beyond to establish standard policies and procedures for auditing Web businesses. The committee is looking to create standard ways to assess how Web businesses authorize users, encrypt information, and store confidential data, such as credit card numbers.

The movement to generate confidence in Web commerce is gaining steam. TRUSTe, a nonprofit Silicon Valley company, has done a good job of bringing the consumer privacy issue to light. By playing the role of "Good Housekeeping Seal of Approval," VeriSign, Inc. is working on an insurance policy to protect users of its digital certificates. And Excite, builder of a very popular search engine and Web site, has a certified merchant program that not only protects consumers for the first $50 not covered by credit card companies in a fraudulent transaction, but will put a red ribbon on merchant sites that meet its encryption and electronic-mail notification requirements. Companies that are able to build trust, whether through the strength of their brand or trusted technology solutions, will have an edge with the consumer.

The notion of liability will become ever more complex. Imagine a Web business or business transaction that is later accused of bad business practices or worse. Who is accountable, the business, the ISP, the bank, or the trust intermediary? Companies must be cognizant of these potential potholes as they deal with suppliers partners, and customers over the Web.

The U.S. House Committee on National Security recently voted to gut the Security and Freedom through Encryption (SAFE) Act. The act was intended to ease encryption export and dissemination. The House Select Committee on Intelligence voted to amend SAFE so domestic encryption technology must enable the FBI to decrypt any and all information moved over the Internet. The SAFE bill still has a number of hurdles to clear before being enacted, but privacy advocates are quite concerned about the issue.

This issue shows the complexity of emerging technologies. The decentralized nature of Internet technologies can be quite empowering, but at the same time criminal elements, the government argues, are also empowered. Fear of unwanted activities will also become visible within organizations, from corporate espionage to surveillance of employees. These same empowering Internet technologies can become vehicles for keeping an eye on people at all times.

Such scenarios will raise very difficult questions that companies are going to confront in the next decade: What will happen to the nation state and the notion of boundaries? Will borders start becoming blurry as will cultures and economies? How does that affect how companies do business? How will cities be affected? With the move to virtual organizations, telecommuting, and purchasing and distribution of goods through electronic means, what will happen to the infrastructure of cities and business themselves? Today, cities are funded by taxes and rely heavily on transportation infrastructure to drive development. The growth and shift toward the virtual might profoundly affect cities as we know them today. As business becomes more virtual and employees work from home more often, tax receipts based on the bricks and mortar of office buildings will begin to shrink. Where will future funds to support the city come from? How will taxation work? Managers are going to have to change their paradigm of work, from "managing" to "enabling," a change that will not come easily to most people and companies.

Internet technologies can be used to enhance the democratic process within society and organizations, for example enabling citizens or employees to brainstorm and understand issues that are of importance to them. With such empowerment and understanding come potentially scary scenarios to those in power. Managers and leaders need to be able to cope with those added voices, which traditionally were silent.

Government and Private Sector Role in the Emerging Digital Economy

Most current government policies have been designed to promote the development of Internet technologies and their applications within a market open to competition. Two examples are the Clinton Administration's Agenda for Action and The Internet Tax Freedom Act. The Agenda for Action relies heavily on private-sector investment in the design and deployment of the Internet technologies. Emphasis is placed on the growth of the Internet and Internet technologies through the private sector, including who will build the actual hardware and what kind of regulation is needed to complement this development. In short, the Administration's view is that "by encouraging private-sector investment, we will promote U.S. competitiveness, job creation, and solutions to pressing social problems." With the Internet Tax Freedom Act, the U.S. Congress proposes a two-year moratorium on state and local taxation of Internet commerce transactions. Congress and the Clinton Administration intend to use this moratorium ostensibly to promote the growth of Internet commerce. Yet at the same time, they plan to use the time to study how best to apply taxation to the international Internet commerce arena.

Unfortunately, as in many areas involving revolutionary social transformations, government policies have so far proved inadequate in achieving the goal of promoting open markets and competition. A case in point is the impact of the Telecommunications Act of 1996. The objective of the act was the continued deregulation of various industry sectors such as telephony, cable, and wireless—with the goal of promoting rapid development of leading-edge telecommunications infrastructure and services. Ironically, the Act's effect seems instead to be a trend towards consolidation in the industry. Mergers and acquisitions have been the primary means by which players in the industry have entered new telecommunications markets. Witness the efforts by WorldCom, GTE, and British Telecom to acquire the networking resources of MCI in late 1997, or the U.S. government's recent experience with auctioning off the RF spectrum. The FCC set aside the C-block for "small business enterprises" in order to ensure that other digital wireless players would be involved in building the digital PCS networks and providing services. Despite this effort, the wireless digital players who won licenses were almost all large companies who could afford the huge bids for obtaining licenses.

The Internet is seen by most managers as a means to bolster U.S. technological and economic competitiveness. The problem with this perspective is two-fold. For one thing, the digital information infrastructure is a global concept and users from all around the world are connected through it. This is clearly seen on the Internet's World Wide Web. Internet technology companies must be mindful of the fact that any policy action or business decisions made within the U.S. will not be enforceable over a global network of users. In this sense, the U.S. is a participant rather than the competitive leader among countries working together in research and in establishing the "game rules" on issues such as network interoperability and security. Secondly, by encouraging private-sector investment to rapidly deploy services on Internet technologies, the potential for convergence of technologies—and thus providers—of these technologies is much greater. This development could mean that a few providers will control the design and eventual structure of the global networks. In turn, what it means to the end user, or consumer, is a potentially chilling effect on free speech through limitations on the diversity of media content.

Furthermore, some U.S. government policies threaten to undermine the current U.S. dominance in worldwide software markets. Prolonged debates over the use of encryption technologies to support network commerce have opened a window of opportunity for non-U.S. software manufacturers to gain a foothold into expanding software markets, e.g., those for server software. Current restrictions on the export of software incorporating encryption technology have limited the ability of U.S. software makers to enter such markets. European and Asian software vendors have seen the provision of encryption products as a first step in building a share in market segments that require applications involving cryptography—not only in the non-U.S. market, but within the U.S. as well, since there are currently no restrictions on the import of such software into the U.S. As non-U.S. software vendors use this foothold as a leverage to sell their other products, they could conceivably slowly chip away at the U.S. vendors' dominance in the software industry.

ENSURING QUALITY, DIVERSITY, AND SECURITY OF INFORMATION AND CONTENT

The Internet has thus far been focused on ways to conduct commerce along traditional lines, such as making transactions or purchases over the Internet. However, this orientation underestimates the Internet by viewing it as simply another broadcast or advertising medium. Rather, as we have frequently pointed out, the interactive nature of the technology transforms the Internet into a two-way street so all users and buyers can also be producers and sellers. The current emphasis on marketing and commerce over the Internet will be balanced by a focus on Internet technologies as an interactive communications medium, where users participate collaboratively in the creation of content and the transmission of information. In order for general users or consumers to become more familiar with these new technologies, the architects of the Internet will continue to research ways to secure networks and ensure that sensitive information is safely protected. This effort will foster continued research on technological, software-based solutions such as file encryption and emerging "privacy protecting methods."

Another issue of security for digital information is that of copyrights and ownership of content. Developers of Internet technologies will be committed to working in conjunction with international collaborative efforts such as the European Imprimatur Project to develop standards for copyrighting, like digital fingerprinting and watermarking. New technologies for tracking the "broadcast" and copying of intellectual property over the Internet are becoming available (e.g., Intersect's MusicReport), which open up the possibility of tracking illegal usage as well as legal uses that are subject to the application of royalties. Lastly, providers, advertisers, the government, and the public will be involved in designing adequate privacy rights measures for users. Privacy issues are becoming more and more of an immediate concern for consumers who often feel private information is being freely made available to market researchers. Advertisers particularly have more control over this information with the Internet, using strategies such as requiring preregistration prior to accessing a Web site to entice consumers to release their most personal information.

MAKING INTERNET TECHNOLOGIES A TRULY PUBLIC GOOD

A necessary condition of making Internet technologies a public good is that services become universally affordable and accessible. To achieve this, pricing schemes will have to be evaluated to ensure that the Internet and other services such as wireless communications are made available to everyone. Such pricing schemes can be worked out by carriers of Internet technologies and the FCC if necessary. The Clinton Administration is promoting access for all schools, colleges, libraries, and other institutions for which information retrieval and exchange are inseparable from research and learning, e.g., the NetDay program.

Ideally, governmental policy will encourage more access to institutions that can provide public benefits through online services and databases or the Internet. This includes the participation of the healthcare industry, government, and community services such as libraries, and education. The potential for transforming these kinds of services is substantial, and the cost savings and information retrieval efficiencies gained by cutting administrative work are only some of the benefits. However, these benefits can be realized only through having these segments actively applying Internet technologies to the various processes necessary for distributing their services.

Ultimately, the key policy key question is, "Can government actions foster a free, competitive market and ubiquitous access to the World Wide Web?" In late 1997, government policies seemed to be hindering rather than helping the development of open markets in electronic commerce, although the tide might eventually turn on this unresolved question. On the encryption issue, for example, recent strong lobbying efforts by U.S. software vendors coupled with aggressive education of government representatives (with an FBI lab devoted to the demonstration and study of encryption) might finally focus the debates and policies towards addressing the real threats to U.S. competitiveness in world software markets.

SUMMARY

How could we possibly summarize this chapter, or this whole book? The search for digital excellence has only just begun.

What's next? Lots of excitement, hundreds of new products and services, thousands of experiments, a few successes, many failures, new laws and regulations, much extended debate, open conflict, new markets, new products, new companies, new lifestyles, plenty of confusion, and loads of opportunity. Fortunes will be made and lost, and thousands of entrepreneurs will enjoy their 15 minutes of global fame.

We believe the birth of the digital economy is the most exciting, most far-reaching revolution the world has ever seen. To paraphrase Charles Dickens, it will be the best of times; it will be the worst of times. But it definitely won't be dull.

SOURCES FOR THINKING ABOUT THE FUTURE

This listing of Web sites, magazines, and books is just a partial compilation of interesting companies or sources of more detailed information about the Web, new technologies, and the future:

WEB SITES

Cambridge Information Network (www.cin.ctp.com)
Cisco Systems, Inc. (www.cisco.com)
Cnet.com (www.cnet.com)
CMPNet (www.techweb.com)

CommerceNet (www.commerce.net)
CyberAtlas.com (www.cyberatlas.com)
Fisher Center for Management and Information Technology
  (www.haas.berkeley.edu/~cmit)
The Gap, Inc. (www.gap.com)
Gartner Group (www.gartner.com)
Information Technology Association of America (www.itaa.org)
The Internet Society (www.isoc.org/indextxt.html)
IS World (www.umich.edu/~isworld/reshome.html)
Levi Strauss, Inc. (www.levistrauss.com)
Microsoft (www.microsoft.com)
Netscape (www.netscape.com)
ONSALE (www.onsale.com)
Society for Information Management (www.simnet.org)
Virtual Vineyards (www.virtualvin.com)

MAGAZINES AND NEWSPAPERS (WEB SITES LISTED IN PARENTHESES)

ASAP (Forbes Quarterly Supplement) (www.forbes.com)
Business Week (www.businessweek.com)
Byte (www.byte.com)
CIO Magazine (www.cio.com)
ComputerWorld (www.computerworld.com)
Datamation (www.datamation.com)
Fast Company (www.fastcompany.com)
Fortune Magazine (www.fortune.com)
Information Week (www.informationweek.com)
Internet Week (www. internetwk.com)
The New York Times (www.nytimes.com)
Red Herring (www.redherring.com)
Upside (www.upside.com)
Wired Magazine (www.wired.com)

BOOKS

The Art of the Long View, by Peter Schwartz, Doubleday: New
  York, 1991.
Competing for the Future, by Gary Hamel and C.K. Prahalad,
  Harvard Business School Press, 1994.

Creating a New Civilization, by Alvin and Heidi Toffler, Turner Publishing: Atlanta, 1994.

The Death of Distance, by Frances Cairncross, Harvard Business School Press, 1997.

The 500 Year Delta, by Jim Taylor and Watts Wacker, HarperBusiness, 1997.

The Digital Economy, by Don Tapscott, McGraw-Hill, 1996.

The Internet Report, by Mary Meeker and Chris DePuy, HarperBusiness: New York, 1996.

Net.Gain, by John Hagel III and Arthur G. Armstrong, Harvard Business School Press, 1997.

Real Time, by Regis McKenna, Harvard Business School Press, 1997.

Rethinking the Future, by Rowan Gibson, Nicholas Brealey Publishing: London, 1997.

The Second Curve, by Ian Morrison, Ballantine Books: New York, 1996.

2020 Vision, by Stan Davis and Bill Davidson, Simon & Schuster: New York, 1991

What Will Be, by Michael Dertouzos, Harvard Business School Press, 1997.

NOTES

[1] "Thin Clients: Behind the Numbers," *Byte*, April 1997, p. 70.

[2] "Windows Everywhere, Thanks to Citrix," *Byte*, April 1997, p. 68.

[3] http://www.rtna.daimlerbenz.com/new/wp970430.html.

[4] "The Body as Password," *Wired*, July 1997 (http://wwww.wired.com/wired/5.07/biometrics.html).

[5] "Break the Bandwidth Barrier," *Byte*, September 1996 (http://www.byte.com/art/9609/sec6/art1.htm).

[6] "Wireless Web Surfing," *The San Francisco Chronicle*, September 16, 1996, p. C1.

[7] Regis McKenna, "Real-Time Marketing," *Harvard Business Review*; v73, N4, July–August 1995.

[8] Peter Schwartz and Peter Leyden, "The Long Boom," *Wired*, July 1997, p. 115.

[9] Raymond Miles and Charles C. Snow, "The new network firm: A spherical structure built on a human investment philosophy," *Organizational Dynamics*, vol. 23, no. 4, Spring 1995, p. 4-18; Nitin Nohria and James Berkley, "The Virtual Organization—Bureaucracy, Technology, and the Implosion of Control," *The Post-Bureaucratic Organization*, Thousand Oaks, Charles Heckscher and Anne Donnelon (eds.), 1994, p. 108-128; Chesbrough, Henry W. Teece, and David J., "When is virtual virtuous? Organizing for innovation," *Harvard Business Review*, vol. 74, no. 1 (Jan/Feb 1996), pp. 65–71.

[10] See B. Gomes-Casseres: Group vs. Group: How Alliance Networks Compete, *Harvard Business Review*, July 1994.

[11] Peter Buxmann and Judith Gebauer. "Internet-based Intermediaries—The Case of the Real Estate Market." Fisher Center for Management and Information Technology, U.C. Berkeley, Working Paper, 98-WP-1027, Berkeley, January 1998.

[12] see "Reachability Management: Choice and Negotiation," Research Project, University of Freiburg, Germany (http://www.iig.uni-freiburg.de /dbskolleg/themen/the21_e.html), also Bill Gates: Looking Forward to a Listed Telephone Number, (1/28), *New York Times Special Features* (http://nytsyn.com/live/Gates2/029_012997?142216?17379.html).

[13] Michael Dertouzos, *What Will Be: How the New World of Information Will Change Our Lives*. New York: HarperCollins, 1997.

[14] Frances Cairncross. *The Death of Distance*, Harvard Business School Press, 1997.

[15] Dertouzos, op cit., pp. 281-282.